AnnualRecipes

INCLUDING PILLSBURY BAKE-OFF® CONTEST WINNERS

Pillsbury Annual Recipes

Our recipes have been tested in the Pillsbury Kitchens and meet our standards of easy preparation, reliability and great taste.

For more great recipes, visit pillsbury.com

PUBLISHED BY
Taste of Home Books
Reiman Media Group, LLC
5400 S. 60th St., Greendale WI 53129
tasteofhome.com

Printed in U.S.A.

Taste of Home® is a registered trademark of Reiman Media Group, LLC.

Bake-Off® is a registered trademark of General Mills.

All recipes were previously published in a slightly different form.

International Standard Book Number:
978-1-61765-176-2
COMPONENT NUMBER : 119000020H00

GENERAL MILLS, INC.
EDITORIAL DIRECTOR: Jeff Nowak
ASSISTANT MANAGER, MARKETING SERVICES: Christine Gray
COOKBOOK EDITOR: Grace Wells
EDITORIAL ASSISTANT: Kelly Gross
DIGITAL ASSETS MANAGER: Carrie Jacobson
RECIPE DEVELOPMENT AND TESTING: Pillsbury Test Kitchens
PHOTOGRAPHY: General Mills Photography Studio

REIMAN MEDIA GROUP, LLC
EDITOR-IN-CHIEF: Catherine Cassidy
EXECUTIVE EDITOR/PRINT & DIGITAL BOOKS:
Stephen C. George
CREATIVE DIRECTOR: Howard Greenberg
EDITORIAL SERVICES MANAGER: Kerri Balliet
SENIOR EDITOR/PRINT & DIGITAL BOOKS: Mark Hagen
EDITOR: Amy Glander
ASSOCIATE CREATIVE DIRECTOR: Edwin Robles Jr.
ART DIRECTORS: Jessie Sharon, Gretchen Trautman
CONTENT PRODUCTION MANAGER: Julie Wagner
LAYOUT DESIGNER: Nancy Novak
COPY CHIEF: Deb Warlaumont Mulvey
CONTRIBUTING PROOFREADER: Victoria Soukup Jensen
EDITORIAL ASSISTANT: Marilyn Iczkowski

READER'S DIGEST NORTH AMERICA
VICE PRESIDENT, BUSINESS DEVELOPMENT: Jonathan Bigham
PRESIDENT, BOOKS AND HOME ENTERTAINING: Harold Clarke
CHIEF FINANCIAL OFFICER: Howard Halligan
VICE PRESIDENT, GENERAL MANAGER,
READER'S DIGEST MEDIA: Marilynn Jacobs
CHIEF MARKETING OFFICER: Renee Jordan
VICE PRESIDENT, CHIEF SALES OFFICER: Mark Josephson
GENERAL MANAGER, MILWAUKEE: Frank Quigley
VICE PRESIDENT, CHIEF CONTENT OFFICER: Liz Vaccariello

THE READER'S DIGEST ASSOCIATION, INC.
PRESIDENT AND CHIEF EXECUTIVE OFFICER:
Robert E. Guth

COVER PHOTOGRAPHY
PHOTOGRAPHER: Jim Wieland
SENIOR FOOD STYLIST: Kathryn Conrad
SET STYLIST: Melissa Haberman

FRONT COVER PHOTOGRAPHS:
Cheese-Crusted Pizza Pot Pies, Pg. 153; Pineapple Pork Burgers, Pg. 137; Harvest Beef and Sweet Potato Stew, Pg. 158; Peanut Butter Boston Cream Cake, Pg. 335; Grilled Steak with Pineapple Salsa, Pg. 180.

PAGE 5 PHOTOGRAPHS:
Split Pea Soup with Sour Cream, Pg. 125; Parmesan-Pecan Fried Chicken, Pg. 160; Curried Lamb-Sweet Potato Stew, Pg. 206; Loaded Calzones, Pg. 160.

BACK COVER PHOTOGRAPHS:
Luscious Caramel-Brownie Bites, Pg. 280; Creole Jambalaya, Pg. 203; Citrus in Vanilla Syrup, Pg. 16; Chicken Italiano Sliders, Pg. 111.

contents

"Satisfy Big Appetites with the Very Best Recipes From Pillsbury!"

introduction

Today, it's easier than ever for home cooks to put a hearty, homemade dinner on the table. That's because with *Pillsbury Annual Recipes*, a delicious meal is only a recipe away.

Packed with 370 sensational specialties, ranging from timeless classics to innovative taste-twists, this colorful collection is the perfect addition to any busy kitchen. Whether you need a quick-to-fix weeknight entree, a crowd-pleasing contribution for a potluck or a simple yet surprising menu for a Saturday night dinner party, this incredible assortment has you covered.

You'll find all of your favorites inside this colossal cookbook: tasty appetizers, bubbling casseroles, weeknight entrees, steaming soups, fresh and colorful salads and sides, oven-fresh breads, delectable sunrise specialties, luscious desserts and other gotta-try-it fare. Best of all, these recipes are quick and versatile and call for common, everyday ingredients to keep things simple and help you stretch your grocery dollars.

Looking for the perfect finger food for your next party? You're sure to dazzle guests with the handheld bites, nifty nibblers and sweet sippers featured in the Appetizers & Beverages and Snacks & Munchies sections. Keep your crew fueled with everything from Gruyère-Bacon Pizza Minis (p. 55) to Devilish Chicken Wings (p. 68).

Suppertime is a snap with the fuss-free standbys featured in the Fast & Easy Entrees chapter. Easy-to-fix recipes such as Steak Kabobs with Guacamole Dip (p. 164) and Orange

Teriyaki Pork Skillet (p. 175) prep in 30 minutes or less and are guaranteed to serve up a big helping of flavor and fulfillment without all the work.

Flip to Slow Cooker Standouts when your hungry clan craves something comforting that will warm them from head to toe. Classics such as Chicken Alfredo Stew (p. 194), Smoked Barbecue Mac 'n Cheese (p. 207) and other hearty slow-cooked sensations make easy work of a homemade meal.

Special occasions call for special food, and the holidays offer the perfect opportunity to experiment. When brisk, wintry days arrive, chase chills with Jack-o'-Lantern Beef and Bean Pots (p. 214) or any of the other cozy creations in Fall & Winter Favorites. When summer's berries are ripe for the picking, indulge your sweet tooth with Strawberry Daiquiri Cocktail Pie (p. 254) from Spring & Summer Specialties.

Life is too short to pass up dessert! Whether you're hosting an elegant dinner party or simply seeking the perfect finale to a weeknight meal, any one of the dreamy delights in Cookies, Bars & More, Pies & Tarts and Delectable Desserts is sure to end dinner on a sweet note.

Featuring everything from savory party snacks you can pop in your mouth to simple-to-make dessert sensations that are guaranteed to leave a sweet impression, *Pillsbury Annual Recipes* is your trusted source for delicious, home-style fare everyone will love!

AT-A-GLANCE ICONS

Want to serve your family a stick-to-your-ribs meal—but your day-to-day routine leaves you too short on time to prepare the home-style classics they've come to adore? Time-crunched cooks, rejoice! Now it's easier than ever to put a deliciously quick supper on the dinner table.

To make things simple, we've highlighted the easy recipes in this book with an icon that looks like the one at left, so you can quickly locate these fuss-free recipes at a glance. These dishes call for 6 ingredients or fewer OR are prepped in 20 minutes or less OR are ready to eat in 30 minutes or less.

At the top of each recipe, we've also included "Prep" and "Ready in" times. This way, you'll know exactly how long it takes to prepare each dish from start to finish.

Are you watching your diet—or cooking for someone who is? As you flip through this book, you'll see the low-fat icon located next to recipes that contain 10 grams of fat or less (main dishes) OR 3 grams of fat or less (all other recipes). We've also included Nutrition Facts with every recipe. With so many delicious slimmed-down recipes, the only hard part will be deciding which one to sample first!

Plus, you'll spot a number of Pillsbury Bake-Off® Contest Winners—the recipes judged to be the very best in our popular contests over the years. Simply look for the Bake-Off® icon next to the recipe title.

HELPFUL INDEXES

This cookbook is indexed in two ways. The alphabetical index starts on page 344, where you can easily locate recipes by their title. The general index starts on page 346, where you can look up any major ingredient or category, such as chicken, chocolate, or nuts & peanut butter, and find a list of recipes starring that item.

Or you may want to simply browse the gorgeous pages of this book, look at the color photographs of the recipes and decide what recipe suits your family best. Whatever Pillsbury dishes you choose to serve, they'll surely turn out to be keepers. They just might become some of your most-cherished recipes ever!

BANANA-WALNUT
PANCAKES
PG. 22

Breakfast Brunch

From coffee cakes to egg bakes, these
a.m. sensations will wake up taste buds.

BACON-EGG BREAKFAST BITES
PG. 12

BUTTERNUT SQUASH BRUNCH BRAID
PG. 18

ALMOND-MACAROON COFFEE CAKE
PG. 8

Almond-Macaroon Coffee Cake

LINDA BIBBO | CHAGRIN FALLS, OH

BAKE-OFF® CONTEST 45, 2012

PREP TIME: 30 MINUTES (READY IN 1 HOUR 25 MINUTES)
SERVINGS: 15

- 2 tablespoons LAND O LAKES® Unsalted or Salted Butter, softened
- 4 tablespoons McCormick® Cinnamon Sugar
- 2 cans Pillsbury® Grands!® Jr. Golden Layers® refrigerated Butter Tastin® biscuits
- 1 ½ cups flaked coconut
- 1 can (14 oz) Eagle Brand® Sweetened Condensed Milk
- 2 LAND O LAKES® Eggs
- 1 ½ teaspoons McCormick® Pure Vanilla Extract
- ½ teaspoon McCormick® Pure Almond Extract
- ½ cup Fisher® Chef's Naturals® Natural Sliced Almonds
- ⅓ cup Hershey's® Special Dark® chocolate baking chips
- Fresh mint leaves, if desired

1) Heat oven to 350°F. Grease bottom and sides of 13x9-inch glass baking dish with 1 tablespoon of the butter. Place 3 tablespoons of the cinnamon sugar in large resealable food-storage plastic bag.

2) Separate dough into 20 biscuits; cut each into quarters. Place in bag with cinnamon sugar; shake to coat. Arrange pieces in dish; sprinkle with coconut.

3) Measure ½ cup of the condensed milk in small microwavable measuring cup; set aside. Pour remaining condensed milk into medium bowl. Add eggs, 1 teaspoon of the vanilla and almond extract; beat with wire whisk until well blended. Spoon over biscuit pieces; sprinkle with almonds and remaining 1 tablespoon cinnamon sugar.

4) Bake 30 to 35 minutes or until golden brown. Cool on cooling rack 20 minutes.

5) Meanwhile, add remaining 1 tablespoon butter and chocolate chips to reserved condensed milk. Microwave on High 30 to 45 seconds or until chips are melted; stir until smooth. Stir in remaining ¼ teaspoon vanilla.

6) To serve, cut into 15 squares. Place on individual plates; drizzle scant tablespoon chocolate mixture over each serving. Garnish with mint. Serve warm.

1 SERVING: Calories 340; Total Fat 16g (Saturated Fat 7g); Sodium 550mg; Total Carbohydrate 43g (Dietary Fiber 1g); Protein 6g. EXCHANGES: 2 Starch, 1 Other Carbohydrate, 3 Fat. CARBOHYDRATE CHOICES: 3.

Biscuit Corn Cakes with Goat Cheese and Blackberry-Thyme Sauce

JANE MICHEL | HOUSTON, TX

Bake-Off®

BAKE-OFF® CONTEST 45, 2012

PREP TIME: 35 MINUTES (READY IN 35 MINUTES)
SERVINGS: 5 (2 CORN CAKES EACH)

1 jar (12 oz) Smucker's® Seedless Blackberry Jam (1 cup)

¼ teaspoon McCormick® Thyme Leaves

2 tablespoons water

2 teaspoons grated lemon peel

¼ cup yellow cornmeal

1 can Pillsbury® Grands!® Jr. Golden Layers® refrigerated buttermilk biscuits

3 tablespoons LAND O LAKES® Unsalted or Salted Butter

1 cup crumbled chèvre (goat) cheese (4 oz)

1 cup fresh blackberries

1) In 1-quart saucepan, stir together blackberry jam, thyme, water and 1 teaspoon of the lemon peel. Bring to a boil over medium heat, stirring frequently. Reduce heat to low; simmer 5 to 10 minutes, stirring frequently, or until slightly thickened. Keep warm.

2) Place cornmeal in shallow dish. Separate dough into 10 biscuits. Gently flatten each biscuit to 3-inch round. Coat both sides of each biscuit with cornmeal, press in lightly.

3) Melt 2 tablespoons of the butter in 10-inch nonstick skillet over medium heat. Place half of the biscuits in skillet and cook 4 to 8 minutes, turning once halfway through cooking, or until browned and lightly puffed. Remove from pan; keep warm. Wipe out skillet with paper towel. Repeat with remaining 1 tablespoon of butter and remaining biscuits.

4) For each serving, place 2 warm corn cakes on plate. Sprinkle each with about 3 tablespoons goat cheese. Drizzle each with about 3 tablespoons blackberry sauce; garnish with blackberries and remaining lemon peel.

1 SERVING: Calories 620; Total Fat 25g (Saturated Fat 13g); Sodium 840mg; Total Carbohydrate 85g (Dietary Fiber 2g); Protein 14g. EXCHANGES: 3 Starch, 2-1/2 Other Carbohydrate, 1/2 Medium-Fat Meat, 4 Fat. CARBOHYDRATE CHOICES: 5-1/2.

French Toast with Berry Syrup

PREP TIME:	10 MINUTES (READY IN 35 MINUTES)
SERVINGS:	4

 EASY   LOW FAT

FRENCH TOAST

- **2 whole eggs plus 1 egg white, lightly beaten, or ½ cup fat-free egg product**
- **1 cup fat-free (skim) milk**
- **2 teaspoons rum extract**
- **¼ teaspoon ground nutmeg**
- **8 slices (1 inch thick) French bread**

SYRUP

- **½ cup frozen (thawed) raspberry blend juice concentrate**
- **½ cup jellied cranberry sauce**
- **1 tablespoon powdered sugar**

1) In medium bowl, beat eggs and egg white, milk, rum extract and nutmeg until well blended. Dip bread slices into egg mixture, coating both sides well. Place in ungreased 11x7-inch (2-quart) glass baking dish. Pour remaining egg mixture over bread. Let stand at room temperature 10 minutes.

2) Heat oven to 425°F. Spray cookie sheet with cooking spray. Remove bread slices from dish; place on cookie sheet.

3) Bake 12 to 15 minutes, turning slices once halfway through baking, or until golden brown.

4) Meanwhile, in 1-quart saucepan, mix syrup ingredients; cook over medium-low heat, stirring occasionally, until cranberry sauce and sugar have melted. Serve French toast with syrup.

1 SERVING: Calories 300; Total Fat 4.5g (Saturated Fat 1.5g); Sodium 340mg; Total Carbohydrate 55g (Dietary Fiber 2g); Protein 10g. EXCHANGES: 1-1/2 Starch, 2 Other Carbohydrate, 1 Medium-Fat Meat. CARBOHYDRATE CHOICES: 3-1/2.

Sausage and Cheese Frittata

PREP TIME: 25 MINUTES (READY IN 50 MINUTES)
SERVINGS: 6

1 lb bulk pork sausage

8 eggs

⅓ cup milk

½ teaspoon pepper

¼ teaspoon salt

1 tablespoon butter

1 cup shredded Cheddar cheese (4 oz)

1) Heat oven to 350°F. In 10-inch ovenproof nonstick skillet, cook sausage over medium-high heat 10 minutes, stirring frequently, until no longer pink; drain. Remove sausage to bowl; set aside. Wipe skillet with paper towels.

2) In medium bowl, beat eggs, milk, pepper and salt with whisk until well blended. In skillet, melt butter over medium heat; remove from heat. Pour half of egg mixture into skillet. Sprinkle with cooked sausage and cheese. Top with remaining egg mixture.

3) Bake uncovered 23 to 25 minutes or until set.

1 SERVING: Calories 353; Total Fat 28g (Saturated Fat 11g); Sodium 673mg; Total Carbohydrate 1g (Dietary Fiber 0g); Protein 23g. EXCHANGES: 1 Medium-Fat Meat, 2 High-Fat Meat, 1 Fat. CARBOHYDRATE CHOICES: 0.

Apple-Cinnamon Doughnut Bites

PREP TIME: 25 MINUTES (READY IN 25 MINUTES)
SERVINGS: 32

 EASY

Oil for deep frying

¼ cup sugar

½ teaspoon ground cinnamon

½ cup apple pie filling (from 21-oz can)

1 can (12.4 oz) Pillsbury® cinnamon rolls with icing

1) In deep fryer or 3-quart heavy saucepan, heat oil to 375°F. In small bowl, mix sugar and cinnamon; set aside.

2) In food processor, place apple pie filling. Cover; process, using quick on-and-off motions, 10 to 20 seconds or until pureed.

3) Set icing from cinnamon rolls aside. Separate dough into 8 rolls; cut each roll into quarters. Fry in hot oil 1 to 2 minutes or until golden brown on all sides. Drain on paper towels. Immediately roll in cinnamon-sugar.

4) Place apple mixture in decorating bag fitted with small round tip #10. Insert tip into side of each doughnut; pipe small amount of apple mixture into doughnut.

5) In small microwavable bowl, heat reserved icing on High 10 to 20 seconds until thin enough to drizzle. Drizzle icing over doughnuts. Serve warm.

1 SERVING: Calories 127; Total Fat 11g (Saturated Fat 1g); Sodium 87mg; Total Carbohydrate 8g (Dietary Fiber 0g); Protein 1g. EXCHANGES: 1/2 Other Carbohydrate, 2 Fat. CARBOHYDRATE CHOICES: 1/2.

Bacon-Egg Breakfast Bites

ERMA INNIS | CEDAR PARK, TX

 Pillsbury Bake-Off

BAKE-OFF® CONTEST 45, 2012

PREP TIME: 20 MINUTES (READY IN 40 MINUTES)
SERVINGS: 12 (2 BREAKFAST BITES EACH)

€ EASY

12 slices precooked bacon
(from 2.1-oz package)

1 can Pillsbury® Place 'n Bake®
refrigerated crescent rounds

24 frozen potato nuggets
(from 2-lb bag)

5 LAND O LAKES® Eggs

¼ teaspoon salt

¼ teaspoon McCormick® Ground
Black Pepper

Chopped fresh parsley, if desired

1) Heat oven to 350°F. Generously spray 24 mini muffin cups with Crisco® Original No-Stick Cooking Spray. Cut each bacon slice in half crosswise. Unroll one crescent round; cut into thirds, forming strips of dough. Place half slice of bacon on 1 dough strip; top with potato nugget and roll up, stretching dough and pinching ends to seal. Place in mini muffin cup, spiral side up. Repeat with remaining crescent rounds, bacon and potato nuggets.

2) In medium bowl, beat eggs, salt and pepper until well blended. Very carefully spoon scant tablespoon egg mixture around each dough-wrapped potato nugget.

3) Bake 13 to 20 minutes or until light brown on top and egg mixture is set. Remove from muffin cups to serving platter. Garnish with parsley. Serve warm.

1 SERVING: Calories 180; Total Fat 11g (Saturated Fat 3.5g); Sodium 440mg; Total Carbohydrate 12g (Dietary Fiber 0g); Protein 7g. EXCHANGES: 1 Starch, 1/2 Medium-Fat Meat, 1-1/2 Fat. CARBOHYDRATE CHOICES: 1.

Cranberry-Orange Shortbread

PREP TIME: 20 MINUTES (READY IN 1 HOUR 30 MINUTES)
SERVINGS: 32 BARS

 EASY

1 cup butter, softened
¾ cup powdered sugar
¼ cup granulated sugar
1 ½ teaspoons grated orange peel
½ teaspoon vanilla
2 cups all-purpose flour
⅓ cup cornstarch
¼ teaspoon salt
½ cup sweetened dried cranberries, chopped

1) Heat oven to 350°F. Line bottom and sides of 13x9-inch pan with foil, leaving foil overhanging at 2 opposite sides of pan; spray foil with cooking spray.

2) In large bowl, beat butter, powdered sugar, granulated sugar and orange peel with electric mixer on low speed until blended. Add vanilla. Beat on medium speed until light and fluffy. Stir in flour, cornstarch and salt. Stir in cranberries. Press dough evenly in pan.

3) Bake 30 to 32 minutes or until set. Cool completely in pan on cooling rack. Use foil to lift out of pan. Cut into 8 rows by 4 rows.

1 BAR: Calories 106; Total Fat 6g (Saturated Fat 4g); Sodium 69mg; Total Carbohydrate 13g (Dietary Fiber 0.5g); Protein 1g. EXCHANGES: 1 Other Carbohydrate, 1 Fat. CARBOHYDRATE CHOICES: 1.

Chocolate-Cherry Stuffed French Toast

BEVERLEY WEAVER ROSSELL | MORGANTOWN, IN BAKE-OFF® CONTEST 45, 2012

PREP TIME: 30 MINUTES (READY IN 1 HOUR)
SERVINGS: 8

1 can Pillsbury® refrigerated crusty French loaf

½ cup coconut milk (from 13.66-oz can)

1 LAND O LAKES® Egg

1 package (8 oz) cream cheese, softened

1 tablespoon sugar

½ teaspoon McCormick® Pure Almond Extract

½ cup flaked coconut

¼ cup Hershey's® milk chocolate baking chips (from 11.5-oz bag)

½ cup Fisher® Roasted and Salted Almonds, chopped

1 jar (12 oz) Smucker's® Cherry Preserves

3 tablespoons LAND O LAKES® Butter

Flaked coconut, if desired

Fresh mint leaves, if desired

1) Heat oven to 350°F. Spray cookie sheet with Crisco® Butter Flavor No-Stick Cooking Spray. Place dough, seam side down, on cookie sheet. Using sharp knife, cut 5 diagonal ½-inch-deep slashes on top of dough. In small bowl, beat together coconut milk and egg. Lightly brush top and sides of loaf with egg mixture; refrigerate remaining egg mixture.

2) Bake 24 to 30 minutes or until golden brown. Transfer loaf to cooling rack. Cool 5 minutes.

3) Meanwhile, in medium bowl, beat cream cheese, sugar and almond extract with electric mixer on medium speed until blended. Stir in coconut, chocolate chips and almonds; set aside.

4) Using sharp bread knife, cut thin slice off each end of loaf; discard. Cut loaf into 8 thick slices. Cut each bread slice crosswise down center to within ¼ inch of bottom to form pocket. Spoon 2 rounded tablespoons cream cheese mixture into each pocket. Press gently to close.

5) Dip stuffed slices in reserved egg mixture. Spray 12-inch skillet generously with Crisco® Butter Flavor Cooking Spray. Cook slices over medium-high heat about 4 minutes, turning once, or until golden brown.

6) Meanwhile, in small saucepan over medium heat, stir together cherry preserves and butter until mixture is warm and butter is melted. Serve French toast slices topped with warm cherry mixture. Garnish with coconut and mint, if desired.

1 SERVING: Calories 520; Total Fat 27g (Saturated Fat 15g); Sodium 420mg; Total Carbohydrate 59g (Dietary Fiber 2g); Protein 8g. EXCHANGES: 2 Starch, 2 Other Carbohydrate, 5 Fat. CARBOHYDRATE CHOICES: 4.

Italian Biscuit Strata

PREP TIME: 25 MINUTES (READY IN 9 HOURS 40 MINUTES)
SERVINGS: 12

4 cans (7.5 oz each) Pillsbury® Simply® refrigerated Buttermilk Biscuits

1 cup chopped sweet onion

1 package (8 oz) sliced fresh mushrooms

1 jar (12 oz) roasted red bell peppers, drained, coarsely chopped

3 cups shredded Italian cheese blend (12 oz)

3 cups milk

1 teaspoon Mediterranean herb seasoning

8 eggs

1) Heat oven to 450°F. Bake biscuits as directed on can; cool. Cut or tear biscuits into quarters; set aside.

2) Coat 12-inch skillet with cooking spray; heat over medium-high heat. Add onion and mushrooms; cook 5 to 6 minutes, stirring occasionally, until tender. Add roasted peppers; cook 1 minute or until thoroughly heated.

3) Spray 13x9-inch (3-quart) glass baking dish with cooking spray. Layer half of the biscuit pieces and onion mixture in baking dish; sprinkle with 1 ½ cups of the cheese. Repeat layers.

4) In large bowl, beat milk, herb seasoning and eggs with wire whisk until well blended. Pour over cheese in dish. Cover; refrigerate at least 8 hours or overnight.

5) Heat oven to 350°F. Uncover baking dish. Bake 1 hour 15 minutes or until top is golden brown and center is set (cover with foil during last 20 minutes of baking to prevent overbrowning, if necessary).

1 SERVING: Calories 401; Total Fat 19g (Saturated Fat 8g); Sodium 1167mg; Total Carbohydrate 37g (Dietary Fiber 1g); Protein 19g. EXCHANGES: 2 Starch, 1 Vegetable, 2 High-Fat Meat, 1/2 Fat. CARBOHYDRATE CHOICES: 2-1/2.

Breakfast Crostatas

BARBARA TARAGNA | COLLEGEVILLE, PA

BAKE-OFF® CONTEST 45, 2012

PREP TIME: 15 MINUTES (READY IN 40 MINUTES)
SERVINGS: 4

e EASY

1 can Pillsbury® refrigerated crusty French loaf

1 ½ teaspoons McCormick® Basil Leaves

½ teaspoon McCormick® Rosemary Leaves, crushed

1 ½ cups diced ham or Canadian bacon

1 ½ cups (6 oz) shredded Gouda cheese or Cheddar cheese

4 LAND O LAKES® Eggs

Dash salt, if desired

Dash McCormick® Ground Black Pepper

1) Heat oven to 350°F. Spray cookie sheet with Crisco® Original No-Stick Cooking Spray. Carefully unroll loaf of dough onto cookie sheet; cut in half lengthwise and crosswise to form 4 squares. Sprinkle dough squares with basil and rosemary. Top dough squares evenly with ham and cheese. Make small well in center of ham and cheese on each square.

2) To form crostatas, fold edges of dough up 1 inch over filling, making pleats and pressing dough firmly. Carefully crack open each egg and drop into well in each crostata. Sprinkle with salt and pepper.

3) Bake 20 to 25 minutes or until bottoms of crostatas are golden brown and egg whites and yolks are firm, not runny.

1 SERVING: Calories 500; Total Fat 23g (Saturated Fat 11g); Sodium 1640mg; Total Carbohydrate 38g (Dietary Fiber 0g); Protein 35g. EXCHANGES: 2 Starch, 1/2 Other Carbohydrate, 1 Lean Meat, 3 Medium-Fat Meat, 1 Fat. CARBOHYDRATE CHOICES: 2-1/2.

Citrus in Vanilla Syrup

PREP TIME: 30 MINUTES (READY IN 30 MINUTES)
SERVINGS: 7

 EASY   LOW FAT

¾ cup sugar

½ cup water

1 tablespoon light corn syrup

1 vanilla bean

3 oranges, peeled

3 red grapefruit, peeled

½ cup pomegranate seeds

1) In 2-quart saucepan, stir sugar, water and corn syrup. Split vanilla bean lengthwise and scrape out seeds; add seeds and bean pod to sugar mixture. Heat to boiling over medium heat; boil 5 minutes or until thick and syrupy. Remove from heat; discard vanilla bean pod.

2) Cut each orange and grapefruit crosswise into ¼ inch thick slices. On rimmed serving platter or in serving bowl, alternately arrange orange and grapefruit slices. Drizzle syrup over fruit. Sprinkle with pomegranate seeds.

1 SERVING: Calories 184; Total Fat 0.5g (Saturated Fat 0g); Sodium 3mg; Total Carbohydrate 49g (Dietary Fiber 8.5g); Protein 1.5g. EXCHANGES: 1-1/2 Fruit, 1-1/2 Other Carbohydrate. CARBOHYDRATE CHOICES: 3.

Great-Start Breakfast Cookies

TERESA RALSTON | NEW ALBANY, OH

Bake-Off®

BAKE-OFF® CONTEST 45, 2012

PREP TIME: 30 MINUTES (READY IN 1 HOUR)
SERVINGS: 12

½ cup Fisher® Chef's Naturals® Chopped Pecans

1 package Pillsbury® Big Deluxe refrigerated oatmeal raisin cookies

1 cup finely shredded carrots

2 ½ cups toasted whole wheat flake cereal, crushed to 1 cup

½ cup flaked coconut

1 tablespoon grated orange peel

½ teaspoon salt

¾ teaspoon McCormick® Ground Cinnamon

1 ½ cups powdered sugar

2 tablespoons fresh orange juice

3 orange slices, if desired

3 large strawberries, if desired

1) Heat oven to 350°F. To toast pecans, spread in 15x10-inch pan with sides. Bake 6 to 10 minutes, stirring occasionally, until brown. Line 2 cookie sheets with cooking parchment paper or spray with Crisco® Original No-Stick Cooking Spray.

2) In large bowl, break up cookie dough. Add carrots, cereal, toasted pecans, coconut, orange peel, salt and cinnamon. Mix with wooden spoon or knead with hands, until well blended. Divide dough into 12 equal portions (rounded ¼ cup each). Place 6 portions of dough on each cookie sheet. Flatten each to 2 ¾-inch round.

3) Bake 14 to 17 minutes or until edges are set and bottoms are golden brown. Cool on cookie sheets 3 minutes. Remove to cooling racks. Cool completely, about 15 minutes.

4) In small bowl, combine powdered sugar and orange juice; blend well. Spoon glaze over cookies. Place cookies on serving platter; garnish with orange slices and strawberries. Store in tightly covered container.

1 SERVING: Calories 300; Total Fat 11g (Saturated Fat 3.5g); Sodium 270mg; Total Carbohydrate 49g (Dietary Fiber 3g); Protein 2g. EXCHANGES: 1/2 Starch, 3 Other Carbohydrate, 2 Fat. CARBOHYDRATE CHOICES: 3.

Butternut Squash Brunch Braid

NATALIE EDWARDS | BOXBOROUGH, MA

Pillsbury Bake-Off® BAKE-OFF® CONTEST 45, 2012

PREP TIME: 35 MINUTES (READY IN 1 HOUR 20 MINUTES)
SERVINGS: 6

2 ½ cups cubed (½ inch) seeded peeled butternut squash

1 tablespoon Crisco® 100% Extra Virgin Olive Oil

1 tablespoon packed brown sugar

¼ teaspoon McCormick® Ground Black Pepper

4 slices bacon, chopped (about 4 oz)

1 medium onion, chopped

½ teaspoon McCormick® Ground Thyme

1 can Pillsbury® Crescent Recipe Creations® refrigerated seamless dough sheet

2 tablespoons grated Parmesan cheese

1 LAND O LAKES® Egg White, beaten

1) Heat oven to 425°F. In medium bowl, combine squash, olive oil, brown sugar and pepper; toss to coat. Spoon mixture into ungreased 15x10-inch pan with sides.

2) Roast 15 to 20 minutes, turning occasionally, or until squash is light brown on edges and tender when pierced with fork. Set aside. Reduce oven temperature to 375°F.

3) Meanwhile, in 10-inch skillet over medium heat, cook bacon until almost crisp. Using slotted spoon, transfer bacon pieces to paper towels. Add onion and thyme to bacon drippings in skillet. Cook and stir onion over medium heat until onion is brown and softened, about 3 minutes. Remove from heat; stir in bacon.

4) Spray large cookie sheet with Crisco® Original No-Stick Cooking Spray. Unroll dough onto cookie sheet; press to 12x8-inch rectangle. Spoon onion mixture in 4-inch-wide strip lengthwise down center of dough. Top onion with butternut squash; sprinkle with Parmesan cheese.

5) With scissors or sharp knife, make cuts 1 inch apart on long sides of dough to within ½ inch of filling. Alternately cross strips over filling; press ends to seal. Brush with egg white.

6) Bake at 375°F 20 to 25 minutes or until deep golden brown. Cool 5 minutes. Cut crosswise into 6 slices.

1 SERVING: Calories 230; Total Fat 11g (Saturated Fat 4g); Sodium 470mg; Total Carbohydrate 26g (Dietary Fiber 1g); Protein 6g. EXCHANGES: 1-1/2 Starch, 1/2 Vegetable, 2 Fat. CARBOHYDRATE CHOICES: 2.

Apple-Raisin Cheese Blintzes

PREP TIME: 20 MINUTES (READY IN 30 MINUTES)
SERVINGS: 5

 EASY

1 container (15 oz) ricotta cheese

4 oz (half of 8-oz package) cream cheese, softened

¼ cup packed brown sugar

1 package (5 oz) prepared crepes

2 tablespoons butter or margarine

1 box (12 oz) frozen cinnamon apples

½ cup raisins

⅔ cup frozen (thawed) whipped topping, if desired

½ cup chopped walnuts, toasted

Powdered sugar, if desired

1) In food processor, place ricotta cheese, cream cheese and brown sugar. Cover; process until smooth. Refrigerate 10 minutes.

2) Spoon 3 tablespoons cheese mixture in center of each crepe. Fold sides and ends of crepe over filling to form a rectangle.

3) In 12-inch nonstick skillet, melt 1 tablespoon of the butter over medium heat. Add 5 blintzes, seam sides down, to skillet; cook 1 to 2 minutes, turning once, until golden brown. Remove from skillet to serving platter; cover to keep warm. Repeat with remaining 1 tablespoon butter and remaining 5 blintzes.

4) Meanwhile, microwave apples as directed on package. Stir in raisins. Spoon apple mixture evenly over blintzes. Top each with dollop of whipped topping; sprinkle with walnuts and powdered sugar.

1 SERVING: Calories 585; Total Fat 31g (Saturated Fat 13g); Sodium 600mg; Total Carbohydrate 63g (Dietary Fiber 3g); Protein 17g. EXCHANGES: 1 Starch, 1 Fruit, 2 Other Carbohydrate, 1-1/2 High-Fat Meat, 3 Fat. CARBOHYDRATE CHOICES: 4.

Caramelized Peach Upside-Down Coffee Cake

BRENDA WATTS | GAFFNEY, SC

BAKE-OFF® CONTEST 45, 2012

PREP TIME: 30 MINUTES (READY IN 1 HOUR 30 MINUTES)
SERVINGS: 8

1 roll Pillsbury® refrigerated sugar cookie dough

¼ cup LAND O LAKES® Unsalted or Salted Butter

⅓ cup packed brown sugar

½ teaspoon McCormick® Ground Cinnamon

1 ½ cups thinly sliced peeled peaches or frozen sliced peaches, thawed

2 teaspoons baking powder

2 LAND O LAKES® Eggs

½ cup half-and-half

⅔ cup Smucker's® Peach Preserves

3 tablespoons orange juice

⅓ cup Fisher® Chef's Naturals® Chopped Pecans

1) Let cookie dough stand at room temperature 10 minutes to soften. Meanwhile, heat oven to 350°F. Line 10-inch springform pan with foil. Lightly spray bottom and side of foil-lined pan with Crisco® Original No-Stick Cooking Spray. In 12-inch skillet over medium heat, melt butter. Stir in brown sugar and cinnamon until blended. Add sliced peaches; cook 4 to 6 minutes or until peaches are tender, stirring occasionally. Spoon and spread peach mixture over bottom of pan.

2) In large bowl, break up cookie dough. Add baking powder and eggs. Beat with electric mixer on medium speed about 1 minute or until well blended. On low speed, beat in half-and-half an additional minute or until cookie dough mixture is smooth and creamy. Pour mixture evenly over peaches in pan.

3) Bake 35 to 50 minutes or until toothpick inserted into center comes out clean. Cool 2 minutes. Place heatproof serving plate upside down over pan; turn plate and pan over. Remove pan. Carefully remove foil. Cool 5 minutes.

4) Meanwhile, in small microwavable bowl, stir peach preserves and orange juice together until blended. Microwave peach mixture on High 30 to 60 seconds or until warm.

5) To serve, drizzle coffee cake with peach mixture and sprinkle with pecans.

1 SERVING: Calories 490; Total Fat 22g (Saturated Fat 8g); Sodium 350mg; Total Carbohydrate 69g (Dietary Fiber 1g); Protein 5g. EXCHANGES: 1-1/2 Starch, 3 Other Carbohydrate, 4 Fat. CARBOHYDRATE CHOICES: 4-1/2.

Easy Danish Kringle

PREP TIME: 15 MINUTES (READY IN 1 HOUR 15 MINUTES)
SERVINGS: 8

 EASY

1 Pillsbury® refrigerated pie crust, softened as directed on box

⅔ cup chopped pecans

⅓ cup packed brown sugar

3 tablespoons butter or margarine, softened

½ cup powdered sugar

¼ teaspoon vanilla

2 to 3 teaspoons milk

3 tablespoons chopped pecans, if desired

1) Heat oven to 375°F. Remove pie crust from pouch; unroll on large ungreased cookie sheet.

2) In medium bowl, mix ⅔ cup pecans, the brown sugar and butter. Sprinkle over half of pie crust to within ¾ inch of edge. Brush edge with water; fold crust over pecan mixture. Move to center of cookie sheet. Press edges with tines of fork to seal; prick top with fork.

3) Bake 17 to 22 minutes or until golden brown. Cool 5 minutes.

4) In small bowl, mix powdered sugar, vanilla and 2 teaspoons milk. Stir in enough remaining milk until glaze is smooth. Drizzle glaze over kringle; sprinkle with 3 tablespoons pecans. Cool 30 minutes before serving.

1 SERVING: Calories 290; Total Fat 18g (Saturated Fat 6g); Sodium 140mg; Total Carbohydrate 31g (Dietary Fiber 0g); Protein 0g. EXCHANGES: 2 Other Carbohydrate, 3-1/2 Fat. CARBOHYDRATE CHOICES: 2.

Pigs-in-a-Blanket Bake

PREP TIME: 15 MINUTES (READY IN 1 HOUR 5 MINUTES)
SERVINGS: 12

 EASY

2 boxes (16.4 oz each) Pillsbury® frozen buttermilk pancakes

4 eggs

1 ½ cups half-and-half

1 package (14 oz) cocktail-size smoked link sausages, chopped

1 cup shredded sharp Cheddar cheese (4 oz)

1 cup buttery maple-flavored syrup

1) Heat oven to 350°F. Lightly grease 13x9-inch (3-quart) glass baking dish with shortening or cooking spray. Remove pancakes from boxes; unwrap and carefully separate. Set aside to partially thaw.

2) In large bowl, beat eggs and half-and-half with whisk. Coarsely chop pancakes. Add pancake pieces and chopped sausage to egg mixture; toss to coat. Let stand 5 minutes. Pour mixture into baking dish. Sprinkle with cheese.

3) Bake uncovered 40 minutes or until edges are set and light golden brown. Let stand 10 minutes. Cut into squares; serve with syrup.

1 SERVING: Calories 452; Total Fat 21g (Saturated Fat 9g); Sodium 748mg; Total Carbohydrate 55g (Dietary Fiber 1g); Protein 13g. EXCHANGES: 2 Starch, 1-1/2 Other Carbohydrate, 1 High-Fat Meat, 2-1/2 Fat. CARBOHYDRATE CHOICES: 3-1/2.

Banana-Walnut Pancakes

PREP TIME: 15 MINUTES (READY IN 15 MINUTES)
SERVINGS: 4

e EASY   **lf** LOW FAT

PANCAKES

2 cups Fiber One® Complete pancake mix (from 28.3-oz box)

1 ⅓ cups cold water

½ cup mashed ripe banana

2 tablespoons chopped walnuts

TOPPING

1 firm ripe banana, sliced

2 teaspoons chopped walnuts

¼ cup fat-free caramel topping

1) Heat griddle or skillet over medium-high heat or to 375°F. Grease with vegetable oil or shortening (or spray with cooking spray before heating).

2) In medium bowl, stir pancake mix and water with fork or wire whisk until smooth (batter will be thin). Stir in banana and 2 tablespoons walnuts.

3) For each pancake, pour slightly less than ¼ cup batter onto hot griddle. Cook until bubbles form on top and edges are dry. Turn and cook other sides until golden brown.

4) Top pancakes with sliced banana, 2 teaspoons walnuts and the caramel topping.

1 SERVING: Calories 340; Total Fat 7g (Saturated Fat 1g); Sodium 520mg; Total Carbohydrate 62g (Dietary Fiber 7g); Protein 7g. EXCHANGES: 2-1/2 Starch, 1-1/2 Other Carbohydrate, 1 Fat. CARBOHYDRATE CHOICES: 4.

Grapefruit Tart

PREP TIME: 25 MINUTES (READY IN 3 HOURS 10 MINUTES)
SERVINGS: 8

CRUST

1 package (5.3 oz) shortbread cookies, crushed (about 1 ⅓ cups)

3 tablespoons sugar

2 tablespoons butter, melted

FILLING

½ cup sugar

6 tablespoons cornstarch

⅛ teaspoon salt

2 cups fresh red grapefruit juice

4 egg yolks

3 tablespoons butter

2 teaspoons grated red grapefruit peel

3 red grapefruit, peeled, sectioned

2 tablespoons sugar

1) Heat oven to 350°F. Spray 9-inch square tart pan with removable bottom with cooking spray. Mix crust ingredients. Press lightly into pan. Bake 10 to 12 minutes or until lightly browned. Cool.

2) In heavy saucepan, mix ½ cup sugar, the cornstarch and salt. Stir in juice and yolks with whisk. Cook over medium-high heat 10 to 12 minutes, stirring constantly, until mixture thickens and boils. Remove from heat; stir in 3 tablespoons butter and the grapefruit peel. Pour filling into baked crust. Cover surface of filling directly with plastic wrap. Refrigerate 2 hours 30 minutes.

3) Place grapefruit sections in large glass bowl; sprinkle with 2 tablespoons sugar. Refrigerate. Before serving, drain grapefruit. Arrange segments on filling.

1 SERVING: Calories 361; Total Fat 15g (Saturated Fat 7g); Sodium 187mg; Total Carbohydrate 55g (Dietary Fiber 2g); Protein 3g. EXCHANGES: 1/2 Starch, 1 Fruit, 2 Other Carbohydrate, 3 Fat. CARBOHYDRATE CHOICES: 3-1/2.

tip

If you like, press raisins into the top of each biscuit and lightly sprinkle with cinnamon before baking.

Key Lime Pie Cinnamon Rolls

ANDREA YACYK | SEBASTIAN, FL

 Bake-Off

BAKE-OFF® CONTEST 45, 2012

PREP TIME: 15 MINUTES (READY IN 30 MINUTES)
SERVINGS: 5

 EASY

---

1 can Pillsbury® Grands!® Flaky Supreme refrigerated cinnamon rolls with icing

⅓ cup graham cracker crumbs

1 tablespoon grated Key lime peel

½ cup Hershey's® premier white baking chips

1 tablespoon Key lime juice

1 Key lime, sliced, if desired

1) Heat oven to 350°F. Line large cookie sheet with cooking parchment paper or lightly spray with Crisco® Original No-Stick cooking spray.

2) Remove dough from can; do not separate dough into rolls. Reserve icing. Unroll cinnamon roll dough on waxed paper. Sprinkle dough evenly with ¼ cup of the graham cracker crumbs, lime peel and white chips; lightly press chips into dough. Reroll dough; using perforations, separate into 5 rolls. Place, cut side up, two inches apart on cookie sheet.

3) Bake 12 to 17 minutes or until golden brown. Cool 5 minutes.

4) Meanwhile, in small bowl, combine reserved icing and lime juice; stir until well blended. Drizzle icing over warm rolls. Sprinkle tops with remaining graham cracker crumbs. Garnish with lime slices. Serve warm.

1 SERVING: Calories 530; Total Fat 26g (Saturated Fat 11g); Sodium 730mg; Total Carbohydrate 67g (Dietary Fiber 1g); Protein 6g. EXCHANGES: 2 Starch, 2-1/2 Other Carbohydrate, 5 Fat. CARBOHYDRATE CHOICES: 4-1/2.

Sausage-Pomodoro Brunch Bake

MARIA VASSEUR | VALENCIA, CA

Bake-Off   BAKE-OFF® CONTEST 45, 2012

PREP TIME: 15 MINUTES (READY IN 50 MINUTES)
SERVINGS: 8

e EASY

1 package (12 oz) bulk reduced-fat pork breakfast sausage

⅓ cup refrigerated basil pesto

1 can Pillsbury® refrigerated crescent dinner rolls

1 can (14.5 oz) Muir Glen® organic diced tomatoes, drained

⅓ cup crumbled feta cheese (1 ½ oz)

1 cup shredded mozzarella cheese (4 oz)

6 LAND O LAKES® Eggs

2 tablespoons milk

3 tablespoons shredded fresh basil leaves

1) Heat oven to 375°F. In 10-inch nonstick skillet, cook sausage 6 to 8 minutes over medium heat or until no longer pink, stirring occasionally. Remove from heat. Stir in pesto. Set aside to cool.

2) Unroll crescent dough into 13x9-inch glass baking dish. Press dough in bottom and ½ inch up sides. Press perforations to seal. Spoon sausage into dough-lined dish. Sprinkle tomatoes and feta cheese over sausage. Top with mozzarella cheese.

3) In medium bowl, beat eggs and milk with wire whisk until well blended. Pour egg mixture evenly over ingredients in dish.

4) Bake 20 to 25 minutes or until dough is golden brown and knife inserted in center comes out clean. Cool 10 minutes. Sprinkle with fresh basil.

1 SERVING: Calories 390; Total Fat 27g (Saturated Fat 9g); Sodium 890mg; Total Carbohydrate 16g (Dietary Fiber 0g); Protein 20g. EXCHANGES: 1 Starch, 2-1/2 Medium-Fat Meat, 3 Fat. CARBOHYDRATE CHOICES: 1.

Citrus Mimosas

PREP TIME: 10 MINUTES (READY IN 10 MINUTES)
SERVINGS: 5 (1 CUP EACH)

e EASY   **f** LOW FAT

1 cup red grapefruit juice, chilled

½ cup orange juice, chilled

¼ cup simple syrup

1 bottle (750 ml) sparkling white wine or champagne, chilled

Red grapefruit or orange wedges or slices, if desired

1) In pitcher, mix juices and syrup. Pour evenly into 5 tall glasses or champagne flutes. Add sparkling wine to fill glasses or flutes. Garnish with citrus wedges or slices. Serve immediately.

1 SERVING: Calories 182; Total Fat 0g (Saturated Fat 0g); Sodium 8mg; Total Carbohydrate 15g (Dietary Fiber 0g); Protein 1g. EXCHANGES: 1/2 Fruit, 1/2 Other Carbohydrate. CARBOHYDRATE CHOICES: 1.

Dark Cherry-Chocolate Breakfast Pastry

MARYANNE SALAWAY | HARVEYS LAKE, PA

BAKE-OFF® CONTEST 45, 2012

PREP TIME: 20 MINUTES (READY IN 1 HOUR 5 MINUTES)
SERVINGS: 8

e EASY

1 can Pillsbury® refrigerated crusty French loaf

4 tablespoons LAND O LAKES® Butter

1 teaspoon grated orange peel

1 cup halved pitted dark sweet cherries

¼ cup Hershey's® mini chips semi-sweet chocolate baking chips

¼ cup Smucker's® Sweet Orange Marmalade

1) Heat oven to 350°F. Lightly spray 15x10-inch pan with sides with Crisco® Original No-Stick Cooking Spray. Carefully unroll loaf of dough in pan; press dough to cover pan. In small microwavable bowl, microwave 2 tablespoons of the butter on High 15 seconds or until melted. Stir in orange peel. Brush butter mixture over dough.

2) Press ½ cup of cherries into half of dough, covering a 10x7 ½-inch area. Sprinkle mini chips over cherries. Fold plain side of dough over cherries. Pinch edges of dough to seal. Cover top of folded dough with remaining cherries; press into dough.

3) In small microwavable bowl, microwave remaining 2 tablespoons of butter and marmalade on High 15 to 30 seconds or until butter is melted; stir to blend well. Carefully brush mixture over cherries and dough.

4) Bake 20 to 30 minutes or until golden brown. Cool on cooling rack 15 minutes.

5) Cut into 8 servings. Serve warm.

1 SERVING: Calories 220; Total Fat 9g (Saturated Fat 5g); Sodium 270mg; Total Carbohydrate 31g (Dietary Fiber 1g); Protein 3g. EXCHANGES: 1 Starch, 1 Other Carbohydrate, 1-1/2 Fat. CARBOHYDRATE CHOICES: 2.

Spanakopita-Style Brunch Squares with Spicy Apricot Sauce

ANN HILLMEYER | SANDIA PARK, NM

BAKE-OFF® CONTEST 45, 2012

PREP TIME: 30 MINUTES (READY IN 1 HOUR)
SERVINGS: 8

4 tablespoons LAND O LAKES® Butter

½ cup chopped onion

1 box (9 oz) frozen chopped spinach, thawed and squeezed to drain

1 ½ teaspoons McCormick® Dill Weed

1 tablespoon Pillsbury BEST® All Purpose Flour

1 cup crumbled feta cheese (4 oz)

2 LAND O LAKES® Eggs, slightly beaten

½ teaspoon McCormick® Garlic Powder

½ teaspoon salt

¼ teaspoon freshly ground McCormick® Black Pepper

2 cans Pillsbury® Crescent Recipe Creations® refrigerated seamless dough sheet

¼ cup Fisher® Chef's Naturals® Natural Sliced Almonds

1 jar (12 oz) Smucker's® Apricot Preserves

¼ cup cider vinegar

¾ teaspoon McCormick® Crushed Red Pepper

1) Heat oven to 375°F. In 2-quart saucepan over medium heat, melt 3 tablespoons of the butter. Add onion; cook and stir until softened, about 3 minutes. Stir in spinach, dill weed and flour. Cook an additional 5 minutes or until most of the liquid is absorbed. Remove from heat; stir in feta cheese, eggs, garlic powder, salt and pepper. Set aside.

2) Lightly spray 13x9-inch glass baking dish with Crisco® Original No-Stick Cooking Spray. Unroll 1 dough sheet in bottom of dish, stretching slightly to fit. Spread spinach mixture over dough. Unroll remaining dough sheet; stretch slightly and place over spinach mixture.

3) In small microwavable bowl, microwave remaining 1 tablespoon butter on High 15 seconds or until melted. Brush butter over top of dough; sprinkle with almonds.

4) Bake 19 to 24 minutes or until filling is set and top is golden brown. Cool 5 minutes.

5) Meanwhile, to make sauce, in 1-quart saucepan over medium heat, cook apricot preserves, vinegar and crushed red pepper. Bring to a boil; reduce heat to low and continue cooking until slightly thickened, 4 to 5 minutes, stirring frequently.

6) To serve, cut spanakopita into 8 squares. Place squares on individual plates; drizzle each with warm sauce.

1 SERVING: Calories 460; Total Fat 22g (Saturated Fat 11g); Sodium 900mg; Total Carbohydrate 58g (Dietary Fiber 2g); Protein 9g. EXCHANGES: 2 Starch, 2 Other Carbohydrate, 1/2 Medium-Fat Meat, 3-1/2 Fat. CARBOHYDRATE CHOICES: 4.

Panko-Topped Curried Eggs Breakfast Pizza

NALINI MENON | VISTA, CA

BAKE-OFF® CONTEST 45, 2012

PREP TIME: 50 MINUTES (READY IN 1 HOUR)
SERVINGS: 8

8 LAND O LAKES® Eggs, hard cooked, peeled, chopped

4 oz (half of 8-oz package) cream cheese, softened

½ cup grated Parmesan cheese

2 tablespoons lemon juice

1 teaspoon McCormick® Ground Black Pepper

1 teaspoon McCormick® Curry Powder

½ teaspoon salt

¼ cup Crisco® 100% Extra Virgin Olive Oil

2 tablespoons refrigerated basil pesto

1 can Pillsbury® refrigerated thin pizza crust

1 ½ cups Progresso® Italian style panko bread crumbs

¼ cup Fisher® Chef's Naturals® Chopped Walnuts

¼ cup LAND O LAKES® Unsalted or Salted Butter, melted

Garnish, if desired

¼ cup finely chopped green onions

4 cherry tomatoes, cut in half

8 sprigs of fresh parsley

1) Heat oven to 425°F. In medium bowl, combine eggs, cream cheese, Parmesan cheese, lemon juice, pepper, curry powder and salt. Using fork, mash all ingredients until well mixed. Cover; refrigerate.

2) In small bowl, beat olive oil and pesto with wire whisk until blended. Brush 1 tablespoon of the pesto mixture onto 15x10-inch pan with sides. Gently unroll pizza crust dough in pan without stretching it; brush remaining pesto mixture over dough.

3) Bake 5 to 8 minutes or until dough is set and puffed. Cool 5 minutes. Meanwhile, in small bowl, stir together bread crumbs, walnuts and butter.

4) Spoon and spread egg mixture over pizza; sprinkle with bread crumb mixture.

5) Bake 5 to 7 minutes or until bread crumbs are golden brown. To serve, cut into 8 squares. Top each serving with green onions, tomato half and sprig of parsley.

1 SERVING: Calories 520; Total Fat 36g (Saturated Fat 11g); Sodium 910mg; Total Carbohydrate 34g (Dietary Fiber 1g); Protein 15g. EXCHANGES: 2-1/2 Starch, 1 Medium-Fat Meat, 5-1/2 Fat. CARBOHYDRATE CHOICES: 2.

tip Curry powder imparts a distinctive flavor and rich golden color to recipes and can be found in both mild and hot versions. Most cooks season dishes lightly with curry powder and add more as desired to reach an acceptable spice level.

Sausage and Zucchini Breakfast Pizza

SUZANNE BECK | DAYTON, OH

Bake-Off®

BAKE-OFF® CONTEST 45, 2012

PREP TIME: 55 MINUTES (READY IN 1 HOUR 15 MINUTES)
SERVINGS: 8

2 tablespoons Crisco® 100% Extra Virgin Olive Oil

1 can Pillsbury® refrigerated classic pizza crust

½ lb bulk spicy Italian pork sausage

4 cups thinly sliced zucchini (about 2 medium)

1 medium onion, thinly sliced

1 medium green bell pepper, cut into 1-inch squares

¼ teaspoon salt

6 LAND O LAKES® Eggs

⅓ cup grated Parmesan cheese

⅛ teaspoon McCormick® Ground Black Pepper

1 cup (4 oz) shredded Cheddar cheese

1) Heat oven to 425°F. Grease large cookie sheet with 1 tablespoon of the oil. Unroll pizza crust dough onto cookie sheet; press into 16x13-inch rectangle.

2) Bake 8 minutes. Meanwhile, in 12-inch nonstick skillet, cook sausage 5 to 7 minutes over medium-high heat or until sausage is no longer pink, stirring frequently. Transfer sausage to small bowl; set aside.

3) Add remaining 1 tablespoon oil to skillet. Cook zucchini, onion, bell pepper and salt over medium heat, stirring frequently, until vegetables are crisp-tender, about 10 minutes. Add sausage to vegetable mixture; stir to combine.

4) In medium bowl, beat eggs with wire whisk. Beat in Parmesan cheese and pepper. Drain vegetable-sausage mixture, if necessary. Add to egg mixture; stir to combine. Cook over medium heat 1 ½ to 2 minutes or until eggs are partially set, stirring occasionally.

5) Spoon vegetable, egg and sausage mixture onto prebaked pizza crust to within ½ inch of edges. Top with Cheddar cheese.

6) Bake 6 to 10 minutes or until egg is set, cheese is melted and crust is golden brown. Let stand 2 minutes before serving.

1 SERVING: Calories 370; Total Fat 21g (Saturated Fat 8g); Sodium 890mg; Total Carbohydrate 29g (Dietary Fiber 2g); Protein 18g. EXCHANGES: 1-1/2 Starch, 1/2 Other Carbohydrate, 2 Medium-Fat Meat, 2 Fat. CARBOHYDRATE CHOICES: 2.

Appetizers & Beverages

Dazzle guests with scrumptious yet easy hors d'oeuvres, the ones that get everyone talking—and munching!

PROSCIUTTO-SPINACH SPIRALS
PG. 32

ICED CARAMEL CAPPUCCINO
PG. 53

MANGO SALSA APPETIZER BITES
PG. 33

SOUTHWESTERN
CORN POPPERS
PG. 36

Prosciutto-Spinach Spirals

TERRI RAPP | WISCONSIN RAPIDS, WI

BAKE-OFF® CONTEST 45, 2012

PREP TIME: 20 MINUTES (READY IN 1 HOUR)
SERVINGS: 16

 EASY

1 can Pillsbury® refrigerated classic pizza crust

1 to 2 teaspoons McCormick® Italian Seasoning

⅓ cup garlic-and-herbs spreadable cheese, softened

2 packages (3 oz each) sliced prosciutto

5 cups loosely packed fresh baby spinach leaves

1 large shallot, finely chopped (¼ cup)

1 jar (14 oz) marinara sauce, warmed

1) Heat oven to 375°F. Lightly spray large cookie sheet with Crisco® Original No-Stick Cooking Spray.

2) Spray 16x12-inch sheet of waxed paper with Crisco® Original No-Stick Cooking spray. Unroll pizza dough onto waxed paper; press dough into 16x12-inch rectangle. Sprinkle half of Italian seasoning over dough. Carefully turn dough upside down onto cookie sheet. Remove waxed paper. Reshape dough, if necessary. Sprinkle dough with remaining Italian seasoning.

3) Spread dough evenly with cheese to within ½ inch from 1 long side. Top cheese with prosciutto, spinach and shallot. Starting on 1 long side, roll dough tightly; press seams to seal. Place roll diagonally on cookie sheet, seam side down.

4) Bake 20 to 30 minutes or until deep golden brown. Remove from oven; cool 10 minutes. Cut diagonally into 1-inch slices. Serve with marinara sauce.

1 SERVING: Calories 120; Total Fat 4g (Saturated Fat 1.5g); Sodium 480mg; Total Carbohydrate 17g (Dietary Fiber 1g); Protein 5g. EXCHANGES: 1 Starch, 1/2 Vegetable, 1/2 Fat. CARBOHYDRATE CHOICES: 1.

Mango Salsa Appetizer Bites

JUDY MORTENSEN | ANTELOPE, CA

 Bake-Off BAKE-OFF® CONTEST 45, 2012

PREP TIME: 55 MINUTES (READY IN 55 MINUTES)
SERVINGS: 24

1 large mango, seed removed, peeled, diced

¼ cup finely chopped red onion

4 teaspoons finely chopped jalapeño chile

½ teaspoon McCormick® Dill Weed

½ teaspoon salt

¼ cup finely chopped fresh cilantro

1 teaspoon grated lime peel

2 tablespoons fresh lime juice

1 Pillsbury® refrigerated pie crust, softened as directed on box

1 large avocado, pitted, peeled and diced

½ cup crumbled chèvre (goat) cheese (2 oz)

Fresh cilantro, if desired

1) In small bowl, combine mango, red onion, jalapeño, dill weed, salt, ¼ cup cilantro, lime peel and 1 tablespoon of the lime juice; mix well. Cover; refrigerate.

2) Heat oven to 450°F. Unroll pie crust. Using 2-inch round cookie cutter, cut 24 rounds from pie crust, rerolling dough if necessary. Press 1 round in bottom and up side of each of 24 ungreased mini muffin cups.

3) Bake 6 to 9 minutes or until golden brown. Cool crusts in cups 15 minutes. Transfer from cups to cooling racks.

4) Meanwhile, in small bowl, combine avocado, goat cheese and remaining 1 tablespoon lime juice. With fork, mash avocado and goat cheese until mixture is smooth. Spoon mixture into small resealable food-storage plastic bag; seal bag. Cut off corner of bag.

5) Pipe 1 teaspoon avocado mixture into each cup; top with scant 1 tablespoon of the mango salsa (cups will be full). Garnish with cilantro. Store covered in refrigerator.

1 SERVING: Calories 60; Total Fat 4g (Saturated Fat 1.5g); Sodium 110mg; Total Carbohydrate 6g (Dietary Fiber 0g); Protein 1g. EXCHANGES: 1/2 Starch, 1/2 Fat. CARBOHYDRATE CHOICES: 1/2.

Salmon Crescent Sushi Rolls

JULIE MCINTIRE | INDEPENDENCE, MO

Pillsbury Bake-Off® — BAKE-OFF® CONTEST 45, 2012

PREP TIME: 30 MINUTES (READY IN 55 MINUTES)
SERVINGS: 24

1 can Pillsbury® Crescent Recipe Creations® refrigerated seamless dough sheet

8 oz salmon fillet (about 5x3x¾ inches), skin removed

¾ cup cooked white rice

3 tablespoons McCormick® Sesame Seed

½ medium avocado, pitted, peeled, cut into 8 slices

¾ teaspoon wasabi paste

3 teaspoons soy sauce

1) Heat oven to 375°F. Unroll dough sheet; press into 10x14-inch rectangle. Cut dough in half lengthwise.

2) Cut salmon lengthwise into 6 pieces. To make each roll, spoon half of rice evenly down 1 long edge of each dough piece in a 1-inch strip to within ¼ inch of edge. Place 3 pieces salmon evenly over rice, overlapping salmon to fit if necessary. Starting at long side topped with salmon, roll up; pinch seam to seal. Sprinkle sesame seed on ungreased cookie sheet; roll and press each log in sesame seed to coat. Place rolls, seam side down, on cookie sheet.

3) Bake 12 to 17 minutes or until golden brown. Cool 5 minutes. Transfer rolls to cutting board. Using serrated knife, cut each roll into 12 slices. Cut each slice of avocado into thirds; place 1 slice on top of each roll. Serve with wasabi and soy sauce.

1 SERVING: Calories 60; Total Fat 3.5g (Saturated Fat 1g); Sodium 125mg; Total Carbohydrate 6g (Dietary Fiber 0g); Protein 3g. EXCHANGES: 1/2 Starch, 1/2 Fat. CARBOHYDRATE CHOICES: 1/2.

Sweet and Spicy Shrimp Cups

AMY ANDREWS | MAPLE VALLEY, WA

Pillsbury Bake-Off

BAKE-OFF® CONTEST 45, 2012

PREP TIME: 30 MINUTES (READY IN 50 MINUTES)
SERVINGS: 24

1 can Pillsbury® Crescent Recipe Creations® refrigerated seamless dough sheet

24 uncooked deveined peeled medium shrimp, thawed if frozen, tail shells removed

2 tablespoons cornstarch

1 tablespoon Crisco® Pure Vegetable Oil

2 oz (¼ of 8-oz package) cream cheese, softened

2 tablespoons mayonnaise

4 teaspoons Smucker's® Sweet Orange Marmalade

2 teaspoons hot chili sauce

4 teaspoons sliced green onions (1 medium)

1) Heat oven to 375°F. Unroll dough; press into 12x8-inch rectangle. Cut dough into 24 squares. Press 1 square in bottom and up side of each of 24 ungreased mini muffin cups.

2) In medium bowl, toss shrimp with cornstarch to lightly coat. In 12-inch nonstick skillet, heat oil over medium-high heat until hot. Add shrimp; cook in single layer for 2 to 3 minutes, turning once or until shrimp turn pink. Remove from heat; drain on paper towels.

3) In small bowl, stir together cream cheese, mayonnaise, marmalade, chili sauce and onions; mix well. Place 1 shrimp in bottom of each dough-lined cup. Spoon 1 rounded teaspoon cream cheese mixture into each cup.

4) Bake 8 to 15 minutes or until edges are golden brown. Cool in pan 5 minutes.

1 SERVING: Calories 60; Total Fat 4g (Saturated Fat 1.5g); Sodium 110mg; Total Carbohydrate 6g (Dietary Fiber 0g); Protein 1g. EXCHANGES: 1/2 Starch, 1/2 Fat. CARBOHYDRATE CHOICES: 1/2.

tip

Shrimp are available fresh or frozen (raw or cooked, peeled or in the shell) or canned. Shrimp in the shell (fresh or frozen) are available in different varieties and sizes (medium, large, extra large, jumbo).

Southwestern Corn Poppers

SINDEE MORGAN | WINDSOR, CA

BAKE-OFF® CONTEST 45, 2012

PREP TIME: 30 MINUTES (READY IN 1 HOUR 5 MINUTES)
SERVINGS: 16

¾ cup finely chopped red bell pepper

1 cup frozen shoepeg white or niblets corn, thawed, drained

1 can (4 oz) diced green chiles, drained

½ cup shredded pepper Jack cheese (2 oz)

1 package (3 oz) cream cheese, softened

2 green onions, thinly sliced (2 tablespoons)

1 tablespoon fresh lime juice

½ teaspoon salt

½ teaspoon McCormick® Basil Leaves

Dash McCormick® Ground Black Pepper

1 can Pillsbury® Place 'n Bake® refrigerated crescent rounds

1 tablespoon finely chopped fresh basil leaves

1) In small bowl, combine ½ cup of the chopped pepper, corn, green chiles, pepper Jack cheese, cream cheese, onions, lime juice, salt, dried basil and pepper; mix well.

2) Heat oven to 375°F. Spray 16 mini muffin cups with Crisco® Original No-Stick Cooking Spray. Remove crescent rounds from can; do not unroll. Using serrated knife, cut roll evenly into 16 rounds; carefully separate rounds. Press each round in bottom and up side of cup. Spoon 2 tablespoons of the corn mixture into each cup (cups will be very full).

3) Bake 17 to 22 minutes or until edges are golden brown. Cool in pans 10 minutes. Transfer from pans to serving platter.

4) In small bowl, mix remaining ¼ cup bell pepper and fresh basil. Top each popper with about ½ teaspoon pepper mixture.

1 SERVING: Calories 100; Total Fat 6g (Saturated Fat 2.5g); Sodium 250mg; Total Carbohydrate 9g (Dietary Fiber 0g); Protein 2g. EXCHANGES: 1/2 Starch, 1 Fat. CARBOHYDRATE CHOICES: 1/2.

Sushi-Style Crescent Crab Rolls

SUSANN STUDZ | BALTIMORE, MD

BAKE-OFF® CONTEST 45, 2012

PREP TIME: 35 MINUTES (READY IN 2 HOURS)
SERVINGS: 24

¾ cup plus 2 tablespoons Progresso® panko bread crumbs

¼ cup mayonnaise

¼ cup finely chopped sweet onion

1 tablespoon Dijon mustard

1 tablespoon fresh lemon juice

1 teaspoon Worcestershire sauce

2 tablespoons finely chopped fresh Italian (flat-leaf) parsley

1 can (6.5 oz) special white lump crabmeat, drained, rinsed

1 can Pillsbury® refrigerated crescent dinner rolls

3 tablespoons LAND O LAKES® Butter, melted

¼ cup finely chopped red bell pepper

1 tablespoon McCormick® Sesame Seed

1 tablespoon McCormick® Black Sesame Seed

Garnish, if desired

Chopped red bell pepper

Chopped fresh Italian (flat-leaf) parsley

1) In small bowl, combine ¼ cup of the bread crumbs, mayonnaise, onion, Dijon, lemon juice, Worcestershire sauce and parsley; mix well. Stir in crabmeat.

2) Unroll crescent dough; separate into 4 rectangles. Firmly press perforations to seal. Brush rectangles with melted butter; sprinkle each with 1 ½ teaspoons bread crumbs. To make each roll, spoon ¼ cup crab mixture on 1 short end of each rectangle, spreading mixture onto ⅓ of rectangle. Starting with crab-filled side, roll up, just covering crab. Spoon 1 tablespoon red pepper next to edge of crab mixture. Roll up completely; press seam to seal. (Refrigerate remaining crab mixture.) In shallow dish, stir together ¼ cup of the bread crumbs, sesame seed and black sesame seed. Brush outsides of rolls with melted butter; roll in sesame seed mixture. Wrap each roll in plastic wrap. Refrigerate 1 hour.

3) Heat oven to 375°F. Using serrated knife, cut each roll into 6 slices. Press cut side of each slice into remaining ¼ cup bread crumbs. Place each slice, crumb side down, in each of 24 ungreased regular-size muffin cups. Spoon ¼ teaspoon reserved crab mixture onto each slice; drizzle with remaining butter.

4) Bake 12 to 17 minutes or until golden brown. Cool in pan on cooling rack 5 minutes.

5) Transfer appetizers to serving platter. Garnish platter with chopped red pepper and parsley. Serve warm.

1 SERVING: Calories 90; Total Fat 6g (Saturated Fat 2g); Sodium 150mg; Total Carbohydrate 7g (Dietary Fiber 0g); Protein 2g. EXCHANGES: 1/2 Starch, 1 Fat. CARBOHYDRATE CHOICES: 1/2.

Caramelized Onion and Peppered Bacon Flatbread

DAWN LOGTERMAN | JANESVILLE, WI   BAKE-OFF® CONTEST 45, 2012

PREP TIME: 45 MINUTES (READY IN 55 MINUTES)
SERVINGS: 24

¼ cup firmly packed brown sugar

¼ teaspoon McCormick® Ground Black Pepper

⅛ teaspoon McCormick® Cayenne Pepper

8 slices thick-sliced bacon

4 cups thinly sliced sweet onion (about 1 lb)

2 cloves garlic, minced

2 tablespoons LAND O LAKES® Butter

1 can Pillsbury® refrigerated thin pizza crust

1 can (14.5 oz) Muir Glen® organic diced tomatoes, drained

2 cups (8 oz) shredded mozzarella cheese

½ cup grated Parmesan cheese

¼ cup thinly sliced fresh basil leaves

1) Heat oven to 400°F. Line 15x10-inch pan with sides with aluminum foil. Place cooling rack in pan.

2) In large resealable food-storage plastic bag, combine brown sugar, black pepper and cayenne; shake to combine. Separate bacon slices and place in bag; shake to coat. Place bacon on rack in pan.

3) Bake 25 to 30 minutes, turning once halfway through baking, or until bacon is browned and thoroughly cooked. Cool completely. Chop bacon; set aside.

4) Meanwhile, in 12-inch skillet, cook onions and garlic in butter over medium heat 15 to 20 minutes, stirring frequently, or until onions are golden brown. Remove from heat; set aside.

5) Spray 15x10-inch pan with sides with Crisco® Original No-Stick Cooking Spray. Unroll pizza crust dough in pan; press dough to edges of pan. Bake 7 minutes. Remove from oven.

6) Spread onion mixture over partially baked crust; top with drained tomatoes. Sprinkle with mozzarella and Parmesan cheeses; top with bacon.

7) Bake 7 to 11 minutes or until crust is golden brown and cheeses are melted.

8) Remove from oven; sprinkle with basil.

1 SERVING: Calories 130; Total Fat 6g (Saturated Fat 3g); Sodium 300mg; Total Carbohydrate 11g (Dietary Fiber 0g); Protein 6g. EXCHANGES: 1 Starch, 1/2 Medium-Fat Meat, 1/2 Fat. CARBOHYDRATE CHOICES: 1.

Spinach Dip Tarts

PREP TIME: 10 MINUTES (READY IN 10 MINUTES)
SERVINGS: 24 TARTS

 EASY   LOW FAT

1 ½ cups refrigerated spinach dip

¼ cup diced celery

24 frozen mini fillo shells (from two 1.9-oz packages), thawed

5 radishes, sliced, slices cut in half

¼ cup matchstick carrots, cut into quarters

1) In small bowl, mix spinach dip and celery. Divide dip evenly among fillo shells, using about 4 ½ teaspoons in each. Garnish tarts with radishes and carrots.

1 TART: Calories 30; Total Fat 2g (Saturated Fat 0g); Sodium 45mg; Total Carbohydrate 3g (Dietary Fiber 0g); Protein 0g. EXCHANGES: 1/2 Fat. CARBOHYDRATE CHOICES: 0.

Shrimp and Dill Toasts

PREP TIME: 15 MINUTES (READY IN 15 MINUTES)
SERVINGS: 16

 EASY   LOW FAT

½ loaf baguette French bread

⅓ cup chives-and-onion cream cheese spread (from 8-oz container)

⅓ cup finely chopped green bell pepper

8 cooked large shrimp, peeled (tail shells removed), cut in half lengthwise

16 fresh dill weed sprigs

1) Heat oven to 350°F. Cut bread into 16 (½-inch) slices. Place on ungreased cookie sheet. Bake 5 minutes; turn. Bake about 7 minutes longer or until crisp and very light brown. Cool.

2) Spread each toast with 1 teaspoon cream cheese spread; top with 1 teaspoon bell pepper and half a shrimp. Top with 1 sprig dill weed.

3) Serve immediately, or cover and refrigerate up to 1 hour.

1 SERVING: Calories 50; Total Fat 2g (Saturated Fat 1g); Sodium 90mg; Total Carbohydrate 6g (Dietary Fiber 0g); Protein 2g. EXCHANGES: 1/2 Starch, 1/2 Fat. CARBOHYDRATE CHOICES: 1/2.

Asian Grilled Chicken Drummies

PREP TIME: 30 MINUTES (READY IN 1 HOUR 30 MINUTES)
SERVINGS: 8

 EASY

½ cup teriyaki sauce

1 tablespoon Thai red curry sauce

24 chicken wing drummettes
(about 2 ½ lb)

2 tablespoons coarsely chopped
fresh cilantro

2 tablespoons chopped salted
dry-roasted peanuts

1) In resealable food-storage plastic bag, mix teriyaki sauce and curry sauce. Add drummettes; seal bag. Shake to coat chicken evenly with sauce mixture. Refrigerate 1 hour.

2) Heat gas or charcoal grill. Remove drummettes from marinade; discard marinade. Place drummettes on grill over medium heat. Cover grill; cook 20 to 25 minutes until chicken is golden brown on outside and no longer pink in center.

3) Place drummettes on serving platter. Sprinkle with cilantro and peanuts.

1 SERVING: Calories 180; Total Fat 11g (Saturated Fat 3g); Sodium 750mg; Total Carbohydrate 3g (Dietary Fiber 0g); Protein 15g. EXCHANGES: 1-1/2 Lean Meat, 1/2 Medium-Fat Meat, 1 Fat. CARBOHYDRATE CHOICES: 0.

tip

If you like, substitute 3 pounds chicken wings for the drummettes. Cut wings into pieces at joints, and discard tips. Continue the recipe as directed.

Crab Cake Crostini with Corn and Bacon Salsa

KELLY MCWHERTER | HOUSTON, TX

BAKE-OFF® CONTEST 45, 2012

PREP TIME: 40 MINUTES (READY IN 1 HOUR 10 MINUTES)
SERVINGS: 24

12 oz fresh cooked lump crabmeat
    (1 ⅓ cups) or 2 cans (6.5 oz each)
    special white lump crabmeat, drained

⅓ cup Progress® Italian style panko
    bread crumbs

½ cup mayonnaise or salad dressing

1 LAND O LAKES® Egg

2 teaspoons lemon juice

¼ teaspoon McCormick® Garlic Salt

1 can Pillsbury® refrigerated crusty
    French loaf

2 tablespoons LAND O LAKES® Butter,
    melted

1 cup fresh or frozen corn, cooked,
    drained

1 medium tomato, seeded, diced

2 green onions, chopped
    (2 tablespoons)

8 slices bacon, crisply cooked,
    crumbled

2 tablespoons chopped fresh cilantro

1) Heat oven to 350°F. Spray large cookie sheets with Crisco® Original No-Stick Cooking Spray.

2) In medium bowl, combine crabmeat, bread crumbs, ⅓ cup of the mayonnaise, egg, lemon juice and ⅛ teaspoon of the garlic salt; mix well. Carefully unroll loaf of dough; spread crab mixture to within ½ inch of long edges. Starting with 1 long side, roll up tightly; pinch seam to seal. Place, seam side down, on cookie sheet.

3) Bake 25 to 30 minutes or until golden brown. Cool 10 minutes; transfer from cookie sheet to cutting board. Using serrated knife, cut loaf into 24 slices about ½ inch thick.

4) Set oven control to broil. Brush slices with 1 tablespoon of the butter. Place on ungreased cookie sheet. Broil 4 to 6 inches from heat 1 to 2 minutes. Turn; brush with remaining 1 tablespoon butter; broil 1 to 2 minutes or until crisp and golden brown. Cool 5 minutes.

5) Meanwhile, in small bowl, combine remaining mayonnaise, corn, tomato, green onions, bacon, cilantro and remaining ⅛ teaspoon garlic salt. Spoon about 1 tablespoon mayonnaise mixture onto each slice.

1 SERVING: Calories 120; Total Fat 7g (Saturated Fat 1.5g); Sodium 250mg; Total Carbohydrate 9g (Dietary Fiber 0g); Protein 5g. EXCHANGES: 1/2 Starch, 1/2 Lean Meat, 1 Fat. CARBOHYDRATE CHOICES: 1/2.

Baked Clam Dip with Crusty French Bread Dippers

CHRISTINE FIELD | SHILLINGTON, PA   BAKE-OFF® CONTEST 45, 2012

PREP TIME: 50 MINUTES (READY IN 2 HOURS 30 MINUTES)
SERVINGS: 30 (5 BREAD DIPPERS AND ABOUT 3 TABLESPOONS DIP)

2 cans Pillsbury® refrigerated crusty French loaf

1 can (18.5 oz) Progresso® Light New England clam chowder soup

1 package (8 oz) ⅓-less-fat cream cheese (Neufchâtel), softened

1 can (10.5 oz) Progresso® white clam sauce

1 cup shredded mozzarella cheese (4 oz)

½ cup grated Parmesan cheese

1 ½ cups Progresso® panko bread crumbs

1 cup LAND O LAKES® Butter, melted

¼ teaspoon McCormick® Parsley Flakes

1 tablespoon McCormick® Garlic Powder

1) Heat oven to 350°F. Spray 1 ½-quart shallow oven-proof serving dish or 9 ½-inch glass deep-dish pie plate with Crisco® Original No-Stick Cooking Spray.

2) Spray 2 large cookie sheets with Crisco® Original No-Stick Cooking Spray. With serrated knife, cut both loaves of dough in half lengthwise. Place 2 pieces of dough, cut sides down, on each cookie sheet; cut 4 or 5 (½-inch-deep) slashes diagonally on top of each loaf.

3) Bake 17 to 20 minutes or until golden brown. Cool on cooling rack.

4) Meanwhile, in food processor bowl, place soup. Cover; process until almost smooth. Add cream cheese; cover and process until well blended. Pour into large bowl; stir in clam sauce, mozzarella cheese, Parmesan cheese and 1 cup of the bread crumbs until well mixed. Pour mixture into serving dish.

5) In small bowl, stir 2 tablespoons of the butter, remaining ½ cup bread crumbs and parsley flakes until well mixed. Sprinkle crumb mixture evenly over clam soup mixture.

6) Bake 35 to 40 minutes or until bubbly and light golden brown around edges. Cool 30 minutes on cooling rack.

7) Meanwhile, in small bowl, stir remaining butter and garlic powder until well mixed. With serrated knife, cut each loaf into 14-inch slices; place on cookie sheets. Brush each slice with garlic-butter mixture (reserve remaining garlic-butter mixture).

8) Bake slices 5 to 8 minutes or until golden brown. Remove from oven; turn slices. Brush with remaining garlic-butter mixture. Bake 5 to 8 minutes or until golden brown and crisp. Cool 5 minutes. Serve bread with warm clam dip. Store any remaining clam dip in refrigerator.

1 SERVING: Calories 180; Total Fat 11g (Saturated Fat 6g); Sodium 400mg; Total Carbohydrate 16g (Dietary Fiber 0g); Protein 5g. EXCHANGES: 1 Starch, 2 Fat. CARBOHYDRATE CHOICES: 1.

Asparagus, Artichoke and Red Pepper Pizza

PREP TIME: 35 MINUTES (READY IN 55 MINUTES)
SERVINGS: 24

8 oz fresh asparagus spears, trimmed

1 large red bell pepper, cut into ½-inch strips

1 tablespoon Crisco® 100% Extra Virgin Olive Oil

¼ teaspoon McCormick® Sea Salt

¼ cup Progresso® panko bread crumbs

1 can Pillsbury® refrigerated classic pizza crust

6 tablespoons whipped cream cheese spread

1 to 2 teaspoons grated lemon peel

1 jar (12 oz) marinated artichoke hearts, drained, chopped

¾ cup shredded Swiss cheese (3 oz)

¾ cup shredded Gruyère cheese (3 oz)

½ teaspoon McCormick® Garlic Powder

1) Heat oven to 400°F. Place asparagus and red pepper in ungreased 13x9-inch pan; drizzle with olive oil and sprinkle with sea salt.

2) Bake vegetables 12 to 16 minutes or until crisp-tender, turning once halfway through baking. Cool 5 minutes.

3) Meanwhile, spray cookie sheet with Crisco® Original No-Stick Cooking Spray. Sprinkle with bread crumbs. Unroll pizza crust dough onto crumb-coated sheet; press into 15x10-inch rectangle. Flute edges of dough.

4) Bake 12 to 16 minutes or until crust is golden brown. Cool 5 minutes.

5) Meanwhile, cut asparagus and red pepper into ½-inch pieces. Spread cream cheese onto warm crust; sprinkle with lemon peel. Arrange half of the artichokes, asparagus and red pepper over cream cheese; sprinkle with half of the Swiss and Gruyère cheeses. Repeat with remaining vegetables and cheeses.

6) Bake 8 to 10 minutes or until edges are golden brown and cheese is melted. Remove from oven; sprinkle with garlic powder.

1 SERVING: Calories 100; Total Fat 4g (Saturated Fat 2g); Sodium 210mg; Total Carbohydrate 11g (Dietary Fiber 2g); Protein 4g. EXCHANGES: 1/2 Starch, 1/2 Vegetable, 1 Fat. CARBOHYDRATE CHOICES: 1.

Mexican Hot Cocoa

PREP TIME: 5 MINUTES (READY IN 2 HOURS 5 MINUTES)
SERVINGS: 7 (1 CUP EACH)

e EASY

4 cups milk or half-and-half

1 ½ cups hot water

¾ cup packed brown sugar

2 tablespoons instant espresso coffee powder or granules

2 teaspoons vanilla

6 oz bittersweet baking chocolate, chopped

9 cinnamon sticks (2 to 3 inch)

1 ancho chile

Frozen whipped topping, thawed, if desired

Ground red pepper (cayenne) or chili powder, if desired

1) Spray 3- to 4-quart slow cooker with cooking spray. In slow cooker, mix milk, hot water, brown sugar, coffee powder, vanilla, chocolate, 2 of the cinnamon sticks and the ancho chile.

2) Cover; cook on Low heat setting 2 to 3 hours. Stir hot cocoa and remove ancho chile before serving. Garnish individual servings with whipped topping, red pepper and remaining cinnamon sticks.

1 SERVING: Calories 311; Total Fat 13g (Saturated Fat 8g); Sodium 73mg; Total Carbohydrate 42.5g (Dietary Fiber 0.5g); Protein 6.5g. EXCHANGES: 2 Other Carbohydrate, 1 Low-Fat Milk, 1-1/2 Fat. CARBOHYDRATE CHOICES: 3.

tip

Mexican hot chocolate is frothy when served. To achieve this effect, vigorously stir hot cocoa with whisk until very frothy. Immediately pour into mugs and serve.

Marmalade-Glazed Asian Meatball Cups

CHERYL LANGLOIS | JEFFERSON, WI

BAKE-OFF® CONTEST 45, 2012

PREP TIME: 20 MINUTES (READY IN 40 MINUTES)
SERVINGS: 24

e EASY

¼ cup Smucker's® Sweet Orange Marmalade

2 tablespoons Chinese plum sauce

1 to 2 teaspoons chili paste

2 cans Pillsbury® Butter Flake refrigerated crescent dinner rolls

24 frozen meatballs (½ oz each), thawed

1 teaspoon McCormick® Sesame Seed

1) Heat oven to 375°F. Lightly spray 24 regular-size muffin cups with Crisco® Original No-Stick Cooking Spray.

2) In small microwavable bowl, microwave marmalade on High 15 to 30 seconds or until melted. Stir in plum sauce and chili paste. Set aside.

3) Remove crescent dough from cans, but do not unroll. Cut each roll into 12 slices. Place 1 slice in bottom of each muffin cup; press ½-inch-wide indentation in center of each slice. Place 1 meatball in each cup; top with scant 1 teaspoon marmalade mixture. Sprinkle with sesame seed.

4) Bake 10 to 15 minutes or until edges are golden brown. Cool 5 minutes. Serve warm.

1 SERVING: Calories 120; Total Fat 6g (Saturated Fat 2g); Sodium 240mg; Total Carbohydrate 12g (Dietary Fiber 0g); Protein 4g. EXCHANGES: 1 Starch, 1 Fat. CARBOHYDRATE CHOICES: 1.

Bacon and Leek Tart

PREP TIME: 35 MINUTES (READY IN 1 HOUR 5 MINUTES)
SERVINGS: 6

1 sheet frozen puff pastry (from 17.3-oz package), thawed

1 egg white, slightly beaten

3 thick slices hickory-smoked bacon

4 medium leeks, sliced

1 cup shredded Gruyère cheese (4 oz)

2 teaspoons chopped fresh thyme leaves

½ teaspoon salt

½ teaspoon pepper

1) Heat oven to 400°F. Unfold pastry sheet; place in 9-inch square tart pan with removable bottom. Brush pastry with egg white. Bake 15 to 20 minutes or until browned.

2) Meanwhile, in 12-inch skillet, cook bacon over medium-high heat 8 to 11 minutes or until crisp; drain on paper towels. Crumble bacon; set aside. Reserve 1 tablespoon bacon drippings in skillet. Add leeks to drippings; cook over medium heat 5 to 7 minutes, stirring occasionally, until tender. Remove from heat. Stir in ½ cup of the cheese, the chopped thyme, salt and pepper.

3) Press pastry with back of spoon to flatten. Spoon leek mixture over pastry; sprinkle with crumbled bacon and remaining ½ cup cheese. Bake 5 to 7 minutes or until cheese is melted. Serve warm.

1 SERVING: Calories 332; Total Fat 21g (Saturated Fat 8g); Sodium 614mg; Total Carbohydrate 23g (Dietary Fiber 2g); Protein 12g. EXCHANGES: 1 Starch, 1-1/2 Vegetable, 1-1/2 High-Fat Meat, 1-1/2 Fat. CARBOHYDRATE CHOICES: 1-1/2.

tip Frozen puff pastry dough is available in sheets or individual shells. It has dozens of paper-thin layers of dough separated by butter. As the pastry bakes, steam created from water in the dough makes the layers rise up and pull apart, resulting in a crisp, flaky pastry.

Baked Brie with Raspberry Preserves

| PREP TIME: | 15 MINUTES (READY IN 55 MINUTES) |
| SERVINGS: | 20 |

 EASY

1 can (8 oz) Pillsbury® Crescent Recipe Creations® refrigerated seamless dough sheet

½ cup raspberry or strawberry preserves

⅓ cup sliced almonds, toasted

1 round (12 to 13 oz) Brie cheese

2 cinnamon sticks (3 inch)

Assorted crackers, baguette slices, or apple slices, as desired

1) Heat oven to 375°F. Unroll dough and roll into 12x8-inch rectangle. Trim dough to 10x8-inch rectangle; reserve dough scraps. Spread ¼ cup of the preserves in 6-inch circle on center of dough rectangle; sprinkle with almonds. Place cheese on center of dough; spread with remaining ¼ cup preserves. Press dough evenly around cheese and press to seal completely.

2) Turn pastry-wrapped cheese upside down onto ungreased cookie sheet. Brush top of pastry with water. With small owl-shaped cookie cutter, cut shape from dough scraps. Arrange cutout on top of pastry. Add cinnamon sticks for branches.

3) Bake 20 to 25 minutes or until golden brown. Cool 15 minutes. Serve warm with crackers. Store any remaining Brie in refrigerator.

1 SERVING: Calories 135; Total Fat 8g (Saturated Fat 4g); Sodium 205mg; Total Carbohydrate 10g (Dietary Fiber 0g); Protein 5g. EXCHANGES: 1/2 Starch, 1/2 High-Fat Meat, 1 Fat. CARBOHYDRATE CHOICES: 1/2.

Beef and Caramelized Onion Canapés

PREP TIME: 45 MINUTES (READY IN 1 HOUR 30 MINUTES)
SERVINGS: 36

1 teaspoon salt

¼ teaspoon garlic powder

¼ teaspoon paprika

¼ teaspoon coarse ground black pepper

1 lb beef tenderloin, trimmed

3 tablespoons butter

1 tablespoon canola oil

2 tablespoons packed brown sugar

3 medium onions, thinly sliced

2 tablespoons dry red wine or water

½ cup sour cream

1 tablespoon prepared horseradish sauce

36 baguette slices

1 ½ cups firmly packed baby spinach leaves

1) Heat oven to 450°F. In small bowl, mix ½ teaspoon of the salt, the garlic powder, paprika and pepper. Rub mixture all over beef. Place beef in small shallow roasting pan; tuck thin end under.

2) Bake 20 to 25 minutes or until meat thermometer inserted in center reads 140°F. Cool completely.

3) Meanwhile, in 12-inch skillet, heat butter and oil over medium heat until butter melts. Add brown sugar and onions; stir to coat. Cook 10 minutes, stirring occasionally, until onions begin to soften. Add wine. Reduce heat to medium-low. Cover; cook 10 to 15 minutes or until onions are very tender.

4) In small bowl, mix sour cream, horseradish and remaining ½ teaspoon salt. To serve, spread baguette slices with sour cream mixture. Top each with spinach leaves. Thinly slice beef; layer over spinach. Top with onions.

1 SERVING: Calories 80; Total Fat 4g (Saturated Fat 1.5g); Sodium 170mg; Total Carbohydrate 7g (Dietary Fiber 0g); Protein 4g. EXCHANGES: 1/2 Starch, 1/2 Very Lean Meat, 1/2 Fat. CARBOHYDRATE CHOICES: 1/2.

Caramelized Onion Dip

PREP TIME: 20 MINUTES (READY IN 8 HOURS 40 MINUTES)
SERVINGS: 28 (1/4 CUP DIP EACH)

 EASY

2 ¾ lb sweet onions, chopped (5 ¾ cups)

½ cup balsamic vinegar

¼ cup butter or margarine, cut into pieces

3 packages (8 oz each) cream cheese, softened

1 cup whipping cream

1 cup crumbled blue cheese (4 oz)

½ teaspoon salt

½ teaspoon freshly ground pepper

4 slices thick-sliced bacon, crisply cooked, crumbled (½ cup)

½ cup chopped fresh parsley

1) Spray 4-quart slow cooker with cooking spray. In slow cooker, mix onions, vinegar and butter. Cover; cook on Low heat setting 8 hours or until onions are golden brown.

2) In large bowl, beat cream cheese with electric mixer on medium speed until creamy. Add whipping cream; beat on low speed until smooth. Stir in blue cheese, salt and pepper until well blended. Add cream cheese mixture to onion mixture in slow cooker; stir until blended.

3) Cover; cook 20 minutes longer or until thoroughly heated. Sprinkle with bacon and parsley.

1 SERVING: Calories 162; Total Fat 14.5g (Saturated Fat 8.5g); Sodium 234mg; Total Carbohydrate 5.5g (Dietary Fiber 0.5g); Protein 3.5g. EXCHANGES: 1 Vegetable, 3 Fat. CARBOHYDRATE CHOICES: 0.

tip

Freeze sweet onions for longer storage. Chop and place in a 15x10x1-inch pan in the freezer. When they're frozen, place in freezer bags or containers and freeze for up to 1 year.

Broccoli-Cheese Bites

PREP TIME: 35 MINUTES (READY IN 35 MINUTES)
SERVINGS: 32 APPETIZERS

Vegetable oil for deep frying

2 teaspoons vegetable oil

1 medium onion, chopped (½ cup)

2 cups baking mix

1 container (8 oz) sour cream

2 eggs

1 cup shredded Cheddar cheese (4 oz)

1 cup chopped fresh broccoli florets

¼ teaspoon ground red pepper (cayenne)

¼ teaspoon salt

1 jar (2 oz) diced pimientos, drained

1) In deep fat fryer or 3-quart heavy saucepan, heat 1 ½ inches oil to 375°F.

2) In 8-inch skillet, heat 2 teaspoons oil over medium-high heat. Cook onion in oil 5 minutes, stirring occasionally, until tender.

3) In large bowl, stir baking mix, sour cream and eggs until blended. Stir in onion, cheese, broccoli, red pepper, salt and pimientos.

4) Drop batter by tablespoonfuls into hot oil. Fry 1 to 2 minutes, turning several times, until golden brown. Drain on paper towels. Serve hot.

1 APPETIZER: Calories 128; Total Fat 11g (Saturated Fat 3g); Sodium 143mg; Total Carbohydrate 6g (Dietary Fiber 0g); Protein 2g. EXCHANGES: 1/2 Starch, 2 Fat. CARBOHYDRATE CHOICES: 1/2.

tip

These savory bites would be delicious served with rémoulade sauce for dipping.

Roasted Lemon-White Bean Dip

PREP TIME: 15 MINUTES (READY IN 40 MINUTES)
SERVINGS: 22 (2 TABLESPOONS DIP EACH)

 e EASY **lf** LOW FAT

2 lemons

4 cloves garlic, peeled

3 tablespoons olive oil

2 cans (15 to 15.5 oz each) cannellini or navy beans, drained, ¼ cup liquid reserved

½ teaspoon salt

½ teaspoon ground red pepper (cayenne)

2 tablespoons chopped fresh parsley

Additional chopped fresh parsley, if desired

Assorted fresh vegetables or pita (pocket) breads, cut into wedges

1) Heat oven to 425°F. Cut lemons in half crosswise. Rub lemons and garlic with 1 tablespoon of the oil. Place lemon halves, cut sides down, and garlic in 9-inch glass pie plate. Roast uncovered 25 minutes or until lemon peel is golden brown and very soft. Cool slightly.

2) Reserve ⅓ cup beans. In food processor, place remaining beans, ¼ cup reserved bean liquid, remaining 2 tablespoons oil, the salt and red pepper. Add roasted garlic. Squeeze juice and pulp from roasted lemons into blender. Cover; process until smooth.

3) Spoon dip into serving bowl; stir in reserved ⅓ cup beans and 2 tablespoons parsley. Sprinkle with additional parsley. Serve with vegetables or pita wedges.

1 SERVING: Calories 49; Total Fat 2g (Saturated Fat 0g); Sodium 146mg; Total Carbohydrate 6g (Dietary Fiber 2g); Protein 2g. EXCHANGES: 1/2 Starch, 1/2 Fat. CARBOHYDRATE CHOICES: 1/2.

Peachy Cream Cheese Appetizers

SHANA BUTLER | SAN DIEGO, CA

BAKE-OFF® CONTEST 45, 2012

PREP TIME: 30 MINUTES (READY IN 40 MINUTES)
SERVINGS: 24

- 2 cans Pillsbury® Crescent Recipe Creations® refrigerated seamless dough sheet
- 2 packages (3 oz each) cream cheese, cut into 24 pieces
- 1 jar (12 oz) Smucker's® Peach Preserves
- 2 tablespoons finely chopped shallots
- 1 medium lime, grated and juiced
- ½ teaspoon McCormick® Chili Powder
- ½ teaspoon McCormick® Ground Cumin
- 2 tablespoons chopped fresh cilantro

1) Heat oven to 350°F. Unroll 1 dough sheet; press into 12x8-inch rectangle. Cut dough sheet into 12 squares. Repeat with remaining dough sheet. Place 1 dough square in bottom and up side of each of 24 ungreased regular-size muffin cups, letting points of dough extend over edge of cup. Place 1 piece of cream cheese in bottom of each cup.

2) Bake 12 to 17 minutes or until golden brown.

3) Meanwhile, in 1-quart saucepan, add peach preserves, shallots, 2 teaspoons lime juice, chili powder and cumin; mix well. Cook over medium-low heat 8 to 10 minutes, stirring occasionally, or until thoroughly heated. Remove from heat; stir in cilantro.

4) Remove cups from pans; place on serving platter. Immediately spoon about 1 teaspoon peach sauce over cream cheese in each cup. Sprinkle each cup with lime peel. Serve warm with remaining sauce.

1 SERVING: Calories 130; Total Fat 5g (Saturated Fat 2.5g); Sodium 180mg; Total Carbohydrate 19g (Dietary Fiber 0g); Protein 1g. EXCHANGES: 1/2 Starch, 1 Other Carbohydrate, 1 Fat. CARBOHYDRATE CHOICES: 1.

Iced Caramel Cappuccino

| PREP TIME: | 5 MINUTES (READY IN 5 MINUTES) |
| SERVINGS: | 4 |

 EASY   LOW FAT

2 tablespoons instant espresso coffee powder or granules

½ cup caramel topping

2 tablespoons sugar

1 cup milk

½ cup whipped cream topping (from aerosol can)

1) In 4-cup microwavable measuring cup, microwave 1 ½ cups water uncovered on High 2 to 3 minutes or until very hot and almost boiling. Stir in espresso powder until dissolved. Stir in ¼ cup of the caramel topping, the sugar and milk.

2) To serve, fill 4 (12-oz) glasses two-thirds with ice. Divide coffee mixture among glasses. Top with whipped cream; drizzle with remaining caramel topping.

1 SERVING: Calories 190; Total Fat 3g (Saturated Fat 2g); Sodium 180mg; Total Carbohydrate 38g (Dietary Fiber 0g); Protein 3g. EXCHANGES: 1/2 Starch, 2 Other Carbohydrate, 1/2 Fat. CARBOHYDRATE CHOICES: 2-1/2.

Almond-Chicken Crescent Crostini

| PREP TIME: | 15 MINUTES (READY IN 35 MINUTES) |
| SERVINGS: | 16 |

 EASY

1 can Pillsbury® Place 'n Bake® refrigerated crescent rounds

½ cup pineapple cream cheese spread (from 8-oz container)

½ cup chèvre (goat) cheese (2 oz)

⅛ teaspoon McCormick® Basil Leaves

Dash McCormick® Ground Thyme

1 can (5 oz) chunk white chicken breast in water, well drained

⅓ cup Fisher® Chef's Naturals® Natural Sliced Almonds, chopped

2 tablespoons chopped fresh parsley

1) Heat oven to 375°F. Prepare and bake crescent rounds as directed on can. Remove to cooling rack; cool 5 minutes.

2) Meanwhile, in medium bowl, beat cream cheese, goat cheese, basil and thyme with electric mixer on low speed until blended. Stir chicken into cream cheese mixture.

3) With serrated knife, cut each round in half horizontally. Place rounds, cut side up, on cookie sheet. Bake 3 to 5 minutes until just starting to brown and surface is crisp. Cool 5 minutes.

4) Spread about 1 tablespoonful cream cheese mixture on each round; sprinkle each 1 with teaspoon almonds.

5) Bake 12 to 15 minutes or until thoroughly heated. Sprinkle appetizers with parsley. Cool 5 minutes. Serve warm.

1 SERVING: Calories 110; Total Fat 7g (Saturated Fat 3g); Sodium 180mg; Total Carbohydrate 6g (Dietary Fiber 0g); Protein 5g. EXCHANGES: 1/2 Starch, 1/2 Very Lean Meat, 1-1/2 Fat. CARBOHYDRATE CHOICES: 1/2.

Brie and Candied Tomato Tartlets

KELLY DROST | EL CAJON, CA

BAKE-OFF® CONTEST 45, 2012

PREP TIME: 45 MINUTES (READY IN 45 MINUTES)
SERVINGS: 24

48 small grape tomatoes (from 12-oz package)

1 tablespoon Crisco® Pure Olive Oil

3 tablespoons sugar

3 tablespoons red wine vinegar

⅛ teaspoon salt

1 tablespoon LAND O LAKES® Unsalted or Salted Butter, softened

1 box Pillsbury® refrigerated pie crusts, softened as directed on box

1 LAND O LAKES® Egg

1 tablespoon water

3 oz Brie cheese, rind removed, cut into 24 cubes

½ cup shaved Parmigiano-Reggiano cheese (2 oz)

1 ½ teaspoons McCormick® Basil Leaves

1) In 2-quart saucepan, cook tomatoes in olive oil over medium-high heat 2 minutes. Stir in sugar and red wine vinegar; bring to a boil. Reduce heat; simmer 10 minutes, stirring occasionally (being careful not to break up tomatoes), or until thoroughly heated. Stir in salt; remove from heat.

2) Heat oven to 425°F. Grease bottoms of 24 regular-size muffin cups with butter. Unroll pie crusts. Using 2 ½-inch round cookie cutter, cut 12 rounds from each pie crust, rerolling dough if necessary. Press 1 round in bottom and halfway up side of each cup. In small bowl, beat egg and water until well blended; brush on crusts.

3) Place 1 cube Brie cheese in each cup. With slotted spoon, place 2 tomatoes into each cup (reserve candied-tomato sauce). Top cups with half of the Parmigiano-Reggiano cheese; sprinkle with basil.

4) Bake 9 to 12 minutes or until crust is golden brown.

5) Top tartlets with remaining Parmigiano-Reggiano cheese. Serve with reserved candied-tomato sauce. Serve warm.

1 SERVING: Calories 110; Total Fat 7g (Saturated Fat 3g); Sodium 160mg; Total Carbohydrate 10g (Dietary Fiber 0g); Protein 2g. EXCHANGES: 1/2 Starch, 1-1/2 Fat. CARBOHYDRATE CHOICES: 1/2.

Gruyère-Bacon Pizza Minis

PEGGY SULLIVAN | RADFORD , VA

BAKE-OFF® CONTEST 45, 2012

PREP TIME: 30 MINUTES (READY IN 45 MINUTES)
SERVINGS: 16

2 tablespoons LAND O LAKES® Unsalted or Salted Butter, melted

2 teaspoons Worcestershire sauce

⅓ cup Progress°® panko bread crumbs

1 tablespoon shredded Parmesan cheese

¼ teaspoon McCormick® Cracked Black Pepper

1 can Pillsbury® refrigerated thin pizza crust

3 slices bacon, cut in half

¼ cup finely chopped sweet onion

⅔ cup refrigerated four-cheese Alfredo pasta sauce

½ cup shredded Gruyère cheese (2 oz)

1) Heat oven to 400°F. Spray cookie sheet with Crisco® Original No-Stick Cooking Spray. In small bowl, stir together butter and 1 teaspoon of the Worcestershire sauce until well blended. In shallow dish, combine bread crumbs, Parmesan cheese and pepper; mix well.

2) Remove pizza crust dough from can, but do not unroll dough. Using sharp knife, cut roll into 16 slices. With hands, flatten each slice into 2 ½-inch round. Brush both sides of each round with butter mixture; coat both sides with bread crumb mixture. Place ½ inch apart on cookie sheet.

3) Bake 4 to 8 minutes or until light golden brown.

4) Meanwhile, in 10-inch skillet over medium heat, cook bacon until crisp. Drain on paper towels; crumble. Reserve 1 teaspoon bacon drippings in skillet. Add onion; cook over medium heat 1 to 2 minutes, stirring frequently, or until tender. Remove from heat; stir in Alfredo sauce, remaining 1 teaspoon Worcestershire sauce and bacon. Spoon about 2 teaspoons bacon mixture onto each round; sprinkle with Gruyère cheese.

5) Bake 7 to 10 minutes or until cheese is melted. Serve warm.

1 SERVING: Calories 140; Total Fat 8g (Saturated Fat 4g); Sodium 220mg; Total Carbohydrate 12g (Dietary Fiber 0g); Protein 4g. EXCHANGES: 1 Starch, 1-1/2 Fat. CARBOHYDRATE CHOICES: 1.

Artichoke-Crab Spread

PREP TIME: 15 MINUTES (READY IN 1 HOUR 30 MINUTES)
SERVINGS: 24 (2 TABLESPOONS SPREAD AND 2 BREAD SLICES EACH)

 EASY

1   cup refrigerated flake-style imitation crabmeat (from 8-oz package)

½   cup grated Parmesan cheese

4   teaspoons lemon juice

4   medium green onions, sliced (¼ cup)

1   can (14 oz) Progresso® artichoke hearts, drained, coarsely chopped

1   package (8 oz) cream cheese, cut into cubes

48 slices French bread baguette or cocktail rye bread

1) Spray 1- to 1 ½-quart slow cooker with cooking spray. In slow cooker, mix all ingredients except bread.

2) Cover and cook on low heat setting 1 to 1 ¼ hours (or high heat setting 30 to 45 minutes) or until cream cheese is melted. Stir until cheese is smooth.

3) Scrape down side of slow cooker with rubber spatula to help prevent edge of spread from scorching. Serve with bread. Spread can be held on Low heat setting up to 3 hours; stir occasionally.

2 TABLESPOONS: Calories 90; Total Fat 4.5g (Saturated Fat 2.5g); Sodium 250mg; Total Carbohydrate 9g (Dietary Fiber 1g); Protein 4g. EXCHANGES: 1/2 Starch, 1 Fat. CARBOHYDRATE CHOICES: 1/2.

tip

Everyone will love this delicious spread. Due to the richness of the cheeses, however, the spread may start to separate and little puddles could appear on the surface. Stir occasionally, and the spread will look as good as new.

Cappuccino Toppers

DAWN ONUFFER | CRESTVIEW, FL

BAKE-OFF® CONTEST 45, 2012

PREP TIME: 30 MINUTES (READY IN 2 HOURS 5 MINUTES)
SERVINGS: 48

1 package Pillsbury® Ready to Bake!™ refrigerated oatmeal chocolate chip cookies

1 package (8 oz) cream cheese, softened

⅓ cup sugar

3 tablespoons instant cappuccino coffee mix

1 ½ cups frozen (thawed) whipped topping (4 oz)

¼ cup Hershey's® mini chips semi-sweet chocolate baking chips

2 tablespoons chocolate sprinkles

1) Heat oven to 350°F. Spray 48 mini muffin cups with Crisco® Original No-Stick Cooking Spray. Cut each cookie in half; press each half into bottom of mini muffin cup.

2) Bake 6 to 9 minutes or until golden brown. Cool 10 minutes in pans. With knife, remove cookies from pans to cooling racks. Cool completely, about 20 minutes.

3) Meanwhile, in medium bowl, beat cream cheese, sugar and cappuccino mix with electric mixer on medium speed until smooth and creamy. Gently fold in whipped topping and mini chips.

4) Spoon or pipe mixture onto each cookie (if piping, fit decorating bag with star tip with ¾-inch opening). Top each with sprinkles. Refrigerate 1 hour before serving. Store covered in refrigerator.

1 SERVING: Calories 80; Total Fat 4.5g (Saturated Fat 2.5g); Sodium 55mg; Total Carbohydrate 10g (Dietary Fiber 0g); Protein 0g. EXCHANGES: 1/2 Other Carbohydrate, 1 Fat. CARBOHYDRATE CHOICES: 1/2.

Tomato-Basil Tart

PREP TIME:	45 MINUTES (READY IN 1 HOUR 25 MINUTES)
SERVINGS:	10

1 Pillsbury® refrigerated pie crust, softened as directed on box

⅓ cup crushed round buttery crackers

¾ cup grated Parmesan cheese

¾ cup mayonnaise

7 plum (Roma) tomatoes, thinly sliced

½ teaspoon salt

½ teaspoon freshly ground pepper

¼ cup fresh basil leaves, thinly shredded

6 slices bacon, crisply cooked, crumbled

Additional shredded fresh basil leaves, if desired

1) Heat oven to 350°F. Place pie crust in 9-inch square tart pan with removable bottom as directed on box for One-Crust Filled Pie; trim edges. Prick crust with fork. Bake 14 minutes or until lightly browned. Sprinkle half of the cracker crumbs over partially baked crust.

2) In small bowl, mix cheese and mayonnaise. Spoon and carefully spread half of the cheese mixture over crumbs. Arrange tomato slices over top; sprinkle evenly with salt and pepper. Sprinkle with ¼ cup basil and the bacon. Spoon and spread remaining cheese mixture on top. Sprinkle with remaining cracker crumbs.

3) Bake 24 to 25 minutes or until browned. Garnish with additional basil. Serve warm.

1 SERVING: Calories 366; Total Fat 30g (Saturated Fat 8g); Sodium 784mg; Total Carbohydrate 17g (Dietary Fiber 1g); Protein 9g. EXCHANGES: 1 Starch, 1 High-Fat Meat, 4 Fat. CARBOHYDRATE CHOICES: 1.

Sweet and Spicy Cocktail Riblets

PREP TIME: 10 MINUTES (READY IN 6 HOURS 10 MINUTES)
SERVINGS: 30

 EASY

3 lb smoked pork loin back ribs, cut in half lengthwise across bones and then into 1 ½-inch pieces

¾ cup ketchup

½ cup pineapple preserves

½ cup teriyaki marinade and sauce (from 10-oz bottle)

¼ cup packed brown sugar

2 cloves garlic, finely chopped

1) Spray inside of 3 ½- to 4-quart slow cooker with cooking spray. Place ribs in slow cooker. In small bowl, mix remaining ingredients; pour over ribs.

2) Cover; cook on Low heat setting 6 to 8 hours or until ribs are tender. Skim fat from cooking liquid, if necessary.

1 SERVING: Calories 110; Total Fat 7g (Saturated Fat 2g); Sodium 430mg; Total Carbohydrate 8g (Dietary Fiber 0g); Protein 4g. EXCHANGES: 1 Fat. CARBOHYDRATE CHOICES: 1/2.

Spiced Cider

PREP TIME: 5 MINUTES (READY IN 4 HOURS 5 MINUTES)
SERVINGS: 14 (1 CUP EACH)

 EASY   LOW FAT

1 container (59 oz) pineapple-orange juice

8 cups apple cider

1 tablespoon honey

1 large orange

2 cinnamon sticks (2 to 3 inch)

½ teaspoon whole cloves

1 slice (1 inch) fresh gingerroot, peeled

7 whole cardamom

2 star anise, if desired

Small pineapple wedges, if desired

1) In 3-quart slow cooker, mix pineapple-orange juice, apple cider and honey. Remove outer peel of orange with citrus zester or vegetable peeler. Cut peel into thin 3- to 4-inch-long strips. Add orange peel, cinnamon sticks, cloves, gingerroot, cardamom and star anise to slow cooker.

2) Cover; cook on Low heat setting 4 hours. Before serving, strain cider to remove whole spices. Serve hot. Garnish with pineapple wedges.

1 SERVING: Calories 137; Total Fat 0g (Saturated Fat 0g); Sodium 27mg; Total Carbohydrate 34g (Dietary Fiber 0.5g); Protein 0g. EXCHANGES: 2 Fruit. CARBOHYDRATE CHOICES: 2.

CHEESY BEAN DIP
PG. 73

Snacks & Munchies

When it comes to casual parties or just tiding over the family until dinner, these small bites go over big.

DEVILISH CHICKEN WINGS
PG. 68

MONSTER BALL
PG. 64

CHOCOLATE-PEANUT
BUTTER HAYSTACKS
PG. 75

Peanut Butter-Graham Cereal Bars

PREP TIME: 15 MINUTES (READY IN 1 HOUR 15 MINUTES)
SERVINGS: 24 BARS

 EASY

1   cup light corn syrup

1   cup sugar

1   cup creamy peanut butter

1   box (12 oz) Golden Grahams® cereal
    (8 cups)

3   cups miniature marshmallows

    Chocolate chips, melted, if desired

1) Lightly butter 13x9-inch pan. In 5-quart Dutch oven, heat corn syrup and sugar to boiling over medium-high heat, stirring constantly. Cook until sugar is dissolved; remove from heat.

2) Add peanut butter; stir until smooth. Add cereal; mix well. Stir in marshmallows, 1 cup at a time.

3) Spoon mixture into pan; using back of spoon, lightly spread mixture evenly and press into pan. Drizzle with melted chocolate chips. Let stand at room temperature at least 1 hour or until firm. Cut into 6 rows by 4 rows. Store loosely covered at room temperature up to 2 days.

1 BAR: Calories 230; Total Fat 6g (Saturated Fat 1g); Sodium 190mg; Total Carbohydrate 41g (Dietary Fiber 1g); Protein 3g. EXCHANGES: 1 Starch, 1-1/2 Other Carbohydrate, 1 Fat. CARBOHYDRATE CHOICES: 3.

To make the bars more special, drizzle with melted chocolate chips. Cheerios® cereal can be substituted for the Golden Grahams® cereal.

Spicy Straw Stacks

PREP TIME: 20 MINUTES (READY IN 30 MINUTES)
SERVINGS: 20

 EASY

½ cup butter or margarine

½ cup sugar

¼ cup dark corn syrup

½ teaspoon ground red pepper (cayenne)

½ teaspoon black pepper

1 can (11.5 oz) mixed nuts

1 cup chow mein noodles

¼ teaspoon kosher (coarse) salt, if desired

1) Line cookie sheet with cooking parchment or waxed paper; spray paper with cooking spray.

2) In 10-inch nonstick skillet, melt butter over medium heat. Stir in sugar, corn syrup, red pepper and black pepper. Cook 4 to 5 minutes, stirring often, until sugar melts and glaze begins to thicken (mixture will look foamy).

3) Remove from heat; stir in nuts and chow mein noodles. Immediately drop in stacks of about 2 tablespoons each onto cookie sheet. Sprinkle with salt. Cool completely. Store tightly covered between layers of waxed paper.

1 SERVING: Calories 190; Total Fat 15g (Saturated Fat 4.5g); Sodium 115mg; Total Carbohydrate 13g (Dietary Fiber 1g); Protein 3g. EXCHANGES: 1 Starch, 2-1/2 Fat. CARBOHYDRATE CHOICES: 1.

Five-Layer Mexican Dip

PREP TIME: 20 MINUTES (READY IN 20 MINUTES)
SERVINGS: 20

 EASY

1 can (16 oz) Old El Paso® refried beans

2 tablespoons Old El Paso® Thick 'n Chunky salsa

1 ½ cups sour cream

1 cup guacamole

1 cup shredded Cheddar cheese (4 oz)

2 medium green onions, chopped (2 tablespoons)

Tortilla chips, if desired

1) In medium bowl, mix refried beans and salsa. In shallow glass serving bowl or 12-inch serving plate, spread bean mixture.

2) Spread sour cream over bean mixture, leaving border of beans around edge. Spread guacamole over sour cream, leaving border of sour cream showing.

3) Sprinkle cheese over guacamole. Sprinkle onions over cheese. Serve immediately, or cover and refrigerate until serving time. Serve with tortilla chips.

1 SERVING: Calories 150; Total Fat 10g (Saturated Fat 4g); Sodium 250mg; Total Carbohydrate 13g (Dietary Fiber 2g); Protein 4g. EXCHANGES: 1 Starch, 2 Fat. CARBOHYDRATE CHOICES: 1.

Monster Ball

PREP TIME: 15 MINUTES (READY IN 2 HOURS 15 MINUTES)
SERVINGS: 24

 EASY

1 container (8 oz) cream cheese spread

2 cups shredded Gouda or Colby cheese (8 oz)

¼ cup chopped fresh chives

¼ cup sliced drained sun-dried tomatoes in oil

¼ teaspoon garlic powder

¼ cup finely chopped fresh chives

Assorted crackers, if desired

1) In medium bowl, mix cream cheese spread and Gouda cheese until blended. Stir in chives, tomatoes and garlic powder.

2) Shape mixture into 1 large or 2 small balls or logs. Roll in chives. Wrap in plastic wrap.

3) Refrigerate at least 2 hours or until firm. Serve with crackers.

1 SERVING: Calories 70; Total Fat 5g (Saturated Fat 3.5g); Sodium 140mg; Total Carbohydrate 0g (Dietary Fiber 0g); Protein 3g. EXCHANGES: 1 Medium-Fat Meat. CARBOHYDRATE CHOICES: 0.

Slow Cooker Spicy Chicken Nachos

PREP TIME: 15 MINUTES (READY IN 3 HOURS)
SERVINGS: 24

 EASY

1 loaf (16 oz) Mexican prepared cheese product with jalapeño peppers, cut into cubes

¾ cup Old El Paso® Thick 'n Chunky salsa

1 can (15 oz) Progresso® black beans, drained, rinsed

1 package (9 oz) frozen cooked chicken breast strips, thawed, cubed

1 container (8 oz) sour cream

1 medium red bell pepper, chopped (1 cup)

3 medium green onions, sliced (3 tablespoons)

Large tortilla chips

1) Spray 3- to 4-quart slow cooker with cooking spray. In slow cooker, mix cheese, salsa, beans and chicken.

2) Cover; cook on Low heat setting 2 hours, stirring after 1 hour.

3) Stir in sour cream, bell pepper and onions. Increase heat setting to High. Cover; cook about 45 minutes longer or until mixture is hot.

4) Serve with tortilla chips. Topping can be kept warm on Low heat setting up to 2 hours; stir occasionally.

1 SERVING: Calories 200; Total Fat 11g (Saturated Fat 4.5g); Sodium 400mg; Total Carbohydrate 17g (Dietary Fiber 2g), Protein 9g. EXCHANGES: 1 Starch, 1 High-Fat Meat, 1/2 Fat. CARBOHYDRATE CHOICES: 1.

tip

Save some prep time by using rotisserie or deli chicken instead of taking time to thaw frozen cooked chicken.

Pull-Apart Web Cheese Sticks

PREP TIME:	10 MINUTES (READY IN 30 MINUTES)
SERVINGS:	4

 EASY

1 can (8 oz) Pillsbury® refrigerated garlic with herbs breadsticks (8 breadsticks)

1 egg

1 tablespoon water

½ cup shredded Cheddar cheese (2 oz)

Pizza sauce or marinara sauce, heated, and garnished with chopped fresh basil leaves or flat-leaf parsley

1) Heat oven to 350°F. Spray large cookie sheet with cooking spray. Separate dough into 8 pieces; roll each piece into 12 to 14-inch rope. On cookie sheet, place 4 dough ropes overlapping to look like asterisk; with remaining 4 dough ropes, make concentric circles to create spider web.

2) In small bowl, beat egg and water; brush over dough. Sprinkle with cheese.

3) Bake 12 to 14 minutes or until golden brown. Immediately remove from cookie sheet. Serve warm with sauce for dipping.

1 SERVING: Calories 283; Total Fat 12g (Saturated Fat 4g); Sodium 884mg; Total Carbohydrate 34g (Dietary Fiber 1g); Protein 12g. EXCHANGES: 2 Starch, 1/2 High-Fat Meat, 1 Fat. CARBOHYDRATE CHOICES: 2.

tip

Choose a large platter for serving these pull-apart cheesy breadsticks so you can show off the whole web.

Trix®-or-Treat Popcorn

PREP TIME: 15 MINUTES (READY IN 1 HOUR 30 MINUTES)
SERVINGS: 16 (1/2 CUP EACH)

 EASY

- 6 cups popped popcorn
- 2 cups Trix® cereal
- ¼ cup butter or margarine
- ½ cup sugar
- 3 tablespoons light corn syrup
- 1 box (4-serving size) orange-flavored gelatin

1) Heat oven to 300°F. Line a 15x10x1-inch pan with cooking parchment paper. In large bowl, mix popcorn and cereal.

2) In 1-quart saucepan, melt butter over medium heat. Add sugar, corn syrup and gelatin; stir until blended. Heat to boiling, stirring constantly. Reduce heat to medium-low; simmer 5 minutes, stirring frequently, until sugar is dissolved.

3) Immediately pour hot sugar mixture over popcorn mixture; toss until completely coated. Spread coated popcorn mixture in pan.

4) Bake 15 minutes or until set. Spread on waxed paper to cool. Break into bite-size pieces. Store tightly covered at room temperature.

1 SERVING: Calories 108; Total Fat 3.5g (Saturated Fat 2g); Sodium 65mg; Total Carbohydrate 20g (Dietary Fiber 1g); Protein 1g. EXCHANGES: 1/2 Starch, 1 Other Carbohydrate, 1/2 High-Fat Meat, 1/2 Fat. CARBOHYDRATE CHOICES: 1-1/2.

Devilish Chicken Wings

PREP TIME: 20 MINUTES (READY IN 55 MINUTES)
SERVINGS: 24

 EASY

12 chicken wings (about 2 lb)

2 tablespoons butter or margarine

½ cup all-purpose flour

½ teaspoon salt

¼ teaspoon pepper

1 cup barbecue sauce

1 tablespoon red pepper sauce

½ teaspoon Cajun seasoning

¼ teaspoon ground cumin

Celery sticks

Blue cheese dressing, if desired

1) Cut each chicken wing at joints to make 3 pieces; discard tip. Cut off and discard excess skin.

2) Heat oven to 425°F. In 13x9-inch pan, melt butter in oven. In large resealable food-storage plastic bag, mix flour, salt and pepper. Add chicken wings; seal bag and shake until chicken is completely coated with flour mixture. Place in pan.

3) Bake uncovered 20 minutes; turn chicken. In small bowl, mix barbecue sauce, pepper sauce, Cajun seasoning and cumin. Pour over chicken; toss until evenly coated with sauce. Bake uncovered 10 to 12 minutes longer or until chicken is no longer pink in center.

4) Serve chicken wings with celery and blue cheese dressing.

1 SERVING: Calories 70; Total Fat 4g (Saturated Fat 1g); Sodium 175mg; Total Carbohydrate 3g (Dietary Fiber 0g); Protein 5g. EXCHANGES: 1 Medium-Fat Meat. CARBOHYDRATE CHOICES: 0.

Pie Poppers

PREP TIME: 30 MINUTES (READY IN 1 HOUR 15 MINUTES)
SERVINGS: 24

 EASY

1 box Pillsbury® refrigerated pie crusts, softened as directed on box

¼ cup canned pie filling

¼ cup lemon curd

½ cup powdered sugar

3 to 4 teaspoons milk

1) Heat oven to 450°F. Remove pie crusts from pouches; unroll on floured work surface. Cut each crust into 12 squares (some of the squares will have a rounded edge). Place 1 teaspoon pie filling or lemon curd on each square.

2) For each popper, bring all sides together in center; press to seal. With fingers, pinch dough firmly about ¼ inch below edges, making a pouch with points extending over top. Place in ungreased mini muffin cups.

3) Bake 11 to 14 minutes or until golden brown. Cool. In small bowl, mix powdered sugar and enough milk until smooth, adding milk until thin enough to drizzle. Drizzle glaze over poppers; let stand until set, about 30 minutes.

1 SERVING: Calories 90; Total Fat 4g (Saturated Fat 1.5g); Sodium 100mg; Total Carbohydrate 13g (Dietary Fiber 0g); Protein 0g. EXCHANGES: 1 Other Carbohydrate, 1 Fat. CARBOHYDRATE CHOICES: 1.

Candied Spiced Nut Mix

PREP TIME: 45 MINUTES (READY IN 1 HOUR 40 MINUTES)
SERVINGS: 15 (1/2 CUP EACH)

 EASY

1 ½ cups sugar

2 teaspoons pumpkin pie spice

½ teaspoon salt

2 egg whites

1 tablespoon water

2 containers (9.5 oz each) mixed nuts with almonds, cashews and pecans

1) Heat oven to 300°F. Line 15x10x1-inch pan with cooking parchment paper. In large bowl, mix sugar, pumpkin pie spice and salt; set aside.

2) In another large bowl, beat egg whites and water with wire whisk until foamy. Add nuts, stirring until evenly coated. Pour nut mixture into colander; drain well. Add nuts to sugar mixture, stirring until coated. With slotted spoon, remove nuts from sugar mixture, shaking to remove excess sugar. Place nuts in single layer in pan.

3) Bake 30 to 35 minutes, stirring after 15 minutes. Cool completely in pan on cooling rack. Break nuts apart. Store tightly covered at room temperature.

1 SERVING: Calories 299; Total Fat 19g (Saturated Fat 3g); Sodium 208mg; Total Carbohydrate 29g (Dietary Fiber 3g); Protein 7g. EXCHANGES: 2 Other Carbohydrate, 1 High-Fat Meat, 2 Fat. CARBOHYDRATE CHOICES: 2.

Cyclops Spirals

PREP TIME: 15 MINUTES (READY IN 1 HOUR 35 MINUTES)
SERVINGS: 14

 EASY

1 tablespoon olive oil

¾ cup chopped onion

½ cup chopped pitted kalamata olives

½ cup crumbled feta cheese (2 oz)

½ teaspoon dried oregano leaves

1 can (8 oz) Pillsbury® refrigerated crescent dinner rolls

7 colossal queen pimiento-stuffed green olives, cut in half crosswise

1) In small nonstick skillet, heat oil over medium-high heat. Cook onion in oil 5 minutes, stirring occasionally, until tender. Remove from heat. In small bowl, mix onion, kalamata olives, cheese and oregano. Cover; refrigerate 1 hour.

2) Heat oven to 350°F. On sheet of lightly floured waxed paper, unroll dough into 1 long 13x7-inch rectangle; firmly press perforations to seal. Spread onion mixture over dough, pressing mixture lightly into dough. Starting at long side, roll up dough; seal long edge.

3) Cut dough into 14 rounds. On ungreased cookie sheet, place slices about 2 inches apart. Place 1 green olive half, cut side up, into center of each slice to look like eyeball. Bake 20 minutes or until golden brown. Serve warm.

1 SERVING: Calories 108; Total Fat 7g (Saturated Fat 2g); Sodium 332; Total Carbohydrate 8g (Dietary Fiber 0g); Protein 2g. EXCHANGES: 1/2 Starch, 1-1/2 Fat. CARBOHYDRATE CHOICES: 1/2.

Pepperoni Pizza Dip

| PREP TIME: | 20 MINUTES (READY IN 3 HOURS 20 MINUTES) | EASY |
| SERVINGS: | 32 (2 TABLESPOONS DIP AND 6 VEGETABLE PIECES EACH) | |

1 jar (14 oz) pizza sauce

1 cup chopped turkey pepperoni
(from 6-oz package)

8 medium green onions, chopped
(½ cup)

½ cup chopped red bell pepper

1 can (2 ¼ oz) sliced ripe olives,
drained

1 cup shredded mozzarella cheese
(4 oz)

1 package (8 oz) cream cheese, cut
into cubes

Broccoli florets, cherry tomatoes
and carrot sticks

1) Spray 1 ½-quart slow cooker with cooking spray. In slow cooker, mix pizza sauce, pepperoni, onions, bell pepper and olives.

2) Cover; cook on Low heat setting 3 to 4 hours.

3) Add mozzarella cheese and cream cheese to dip; stir until melted. Serve with vegetables. Dip can be held on Low heat setting up to 2 hours.

1 SERVING: Calories 70; Total Fat 4g (Saturated Fat 2g); Sodium 190mg; Total Carbohydrate 6g (Dietary Fiber 2g); Protein 4g. EXCHANGES: 1 Vegetable, 1 Fat. CARBOHYDRATE CHOICES: 1/2.

Crunchy Curried Snack Mix

PREP TIME: 10 MINUTES (READY IN 3 HOURS 10 MINUTES)
SERVINGS: 20 (1/2 CUP EACH)

 EASY

4 cups Corn Chex® cereal

1 package (3.2 to 3.5 oz) sesame rice crunch crackers, broken in half (about 3 cups)

2 cups small pretzel twists

1 package (8 oz) slivered almonds (1 ½ cups)

¼ cup butter or margarine

1 tablespoon packed brown sugar

2 tablespoons soy sauce

1 teaspoon curry powder

½ teaspoon garlic powder

1) Spray 5- to 6-quart slow cooker with cooking spray. In slow cooker lightly mix cereal, crackers, pretzels and almonds.

2) In small microwavable bowl, microwave butter on High 30 to 45 seconds until melted. Stir in brown sugar, soy sauce, curry powder and garlic powder. Pour over cereal mixture, stirring gently until evenly coated.

3) Cook uncovered on Low heat setting 3 to 4 hours (or on High heat setting 2 to 2 hours 30 minutes), stirring every 30 minutes. (It's important to stir this mixture or it may scorch where slow cooker's heater is located. Cooking it uncovered allows the excess moisture to evaporate, and makes for a crisp, toasted snack.) If desired, keep snack mix warm on Low heat setting for serving.

1 SERVING: Calories 150; Total Fat 8g (Saturated Fat 1.5g); Sodium 260mg; Total Carbohydrate 15g (Dietary Fiber 2g); Protein 4g. EXCHANGES: 1 Starch, 1-1/2 Fat. CARBOHYDRATE CHOICES: 1.

Black Widow Spider Bruschetta

PREP TIME: 20 MINUTES (READY IN 20 MINUTES)
SERVINGS: 24

 EASY   LOW FAT

12 slices pumpernickel bread

2 tablespoons olive oil

3 medium tomatoes, chopped (2 cups)

2 cloves garlic, finely chopped

1 tablespoon chopped fresh basil leaves

2 teaspoons olive oil

2 teaspoons balsamic vinegar

½ teaspoon salt

¼ teaspoon pepper

1) Heat oven to 450°F. With spider-shaped cookie cutter, cut 2 spider shapes from each bread slice. Brush both sides of shapes with 2 tablespoons oil. Place on ungreased cookie sheet.

2) Bake 4 minutes, turning once, until toasted.

3) Meanwhile, in small bowl, mix remaining ingredients. Arrange toasted bread on serving platter; spoon tomato mixture on each piece. Serve warm.

1 SERVING: Calories 50; Total Fat 2g (Saturated Fat 0.5g); Sodium 137mg; Total Carbohydrate 7g (Dietary Fiber 1g); Protein 1g. EXCHANGES: 1/2 Starch, 1/2 Fat. CARBOHYDRATE CHOICES: 1/2.

Cheesy Bean Dip

PREP TIME:	15 MINUTES (READY IN 15 MINUTES)
SERVINGS:	32

 EASY   LOW FAT

1 can (16 oz) Old El Paso® refried beans

1 can (4.5 oz) Old El Paso® chopped green chiles

2 cups shredded Mexican cheese blend (8 oz)

½ medium red bell pepper, chopped

OPTIONAL

Chopped fresh cilantro

Tortilla chips

1) In ungreased 9-inch microwavable dish, mix beans and green chiles; spread evenly in dish. Cover with microwavable waxed paper. Microwave on High 2 minutes to 2 minutes 30 seconds or until dip is warm.

2) Sprinkle with cheese. Top with bell pepper. Cover; microwave on Medium (50%) 3 to 4 minutes longer or until cheese is almost melted. Lift waxed paper slowly to allow steam to escape. Dish will be hot; carefully remove from microwave. Let dip stand 2 minutes; uncover.

3) Sprinkle with cilantro. Serve with tortilla chips, if desired.

1 SERVING: Calories 40; Total Fat 2g (Saturated Fat 1.5g); Sodium 130mg; Total Carbohydrate 2g (Dietary Fiber 0g); Protein 2g. EXCHANGES: 1/2 Fat. CARBOHYDRATE CHOICES: 0.

tip

To prepare in oven, heat oven to 350°F. In ungreased 9- or 10-inch quiche dish or glass pie plate, mix beans and green chiles; spread evenly in dish. Sprinkle with cheese. Top with bell pepper. Bake uncovered about 15 minutes or until cheese is melted.

Raspberry-White Chocolate Pie Pops

PREP TIME: 20 MINUTES (READY IN 45 MINUTES)
SERVINGS: 8 PIE POPS

 EASY

1 box Pillsbury® refrigerated pie crusts, softened as directed on box

24 fresh raspberries

8 white candy melts or coating wafers (1.6 oz), chopped

8 craft sticks (flat wooden sticks with round ends)

1 egg, beaten

2 tablespoons coarse white sparkling sugar

1) Heat oven to 450°F. Spray cookie sheet with cooking spray.

2) Remove pie crusts from pouches; unroll on floured work surface. With 3 ½-inch round cutter, cut out 8 rounds from each crust. Place 8 rounds on cookie sheet. Place 3 raspberries in center of each round; sprinkle chopped candy melts evenly over raspberries.

3) Place 1 craft stick on each round, so tip of stick is in center of round. Top each with 1 remaining round. Press edges together; seal and flute. Cut 4 or 5 small slits in top crust. Brush tops with egg; sprinkle with sugar.

4) Bake 10 to 13 minutes or until golden brown. Remove from cookie sheet to cooling rack; cool 10 minutes before serving.

1 PIE POP: Calories 271; Total Fat 16g (Saturated Fat 7g); Sodium 285mg; Total Carbohydrate 32g (Dietary Fiber 0g); Protein 3g. EXCHANGES: 1-1/2 Starch, 1/2 Other Carbohydrate, 3 Fat. CARBOHYDRATE CHOICES: 2.

Chocolate-Peanut Butter Haystacks

PREP TIME: 10 MINUTES (READY IN 40 MINUTES)
SERVINGS: 22

 EASY

1 bag (12 oz) semisweet chocolate chips (2 cups)

1 bag (10 oz) peanut butter chips (1 ⅔ cups)

2 cups miniature marshmallows (from 10.5-oz bag)

2 cups broken pretzel sticks

1 cup lightly salted dry-roasted peanuts

1) Line cookie sheet with waxed paper. In medium microwavable bowl, microwave chocolate chips and peanut butter chips uncovered on High 1 to 2 minutes, stirring once, until softened and chips can be stirred smooth.

2) Stir in remaining ingredients until well coated. Drop mixture by ¼ cupfuls onto cookie sheet. Refrigerate until firm, about 30 minutes. Store covered in refrigerator.

1 SERVING: Calories 206; Total Fat 10g (Saturated Fat 8g); Sodium 116mg; Total Carbohydrate 25g (Dietary Fiber 1g); Protein 5g. EXCHANGES: 1-1/2 Other Carbohydrate, 2 Fat. CARBOHYDRATE CHOICES: 2.

Mini Tostada Bites

PREP TIME: 15 MINUTES (READY IN 15 MINUTES)
SERVINGS: 16 APPETIZERS

 EASY LOW FAT

16 restaurant-style tortilla chips

½ cup refrigerated guacamole

½ cup Progresso® black beans (from 15-oz can), drained, rinsed

1 cup shredded deli rotisserie chicken

3 tablespoons chopped fresh cilantro

OPTIONAL

Old El Paso® salsa

1) Place tortilla chips on large serving tray. Top each chip with 1 ½ teaspoons guacamole, 1 ½ teaspoons beans and 1 tablespoon chicken. Sprinkle with cilantro. Serve with salsa.

2) Serve immediately, or cover and refrigerate up to 30 minutes before serving.

1 APPETIZER: Calories 45; Total Fat 2g (Saturated Fat 0g); Sodium 100mg; Total Carbohydrate 4g (Dietary Fiber 1g); Protein 3g. EXCHANGES: 1/2 Starch, 1/2 Fat. CARBOHYDRATE CHOICES: 0.

Make quick nacho bites by following directions to the left and topping with shredded Cheddar cheese. Heat under broiler about 1 minute or until cheese is melted.

Breads *&* Side Dishes

Look here for everything from special breads to quick veggies that will make any meal memorable.

CLASSIC BAKED CORN PUDDING
PG. 86

ROASTED ROSEMARY-ONION POTATOES
PG. 82

STUFFED THREE-SEED BRAID
PG. 83

MONKEY BREAD
PG. 81

Bacon-Date Scones with Orange Marmalade Glaze

JOANNE OPDAHL | VENICE, CA

BAKE-OFF® CONTEST 45, 2012

PREP TIME: 20 MINUTES (READY IN 35 MINUTES)
SERVINGS: 16

 EASY

SCONES

2 ¼ cups Pillsbury BEST® All Purpose Flour

⅓ cup sugar

4 teaspoons baking powder

6 tablespoons LAND O LAKES® Butter

½ cup chopped precooked bacon

½ cup chopped pitted dates

½ cup Fisher® Chef's Naturals® Chopped Walnuts

¾ cup whipping cream

1 LAND O LAKES® Egg

GLAZE

½ cup Smucker's® Sweet Orange Marmalade

2 tablespoons LAND O LAKES® Butter

1) Heat oven to 400°F. Spray 1 large cookie sheet with Crisco® Original No-Stick Cooking Spray. In large bowl, combine flour, sugar and baking powder; mix well. Using pastry blender or fork, cut in 6 tablespoons butter until mixture looks like coarse crumbs.

2) In small bowl, stir together bacon, dates and nuts. Stir 1 cup of bacon mixture into flour mixture; set remaining bacon mixture aside. Make a well in center of flour mixture. In small bowl, lightly beat cream and egg together with wire whisk. Pour into well of flour mixture. Stir with fork until flour mixture is moistened. Gently form into 2 balls.

3) Place balls about 3 ½ inches apart on cookie sheet; pat each into 8-inch round. Using knife dipped in flour, cut each round into 8 wedges; do not separate. Sprinkle top of each round with remaining bacon mixture. Press mixture into dough.

4) Bake 14 to 16 minutes or until edges are light golden brown.

5) In small microwavable bowl, microwave glaze ingredients on High 20 to 30 seconds or until melted, stirring until smooth. Spread glaze evenly over the 2 rounds. Carefully separate into 16 wedges. Serve warm.

1 SERVING: Calories 250; Total Fat 13g (Saturated Fat 7g); Sodium 230mg; Total Carbohydrate 29g (Dietary Fiber 1g); Protein 4g. EXCHANGES: 1-1/2 Starch, 1/2 Other Carbohydrate, 2-1/2 Fat. CARBOHYDRATE CHOICES: 2.

tip To prevent sticking when slicing or chopping dates, spray your scissors or knife with cooking spray or frequently dip in cold water. Dried dates stay fresh for 1 year in the refrigerator and for up to 5 years in the freezer.

Chocolate and Caramel-Cinnamon Roll Skewers

FRANCES BLACKWELDER | GRAND JUNCTION, CO

BAKE-OFF® CONTEST 45, 2012

Bake-Off®
Pillsbury

PREP TIME:	30 MINUTES
SERVINGS:	5

1 can Pillsbury® Grands!® Flaky Supreme refrigerated cinnamon rolls with icing

5 (12- or 10-inch) wooden skewers

25 caramels, unwrapped (from 14-oz bag)

1 tablespoon milk

¾ cup Fisher® Chef's Naturals® Chopped Pecans

¾ cup Hershey's® milk chocolate baking chips

1 teaspoon Crisco® Pure Vegetable Oil

1) Heat oven to 350°F. Line large cookie sheet with cooking parchment paper or spray with Crisco® Original No-Stick Cooking Spray. Separate dough into 5 rolls; reserve icing. Unroll each roll into a strip; thread each strip onto wooden skewer. Place on cookie sheet.

2) Bake 13 to 19 minutes or until golden brown. Place piece of waxed paper under cooling rack. Transfer skewers from cookie sheet to cooling rack.

3) Meanwhile, in 2-quart saucepan over low heat, heat caramels and milk, stirring occasionally, until caramels are melted. Place pecans on piece of waxed paper. Generously drizzle caramel mixture lengthwise over cinnamon roll strips; roll in pecans. Return to cooling rack.

4) In small resealable freezer plastic bag, place chocolate chips and oil; seal bag. Microwave on High 15 to 25 seconds or until softened. Gently squeeze bag until chocolate is smooth; cut off tiny corner of bag. Squeeze bag to drizzle chocolate crosswise over cinnamon roll strips.

5) Place reserved icing in small resealable freezer plastic bag; seal bag. Microwave on High 10 seconds or until softened. Gently squeeze bag until icing is smooth; cut off tiny corner of bag. Squeeze bag to drizzle icing crosswise over cinnamon roll skewers. Serve warm.

1 SERVING: Calories 850; Total Fat 44g (Saturated Fat 12g); Sodium 800mg; Total Carbohydrate 104g (Dietary Fiber 3g); Protein 10g. EXCHANGES: 3 1/2 Starch, 3 1/2 Other Carbohydrate, 8 Fat. CARBOHYDRATE CHOICES: 7.

Multi-Grain Cheese Crostini

DENISE POUNDS | HUTCHINSON, KS

BAKE-OFF® CONTEST 45, 2012

PREP TIME:	30 MINUTES (READY IN 1 HOUR 40 MINUTES)
SERVINGS:	30

⅓ cup Fisher® Roasted and Salted Almonds, finely chopped

2 tablespoons quick-cooking oats

1 tablespoon cornmeal

1 tablespoon McCormick® Sesame Seed

1 tablespoon McCormick® Poppy Seed

1 tablespoon flaxseed meal

1 can Pillsbury® refrigerated crusty French loaf

2 tablespoons water

4 oz Gruyère cheese, shredded (1 cup)

2 tablespoons Crisco® 100% Extra Virgin Olive Oil

¼ teaspoon McCormick® Sea Salt

1) Heat oven to 350°F. Line cookie sheets with cooking parchment paper. In small bowl, combine almonds, oats, cornmeal, sesame seed, poppy seed and flaxseed meal; mix well. Set aside.

2) Carefully unroll loaf of dough; press into 15x12-inch rectangle. Brush dough with 1 tablespoon of the water. Reserve 2 tablespoons of almond mixture; set aside. Sprinkle remaining almond mixture over dough; top with cheese. Starling on one long side, tightly roll up dough; pinch seam firmly to seal. Brush roll with remaining 1 tablespoon water. Roll loaf in reserved almond mixture; press mixture into dough. Place, seam side down, on cookie sheet.

3) Bake 20 to 28 minutes or until golden brown. Cool on cooling rack 20 minutes.

4) Using serrated knife, cut bread into 30 (½-inch) slices. Place slices on cookie sheets. Brush both sides of each slice with olive oil; lightly sprinkle with salt.

5) Bake an additional 16 to 19 minutes, turning once halfway through baking, or until slices are crisp and golden brown.

6) If desired, serve with your favorite dip or topping. Store tightly covered.

1 SERVING: Calories 70; Total Fat 3.5g (Saturated Fat 1g); Sodium 95mg; Total Carbohydrate 6g (Dietary Fiber 0g); Protein 2g. EXCHANGES: 1/2 Starch, 1/2 Fat. CARBOHYDRATE CHOICES: 1/2.

Monkey Bread

PREP TIME: 20 MINUTES (READY IN 1 HOUR)
SERVINGS: 12

 EASY

¾ cup butter (do not use margarine)

1 cup packed brown sugar

2 tablespoons whipping cream

½ cup coarsely chopped pecans

3 ½ cups baking mix

½ cup milk

6 tablespoons granulated sugar

3 tablespoons butter, softened
(do not use margarine)

1 teaspoon vanilla

1 egg

½ teaspoon ground cinnamon

1) Heat oven to 350°F. Spray 12-cup fluted tube cake pan with cooking spray.

2) In 2-quart saucepan, melt ¾ cup butter. Add brown sugar and whipping cream; heat to boiling over medium heat, stirring constantly. Boil 2 minutes; remove from heat. Pour into pan; sprinkle with pecans.

3) In large bowl, stir baking mix, milk, 2 tablespoons of the granulated sugar, 3 tablespoons butter, the vanilla and egg until soft dough forms. Shape dough into 1-inch balls. In small bowl, mix remaining 4 tablespoons granulated sugar and the cinnamon. Roll each ball in cinnamon-sugar; place randomly in pan. Sprinkle with any remaining cinnamon-sugar.

4) Bake 22 to 28 minutes or until golden brown. Cool 10 minutes. Place heatproof serving plate upside down over pan; turn plate and pan over. Remove pan. Serve warm.

1 SERVING: Calories 420; Total Fat 23g (Saturated Fat 11g); Sodium 550mg; Total Carbohydrate 49g (Dietary Fiber 1g); Protein 4g. EXCHANGES: 1-1/2 Starch, 1-1/2 Other Carbohydrate, 4-1/2 Fat. CARBOHYDRATE CHOICES: 3.

Roasted Rosemary-Onion Potatoes

PREP TIME: 10 MINUTES (READY IN 35 MINUTES)
SERVINGS: 4

 EASY

4 medium red potatoes (1 ⅓ lb)

1 small onion, finely chopped (¼ cup)

2 tablespoons olive or vegetable oil

2 tablespoons chopped fresh or 2 teaspoons dried rosemary leaves, crushed

1 teaspoon chopped fresh or ¼ teaspoon dried thyme leaves, crushed

¼ teaspoon salt

⅛ teaspoon pepper

1) Heat oven to 450°F. Spray 15x10x1-inch pan with cooking spray.

2) Cut potatoes into 1-inch pieces. In large bowl, mix remaining ingredients. Add potatoes; toss to coat. Spread potatoes in single layer in pan.

3) Roast uncovered 20 to 25 minutes, turning occasionally, until potatoes are light brown and tender when pierced with fork.

1 SERVING: Calories 180; Total Fat 7g (Saturated Fat 1g); Sodium 160mg; Total Carbohydrate 27g (Dietary Fiber 3g); Protein 3g. EXCHANGES: 1 Starch, 1 Other Carbohydrate, 1 Fat. CARBOHYDRATE CHOICES: 2.

Easy Cinnamon Rolls

PREP TIME: 20 MINUTES (READY IN 55 MINUTES)
SERVINGS: 12

 EASY

1 can (11 oz) Pillsbury® refrigerated crusty French loaf

½ cup honey nut cream cheese spread (from 8-oz container), softened

¼ cup packed light brown sugar

1 teaspoon ground cinnamon

2 tablespoons granulated sugar

1 tablespoon butter or margarine, melted

⅔ cup powdered sugar

1 tablespoon milk

1) Heat oven to 375°F. Lightly grease 9-inch round cake pan with shortening or cooking spray.

2) On lightly floured surface, unroll dough. In small bowl, mix cream cheese spread, brown sugar and cinnamon until smooth. Spread cheese mixture over dough, leaving ¼-inch border around edges. Sprinkle with granulated sugar.

3) Gently roll up dough, starting with long side. Cut into 12 (1 ¼-inch) slices. Place in pan. Brush tops of slices with butter.

4) Bake 28 to 32 minutes or until golden.

5) In small bowl, stir powdered sugar and milk until smooth. Drizzle glaze over rolls. Serve warm.

1 SERVING: Calories 156; Total Fat 4g (Saturated Fat 2g); Sodium 202mg; Total Carbohydrate 28g (Dietary Fiber 1g); Protein 2g. EXCHANGES: 1 Starch, 1 Other Carbohydrate, 1 Fat. CARBOHYDRATE CHOICES: 2.

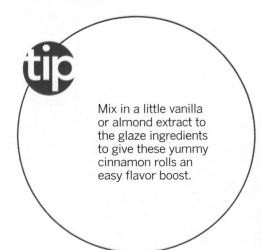

tip

Mix in a little vanilla or almond extract to the glaze ingredients to give these yummy cinnamon rolls an easy flavor boost.

Stuffed Three-Seed Braid

KATHY AULT | EDMOND, OK

BAKE-OFF® CONTEST 45, 2012

Bake-Off®

🄴 EASY

PREP TIME:	20 MINUTES (READY IN 50 MINUTES)
SERVINGS:	8

1 can Pillsbury® refrigerated crusty French loaf

4 ½ sticks (4 ½ oz) string cheese

1 LAND O LAKES® Egg

1 teaspoon water

1 teaspoon McCormick® Sesame Seed

¾ teaspoon McCormick® Fennel Seed

½ teaspoon McCormick® Poppy Seed

1) Heat oven to 350°F. Lightly spray cookie sheet with Crisco® Original No-Stick Cooking Spray. Cut dough lengthwise into thirds, forming 3 long strips. Press out strips to flatten to 2 ½-inch width.

2) Cut cheese sticks into 18 (about 1-inch) pieces. Place 6 pieces of the cheese evenly along length of one dough strip to within 1 inch of each end. Pull up long sides of dough strip and pinch to seal seam, encasing cheese in dough. Repeat with remaining dough and cheese.

3) In small bowl, beat egg and water with wire whisk. Brush egg mixture over strips. Sprinkle one strip with sesame seed, one with fennel seed and one with poppy seed. On cookie sheet, braid dough strips, seam sides up, pinching seams to seal, if necessary; tuck ends under.

4) Bake 18 to 24 minutes or until golden brown. Cool 5 minutes. Cut crosswise into slices. Serve warm.

1 SERVING: Calories 160; Total Fat 5g (Saturated Fat 2.5g); Sodium 320mg; Total Carbohydrate 19g (Dietary Fiber 0g); Protein 8g. EXCHANGES: 1-1/2 Starch, 1/2 Lean Meat, 1/2 Fat. CARBOHYDRATE CHOICES: 1.

Simple Yeast Rolls

PREP TIME: 30 MINUTES (READY IN 2 HOURS 30 MINUTES)
SERVINGS: 18

4 ½ cups all-purpose flour

2 ½ teaspoons regular active dry yeast

1 ¼ teaspoons salt

1 cup refrigerated mashed potatoes

1 cup milk

3 tablespoons honey

6 tablespoons butter or margarine, softened

2 eggs

Cooking spray

1) In large bowl, mix 1 ½ cups of the flour, the yeast and salt. In medium microwavable bowl, mix potatoes, milk, honey and ¼ cup of the butter. Microwave uncovered on High 1 minute or until mixture reaches 110°F. Add potato mixture to flour mixture, stirring until blended. Stir in eggs.

2) Add 2 cups flour to potato mixture, stirring until soft dough forms. On floured surface, knead dough 10 minutes or until smooth and springy, adding enough of remaining 1 cup flour to prevent hands from sticking to dough (dough will be soft).

3) In greased bowl, place dough; turn greased side up. Cover; let rise in warm place (80°F to 85°F) 1 hour or until doubled in size. (Dough is ready if indentation remains when touched.) Punch dough down; let rest 5 minutes. Spray 2 (8-inch) square pans with cooking spray. Divide dough into 18 equal portions; shape each into a ball. Place in pans; spray tops of balls with cooking spray. Cover; let rise 30 minutes or until doubled.

4) Heat oven to 350°F. Bake rolls 30 minutes or until browned. Melt remaining 2 tablespoons butter; brush over rolls. Serve warm.

1 SERVING: Calories 176; Total Fat 5g (Saturated Fat 3g); Sodium 260mg; Total Carbohydrate 28g (Dietary Fiber 1g); Protein 5g. EXCHANGES: 2 Starch, 1 Fat. CARBOHYDRATE CHOICES: 2.

Creamy Squash Casserole

PREP TIME: 30 MINUTES (READY IN 1 HOUR 20 MINUTES)
SERVINGS: 12

6 tablespoons butter or margarine

1 large onion, chopped (1 cup)

4 lb yellow summer squash, sliced (13 cups)

1 container (8 oz) sour cream

2 cups shredded Italian cheese blend (8 oz)

1 teaspoon savory herb with garlic soup mix (from 2.4-oz box)

2 eggs

½ teaspoon salt

2 cups crushed round buttery crackers (45 crackers)

1) Heat oven to 350°F. Spray 13x9-inch (3-quart) glass baking dish with cooking spray.

2) In 4-quart Dutch oven, melt 2 tablespoons of the butter over medium-high heat. Cook onion in butter 3 minutes, stirring occasionally. Add squash; cook 10 minutes, stirring frequently, until tender. Remove from heat; stir in sour cream, cheese, soup mix, eggs and salt. Spread in baking dish.

3) In medium microwavable bowl, microwave remaining ¼ cup butter covered on High 30 seconds or until melted. Stir in crushed crackers. Sprinkle over casserole.

4) Bake uncovered 40 minutes or until bubbly and set. Let stand 10 minutes before serving.

1 SERVING: Calories 253; Total Fat 18g (Saturated Fat 10g); Sodium 429mg; Total Carbohydrate 16g (Dietary Fiber 2g); Protein 9g. EXCHANGES: 1/2 Starch, 1-1/2 Vegetable, 1 High-Fat Meat, 2 Fat. CARBOHYDRATE CHOICES: 1.

Classic Baked Corn Pudding

PREP TIME: 20 MINUTES (RFADY IN 1 HOUR 35 MINUTES)
SERVINGS: 16

 EASY

½ cup butter or margarine

1 small onion, chopped (¼ cup)

½ cup all-purpose flour

½ teaspoon salt

½ teaspoon pepper

4 cups (1 quart) milk

6 eggs, slightly beaten

2 cups shredded Cheddar cheese (8 oz)

2 cans (15.25 oz each) Green Giant® whole kernel sweet corn, drained

½ cup chopped fresh parsley or 2 tablespoons parsley flakes

¾ cup Progresso® plain bread crumbs

3 tablespoons butter or margarine, melted

1) Heat oven to 350°F. Spray 3-quart casserole with cooking spray.

2) In 4-quart Dutch oven, melt ½ cup butter over medium heat. Cook onion in butter 3 to 4 minutes, stirring frequently, until tender. Stir in flour, salt and pepper until well blended. Stir in milk. Cook 4 to 5 minutes, stirring constantly, until thickened. Gradually stir in eggs and cheese. Stir in corn and parsley. Pour into casserole.

3) In small bowl, mix bread crumbs and melted butter; sprinkle over corn mixture.

4) Bake uncovered 55 to 65 minutes or until set and knife inserted in center comes out clean. Let stand 5 to 10 minutes before serving.

1 SERVING: Calories 270; Total Fat 16g (Saturated Fat 10g); Sodium 310mg; Total Carbohydrate 18g (Dietary Fiber 1g); Protein 10g. EXCHANGES: 1 Starch, 1 High-Fat Meat, 1-1/2 Fat. CARBOHYDRATE CHOICES: 1.

Hoppin' John

PREP TIME: 15 MINUTES (READY IN 15 MINUTES)
SERVINGS: 4

 EASY

1 large sweet onion, finely chopped (1 cup)

2 tablespoons bacon drippings or oil

1 package (8.5 oz) ready-to-serve jasmine rice

1 can (15 oz) black-eyed peas, drained

¼ teaspoon salt

¼ teaspoon pepper

Chopped fresh parsley, if desired

1) In large skillet, cook onion in bacon drippings over medium-high heat 5 minutes, stirring frequently, until golden.

2) Stir in rice and black-eyed peas. Cook 5 minutes, stirring gently, until thoroughly heated. Season with salt and pepper. Sprinkle with chopped parsley.

1 SERVING: Calories 252; Total Fat 8g (Saturated Fat 3g); Sodium 460mg; Total Carbohydrate 40g (Dietary Fiber 4g); Protein 6g. EXCHANGES: 2-1/2 Starch, 1 Fat. CARBOHYDRATE CHOICES: 2 1/2.

Chili-Fried Potatoes

PREP TIME: 15 MINUTES (READY IN 25 MINUTES)
SERVINGS: 4

 EASY

3 cups cubed unpeeled baking potatoes (about 1 lb)

½ teaspoon olive oil

1 small onion, halved, thinly sliced and separated into rings

1 teaspoon chili powder

½ teaspoon salt

1 cup shredded sharp Cheddar cheese (4 oz)

Sliced green onions, if desired

1) In 2-quart saucepan, place steamer basket; add ½ inch water (water should not touch bottom of basket). Place potatoes in basket; cover tightly and heat to boiling. Reduce heat; steam covered 10 minutes or until tender. Remove from heat.

2) In 12-inch nonstick skillet, heat oil over medium-high heat. Cook onion in oil 3 minutes, stirring frequently, until tender. Add potatoes, chili powder and salt. Cook 5 minutes, stirring frequently, until potatoes are lightly browned. Sprinkle cheese over potato mixture. Cover; remove from heat. Let stand 1 minute or until cheese is melted. Sprinkle with green onions.

1 SERVING: Calories 219; Total Fat 11g (Saturated Fat 6g); Sodium 487mg; Total Carbohydrate 21g (Dietary Fiber 2g); Protein 9g. EXCHANGES: 1-1/2 Starch, 1/2 High-Fat Meat, 1 Fat. CARBOHYDRATE CHOICES: 1-1/2.

Cheesy Sausage Muffins

PREP TIME: 15 MINUTES (READY IN 40 MINUTES)
SERVNGS 12 MUFFINS

 EASY

½ lb bulk pork sausage

2 cups baking mix

1 ½ cups shredded sharp Cheddar cheese (6 oz)

⅛ teaspoon ground red pepper (cayenne)

¾ cup milk

2 tablespoons butter or margarine, melted

½ teaspoon Dijon mustard

1 egg

1) Heat oven to 400°F. Spray 12 regular-size muffin cups with cooking spray.

2) In 10-inch skillet, cook sausage over medium-high heat 5 to 6 minutes, stirring to crumble, until no longer pink; drain.

3) In large bowl, stir baking mix, cheese and red pepper. In medium bowl, beat milk, butter, mustard and egg with fork or wire whisk. Add milk mixture to baking mixture, stirring just until moistened. Stir in sausage. Spoon evenly into muffin cups.

4) Bake 17 to 20 minutes or until golden brown. Cool in pan 5 minutes. Serve warm.

1 MUFFIN: Calories 208; Total Fat 14g (Saturated Fat 6g); Sodium 462mg; Total Carbohydrate 15g (Dietary Fiber 0g); Protein 8g. EXCHANGES: 1 Starch, 1 High-Fat Meat, 1 Fat. CARBOHYDRATE CHOICES: 1.

Maple Sweet Potato Cups

PREP TIME: 15 MINUTES (READY IN 25 MINUTES)
SERVINGS: 8

 EASY

2 packages (24 oz each) refrigerated mashed sweet potatoes

⅓ cup butter, softened

⅓ cup packed light brown sugar

⅓ cup real maple syrup

3 teaspoons grated orange peel

1 teaspoon salt

4 egg whites

½ cup granulated sugar

1) Heat oven to 400°F. Microwave sweet potatoes as directed on package. In large bowl, stir sweet potatoes, butter, brown sugar, syrup, orange peel and salt.

2) Spoon mixture into 8 (6-oz) custard cups or individual baking dishes (ramekins). Place on 15x10x1-inch pan. In small bowl, beat egg whites with electric mixer on high speed until foamy. Add granulated sugar, 1 tablespoon at a time, beating until stiff peaks form and sugar is dissolved. Spread meringue over sweet potato mixture.

3) Bake 5 minutes or until golden brown.

1 SERVING: Calories 320; Total Fat 8g (Saturated Fat 5g); Sodium 436mg; Total Carbohydrate 59g (Dietary Fiber 4g); Protein 3g. EXCHANGES: 2 Starch, 2 Other Carbohydrate, 1-1/2 Fat. CARBOHYDRATE CHOICES: 4.

tip

Make this casserole up to 24 hours ahead of time; cover and refrigerate. You'll need to increase the bake time by about 15 minutes.

Cheesy Mashed Potato Casserole

PREP TIME: 15 MINUTES (READY IN 45 MINUTES)
SERVINGS: 8

 EASY

2 teaspoons butter or margarine

8 medium green onions, sliced (½ cup)

1 medium yellow or orange bell pepper, chopped (1 cup)

3 cups hot water

1 cup half-and-half or whole milk

¼ cup butter or margarine

1 box (7.2 oz) roasted garlic mashed potato mix (2 pouches)

1 ½ cups shredded Cheddar cheese (6 oz)

1) Heat oven to 350°F. Spray 2-quart casserole with cooking spray.

2) In 10-inch nonstick skillet, melt 2 teaspoons butter over medium-high heat. Cook onions and bell pepper in butter 1 minute, stirring occasionally. Remove from heat; set aside.

3) In 2-quart saucepan, heat water, half-and-half and ¼ cup butter to boiling; remove from heat. Stir in both pouches of potatoes and seasoning just until moistened. Let stand about 1 minute or until liquid is absorbed. Beat with fork until smooth.

4) Spoon 1 ⅓ cups of the potatoes into casserole; top with half of the onion mixture and ¾ cup of the cheese. Spoon another 1 ⅓ cups potatoes over cheese; carefully spread to cover. Sprinkle evenly with remaining onion mixture. Top with remaining potatoes; carefully spread to cover. Sprinkle with remaining ¾ cup cheese.

5) Bake uncovered about 30 minutes or until hot.

1 SERVING: Calories 296; Total Fat 21g (Saturated Fat 12g); Sodium 749mg; Total Carbohydrate 21g (Dietary Fiber 2g); Protein 8g. EXCHANGES: 1-1/2 Starch, 1/2 High-Fat Meat, 3 Fat. CARBOHYDRATE CHOICES: 1-1/2.

Broccoli-Cauliflower Tetrazzini

BARBARA VAN ITALLIE | POUGHKEEPSIE, NY

BAKE-OFF® CONTEST 33, 1988

PREP TIME: 30 MINUTES (READY IN 50 MINUTES)
SERVINGS: 8

- **8** oz uncooked spaghetti, broken into thirds
- **1** bag (1 lb) frozen broccoli, carrots and cauliflower or 4 cups frozen cut broccoli
- **2** tablespoons butter or margarine
- **3** tablespoons all-purpose flour
- **2** cups fat-free (skim) milk
- **½** cup grated Parmesan cheese
  Dash pepper
- **1** jar (4.5 oz) Green Giant® sliced mushrooms, drained
- **2** tablespoons grated Parmesan cheese

1) Heat oven to 400°F. Spray 13x9-inch (3-quart) glass baking dish with cooking spray. Cook and drain spaghetti as directed on package, using minimum cook time; cover to keep warm. Meanwhile, cook vegetables until crisp-tender as directed on bag; drain.

2) In 2-quart saucepan, melt butter over medium heat. Stir in flour until smooth. Gradually add milk, stirring until well blended. Cook 6 to 10 minutes, stirring constantly, until mixture boils and thickens. Stir in ½ cup cheese and the pepper.

3) Spoon cooked spaghetti into baking dish. Top with cooked vegetables and mushrooms. Pour white sauce over top. Sprinkle with 2 tablespoons cheese.

4) Bake uncovered 15 to 20 minutes or until hot and bubbly around edges.

1 SERVING: Calories 240; Total Fat 6g (Saturated Fat 3.5g); Sodium 350mg; Total Carbohydrate 34g (Dietary Fiber 3g); Protein 12g. EXCHANGES: 2 Starch, 1 Vegetable, 1/2 Lean Meat, 1/2 Fat. CARBOHYDRATE CHOICES: 2.

Orange Marmalade Cornmeal Muffins

PAULA MAHAGNOUL | SIOUX FALLS, SD

BAKE-OFF® CONTEST 45, 2012

PREP TIME: 30 MINUTES (READY IN 1 HOUR)
SERVINGS: 6

MUFFINS

½ cup LAND O LAKES® Butter, softened

½ cup Smucker's® Sweet Orange Marmalade

1 LAND O LAKES® Egg

1 tablespoon grated orange peel

½ teaspoon McCormick® Pure Orange Extract

⅛ teaspoon kosher (coarse) salt

⅓ cup yellow cornmeal

2 teaspoons baking powder

⅔ cup orange juice

1 ¼ cups Pillsbury BEST® All Purpose Flour

CANDIED ORANGE PEEL

Peel from 1 large orange

3 tablespoons granulated sugar

¼ cup water

GLAZE

¾ cup powdered sugar

2 tablespoons orange juice

ORANGE BUTTER

6 tablespoons LAND O LAKES® Butter, softened

¼ cup Smucker's® Sweet Orange Marmalade

1) Heat oven to 350°F. Spray 6 jumbo muffin cups with Crisco® Butter Flavor No-Stick Cooking Spray. In large bowl, beat ½ cup butter and ½ cup orange marmalade until blended. Stir in egg, 1 tablespoon orange peel, orange extract and salt until well blended. Add cornmeal and baking powder; mix well. Alternately add ⅔ cup orange juice and flour, stirring just until moistened. Spoon rounded ⅓ cup batter into each muffin cup.

2) Bake 20 to 24 minutes or until toothpick inserted in center comes out clean. Cool in cups 15 minutes. Remove from cups to cooling rack.

3) Meanwhile, to make candied orange peel, using vegetable peeler, cut ½-inch-wide strips of peel from orange. Using knife, cut orange peel into fine strips. In 1-quart saucepan, bring granulated sugar, orange peel strips and water to a boil over medium-high heat. Reduce heat to low; simmer 10 minutes. With slotted spoon, remove peel from syrup. Cool on waxed paper.

4) In small bowl, combine glaze ingredients; mix well. Set aside. In another small bowl, beat together orange butter ingredients until light and fluffy. Set aside.

5) Drizzle glaze over tops of muffins. Garnish each with candied orange peel. Serve with orange butter.

1 SERVING: Calories 530; Total Fat 21g (Saturated Fat 12g); Sodium 370mg; Total Carbohydrate 81g (Dietary Fiber 2g); Protein 5g. EXCHANGES: 2 Starch, 3-1/2 Other Carbohydrate, 4 Fat. CARBOHYDRATE CHOICES: 5-1/2.

Asian Scallion Buns with Sweet and Sour Sauce

NANCY OLSON | KINGWOOD, TX

BAKE-OFF® CONTEST 45, 2012

PREP TIME: 30 MINUTES (READY IN 40 MINUTES)
SERVINGS: 12

2 tablespoons Crisco® Pure Canola Oil

1 can Pillsbury® refrigerated crescent dinner rolls

2 tablespoons sesame oil

¾ cup thinly sliced green onions (12 medium)

¼ teaspoon McCormick® Ground Black Pepper

2 tablespoons Pillsbury BEST® All Purpose Flour

2 tablespoons McCormick® Sesame Seed

½ cup Smucker's® Simply Fruit® Apricot Spreadable Fruit

¼ cup water

2 tablespoons reduced-sodium soy sauce

½ teaspoon McCormick® Ground Ginger

¼ cup rice vinegar

Dash McCormick® Crushed Red Pepper

1) Heat oven to 350°F. Brush 2 large cookie sheets with canola oil. Unroll crescent dough; separate into 4 rectangles. Firmly press perforations to seal. Brush rectangles with 1 tablespoon of the sesame oil. Top each rectangle with 3 tablespoons green onion; sprinkle with pepper. Starting with 1 long side of each rectangle, roll up. Cut each roll into 3 pieces. Twist each dough piece into 4-inch rope. Lightly coil each rope into small bun. On floured work surface, press each bun into 3-inch round. Place 2 inches apart onto cookie sheets. Brush buns with remaining sesame oil; sprinkle with sesame seed.

2) Bake 10 to 14 minutes or until golden brown.

3) Meanwhile, in 1-quart saucepan, heat spreadable fruit, water, soy sauce, ginger and vinegar over medium heat 3 minutes, stirring frequently, or until thoroughly heated; stir in red pepper. Transfer sauce to small serving bowl. Serve warm buns with sauce.

1 SERVING: Calories 170; Total Fat 10g (Saturated Fat 2g); Sodium 240mg; Total Carbohydrate 18g (Dietary Fiber 0g); Protein 2g. EXCHANGES: 1 Starch, 2 Fat. CARBOHYDRATE CHOICES: 1.

Parmesan Corn Pudding

PREP TIME: 10 MINUTES (READY IN 55 MINUTES)
SERVINGS: 8

 EASY

2 bags (12 oz each) Green Giant® Valley Fresh Steamers® Select® frozen shoepeg white corn, thawed

⅓ cup sugar

¼ cup all-purpose flour

2 tablespoons yellow cornmeal

½ teaspoon salt

6 tablespoons butter, melted

1 ½ cups milk

4 eggs

2 tablespoons chopped fresh chives

½ cup shredded Parmesan cheese (2 oz)

Additional chopped fresh chives, if desired

1) Heat oven to 350°F. Spray 2-quart casserole with cooking spray. In food processor, place 1 bag of the corn, the sugar, flour, cornmeal, salt, butter, milk and eggs. Cover; process until smooth, stopping occasionally to scrape down sides.

2) Transfer mixture to large bowl; stir in 2 tablespoons chives and second bag of corn. Pour into casserole; sprinkle with cheese.

3) Bake uncovered 40 to 45 minutes or until set. Sprinkle with additional chives.

1 SERVING: Calories 311; Total Fat 15g (Saturated Fat 8g); Sodium 407mg; Total Carbohydrate 35g (Dietary Fiber 2g); Protein 10g. EXCHANGES: 1-1/2 Starch, 1/2 Other Carbohydrate, 1 Medium-Fat Meat, 2 Fat. CARBOHYDRATE CHOICES: 2.

Skin-On Mashed Potatoes

PREP TIME: 15 MINUTES (READY IN 35 MINUTES)
SERVINGS: 4

 EASY   LOW FAT

3 cups cubed (1 to 1 ½ inch) unpeeled red potatoes (1 ¼ lb)

½ cup plain low-fat yogurt

¼ cup shredded Gruyère or Swiss cheese (1 oz)

2 tablespoons fat-free (skim) milk

½ teaspoon salt

Dash pepper

2 medium green onions, sliced (2 tablespoons)

1 tablespoon chopped fresh or 1 teaspoon dried basil leaves

1) In 3-quart saucepan, place potatoes and enough water to cover. Heat to boiling; reduce heat. Cover; simmer 15 to 20 minutes or until tender. Drain thoroughly.

2) In same saucepan or large bowl, mash hot potatoes. Add yogurt, cheese, milk, salt and pepper; beat until light and fluffy. Add onions and basil; mix well.

1 SERVING: Calories 180; Total Fat 3g (Saturated Fat 2g); Sodium 330mg; Total Carbohydrate 32g (Dietary Fiber 3g); Protein 7g. EXCHANGES: 2 Starch, 1/2 Fat. CARBOHYDRATE CHOICES: 2.

Yellow Squash Casserole

PREP TIME: 10 MINUTES (READY IN 40 MINUTES)
SERVINGS: 10

 EASY

2 ½ lb yellow summer squash, sliced

¾ cup chopped green onions (12 medium)

1 cup mayonnaise

2 eggs, slightly beaten

1 tablespoon all-purpose flour

½ teaspoon salt

2 ½ cups shredded sharp Cheddar cheese (10 oz)

1 cup soft bread crumbs (about 1 ½ slices bread)

2 tablespoons butter, melted

1) In large microwavable bowl, place squash and onions. Cover tightly with microwavable plastic wrap, folding back one edge or corner ¼ inch to vent steam. Microwave on High 8 minutes or until squash is tender. (Do not drain.)

2) Spray 11x7-inch microwavable dish with cooking spray. In large bowl, stir together mayonnaise, eggs, flour and salt; stir in squash mixture and cheese. Spoon mixture into baking dish. Cover tightly with microwavable plastic wrap, folding back one edge or corner ¼ inch to vent steam. Microwave on High 10 minutes or until set; let stand 10 minutes.

3) In small microwavable bowl, mix bread crumbs and melted butter. Microwave on High 2 minutes. Sprinkle over casserole or over individual serving.

1 SERVING: Calories 356; Total Fat 32g (Saturated Fat 10g); Sodium 509mg; Total Carbohydrate 8g (Dietary Fiber 2g); Protein 9g. EXCHANGES: 1 Vegetable, 1 High-Fat Meat, 5 Fat. CARBOHYDRATE CHOICES: 1/2.

Praline-Topped Sweet Potatoes

PREP TIME: 10 MINUTES (READY IN 55 MINUTES)
SERVINGS: 12

 EASY

1 cup all-purpose flour

¾ cup packed brown sugar

½ cup chopped pecans, toasted

½ cup butter, melted

½ teaspoon ground cinnamon

2 containers (24 oz each) refrigerated mashed sweet potatoes

1 teaspoon vanilla

1) Heat oven to 350°F. Spray shallow 2 ½-quart casserole with cooking spray.

2) In medium bowl, mix flour, brown sugar, pecans, butter and cinnamon until blended. In large bowl, mix sweet potatoes, vanilla and ½ cup of the streusel mixture. Spoon sweet potato mixture into casserole; sprinkle with remaining streusel mixture.

3) Bake uncovered 45 minutes or until thoroughly heated and streusel is crisp.

1 SERVING: Calories 287; Total Fat 12g (Saturated Fat 5g); Sodium 218mg; Total Carbohydrate 42g (Dietary Fiber 3g); Protein 3g. EXCHANGES: 2 Starch, 1 Other Carbohydrate, 2 Fat. CARBOHYDRATE CHOICES: 3.

tip

Toasting pecans and other nuts brings out their flavor. To toast pecans, spread in ungreased shallow pan. Bake uncovered at 350°F 6 to 10 minutes, stirring occasionally, until golden brown.

Mango-Lemon Drop Sunshine Puffs

AMBER SCHOFIELD | ATHENS, AL

Bake-Off   BAKE-OFF® CONTEST 45, 2012

PREP TIME: 40 MINUTES (READY IN 55 MINUTES)
SERVINGS: 16

1 package (3 oz) cream cheese, softened

⅓ cup powdered sugar

2 tablespoons lemon juice

⅛ teaspoon grated lemon peel

1 cup flaked coconut

1 can Pillsbury® Big & Buttery refrigerated crescent dinner rolls

⅔ cup Hershey's® premier white baking chips

⅓ cup Smucker's® Mango Jam or Sweet Orange Marmalade

1) Heat oven to 350°F. In small bowl, beat cream cheese and powdered sugar with electric mixer on medium speed until smooth. Beat in lemon juice on low speed. Stir in lemon peel and coconut until well mixed. Set aside.

2) Unroll crescent dough onto ungreased cookie sheet; separate into 4 rectangles. Firmly press perforations to seal. Cut each rectangle into 8 squares. Place 16 of the squares 2 inches apart on cookie sheet. Spoon heaping teaspoon of cream cheese mixture in center of each square. Top cream cheese mixture with remaining dough squares, placing each of the squares at an angle so points of the square hang over the middles of the sides of the bottom square to look like shape of the sun. Press edges of dough around cream cheese mixture to seal.

3) Bake 9 to 14 minutes or until light golden brown. Cool 5 minutes.

4) Meanwhile, in 1-quart saucepan over low heat, melt white chips and mango jam, stirring constantly, until melted and smooth. Spread glaze over rolls. Serve warm.

1 SERVING: Calories 200; Total Fat 10g (Saturated Fat 7g); Sodium 220mg; Total Carbohydrate 25g (Dietary Fiber 0g); Protein 2g. EXCHANGES: 1/2 Starch, 1 Other Carbohydrate, 2 Fat. CARBOHYDRATE CHOICES: 1-1/2.

Soups, Salads & Sandwiches

These standout specialties will complete your menu...or even make a meal by themselves!

TEXAS NO-BEAN CHILI
PG. 100

WICKED TERIYAKI STEAK SALAD
PG. 110

CHICKEN ITALIANO SLIDERS
PG. 111

SOUTHWEST
POTATO-CORN
CHOWDER
PG. 103

Citrus-Shrimp Wraps

SANDRA GALLANT | FORESTVILLE, CA

Bake-Off®

BAKE-OFF® CONTEST 45, 2012

PREP TIME: 30 MINUTES (READY IN 40 MINUTES)
SERVINGS: 4

¾ cup lightly packed fresh parsley leaves

½ cup Smucker's® Apricot Preserves

⅓ cup reduced-sodium soy sauce

4 tablespoons fresh lemon juice

2 teaspoons fresh lime juice

½ teaspoon McCormick® Ground Mustard

½ teaspoon McCormick® Ground Ginger

¾ lb cooked deveined peeled medium shrimp, thawed if frozen, tail shells removed

¾ cup lightly packed fresh cilantro

½ cup lightly packed fresh mint leaves

¼ cup Crisco® 100% Extra Virgin Olive Oil

3 cloves garlic

¼ teaspoon salt

1 can Pillsbury® refrigerated thin pizza crust

1 cup shredded red cabbage

⅔ cup shredded carrot

¼ cup Fisher® Cashews, Halves and Pieces, coarsely chopped

1) Chop 2 tablespoons of the parsley leaves; set aside. In 1-quart saucepan, stir together apricot preserves, soy sauce, 2 tablespoons of the lemon juice, lime juice, mustard and ginger. Cook and stir over medium heat until slightly thickened, about 5 minutes. Stir in 2 tablespoons chopped parsley and shrimp. Transfer to bowl; set aside.

2) To make fresh herb dressing, in food processor or blender, combine remaining parsley leaves, cilantro, mint, olive oil, garlic, salt and remaining 2 tablespoons lemon juice. Cover; process until herbs are finely chopped, scraping down side of bowl if necessary. Set aside.

3) Heat oven to 350°F. Line large cookie sheet with cooking parchment paper or spray with Crisco® Original No-Stick Cooking Spray. Unroll pizza crust dough. Cut dough in half lengthwise and crosswise, forming 4 rectangles. Place on cookie sheet.

4) Bake 4 minutes. Turn dough over; bake an additional 4 to 6 minutes or until light golden brown. With tongs, transfer warm pizza crusts to 4 (2 ½- to 3-inch diameter) drinking glasses, draping crust lengthwise to form "U" shape.

5) With slotted spoon, remove shrimp from marinade; discard marinade. To make each wrap, spread about 2 tablespoons herb dressing evenly over inside of wrap; top with ¼ cup of cabbage, about 2 tablespoons carrot and ¼ of the shrimp. Sprinkle each with cashews. Fold long edges together to form wrap.

1 SERVING: Calories 620; Total Fat 25g (Saturated Fat 4g); Sodium 1520mg; Total Carbohydrate 73g (Dietary Fiber 3g); Protein 27g. EXCHANGES: 3-1/2 Starch, 1 Other Carbohydrate, 1 Vegetable, 2 Very Lean Meat, 4-1/2 Fat. CARBOHYDRATE CHOICES: 5.

Beefy French Onion Soup

PREP TIME: 15 MINUTES (READY IN 9 HOURS 30 MINUTES)
SERVINGS: 8

 EASY

7 small onions, cut in half, thinly sliced (about 7 cups)

1 tablespoon butter or margarine, melted

2 tablespoons sugar

2 dried bay leaves

1 ½ lb beef stew meat

3 cans (10 ½ oz each) condensed beef broth

1 cup apple juice

¼ cup dry sherry or additional apple juice

¼ teaspoon dried thyme leaves

8 slices (½ inch thick) French bread, toasted

2 cups shredded Swiss cheese (8 ounces)

Fresh thyme springs, if desired

1) Spray 5- to 6-quart slow cooker with cooking spray. In slow cooker, toss onions, butter and sugar. Top with bay leaves and beef.

2) Cover; cook on Low heat setting 9 to 10 hours or until onions are deep brown.

3) Stir in beef broth, apple juice, sherry and dried thyme into beef. Increase heat setting to High. Cover; cook 10 minutes or until hot. Remove bay leaves.

4) Set oven control to broil. Ladle 1 cup soup into each of 8 ovenproof soup bowls. Top with 1 slice of toast and ¼ cup cheese. Broil tops 6 inches from heat 3 to 5 minutes or until cheese is bubbly and begins to brown. Garnish with thyme springs.

1 SERVING: Calories 440; Total Fat 20g (Saturated Fat 10g); Sodium 910mg; Total Carbohydrate 31g (Dietary Fiber 2g); Protein 34g. EXCHANGES: 2 Vegetable, 4 Lean Meat, 1 Fat. CARBOHYDRATE CHOICES: 2.

Texas No-Bean Chili

PREP TIME: 25 MINUTES (READY IN 8 HOURS 25 MINUTES)
SERVINGS: 12 (1 CUP EACH)

 LOW FAT

3 lb lean (at least 80%) ground beef

2 ½ cups finely chopped onions

4 large cloves garlic, finely chopped

1 small jalapeño chile, seeded, chopped

1 can (6 oz) tomato paste

2 cans (14.5 oz each) diced tomatoes in sauce

3 ½ cups Progresso® beef-flavored broth (from 32-oz carton)

¼ cup Mexican chili powder

1 tablespoon ground cumin

Shredded Cheddar cheese, if desired

Sliced green onions, if desired

1) Spray 5-quart slow cooker with cooking spray. In 12-inch skillet, cook half of the beef over medium-high heat 5 to 7 minutes, stirring occasionally, until thoroughly cooked; drain. Remove beef from skillet to slow cooker. Repeat with remaining beef. Add onions, garlic, chile, tomato paste, tomatoes, broth, chili powder and cumin to slow cooker; mix well.

2) Cover; cook on Low heat setting 8 hours. Garnish individual servings with cheese and green onions.

1 SERVING: Calories 251; Total Fat 10.5g (Saturated Fat 4g); Sodium 737mg; Total Carbohydrate 13g (Dietary Fiber 3g); Protein 23.5g. EXCHANGES: 1/2 Other Carbohydrate, 1 Vegetable, 3 Lean Meat. CARBOHYDRATE CHOICES: 1.

Greek Chicken Faux-coccia Sandwiches

STEPHANIE BRIGHT | SIMPSONVILLE, SC

BAKE-OFF® CONTEST 45, 2012

PREP TIME: 30 MINUTES (READY IN 55 MINUTES)
SERVINGS: 8

4 tablespoons Crisco® 100% Extra Virgin Olive Oil

1 teaspoon McCormick® Rosemary Leaves, crushed

1 teaspoon McCormick® Oregano Leaves

4 boneless skinless chicken breasts (about 1 ¼ lb)

2 tablespoons Pillsbury BEST® All Purpose Flour

1 can Pillsbury® Grands!® Homestyle refrigerated Southern Style biscuits

½ teaspoon McCormick® Garlic Powder

½ medium red onion, thinly sliced (about 1 cup)

½ cup crumbled feta cheese (2 oz)

1 package (8 oz) cream cheese, softened

2 cloves garlic, finely chopped

⅓ cup pitted kalamata olives, chopped

2 cups shredded iceberg lettuce

1) Heat oven to 325°F. Grease 2 large cookie sheets with 1 tablespoon of the olive oil.

2) In small bowl, stir together rosemary and oregano. Rub chicken breasts with 1 tablespoon of olive oil; rub rosemary mixture over chicken.

3) In 12-inch nonstick skillet or grill pan, cook chicken 3 to 4 minutes on each side over medium-high heat or until juice of chicken is clear when center of thickest part is cut (165°F). Remove chicken from skillet; let stand 10 minutes. Slice each chicken breast into ½-inch slices; cover to keep warm.

4) Meanwhile, lightly flour work surface and rolling pin. Roll each biscuit into 6-inch round. Using fingertips, make dimples in each biscuit. Brush tops with remaining 2 tablespoons of olive oil. Sprinkle with garlic powder and about ⅓ cup thinly sliced onions; press into dough. Place on cookie sheets. Place cookie sheets on separate oven racks.

5) Bake 14 to 17 minutes or until light golden brown, changing position of cookie sheets halfway through baking. Meanwhile, in small bowl, stir together feta cheese, cream cheese and garlic.

6) To assemble sandwiches, place faux-coccias, onion side down; spread feta mixture over each. Sprinkle with olives. On half of each faux-coccia, layer ⅛ of warm chicken, lettuce and remaining onion slices. Fold in half to form sandwich.

1 SERVING: Calories 550; Total Fat 33g (Saturated Fat 11g); Sodium 1100mg; Total Carbohydrate 38g (Dietary Fiber 0g); Protein 25g. EXCHANGES: 2-1/2 Starch, 2-1/2 Very Lean Meat, 6 Fat. CARBOHYDRATE CHOICES: 2-1/2.

Kickin' Chicken Sandwiches with Cucumber Topping

PAULINE PORTERFIELD | ROXBORO, NC

PREP TIME: 35 MINUTES (READY IN 35 MINUTES)
SERVINGS: 6

- 1 can Pillsbury® refrigerated crusty French loaf
- 1 tablespoon Crisco® 100% Extra Virgin Olive Oil
- 1 LAND O LAKES® Egg
- 1 tablespoon water
- 3 cups shredded deli rotisserie chicken (from 2-lb chicken)
- ¼ teaspoon McCormick® Garlic Powder
- ⅛ teaspoon salt
- ⅛ teaspoon McCormick® Ground Black Pepper
- ¼ cup hot red pepper sauce
- ¼ cup LAND O LAKES® Unsalted or Salted Butter
- 1 tablespoon honey
- 2 cups thinly sliced English (seedless) cucumber
- ¼ cup diced celery
- ⅓ cup blue cheese dressing
- ½ teaspoon McCormick® Dill Weed

1) Heat oven to 350°F. Spray cookie sheet with Crisco® Original No-Stick Cooking Spray. Carefully unroll loaf of dough; press into 15x9-inch rectangle. Cut in half lengthwise; cut crosswise into thirds, forming 6 pieces. Brush each piece with olive oil. To make rolls, fold each piece of dough almost in half crosswise, bringing top end of dough to within ¼ inch of bottom end (oiled surfaces will be touching). Place on cookie sheet. In small bowl, beat egg and water with fork; brush on tops of rolls.

2) Bake 15 to 20 minutes or until rolls are golden brown. Cool 5 minutes.

3) Meanwhile, in large bowl, stir together chicken, garlic powder, salt and pepper; mix well. In small microwavable bowl, microwave pepper sauce, butter and honey on High 15 to 30 seconds or until butter is melted; stir. Add to chicken mixture; mix well. In another medium bowl, add cucumber, celery, dressing and dill; toss to combine.

4) To serve, gently open sandwich rolls. Fill each with about ⅓ cup chicken mixture; top with scant ¼ cup of the cucumber mixture. Serve with any remaining cucumber mixture.

1 SERVING: Calories 440; Total Fat 24g (Saturated Fat 8g); Sodium 1310mg; Total Carbohydrate 30g (Dietary Fiber 0g); Protein 25g. EXCHANGES: 1 Starch, 1 Other Carbohydrate, 1/2 Vegetable, 1-1/2 Very Lean Meat, 1-1/2 Lean Meat, 3-1/2 Fat. CARBOHYDRATE CHOICES: 2.

tip

Chill cucumbers overnight in ice water so they stay cool and crispy when added to the dressing.

Southwest Potato-Corn Chowder

PREP TIME: 35 MINUTES (READY IN 35 MINUTES)
SERVINGS: 5

If LOW FAT

6 medium unpeeled red potatoes (1 ½ lb), cut into ½-inch cubes

3 cups Progresso® chicken broth

1 ¼ teaspoons sugar

½ teaspoon garlic salt

¼ teaspoon black pepper

⅛ to ¼ teaspoon ground red pepper (cayenne)

1 ½ cups Green Giant® Valley Fresh Steamers® Niblets® frozen corn (from 12-oz bag)

⅓ cup chopped roasted red bell peppers

⅓ cup all-purpose flour

1 cup milk

1 cup shredded reduced-fat sharp Cheddar cheese (4 oz)

1 container (6 oz) Yoplait® Greek Fat Free plain yogurt

4 medium green onions, finely chopped (¼ cup)

3 tablespoons chopped fresh cilantro

4 slices bacon, crisply cooked, crumbled

1) In 3-quart saucepan, place potatoes. Add water to cover. Heat to boiling; reduce heat. Cover; simmer 15 minutes or until tender. Drain. In small bowl, mash 1 cup potatoes. Return all potatoes to pan. Stir in broth, sugar, garlic salt, black and red pepper, corn and roasted peppers. Cook over medium heat 5 minutes, stirring occasionally.

2) In small bowl, stir flour and milk with whisk; stir into potato mixture. Cook over medium heat, stirring frequently, until mixture thickens and boils. Stir in cheese. Remove from heat; stir in yogurt, onions and cilantro. Top with bacon.

1 SERVING: Calories 320; Total Fat 6g (Saturated Fat 3g); Sodium 1040mg; Total Carbohydrate 48g (Dietary Fiber 5g); Protein 18g. EXCHANGES: 2 Starch, 1/2 Low-Fat Milk, 2-1/2 Vegetable, 1/2 Medium-Fat Meat. CARBOHYDRATE CHOICES: 3.

tip

For a healthier topping to use instead of the bacon, top off bowls of steaming chowder with seasoned croutons or fish-shaped crackers.

Orange-Coconut Fish Po'Boys

JONE SCHUMACHER | CHAPIN, IL

PREP TIME: 30 MINUTES (READY IN 1 HOUR 30 MINUTES)
SERVINGS: 4

SANDWICHES

7 tablespoons LAND O LAKES® Butter, melted

1 teaspoon McCormick® Imitation Coconut Extract

1 can Pillsbury® refrigerated crusty French loaf

4 frozen breaded fish fillets (about 3 oz each)

⅓ cup Smucker's® Low Sugar™ Sweet Orange Marmalade

¼ teaspoon salt

½ cup flaked coconut

SPREAD AND TOPPING

4 slices (1 oz each) Swiss cheese, each cut into fourths

2 tablespoons mayonnaise

2 tablespoons Smucker's® Low Sugar™ Sweet Orange Marmalade

4 large tomato slices

4 tablespoons chopped green onions, if desired

1) Heat oven to 350°F. Line cookie sheet with cooking parchment paper. In small bowl, stir together 4 tablespoons of the butter and ½ teaspoon of the coconut extract. Remove dough from can. Stretch dough to 16-inch length. Cut loaf crosswise into 4 pieces. Press down on each piece to flatten slightly. Cut 3 diagonal ¼-inch-deep slashes on top of each piece of dough. Lightly brush bottom of each piece of dough with butter mixture; place on cookie sheet. Lightly brush tops of dough with butter mixture. Reserve remaining butter mixture.

2) Bake 18 to 20 minutes or until golden brown. Lightly brush hot rolls with butter mixture. Cool.

3) Increase oven temperature to 400°F. Place fish fillets on same paper-lined cookie sheet. Bake 10 minutes.

4) Meanwhile, in small bowl, stir together ⅓ cup marmalade, remaining 3 tablespoons melted butter and ½ teaspoon coconut extract and salt; blend well. Remove fish from oven; brush with marmalade mixture. Return to oven; bake an additional 10 minutes. Remove fish from oven; turn and brush with marmalade mixture. Top each fillet with 1 tablespoon of the coconut. Return to oven; bake 5 to 6 minutes or until coconut is lightly browned. Remove from oven; turn fish. Brush tops of fillets with orange marmalade; top each with 1 tablespoon coconut. Return to oven; bake 5 to 6 minutes or until coconut is lightly browned. Place four pieces of Swiss cheese on each fish fillet. Bake 3 to 4 minutes or until cheese is melted.

5) Meanwhile, in small bowl stir together mayonnaise and 2 tablespoons marmalade; mix well.

6) Set oven control to broil. Cut each bread piece in half horizontally. Brush cut sides with remaining flavored butter; place, cut side up, on cookie sheet. Broil 3 to 4 inches from heat 2 to 3 minutes or until toasted. Spread 1 tablespoon mayonnaise mixture on bottom of each bun; top each with fish fillet, tomato slice and 1 tablespoon of onion and top of bun.

1 SERVING: Calories 860; Total Fat 51g (Saturated Fat 24g); Sodium 1240mg; Total Carbohydrate 79g (Dietary Fiber 1g); Protein 21g. EXCHANGES: 5-1/2 Other Carbohydrate, 2 Lean Meat, 1 High-Fat Meat, 7-1/2 Fat. CARBOHYDRATE CHOICES: 5.

Grilled Pimiento Cheese Sandwiches

PREP TIME: 40 MINUTES (READY IN 40 MINUTES)
SERVINGS: 8

 EASY

1 ¼ cups mayonnaise

1 jar (4 oz) diced pimientos, drained

1 teaspoon Worcestershire sauce

1 teaspoon finely grated onion

4 cups shredded sharp Cheddar cheese (16 oz)

16 slices white bread

1) In small bowl, mix 1 cup of the mayonnaise, the pimientos, Worcestershire sauce and onion. Stir in cheese. (Store in airtight container in refrigerator up to 1 week, if desired.)

2) For each sandwich, spread ¼ cup pimiento cheese mixture on 1 side of a bread slice; top with a second bread slice. Lightly spread outsides of sandwiches with remaining ¼ cup mayonnaise.

3) Heat griddle or large nonstick skillet over medium heat. Cook sandwiches in batches 8 to 10 minutes, turning once, until golden brown and cheese is melted.

1 SERVING: Calories 490; Total Fat 36g (Saturated Fat 13g); Sodium 722mg; Total Carbohydrate 26g (Dietary Fiber 1g); Protein 14g. EXCHANGES: 2 Starch, 1 High-Fat Meat, 5-1/2 Fat. CARBOHYDRATE CHOICES: 2.

Mandarin-Chicken Salad Sandwiches

PREP TIME: 10 MINUTES (READY IN 10 MINUTES)
SERVINGS: 4

EASY

2 snack-size containers (4 oz each) mandarin orange segments, drained (about ⅔ cup)

1 pint (2 cups) chicken salad (from deli)

4 slices cinnamon-raisin bread, toasted

4 leaves romaine lettuce, shredded

¼ cup chopped smoked almonds (about 1.25 oz)

1) In small bowl, mix oranges and chicken salad. Spread ½ cup chicken mixture on each toast slice.

2) Arrange shredded lettuce evenly over chicken salad; sprinkle each with 1 tablespoon almonds.

1 SERVING: Calories 350; Total Fat 21g (Saturated Fat 3.5g); Sodium 340mg; Total Carbohydrate 23g (Dietary Fiber 3g); Protein 17g. EXCHANGES: 1/2 Starch, 1 Other Carbohydrate, 1/2 Vegetable, 1 Very Lean Meat, 1 Lean Meat, 3-1/2 Fat. CARBOHYDRATE CHOICES: 1-1/2.

Mixed Greens with Cranberry Vinaigrette

PREP TIME: 20 MINUTES (READY IN 20 MINUTES)
SERVINGS: 12

 EASY

VINAIGRETTE

- ⅓ cup vegetable oil
- ¼ cup frozen (thawed) cranberry juice concentrate
- 1 teaspoon Dijon mustard
- ¼ teaspoon salt
- ½ cup sweetened dried cranberries

SALAD

- 2 bags (5 oz each) mixed spring greens
- 1 small bunch watercress, torn into pieces
- 2 tart red apples, thinly sliced, slices cut in half
- 1 avocado, pitted, peeled and sliced

1) In small bowl, beat all vinaigrette ingredients except cranberries with wire whisk until smooth. Stir in cranberries.

2) In serving bowl, toss all salad ingredients with vinaigrette just before serving.

1 SERVING: Calories 130; Total Fat 8g (Saturated Fat 1g); Sodium 70mg; Total Carbohydrate 12g (Dietary Fiber 2g); Protein 0g. EXCHANGES: 1/2 Other Carbohydrate, 1 Vegetable, 1-1/2 Fat. CARBOHYDRATE CHOICES: 1.

Watercress has small, crisp, dark green leaves and a peppery flavor. It is sold in small bunches in the produce section of the supermarket.

French Dip Roll

JULIE MERRIMAN | COLD BROOK, NY

Pillsbury Bake-Off · BAKE-OFF® CONTEST 45, 2012

PREP TIME: 35 MINUTES (READY IN 1 HOUR)
SERVINGS: 6

1   can Pillsbury® refrigerated crusty French loaf

1   lb sliced roast beef (from deli)

6   oz fontina cheese, shredded (1 ½ cups)

4   tablespoons LAND O LAKES® Butter

¼   cup grated Parmesan cheese

1   tablespoon McCormick® Basil Leaves

2   tablespoons Pillsbury BEST® All Purpose Flour

1   can (18.5 oz) Progresso® Vegetable Classics French onion soup

1) Heat oven to 350°F. Carefully unroll loaf of dough. Place half of roast beef slices over dough to within ½ inch of 1 long side. Sprinkle with fontina cheese; top with remaining roast beef. Starting on long side with filling, roll up. Press seam firmly to seal. Place diagonally, seam side down, on ungreased 15x10-inch pan with sides. In small microwavable bowl, microwave 2 tablespoons of the butter on High 15 to 20 seconds or until melted. Brush over loaf; sprinkle with Parmesan cheese and basil.

2) Bake 25 to 30 minutes or until golden brown. Cover with aluminum foil; bake an additional 10 minutes.

3) Meanwhile, to make dipping sauce, in 2-quart saucepan, melt remaining 2 tablespoons butter over medium heat. Stir in flour with wire whisk. Cook 2 minutes, stirring constantly. Stir in soup with wire whisk. Bring to a boil over medium-high heat, stirring constantly. Reduce to simmer; cook until thickened, about 10 minutes, stirring occasionally.

4) Remove loaf from oven. Cool 5 minutes. Cut into 6 slices. Serve with dipping sauce.

1 SERVING: Calories 440; Total Fat 22g (Saturated Fat 12g); Sodium 1750mg; Total Carbohydrate 31g (Dietary Fiber 0g); Protein 28g. EXCHANGES: 1-1/2 Starch, 1/2 Other Carbohydrate, 2-1/2 Lean Meat, 1 High-Fat Meat, 1 Fat. CARBOHYDRATE CHOICES: 2.

Smoky Chicken Salad

| PREP TIME: | 15 MINUTES (READY IN 15 MINUTES) |
| SERVINGS: | 4 |

 EASY

¾ cup ranch dressing

2 chipotle chiles in adobo sauce (from 7-oz can), chopped

2 cups Green Giant® Niblets® frozen corn (from 12-oz bag), thawed

8 cups torn romaine lettuce

2 cups shredded smoked chicken

1 large tomato, chopped (1 ½ cups)

⅓ cup thinly sliced red onion

1 cup multicolored tortilla strips

1) In small bowl, mix ranch dressing and chipotle chiles; set aside.

2) Heat 10-inch nonstick skillet over medium-high heat. Add corn; cook 5 minutes, stirring frequently, until lightly browned.

3) Divide lettuce evenly among 4 salad plates. Top evenly with chicken, corn, tomato and onion. Drizzle each salad with 3 tablespoons dressing. Sprinkle with tortilla strips.

1 SERVING: Calories 463; Total Fat 28g (Saturated Fat 4.5g); Sodium 824mg; Total Carbohydrate 26g (Dietary Fiber 5.5g); Protein 30g. EXCHANGES: 1 Starch, 1 Vegetable, 3 Very Lean Meat, 4 High-Fat Meat, 5 Fat. CARBOHYDRATE CHOICES: 2.

Turkey and Pepper Hoagies

| PREP TIME: | 15 MINUTES (READY IN 15 MINUTES) |
| SERVINGS: | 4 |

 EASY   LOW FAT

½ cup fat-free mayonnaise or salad dressing

1 teaspoon Italian seasoning

½ lb sliced smoked turkey breast, cut into strips

2 cups frozen pepper stir-fry (from 1-lb bag)

4 hoagie buns (6 to 7 inch) split

1) In small bowl, mix mayonnaise and Italian seasoning; set aside.

2) Spray 10-inch skillet with cooking spray; heat over medium-high heat. Add turkey and pepper stir-fry; cook and stir 1 minute. Cover; cook 2 minutes. Uncover; cook 1 to 3 minutes longer, stirring constantly, until liquid is evaporated and peppers are tender.

3) Spread 1 tablespoon mayonnaise mixture on cut side of each bun. Divide turkey mixture evenly among bun bottoms. Cover with bun tops.

1 SERVING: Calories 350; Total Fat 6g (Saturated Fat 1g); Sodium 1390mg; Total Carbohydrate 57g (Dietary Fiber 4g); Protein 17g. EXCHANGES: 3-1/2 Starch, 3-1/2 Other Carbohydrate, 1 Vegetable, 1 Very Lean Meat. CARBOHYDRATE CHOICES: 4.

Crunchy Carrot-Beet Salad

PREP TIME: 20 MINUTES (READY IN 20 MINUTES)
SERVINGS: 6

 EASY

½ cup coarsely chopped walnuts

½ cup olive oil

¼ cup fresh lemon juice

1 shallot, finely chopped

1 tablespoon packed brown sugar

1 teaspoon Dijon mustard

Dash salt

Dash pepper

2 medium fresh beets, peeled

2 large carrots

1 bag (5 oz) arugula

1 cup loosely packed fresh parsley leaves

1) Sprinkle walnuts in ungreased heavy skillet. Cook over medium heat 5 to 7 minutes, stirring frequently until nuts begin to brown, then stirring constantly until nuts are light brown.

2) Meanwhile, in small bowl, mix oil, lemon juice, shallot, brown sugar, mustard, salt and pepper with whisk.

3) Cut beets and carrots into thin slices, using mandoline or sharp knife. (To prevent hands from being stained, hold beets with paper towel or wear rubber gloves while slicing.) Toss arugula with small amount of vinaigrette. Arrange arugula on serving platter. Toss beets, carrots and parsley with desired amount of vinaigrette. Spoon mixture over arugula; sprinkle with walnuts. Season with salt and pepper, if desired. Serve immediately with any remaining vinaigrette.

1 SERVING: Calories 264; Total Fat 25g (Saturated Fat 3g); Sodium 112mg; Total Carbohydrate 10g (Dietary Fiber 2g); Protein 3g. EXCHANGES: 1-1/2 Vegetable, 5 Fat. CARBOHYDRATE CHOICES: 1/2.

Wicked Teriyaki Steak Salad

PREP TIME: 25 MINUTES (READY IN 25 MINUTES)
SERVINGS: 6

 EASY   LOW FAT

¼ cup citrus vinaigrette dressing

¼ cup teriyaki marinade and sauce (from 10-oz bottle)

1 lb beef strips for stir-fry

1 package (3 oz) Oriental-flavor ramen noodle soup mix

1 bag (10 oz) romaine and leaf lettuce mix

1 cup fresh snow pea pods, strings removed

½ cup julienne carrots (from 10-oz bag)

1 can (11 oz) mandarin orange segments, drained

1) In small bowl, mix dressing and teriyaki marinade; set aside.

2) Spray 12-inch skillet with cooking spray; heat over medium-high heat. Place beef in skillet; sprinkle with 1 teaspoon seasoning from soup mix. (Discard remaining seasoning packet.) Cook beef 4 to 6 minutes, stirring occasionally, until brown. Stir in 1 tablespoon of the teriyaki mixture.

3) Into large bowl, break block of noodles into small pieces. Add lettuce, pea pods, carrots and orange segments. Add remaining teriyaki mixture; toss until well coated. Divide mixture among 6 plates; top with beef.

1 SERVING: Calories 200; Total Fat 8g (Saturated Fat 1.5g); Sodium 770mg; Total Carbohydrate 11g (Dietary Fiber 2g); Protein 20g. EXCHANGES: 1/2 Other Carbohydrate, 1 Vegetable, 2-1/2 Lean Meat. CARBOHYDRATE CHOICES: 1.

tip For a stylish Asian dinner, set the table with chopsticks and brew a pot of jasmine tea. For dessert, set out a plate of pineapple chunks or fresh orange wedges.

Chicken Italiano Sliders

JULIE BECKWITH | CRETE, IL

BAKE-OFF® CONTEST 45, 2012

PREP TIME: 30 MINUTES (READY IN 1 HOUR 10 MINUTES)
SERVINGS: 16

4 oz fresh mozzarella cheese

⅓ cup mayonnaise

1 small clove garlic, finely chopped

¼ teaspoon salt

⅛ teaspoon McCormick® Ground Black Pepper

1 teaspoon lemon juice

3 tablespoons finely chopped fresh basil leaves

2 cans Pillsbury® Place 'n Bake® refrigerated crescent rounds

3 tablespoons Crisco® 100% Extra Virgin Olive Oil

½ teaspoon McCormick® Italian Seasoning

1 package (9 oz) refrigerated cooked Italian-style chicken breast strips, finely chopped

2 medium plum (Roma) tomatoes, cut into 16 slices

1) Heat oven to 375°F. Lightly spray 2 cookie sheets with Crisco® Original No-Stick Cooking Spray. Freeze mozzarella cheese 30 minutes.

2) Meanwhile, in small bowl, combine mayonnaise, garlic, salt, pepper, lemon juice and 1 tablespoon of the chopped basil; mix well. Cover; refrigerate.

3) Place crescent rounds 2 inches apart on cookie sheets. In small bowl, stir together olive oil and Italian seasoning. Lightly brush tops of rounds with 1 tablespoon of the oil mixture.

4) Bake 8 to 10 minutes or until light golden brown. Cool 5 minutes.

5) Using serrated knife, cut crescent rounds in half horizontally. Place 16 crescent halves, cut side up, on cookie sheets. Lightly brush with oil mixture. Bake 5 to 9 minutes or until golden brown. Repeat with remaining crescent halves and oil mixture.

6) Shred mozzarella cheese. Spread about ½ teaspoon of the mayonnaise mixture on each cut side of crescent rounds. Top bottom of each crescent round with 1 rounded tablespoon chicken, 1 tomato slice and 1 tablespoon shredded mozzarella. Place on cookie sheets.

7) Set oven control to broil. Broil 4 to 6 inches from heat 2 to 3 minutes or until cheese is melted. Remove from oven; top with remaining basil and crescent round tops. Secure sliders with cocktail toothpicks.

1 SERVING: Calories 210; Total Fat 14g (Saturated Fat 4g); Sodium 400mg; Total Carbohydrate 12g (Dietary Fiber 0g); Protein 7g. EXCHANGES: 1 Starch, 1/2 Very Lean Meat, 2-1/2 Fat. CARBOHYDRATE CHOICES: 1.

Falafel Sandwiches with Fire-Roasted Tomato Aioli

ELIZABETH DEHART | WEST JORDAN, UT

BAKE-OFF® CONTEST 45, 2012

Pillsbury Bake-Off®

PREP TIME: 45 MINUTES (READY IN 45 MINUTES)
SERVINGS: 8

½ cup mayonnaise

½ cup Muir Glen® organic fire roasted crushed tomatoes (from 14.5-oz can), drained

¾ teaspoon McCormick® Minced Garlic

1 can (16.3 oz) Pillsbury® Grands!® Homestyle refrigerated buttermilk biscuits

5 tablespoons Crisco® Light Olive Oil

1 can (15 oz) Progresso® chick peas (garbanzo beans), rinsed, drained

½ red onion, chopped

¼ cup fresh Italian (flat-leaf) parsley, chopped

1 teaspoon McCormick® Chili Powder

¾ teaspoon McCormick® Ground Turmeric

½ teaspoon McCormick® Ground Cumin

½ teaspoon McCormick® Ground Roasted Coriander

4 tablespoons Pillsbury BEST® All Purpose Flour

1 cup fresh baby spinach leaves

1) To prepare aioli, place mayonnaise, tomatoes and ½ teaspoon of the minced garlic in food processor or blender. Cover; process until smooth. Cover and refrigerate.

2) Heat oven to 350°F. Place biscuits on ungreased cookie sheet. Brush tops of biscuits with 1 tablespoon of the olive oil.

3) Bake 11 to 15 minutes or until golden brown. Meanwhile, in food processor, place chick peas, onion, remaining ¼ teaspoon minced garlic, parsley, chili powder, turmeric, cumin and coriander. Cover; process, using quick on-and-off motions, adding flour 1 tablespoon at a time until mixture is well blended.

4) With wet hands, form about 3 tablespoons chick pea mixture into 3-inch patty. Repeat to make 7 more patties. In 12-inch skillet, heat remaining 4 tablespoons olive oil over medium-high heat. Cook patties in oil 6 to 8 minutes, turning once, or until golden brown.

5) Split biscuits; spread a generous tablespoon aioli on bottom half of each biscuit. Top each with patty, spinach leaves and top of biscuit.

1 SERVING: Calories 430; Total Fat 26g (Saturated Fat 7g); Sodium 770mg; Total Carbohydrate 41g (Dietary Fiber 3g); Protein 7g. EXCHANGES: 1-1/2 Starch, 1 Other Carbohydrate, 1 Vegetable, 5 Fat. CARBOHYDRATE CHOICES: 3.

Chicken Primavera Crescent Braid

CHERYL KASSIN | STERLING HEIGHTS, MI

Bake-Off®   BAKE-OFF® CONTEST 45, 2012

PREP TIME: 30 MINUTES (READY IN 1 HOUR)
SERVINGS: 6

2 tablespoons LAND O LAKES® Butter

2 small green onions, finely chopped

½ cup chopped fresh asparagus

½ cup sliced fresh sugar snap peas

¼ cup chopped red bell pepper

¼ teaspoon McCormick® Cayenne Pepper

¼ teaspoon McCormick® Basil Leaves

¼ teaspoon McCormick® Ground Sage

⅛ teaspoon McCormick® Ground Black Pepper

2 cups finely chopped cooked chicken

½ cup savory garlic cooking creme (from 10-oz container)

½ cup shredded Colby-Monterey Jack cheese blend (2 oz)

¼ cup grated Parmesan cheese

1 can Pillsbury® Butter Flake refrigerated crescent dinner rolls

½ teaspoon McCormick® Sesame Seed

1) Heat oven to 350°F. In 3-quart saucepan, melt 1 tablespoon of the butter over medium heat. Add onions; cook and stir 1 minute. Add asparagus, snap peas and bell pepper; cook and stir an additional minute. Stir in cayenne pepper, basil, sage and black pepper. Add chicken, cooking creme, shredded cheese and Parmesan. Cook, stirring constantly, or until thoroughly heated and cheese is melted, 1 to 3 minutes. Remove from heat.

2) Line cookie sheet with cooking parchment paper or spray with Crisco® Original No-Stick Cooking Spray. Unroll crescent dough on cookie sheet. Firmly press perforations to seal. Press dough to 14x10-inch rectangle. Spoon chicken mixture down center of rectangle in 4-inch-wide strip. Using kitchen scissors or sharp knife, make cuts 1 inch apart on each long side of rectangle to within ½ inch of filling. Fold dough strips over filling, pulling gently to overlap slightly in the center.

3) In small microwavable bowl, microwave remaining 1 tablespoon of butter on High 10 to 15 seconds or until melted. Brush dough with butter; sprinkle with sesame seed.

4) Bake 15 to 25 minutes or until edges are golden brown and center is light golden brown. Cool on pan 10 minutes. Cut crosswise into slices.

1 SERVING: Calories 360; Total Fat 22g (Saturated Fat 10g); Sodium 650mg; Total Carbohydrate 18g (Dietary Fiber 0g); Protein 21g. EXCHANGES: 1 Starch, 1/2 Vegetable, 2 Lean Meat, 1/2 High-Fat Meat, 2-1/2 Fat. CARBOHYDRATE CHOICES: 1.

Cilantro-Peanut Slaw

PREP TIME: 10 MINUTES (READY IN 10 MINUTES)
SERVINGS: 10 (1/2 CUP EACH)

 EASY

1 bag (16 oz) coleslaw mix (shredded cabbage and carrots)

½ cup sweet-spicy French dressing

¼ cup chopped red bell pepper

¼ cup loosely packed fresh cilantro leaves, coarsely chopped

¼ cup coarsely chopped salted dry-roasted peanuts

1) In 2-quart bowl, mix coleslaw mix and dressing. Top with bell pepper, cilantro and peanuts. Toss just before serving.

1 SERVING: Calories 90; Total Fat 7g (Saturated Fat 1g); Sodium 135mg; Total Carbohydrate 4g (Dietary Fiber 0g); Protein 1g. EXCHANGES: 1/2 Other Carbohydrate, 1-1/2 Fat. CARBOHYDRATE CHOICES: 0.

Curried Turkey Salad Sandwiches

PREP TIME: 20 MINUTES (READY IN 20 MINUTES)
SERVINGS: 4

 EASY

1 ½ cups diced cooked turkey

½ cup diced unpeeled apple

½ cup mayonnaise or salad dressing

1 ½ teaspoons curry powder

¼ teaspoon ground ginger

¼ teaspoon pepper

1 medium stalk celery, chopped (½ cup)

2 medium green onions, chopped (2 tablespoons)

8 slices whole-grain bread

1) In medium bowl, mix all ingredients except bread.

2) Divide turkey mixture evenly among 4 slices bread. Top with remaining bread.

1 SERVING: Calories 460; Total Fat 28g (Saturated Fat 5g); Sodium 510mg; Total Carbohydrate 31g (Dietary Fiber 5g); Protein 21g. EXCHANGES: 2 Starch, 2 Lean Meat, 4 Fat. CARBOHYDRATE CHOICES: 2.

tip

Skip the bread and serve this turkey salad on a lettuce-lined plate with cut-up fresh vegetables or fruit.

Sloppy Jose Gorditas

NAYLET LAROCHELLE | MIAMI, FL

BAKE-OFF® CONTEST 45, 2012

PREP TIME: 40 MINUTES (READY IN 1 HOUR 5 MINUTES)
SERVINGS: 8

1 tablespoon Crisco® Pure Olive Oil

½ cup diced onion

1 lb ground beef

1 can (8 oz) Muir Glen® organic tomato sauce

1 teaspoon McCormick® Oregano Leaves

½ teaspoon McCormick® Ground Cumin

¼ teaspoon salt

¼ teaspoon McCormick® Ground Cinnamon

1 can (15 oz) Progresso® black beans, rinsed, drained

⅓ cup raisins

1 can Pillsbury® Grands!® Flaky Layers refrigerated honey butter biscuits

1 LAND O LAKES® Egg White, lightly beaten

1 ½ cups shredded lettuce

½ cup crumbled cotija (white Mexican) cheese or queso fresco cheese

2 tablespoons finely chopped fresh cilantro

½ cup sour cream, if desired

8 lime wedges, if desired

1) Heat oven to 350°F. Heat olive oil in 12-inch nonstick skillet over medium-high heat. Add onion; cook, stirring occasionally, 3 to 4 minutes or until softened. Stir in ground beef; cook 5 to 7 minutes, stirring frequently, until browned and no longer pink. Drain. Reduce heat to low.

2) Return skillet with browned meat to stove. Stir in tomato sauce, oregano, cumin, salt, cinnamon, black beans and raisins. Cook 5 to 8 minutes, stirring occasionally, until thoroughly heated. Remove from heat; cover to keep warm.

3) Meanwhile, using a rolling pin, roll out each biscuit into 6-inch round. Lightly brush top side of each biscuit with egg white; fold biscuit in half. Place folded biscuits on large ungreased cookie sheet.

4) Bake 13 to 18 minutes or until golden brown. Remove to cooling rack; cool 5 minutes.

5) Using a small serrated knife, make a 5-inch slit in center of curved side of each biscuit. Spoon about ½ cup ground beef mixture into opening. Evenly divide lettuce among gorditas. Top each with 1 tablespoon cheese. Place gorditas on serving platter; sprinkle with cilantro. Serve with sour cream and lime wedges.

1 SERVING: Calories 430; Total Fat 17g (Saturated Fat 7g); Sodium 870mg; Total Carbohydrate 49g (Dietary Fiber 7g); Protein 20g. EXCHANGES: 3 Starch, 1/2 Vegetable, 1-1/2 Medium-Fat Meat, 1-1/2 Fat. CARBOHYDRATE CHOICES: 3.

Bacon-Chicken Sliders with Raspberry-Onion Spread

CAMERON BAILEY | SALT LAKE CITY, UT

BAKE-OFF® CONTEST 45, 2012

PREP TIME: 45 MINUTES (READY IN 45 MINUTES)
SERVINGS: 8

- 1 can Pillsbury® Place 'n Bake® refrigerated crescent rounds
- 1 LAND O LAKES® Egg, beaten
- 1 to 2 teaspoons McCormick® Poppy Seed
- 1 tablespoon Crisco® Pure Vegetable Oil
- 1 cup chopped red onions
- ⅛ teaspoon salt
- ⅛ teaspoon McCormick® Ground Black Pepper
- 1 cup Progresso® chicken broth
- 2 tablespoons balsamic vinegar
- ¼ cup Smucker's® Red Raspberry Preserves
- ¼ cup Smucker's® Apricot Preserves
- 1 boneless skinless chicken breast, cooked, thinly sliced
- 4 slices hickory-smoked bacon, crisply cooked, broken in half
- ¼ cup fresh cilantro leaves

1) Heat oven to 375°F. Line large cookie sheet with cooking parchment paper. Place crescent rounds on cookie sheet; press each crescent into 2 ½-inch round. Brush with egg; sprinkle with poppy seed.

2) Bake 8 to 13 minutes or until golden brown. Remove from cookie sheet to cooling rack.

3) Meanwhile, in 10-inch skillet, heat oil over medium heat. Add onions, salt and pepper; cook 3 to 5 minutes, stirring frequently, or until onions are tender. Add chicken broth and balsamic vinegar; cook 12 to 17 minutes or until sauce is reduced by half. Stir in red raspberry and apricot preserves; cook 2 to 3 minutes, stirring frequently, or until slightly thickened. Cool 5 minutes.

4) Cut each crescent round in half horizontally. Place bottoms of buns on serving platter; top each with 2 teaspoons of the onion mixture, chicken, bacon, cilantro and top of bun.

1 SERVING: Calories 250; Total Fat 11g (Saturated Fat 3g); Sodium 500mg; Total Carbohydrate 28g (Dietary Fiber 0g); Protein 8g. EXCHANGES: 2 Starch, 2 Fat. CARBOHYDRATE CHOICES: 2.

Spicy Cheeseburger Soup

PREP TIME: 15 MINUTES (READY IN 5 HOURS 15 MINUTES)
SERVINGS: 6 (1 CUP EACH)

 EASY

1 lb lean (at least 80%) ground beef

3 cups half-and-half

¼ teaspoon freshly ground pepper

1 loaf (16 oz) spicy Buffalo prepared cheese product, cut into cubes

3 plum (Roma) tomatoes, chopped (¾ cup)

1½ cups shredded lettuce

½ cup chopped red onion

18 slices dill pickles

1) Spray 3-quart slow cooker with cooking spray. In 10-inch skillet, cook beef over medium-high heat 5 to 7 minutes, stirring frequently, until thoroughly cooked; drain. In slow cooker, stir beef, half-and-half, pepper and cheese until blended.

2) Cover; cook on Low heat setting 5 hours. About 5 minutes before serving, stir soup. Top individual bowls with tomatoes, lettuce, onion and pickles.

1 SERVING: Calories 511; Total Fat 34.5g (Saturated Fat 20.5g); Sodium 1086mg; Total Carbohydrate 16.5g (Dietary Fiber 1g); Protein 31g. EXCHANGES: 1/2 Starch, 1/2 Milk, 2 Medium-Fat Meat, 2 High-Fat Meat, 1 Fat. CARBOHYDRATE CHOICES: 1.

tip

All the elements that make a great cheeseburger are present in this slow cooker soup. If you prefer a milder soup, use regular prepared cheese product instead of the spicy variety.

Thai Chicken Subs

NADINE CLARK | QUAKERTOWN, PA

BAKE-OFF® CONTEST 45, 2012

PREP TIME: 40 MINUTES (READY IN 40 MINUTES)
SERVINGS: 6

2 cans Pillsbury® refrigerated crusty French loaf

1 cup coleslaw mix

1 small red onion (halved lengthwise), cut into thin wedges (1 cup)

1 medium red bell pepper, cut into ⅛-inch strips (1 cup)

½ medium English (seedless) cucumber, cut into 2x¼x¼-inch pieces (1 cup)

¼ cup fresh cilantro, chopped

¾ cup soy-teriyaki blend or ¾ cup stir-fry sauce plus 2 teaspoons sesame seed

¾ cup seasoned rice vinegar

2 tablespoons packed brown sugar

1 ½ teaspoons hot chili sauce

¼ cup Jif® Creamy Peanut Butter

1 tablespoon Crisco® Pure Vegetable Oil

1 ½ lb uncooked chicken breast tenders (not breaded)

1) Heat oven to 350°F. Spray large cookie sheet with Crisco® Original No-Stick Cooking Spray. Place loaves, seam side down on cookie sheet, about 3 inches apart. Using sharp knife, cut 5 diagonal ½-inch-deep slashes on top of dough.

2) Bake 26 to 30 minutes or until golden brown.

3) Meanwhile, in medium bowl, combine coleslaw mix, onion, bell pepper, cucumber and cilantro. In 2-cup measuring cup, combine ½ cup of the soy-teriyaki blend, ½ cup of the rice vinegar, 1 tablespoon of the brown sugar and 1 teaspoon of the chili sauce. Beat well with wire whisk. Pour over vegetable mixture; stir to combine. Set aside, stirring occasionally.

4) In 1-quart saucepan, combine peanut butter, remaining ¼ cup soy-teriyaki blend, ¼ cup rice vinegar, 1 tablespoon brown sugar and ½ teaspoon chili sauce. Cook over medium heat 4 to 5 minutes, stirring occasionally, until smooth. Set aside.

5) In 12-inch skillet, heat oil over medium-high heat. Add chicken tenders; cook 7 to 10 minutes, turning once, until chicken is no longer pink in center. Add peanut sauce; stir to coat. Remove from heat.

6) Cut each loaf crosswise into thirds. Cut each piece of bread in half lengthwise down center to within ½ inch of bottom. To make each sub, spoon ⅙ of chicken mixture into each piece of bread. With slotted spoon, top each with about ½ cup vegetable mixture. Serve any remaining sauce as a dipping sauce.

1 SERVING: Calories 520; Total Fat 12g (Saturated Fat 2.5g); Sodium 1860mg; Total Carbohydrate 67g (Dietary Fiber 2g); Protein 35g. EXCHANGES: 3 Starch, 1 Other Carbohydrate, 1 Vegetable, 3 Very Lean Meat, 1/2 High-Fat Meat, 1 Fat. CARBOHYDRATE CHOICES: 4-1/2.

Turkey Chowder

PREP TIME: 15 MINUTES (READY IN 6 HOURS 35 MINUTES)
SERVINGS: 6

 EASY   LOW FAT

2 turkey breast tenderloins ($^3/_4$ lb each), cut into 1-inch pieces

$^3/_4$ teaspoon garlic-pepper blend

1 teaspoon salt

6 to 8 small red potatoes, cut into 1-inch pieces

2 medium carrots, sliced (1 cup)

1 medium onion, chopped ($^1/_2$ cup)

2 teaspoons dried dill weed

2 $^1/_2$ cups Progresso® chicken broth (from 32-oz carton)

1 can (15.25 oz) Green Giant® whole kernel corn, drained

1 cup half-and-half

3 tablespoons cornstarch

1) Spray 4- to 5-quart slow cooker with cooking spray. Place turkey in slow cooker; sprinkle with garlic-pepper blend and salt. Stir in remaining ingredients except half-and-half and cornstarch.

2) Cover; cook on Low heat setting 6 to 8 hours.

3) In small bowl, mix half-and-half and cornstarch until smooth; gradually stir into chowder until blended. Increase heat setting to High. Cover; cook about 20 minutes longer, stirring occasionally, until thickened.

1 SERVING: Calories 400; Total Fat 7g (Saturated Fat 3.5g); Sodium 1090mg; Total Carbohydrate 50g (Dietary Fiber 6g); Protein 33g. EXCHANGES: 2 Starch, 1 Other Carbohydrate, 1 Vegetable, 3-1/2 Very Lean Meat, 1/2 Fat. CARBOHYDRATE CHOICES: 3.

Greens, Beans and Bacon Soup

PREP TIME: 15 MINUTES (READY IN 40 MINUTES)
SERVINGS: 3

 EASY   LOW FAT

3 slices bacon, cut crosswise into $^1/_4$-inch pieces

3 cups packed chopped kale

2 $^1/_4$ cups water

1 can (15 oz) cannellini beans, drained, rinsed

1 can (14 oz) roasted garlic-seasoned chicken broth

1 cup frozen chopped onion

$^1/_4$ teaspoon pepper

Red pepper sauce, if desired

1) In large saucepan, cook bacon over medium-high heat 8 minutes or until crisp. Reserve 2 teaspoons drippings in pan; discard excess drippings.

2) Add kale, water, beans, broth, onion and pepper to bacon and drippings in pan. Stir in pepper sauce. Heat to boiling over high heat; reduce heat. Cover; simmer 25 minutes. Serve immediately.

1 SERVING: Calories 240; Total Fat 7g (Saturated Fat 2g); Sodium 947mg; Total Carbohydrate 31g (Dietary Fiber 8g); Protein 14g. EXCHANGES: 1-1/2 Starch, 1-1/2 Vegetable, 1 Very Lean Meat, 2-1/2 Fat. CARBOHYDRATE CHOICES: 2.

Turkey Chile Verde

PREP TIME: 20 MINUTES (READY IN 8 HOURS 20 MINUTES)
SERVINGS: 7 (1 CUP EACH)

 EASY   LOW FAT

1 tablespoon vegetable oil

1 turkey breast tenderloin (1 lb), cut into 1-inch pieces

2 cups Progresso® reduced-sodium chicken broth (from 32-oz carton)

1 cup Old El Paso® salsa verde

1 container (8 oz) refrigerated prechopped onion

1 ½ teaspoons ground cumin

½ teaspoon pepper

1 can (11 oz) Green Giant® chipotle white corn, drained

1 can (4.5 oz) Old El Paso® chopped green chiles

2 cans (15 oz each) reduced-sodium cannellini beans, drained, rinsed

Light sour cream, if desired

1) Spray 4-quart slow cooker with cooking spray. In 12-inch nonstick skillet, heat oil over medium-high heat. Cook turkey in oil 6 to 8 minutes, stirring often, until browned. In slow cooker, mix turkey, broth, salsa, onion, cumin, pepper, corn and chiles.

2) Cover; cook on Low heat setting 7 hours.

3) Stir 1 can of the beans into soup. Mash remaining can of beans; stir into soup. Cover; cook 1 hour longer or until thickened. Serve with sour cream.

1 SERVING: Calories 244; Total Fat 3.5g (Saturated Fat 0.5g); Sodium 784mg; Total Carbohydrate 29.5g (Dietary Fiber 6.5g); Protein 24g. EXCHANGES: 1-1/2 Starch, 1-1/2 Vegetable, 2-1/2 Very Lean Meat. CARBOHYDRATE CHOICES: 2.

tip Unless the recipe instructs you to stir in or add ingredients, refrain from lifting the lid while the slow cooker is cooking. Every time you lift the lid, steam is lost and you add 15 to 30 minutes of cooking time.

Three-Cheese Broccoli Soup

PREP TIME: 20 MINUTES (READY IN 2 HOURS 20 MINUTES)
SERVINGS: 9 (1 CUP EACH)

 EASY

2 tablespoons butter or margarine

1 large onion, chopped (1 cup)

⅓ cup all-purpose flour

2 cups half-and-half

3 cups Progresso® chicken broth
(from 32-oz carton)

1 bag (12 oz) fresh broccoli florets,
chopped

1 loaf (8 oz) prepared cheese product,
cut into cubes

4 oz white Cheddar cheese, shredded
(1 cup)

4 oz Gruyère cheese, shredded (1 cup)

1 cup freshly shredded Parmesan
cheese (4 oz)

Additional freshly shredded
Parmesan cheese, if desired

1) Spray 3 ½-quart slow cooker with cooking spray. In 1-quart saucepan, melt butter over medium-high heat. Cook onion in butter 3 minutes, stirring occasionally, until tender. Stir in flour; cook and stir 1 minute. Reduce heat to medium. Gradually stir in half-and-half; cook 3 to 5 minutes, stirring constantly, until thickened. Pour into slow cooker. Stir in broth and broccoli.

2) Cover; cook on Low heat setting 2 hours or until broccoli is tender.

3) Add cheese product, Cheddar cheese, Gruyère cheese and 1 cup Parmesan cheese; stir until cheeses are melted. Sprinkle individual servings with additional Parmesan cheese.

1 SERVING: Calories 363; Total Fat 26g (Saturated Fat 15.5g); Sodium 1065mg; Total Carbohydrate 12.5g (Dietary Fiber 1.5g); Protein 21g. EXCHANGES: 1/2 Starch, 1 Vegetable, 2-1/2 High-Fat Meat, 2 Fat. CARBOHYDRATE CHOICES: 1.

TURKEY CONFETTI PIZZA
PG. 134

Main Dishes

Families come running for hearty helpings of these skillet suppers, pasta dishes, meat pies and more!

INDONESIAN CHICKEN TURNOVERS
WITH SPICY PEANUT SAUCE
PG. 133

MEATBALL MINESTRONE BAKE
PG. 136

CHICKEN FETTUCCINE
PG. 137

Stuffed Onion Packets with Cheese Sauce

DONNA NEWCOMER | BUFFALO, NY

BAKE-OFF® CONTEST 45, 2012

PREP TIME: 45 MINUTES (READY IN 1 HOUR 30 MINUTES)
SERVINGS: 4

- 4 large (about 1 lb each) sweet onions
- 5 oz bulk Italian pork sausage
- 4 oz lean (at least 80%) ground beef
- 4 oz (half of 8-oz package) cream cheese
- 1 cup chopped drained roasted red bell peppers (from a jar)
- 1 ½ cups shredded Swiss cheese (6 oz)
- 2 tablespoons Progresso® Italian style bread crumbs
- 1 can Pillsbury® refrigerated classic pizza crust
- 1 jar (15 oz) cheese dip
- ¾ cup milk
- 1 teaspoon prepared horseradish
- ⅛ teaspoon McCormick® Parsley Flakes, if desired

1) Fill 4- to 5-quart Dutch oven ¾ full with water. Bring to a boil over medium-high heat.

2) Meanwhile, slice bottom and top off each onion, leaving outer skin on. To hollow out onions, with knife, cut an "X" through center of each onion, cutting up to but not through 2 outer rings of onion. Run knife around the inside of second outer ring to loosen middle of onion; with thumbs, push middle part of onion out. (Save insides of onions for another use.) Gently drop onions into boiling water; boil 12 to 13 minutes. (Onions will be slightly soft but retain their shape.) With slotted spoon, remove onions from water. Cool 10 minutes. Remove onion skins.

3) Meanwhile, heat oven to 350° F. In 10-inch skillet, cook and stir sausage and ground beef over medium-high heat 6 to 7 minutes or until no longer pink, breaking up any large chunks. Remove from skillet; set aside. In large microwavable bowl, microwave cream cheese on High 30 to 40 seconds or until very soft. Stir in cooked meat, ⅓ cup of the roasted peppers, Swiss cheese and bread crumbs until well mixed.

4) Unroll pizza dough. Cut in half lengthwise and crosswise, forming 4 rectangles. Press out each to 8x6-inch rectangle. One at a time, place rectangle on large ungreased cookie sheet. Place 1 onion in center of dough. Fill onion with ¼ of meat filling, mounding filling on top of onion. Bring 2 opposite corners of dough together over top of onion; pinch to seal. Repeat with remaining corners; pinch top and sides to seal. Repeat with remaining dough, onions and filling. Using fork, poke several holes in top of dough in each packet.

5) Bake 30 to 40 minutes or until golden brown.

6) Meanwhile, to make sauce, in medium microwavable bowl microwave cheese dip, milk and remaining ⅔ cup roasted peppers uncovered on High 2 minutes 30 seconds to 3 minutes, stirring once halfway through cooking or until melted. Stir in horseradish. To serve, spoon ¼ cup of the sauce in center of each of 4 individual plates. Place packets on sauce; sprinkle with parsley flakes. Serve with remaining sauce.

1 SERVING: Calories 990; Total Fat 58g (Saturated Fat 31g); Sodium 2330mg; Total Carbohydrate 74g (Dietary Fiber 4g); Protein 42g. EXCHANGES: 4 Starch, 1/2 Low-Fat Milk, 1-1/2 Vegetable, 2 Lean Meat, 1-1/2 High-Fat Meat, 7 Fat. CARBOHYDRATE CHOICES: 5.

Chicago Deep-Dish Sausage Pizza

PREP TIME:	25 MINUTES (READY IN 50 MINUTES)
SERVINGS:	6

1 lb bulk Italian pork sausage

1 small bell pepper (any color), chopped (½ cup)

1 cup sliced fresh mushrooms (3 oz)

1 can (8 oz) pizza sauce

1 can (13.8 oz) Pillsbury® refrigerated classic pizza crust

1 ½ cups shredded mozzarella cheese (6 oz)

2 medium plum (Roma) tomatoes, chopped

¼ cup sliced ripe olives, if desired

2 medium green onions, chopped (2 tablespoons)

1) Heat oven to 400°F. Spray 9-inch square pan with cooking spray. In 10-inch nonstick skillet, cook sausage and bell pepper over medium-high heat 7 to 9 minutes, stirring frequently, until sausage is no longer pink. Stir in mushrooms and pizza sauce. Keep warm over low heat.

2) Unroll dough; place in pan. Starting at center, press out dough to edges of pan, pressing up sides at least 1 inch, folding edge under to form crust. Sprinkle ½ cup of the cheese evenly in bottom of crust. Spoon hot sausage mixture over cheese. Top with remaining 1 cup cheese, the tomatoes and olives.

3) Bake 15 to 20 minutes or until crust is golden brown. Sprinkle with onions. Let stand 5 minutes before cutting.

1 SERVING: Calories 390; Total Fat 18g (Saturated Fat 7g); Sodium 1050mg; Total Carbohydrate 37g (Dietary Fiber 1g); Protein 25g. EXCHANGES: 2 Starch, 1/2 Other Carbohydrate, 2 1/2 High-Fat Meat. CARBOHYDRATE CHOICES: 2-1/2.

Loaded Nacho Burgers

PAM WILKINSON | TRACY, CA

Pillsbury Bake-Off®   BAKE-OFF® CONTEST 45, 2012

PREP TIME: 45 MINUTES (READY IN 45 MINUTES)
SERVINGS: 8

½ cup crushed nacho-flavored tortilla chips (about 25 chips)

1 can (16.3 oz) Pillsbury® Grands!® Homestyle refrigerated buttermilk biscuits

¾ cup sliced mild banana pepper rings (from 16-oz jar), drained

1 lb lean (at least 80%) ground beef

¾ cup nacho cheese sauce or dip

¼ teaspoon McCormick® Chili Powder

¼ teaspoon McCormick® Ground Cumin

2 oz (¼ of 8-oz package) cream cheese, softened

¼ cup finely chopped red onion

⅓ cup diced seeded tomato

¼ cup crumbled cooked bacon

1 medium ripe avocado, pitted, peeled and diced

1) Heat oven to 350°F. Place crushed nacho chips in shallow dish. Press both sides of each biscuit into crushed chips. Bake biscuits on ungreased cookie sheet 13 to 17 minutes or until golden brown. Remove from cookie sheet to cooling rack.

2) Meanwhile, finely chop enough banana pepper rings to equal ¼ cup. In large bowl, mix ground beef, ¼ cup of the nacho cheese sauce, ¼ cup chopped banana peppers, chili powder, and cumin. Shape mixture into 8 patties, 3 ½ inches in diameter.

3) In nonstick skillet, cook patties over medium-high heat 5 to 7 minutes, turning once, or until meat thermometer inserted in center of patties reads 160°F.

4) In small microwavable bowl, microwave remaining ½ cup nacho cheese sauce on High 30 to 45 seconds or until warm; stir. Split biscuits. Lightly spread cream cheese on cut sides of biscuit halves. Top bottom of each biscuit with burger, nacho cheese sauce, onion, tomato, bacon, avocado, remaining banana pepper rings and biscuit tops.

1 SERVING: Calories 410; Total Fat 24g (Saturated Fat 8g); Sodium 860mg; Total Carbohydrate 32g (Dietary Fiber 2g); Protein 17g. EXCHANGES: 1 Starch, 1 Other Carbohydrate, 1/2 Vegetable, 1 Lean Meat, 1 High-Fat Meat, 2-1/2 Fat. CARBOHYDRATE CHOICES: 2.

Indonesian Chicken Turnovers with Spicy Peanut Sauce

LINDA BLAKELY | BERNE, NY

Pillsbury Bake-Off®

PREP TIME: 50 MINUTES (READY IN 1 HOUR)
SERVINGS: 8 (2 TURNOVERS EACH)

8 tablespoons Crisco® Pure Canola Oil

¾ cup finely chopped onions

2 cups shredded rotisserie chicken (from 2-lb chicken)

1 tablespoon McCormick® Curry Powder

¾ teaspoon McCormick® Garlic Powder

½ teaspoon McCormick® Cayenne Pepper

1 can (6 oz) pineapple juice

¼ cup canned crushed pineapple

¼ cup raisins

1 tablespoon shredded coconut

2 tablespoons coarsely chopped bread-and-butter pickles (not pickle relish)

2 cans Pillsbury® refrigerated crescent dinner rolls

¼ cup Jif® Creamy Peanut Butter

2 tablespoons soy sauce

2 tablespoons sugar

2 teaspoons white vinegar

1 tablespoon finely chopped green onion with top

1) In 10-inch skillet, heat 3 tablespoons of the oil over medium heat. Add ¾ cup onions; cook 2 to 3 minutes, stirring frequently, or until onions are softened. Add chicken, curry powder, garlic powder, and ¼ teaspoon of the cayenne pepper; cook 2 minutes, stirring constantly. Stir in pineapple juice, crushed pineapple, raisins, coconut and pickles. Bring to a boil. Reduce heat to medium-low; simmer uncovered 7 to 10 minutes, stirring occasionally, or until liquid is absorbed. Remove from heat.

2) Heat oven to 350°F. Unroll both cans of crescent dough; separate dough into 8 rectangles. Firmly press perforations to seal. Press each piece of dough into 7x3 ½-inch rectangle. Cut each rectangle crosswise into 2 squares. Place about 2 tablespoons of chicken mixture onto center of each square; fold dough in half diagonally to form a triangle. With fork, seal edges. Place 2 inches apart on ungreased cookie sheet.

3) Bake 11 to 15 minutes or until light golden brown.

4) Meanwhile, in 1-quart saucepan, combine peanut butter, remaining 5 tablespoons oil, soy sauce, sugar, vinegar, remaining ¼ teaspoon cayenne pepper, and green onion. Cook over medium heat, stirring constantly with wire whisk, or until thoroughly heated.

5) To serve, place 2 turnovers on each of 8 plates. Drizzle each turnover with 1 teaspoon of the sauce. Serve with remaining sauce. Sprinkle turnovers with additional chopped green onion, if desired.

1 SERVING: Calories 510; Total Fat 33g (Saturated Fat 7g); Sodium 900mg; Total Carbohydrate 37g (Dietary Fiber 1g); Protein 15g. EXCHANGES: 1-1/2 Starch, 1 Other Carbohydrate, 1-1/2 Lean Meat, 5-1/2 Fat. CARBOHYDRATE CHOICES: 2-1/2.

Turkey Confetti Pizza

ALECIA FIELDS | GREENWOOD, IN

BAKE-OFF® CONTEST 45, 2012

PREP TIME: 30 MINUTES (READY IN 55 MINUTES)
SERVINGS: 8

1 lb lean (at least 90%) ground turkey

2 tablespoons Crisco® Pure Canola Oil

1 can (11 oz) mandarin orange segments, drained, reserving liquid, chopped

⅓ cup sweetened dried cranberries

¼ cup chopped drained roasted red bell peppers (from a jar)

¼ cup sliced green olives

½ teaspoon McCormick® Garlic Powder

1 teaspoon McCormick® Crushed Red Pepper

1 teaspoon McCormick® Perfect Pinch® Caribbean Jerk Seasoning

3 tablespoons balsamic vinegar

½ cup Smucker's® Simply Fruit® Apricot Spreadable Fruit

4 tablespoons chopped fresh cilantro

1 can Pillsbury® refrigerated classic pizza crust

3 tablespoons shredded Parmesan cheese

1 cup shredded mozzarella cheese (4 oz)

1 cup shredded mild Cheddar cheese (4 oz)

⅓ cup crumbled feta cheese

1) Heat oven to 425°F. Spray large cookie sheet with Crisco® Original No-Stick Cooking Spray.

2) In 10-inch skillet, cook turkey in oil over medium heat 5 to 7 minutes, stirring frequently, or until turkey is no longer pink. In large bowl, combine cooked turkey, mandarin oranges, dried cranberries, roasted peppers, olives, garlic powder, crushed red pepper and jerk seasoning; mix well. Remove turkey from skillet; set aside.

3) To warm skillet, add vinegar and reserved mandarin orange liquid; bring to a boil over medium heat. Stir in apricot fruit spread until blended.

4) Add turkey mixture to skillet; mix well. Bring to a boil over medium-high heat. Reduce heat; simmer 10 to 15 minutes or until liquid is absorbed. Stir in 2 tablespoons of the cilantro.

5) Unroll pizza crust dough on cookie sheet; press dough into 13x10-inch rectangle. Bake 6 to 10 minutes or until edges are light brown. Remove from oven. Sprinkle crust with Parmesan cheese. Top with turkey mixture. Top with mozzarella, Cheddar and feta cheeses; sprinkle with remaining 2 tablespoons cilantro.

6) Bake 10 to 14 minutes or until crust is golden brown and cheeses are melted.

1 SERVING: Calories 460; Total Fat 18g (Saturated Fat 8g); Sodium 780mg; Total Carbohydrate 48g (Dietary Fiber 2g); Protein 25g. EXCHANGES: 1-1/2 Starch, 1/2 Fruit, 1 Other Carbohydrate, 2 Lean Meat, 1/2 Medium-Fat Meat, 1/2 High-Fat Meat, 1 Fat. CARBOHYDRATE CHOICES: 3.

Pork Picadillo Empanadas

PREP TIME: 25 MINUTES (READY IN 8 HOURS 50 MINUTES)
SERVINGS: 16

(f) LOW FAT

³/₄ lb ground pork

1 small jalapeño chile, seeded, finely chopped

1 teaspoon chili powder

1 teaspoon ground cumin

³/₄ teaspoon ground cinnamon

¼ teaspoon salt

¼ cup golden raisins

2 cups chipotle salsa

2 tablespoons fresh lime juice

3 tablespoons chopped almonds, toasted

¼ cup sour cream

1 can (16.3 oz) Pillsbury® refrigerated buttermilk biscuits

1 egg, slightly beaten

1) In 10-inch nonstick skillet, cook pork over medium-high heat 8 to 10 minutes, stirring occasionally, until no longer pink; drain. Add chile, chili powder, cumin, cinnamon and salt; cook 2 minutes, stirring occasionally. Stir in raisins, ½ cup of the salsa and the lime juice. Remove from heat; stir in almonds and sour cream. Cool.

2) Separate dough into 8 biscuits. Split each biscuit in half to make 16 rounds. On lightly floured surface, roll each round to 4-inch diameter. Spoon pork mixture evenly in center of dough. Fold dough over filling, pressing edges with fork to seal. Wrap in plastic wrap; refrigerate up to 8 hours.

3) Heat oven to 350°F. Spray cookie sheet with cooking spray. Place empanadas on cookie sheet. Brush tops with beaten egg. Bake 15 to 20 minutes or until golden. Cool 5 minutes. Serve empanadas with remaining 1 ½ cups salsa.

1 SERVING: Calories 120; Total Fat 7g (Saturated Fat 3g); Sodium 112mg; Total Carbohydrate 12g (Dietary Fiber 0g); Protein 2g. EXCHANGES: 1/2 Starch, 1/2 Other Carbohydrate, 1-1/2 Fat. CARBOHYDRATE CHOICES: 1.

Meatball Minestrone Bake

DINAH SURH | STATEN ISLAND, NY

PREP TIME: 25 MINUTES (READY IN 1 HOUR 20 MINUTES)
SERVINGS: 8

- ¾ teaspoon McCormick® Oregano Leaves
- ¼ teaspoon McCormick® Basil Leaves
- ¼ teaspoon McCormick® Garlic Powder
- ¼ teaspoon McCormick® California Lemon Peel
- ¼ teaspoon McCormick® Ground Black Pepper
- 1 ½ lb extra lean (at least 90%) ground beef
- ¾ cup Progresso® Italian style bread crumbs
- ¼ cup chopped onion
- ¾ cup milk
- 1 LAND O LAKES® Egg
- 1 teaspoon kosher (coarse) salt
- 1 can (19 oz) Progresso® High Fiber homestyle minestrone soup
- 2 tablespoons grated Parmesan cheese
- 1 can Pillsbury® Place 'n Bake® refrigerated crescent rounds
- 1 tablespoon Crisco® 100% Extra Virgin Olive Oil
- 2 cups shredded Italian cheese blend (8 oz)

1) Heat oven to 400°F. In small bowl, stir together oregano, basil, garlic powder, lemon peel and pepper. Reserve ¾ teaspoon of mixture; set aside. In large bowl, mix ground beef, bread crumbs, onion, milk, egg, salt and remaining seasoning mix until thoroughly combined. Form into sixteen 2-inch meatballs. Pour soup into ungreased 13x9-inch (3-quart) glass baking dish; top with meatballs.

2) Bake 35 minutes or until bubbly.

3) Meanwhile, in small bowl, mix reserved ¾ teaspoon seasoning mixture and Parmesan cheese. Unroll each crescent round to make a strip; place strips on piece of foil. Brush strips with olive oil; sprinkle generously with Parmesan cheese mixture.

4) Remove baking dish from oven. Reduce oven temperature to 350°F. Sprinkle meatballs with Italian cheese. Place seasoned crescent strips in a diagonal pattern on top of cheese, cutting to fit if necessary and not crisscrossing the strips.

5) Bake an additional 20 to 24 minutes or until cheese is melted and strips are golden brown. Serve in bowls.

1 SERVING: Calories 480; Total Fat 26g (Saturated Fat 11g); Sodium 1270mg; Total Carbohydrate 27g (Dietary Fiber 2g); Protein 35g. EXCHANGES: 1 Starch, 1/2 Other Carbohydrate, 4-1/2 Very Lean Meat, 4-1/2 Fat. CARBOHYDRATE CHOICES: 2.

Chicken Fettuccine

PREP TIME: 15 MINUTES (READY IN 15 MINUTES)
SERVINGS: 4

 EASY

1 package (9 oz) refrigerated fettuccine, cut into thirds

2 teaspoons vegetable oil

3 individually wrapped boneless skinless roasted garlic with white wine chicken breasts (4.8 oz each), sliced

½ cup milk

1 container (10 oz) savory garlic cooking creme

1 cup grape tomatoes, cut in half

¼ cup shredded fresh basil leaves

2 tablespoons pine nuts, toasted

1) In Dutch oven or 3-quart saucepan, cook and drain fettuccine as directed on package; return to Dutch oven.

2) Meanwhile, in 10-inch nonstick skillet, heat oil over medium-high heat. Cook chicken in oil 3 minutes, stirring constantly, until browned. Reduce heat to medium. Gradually add milk, stirring constantly 1 minute. Add cooking creme; cook and stir 1 minute or until bubbly.

3) Pour sauce over cooked fettuccine. Add tomatoes and basil; toss gently to coat. Sprinkle with pine nuts.

1 SERVING: Calories 453; Total Fat 18g (Saturated Fat 7g); Sodium 773mg; Total Carbohydrate 43g (Dietary Fiber 2g); Protein 2g. EXCHANGES: 2-1/2 Starch, 1-1/2 Other Carbohydrate, 3 Fat. CARBOHYDRATE CHOICES: 3.

Pineapple Pork Burgers

PREP TIME: 20 MINUTES (READY IN 20 MINUTES)
SERVINGS: 4 BURGERS

 EASY

1 lb ground pork

2 tablespoons dry applewood rub seasoning

1 can (8 oz) pineapple slices in juice, drained and 2 tablespoons juice reserved

4 onion or plain hamburger buns, split

4 leaves lettuce

1) Heat gas or charcoal grill. In medium bowl, mix pork, seasoning and 2 tablespoons reserved pineapple juice. Shape mixture into 4 patties, about ½ inch thick.

2) Place patties on grill over medium heat. Cover grill; cook 6 to 7 minutes, turning once, until no longer pink in center and meat thermometer inserted in center of patties reads 160°F. During last 4 minutes of cooking time, add pineapple slices to grill, turning once.

3) On bun bottoms, place lettuce, burger and pineapple slice. Cover with bun tops.

1 BURGER: Calories 380; Total Fat 18g (Saturated Fat 6g); Sodium 630mg; Total Carbohydrate 31g (Dietary Fiber 2g); Protein 24g. EXCHANGES: 1 Starch, 1/2 Fruit, 1/2 Other Carbohydrate, 1/2 Vegetable, 1-1/2 Lean Meat, 1-1/2 Medium-Fat Meat, 1 Fat. CARBOHYDRATE CHOICES: 2.

Tuscan Stromboli

KATHRYN FRIEDL | LAWTON, OK

Bake-Off®

BAKE-OFF® CONTEST 45, 2012

PREP TIME: 25 MINUTES (READY IN 1 HOUR 5 MINUTES)
SERVINGS: 6

1 can Pillsbury® refrigerated classic pizza crust

4 oz (half of 8-oz package) cream cheese, softened

⅓ cup sun-dried tomatoes in oil, sliced

15 slices (1 ½-inch size) pepperoni

2 tablespoons finely chopped red onion

½ cup drained finely chopped artichoke hearts (from 14-oz can)

1 cup cooked chicken, diced

4 oz fresh mozzarella cheese, diced (about 1 cup)

1 teaspoon McCormick® Italian Seasoning

1 teaspoon McCormick® Garlic Salt

1 tablespoon Crisco® Pure Olive Oil

½ teaspoon McCormick® Rosemary Leaves

1) Heat oven to 400°F. Line cookie sheet with cooking parchment paper or spray with Crisco® Original No-Stick Cooking Spray. Unroll pizza crust dough; press dough into 15x9-inch rectangle.

2) In small bowl, combine cream cheese and sun-dried tomatoes; mix well. Spread over dough to within ½ inch of edges. Top with pepperoni, onion, artichokes, chicken and mozzarella cheese. Sprinkle with Italian seasoning and ½ teaspoon of the garlic salt. Starting on 1 long side, roll up. Press seam firmly to seal. Place, seam side down, on cookie sheet. Brush top with olive oil. Sprinkle with remaining ½ teaspoon garlic salt and rosemary; press rosemary into dough.

3) Bake 20 to 30 minutes or until deep golden brown. Cool 10 minutes.

1 SERVING: Calories 440; Total Fat 23g (Saturated Fat 10g); Sodium 1070mg; Total Carbohydrate 36g (Dietary Fiber 2g); Protein 21g. EXCHANGES: 2 Starch, 1/2 Other Carbohydrate, 2 Medium-Fat Meat, 2-1/2 Fat. CARBOHYDRATE CHOICES: 2-1/2.

Chicken Empanada Cones

DONNA WOLFE | HAMILTON, NJ

BAKE-OFF® CONTEST 45, 2012

PREP TIME: 1 HOUR (READY IN 1 HOUR 15 MINUTES)
SERVINGS: 8

⅓ cup water

2 teaspoons golden raisins

3 tablespoons LAND O LAKES® Butter

4 teaspoons agave sweetener or honey

⅓ cup fresh cilantro

¾ cup chopped onions

1 tablespoon Pillsbury BEST® Unbleached Flour

1 can (18.5 oz) Progresso® World Recipes frijoles negros y jalapeño soup, drained, reserving liquid

2 cups diced cooked chicken breast

½ cup frozen corn, thawed

½ cup chopped roasted red bell peppers (from a jar)

½ teaspoon McCormick® Garlic Salt

¼ teaspoon McCormick® Ground Cumin

1 teaspoon red pepper sauce

2 tablespoons cornmeal

1 box Pillsbury® refrigerated pie crusts, softened as directed on box

1 cup salsa

½ cup sour cream

1) In 1-cup microwavable measuring cup, microwave water on High 1 minute. Add raisins; set aside. In small microwavable bowl, microwave 1 tablespoon of the butter on High 10 to 20 seconds or until melted. Stir in agave sweetener; set aside. Chop enough cilantro to measure 1 tablespoon; set aside.

2) In 10-inch skillet over medium heat, melt remaining 2 tablespoons butter. Add onions; cook 2 to 3 minutes, stirring frequently or until onions are softened. Sprinkle with flour; cook and stir 3 minutes. Stir in reserved liquid from can of frijoles negros. Reduce heat to medium-low; cook until thickened, about 4 minutes. Stir in the frijoles negros, chicken, corn, roasted peppers, 1 tablespoon chopped cilantro, garlic salt, cumin and pepper sauce. Bring to a boil; reduce heat to medium-low. Simmer 10 to 15 minutes, stirring frequently or until most of the liquid is absorbed. Drain raisins; chop raisins and stir into chicken mixture. Cool slightly.

3) Heat oven to 450°F. Line 2 large cookie sheets with cooking parchment paper or spray with Crisco® Original No-Stick Cooking Spray. Sprinkle cookie sheets with cornmeal. Unroll pie crusts. Roll each into 13-inch round; cut each round into quarters. To make each empanada, place piece of pie crust on cookie sheet, pressing into cornmeal. Brush center with agave mixture. Spoon rounded ⅓ cup of the chicken mixture in center. Bring long sides of dough together, forming a cone shape. Press to seal, leaving rounded end open. Repeat with remaining pie crust, agave mixture and chicken mixture.

4) Bake 13 to 18 minutes or until golden brown. Serve empanadas with salsa, sour cream and remaining cilantro.

1 SERVING: Calories 430; Total Fat 21g (Saturated Fat 10g); Sodium 800mg; Total Carbohydrate 44g (Dietary Fiber 3g); Protein 15g. EXCHANGES: 2-1/2 Starch, 1 Vegetable, 1 Very Lean Meat, 4 Fat. CARBOHYDRATE CHOICES: 3.

Southwestern Beef Chili with Corn

PREP TIME: 35 MINUTES (READY IN 35 MINUTES)
SERVINGS: 4

½ lb lean (at least 80%) ground beef

1 tablespoon olive oil

2 carrots, chopped

1 medium onion, chopped (½ cup)

2 cloves garlic, finely chopped

1 poblano chile, seeded and chopped, or 1 small green bell pepper, chopped

¼ cup tomato paste

2 cans (15 oz each) Progresso® black beans, drained, rinsed

½ cup Green Giant® Valley Fresh Steamers® Niblets® frozen corn, thawed

1 tablespoon chili powder

3 cups reduced-sodium beef broth

½ teaspoon kosher (coarse) salt

¼ teaspoon pepper

½ cup shredded Cheddar cheese (2 oz)

Chopped red onion, if desired

Chopped jalapeño chiles, if desired

1) In 3-quart saucepan, cook beef over medium-high heat 5 to 7 minutes, stirring occasionally, until thoroughly cooked; drain. Remove beef from pan; set aside.

2) In same pan, heat oil over medium-high heat. Add carrots, onion, garlic and poblano chile; cook 3 minutes, stirring constantly. Stir in tomato paste; cook until slightly darkened, about 1 minute. Add cooked beef, the beans, corn, chili powder, broth, salt and pepper. Reduce heat to medium. Simmer uncovered 10 minutes, stirring occasionally, until vegetables are tender.

3) Ladle chili into 4 bowls. Sprinkle with cheese. Garnish with red onion and jalapeños.

1 SERVING: Calories 343; Total Fat 15g (Saturated Fat 5g); Sodium 893mg; Total Carbohydrate 34g (Dietary Fiber 11g); Protein 23g. EXCHANGES: 2 Starch, 1 Vegetable, 2 Lean Meat, 1-1/2 Fat. CARBOHYDRATE CHOICES: 2.

tip

Looking for a fun way to serve chili? Put a dollop of mashed potatoes in soup bowls, then put the chili on top and sprinkle with Cheddar cheese.

Elbows and Cheese

PREP TIME: 20 MINUTES (READY IN 20 MINUTES)
SERVINGS: 4

 EASY

2 cups uncooked elbow macaroni (about 8 oz)

1 ¼ cups whipping cream

1 jar (4 oz) diced pimientos, drained

1 cup shredded sharp Cheddar cheese (4 oz)

¼ cup freshly grated Parmesan cheese

½ teaspoon salt

1) Cook and drain macaroni as directed on package; cover to keep warm in colander.

2) Add whipping cream and pimientos to saucepan. Cook over medium-high heat 2 minutes. Stir in cheeses, salt and cooked macaroni. Cook and stir 2 minutes or until cheese is melted. Serve hot.

1 SERVING: Calories 395; Total Fat 25g (Saturated Fat 15g); Sodium 365mg; Total Carbohydrate 31g (Dietary Fiber 1.5g); Protein 11g. EXCHANGES: 2 Starch, 1/2 High-Fat Meat, 3-1/2 Fat. CARBOHYDRATE CHOICES: 2.

Home-Style Meat Loaf

PREP TIME: 15 MINUTES (READY IN 1 HOUR 25 MINUTES)
SERVINGS: 6

 EASY

1 lb lean (at least 80%) ground beef

2 eggs

1 cup Progresso® plain bread crumbs

¼ cup grated Parmesan cheese

1 small onion, finely chopped (¼ cup)

1 tablespoon Italian seasoning

1 jar (14 oz) marinara sauce

1) Heat oven to 350°F. In large bowl, mix all ingredients except marinara sauce. Add 1 cup of the marinara sauce; mix well.

2) Press mixture into ungreased 8x4-inch loaf pan.

3) Bake 40 minutes. Pour remaining marinara sauce over loaf. Bake 15 to 20 minutes longer or until meat thermometer inserted in center of loaf reads 160°F. Let stand 10 minutes before serving.

1 SERVING: Calories 288; Total Fat 13g (Saturated Fat 5g); Sodium 587mg; Total Carbohydrate 20g (Dietary Fiber 3g); Protein 22g. EXCHANGES: 1 Starch, 2-1/2 Medium-Fat Meat. CARBOHYDRATE CHOICES: 1.

Turkey Upside-Down Burgers

DONNA STAHL | BELLEVUE, KY

BAKE-OFF® CONTEST 45, 2012

PREP TIME: 40 MINUTES (READY IN 1 HOUR 5 MINUTES)
SERVINGS: 8 (2 BURGERS)

2 tablespoons Crisco® Light Olive Oil

2 medium onions, thinly sliced

1 lb ground turkey breast

½ cup chunky applesauce

¾ cup real maple syrup

1 LAND O LAKES® Egg

½ teaspoon McCormick® Onion Salt

½ teaspoon McCormick® Garlic Powder

1 ½ cups Progresso® panko bread crumbs

1 can Pillsbury® Place 'n Bake® refrigerated crescent rounds

4 slices (1 oz each) Swiss cheese, cut into quarters

½ cup mayonnaise

1 tablespoon yellow mustard

½ cup finely chopped, seeded tomato

1) Spray 16 regular-size muffin cups with Crisco® Original No-Stick Cooking Spray. Heat oil in 10-inch skillet over medium heat. Cook onions in oil 15 to 20 minutes or until transparent, stirring occasionally. Set aside.

2) Heat oven to 350°F. In large bowl, combine turkey, applesauce, ¼ cup of the maple syrup, egg, onion salt, garlic powder and bread crumbs; mix thoroughly. Fill each muffin cup with about ¼ cup of meat mixture; press firmly into cup.

3) Bake 10 minutes. Meanwhile, remove crescent rounds from can; do not unroll. Using serrated knife, cut roll evenly into 16 rounds; carefully separate rounds.

4) Remove burgers from oven. Evenly divide onions among tops of burgers in cups. Top each with 1 square of cheese and 1 crescent round.

5) Bake an additional 14 to 20 minutes or until thermometer inserted in center of turkey burgers reads 165°F and crescents are golden brown. Meanwhile, in small bowl, beat together remaining ½ cup maple syrup, mayonnaise and mustard with wire whisk until blended.

6) Remove burgers from oven; let stand 5 minutes. With thin metal spatula, remove each burger from cup and turn upside down onto individual serving plate. Top each with tomato. Serve with maple-mustard sauce.

1 SERVING: Calories 560; Total Fat 30g (Saturated Fat 8g); Sodium 530mg; Total Carbohydrate 53g (Dietary Fiber 1g); Protein 20g. EXCHANGES: 2 Starch, 1-1/2 Other Carbohydrate, 1/2 Vegetable, 1-1/2 Lean Meat, 1/2 High-Fat Meat, 4 Fat. CARBOHYDRATE CHOICES: 3-1/2.

Shrimp, Peas and Pesto Pasta

PREP TIME: 20 MINUTES (READY IN 20 MINUTES)
SERVINGS: 4

 EASY

- 1 package (9 oz) refrigerated linguine
- 1 lb uncooked deveined peeled medium shrimp, thawed if frozen, tail shells removed
- 1 container (7 oz) refrigerated basil pesto
- 2 cups Green Giant® Valley Fresh Steamers™ frozen sweet peas (from 12-oz bag), thawed
- ¼ cup shredded Parmesan cheese (1 oz)

1) Cook linguine as directed on package. Drain, reserving ⅓ cup of the cooking water. Rinse linguine with hot water; cover to keep warm.

2) Meanwhile, in 12-inch nonstick skillet, cook shrimp with 1 tablespoon of the pesto over medium-high heat 2 to 3 minutes, stirring frequently, until pink. Add peas; cook 2 to 3 minutes or until thoroughly heated.

3) Stir remaining pesto and ⅓ cup reserved cooking water into linguine; toss with shrimp and peas. Spoon into 4 bowls; top each with 1 tablespoon cheese.

1 SERVING: Calories 600; Total Fat 30g (Saturated Fat 7g); Sodium 870mg; Total Carbohydrate 46g (Dietary Fiber 5g); Protein 34g. EXCHANGES: 3 Starch, 1/2 Vegetable, 3 Very Lean Meat, 1/2 Lean Meat, 5 Fat. CARBOHYDRATE CHOICES: 3.

Cold Thai Noodles with Shrimp

PREP TIME: 20 MINUTES (READY IN 20 MINUTES)
SERVINGS: 4 (1 CUP EACH)

 EASY   LOW FAT

4 oz uncooked spaghetti

4 oz fresh snow pea pods, trimmed, cut diagonally into thirds

½ medium red bell pepper, cut into thin lengthwise strips

½ lb cooked deveined peeled medium shrimp, thawed if frozen, tail shells removed

½ cup Thai peanut sauce

1) Cook and drain spaghetti as directed on package. Rinse with cold water to cool; drain.

2) In large bowl, mix remaining ingredients. Add cooked spaghetti; toss gently to mix. Serve immediately, or cover and refrigerate up to 2 hours.

1 SERVING: Calories 270; Total Fat 9g (Saturated Fat 2g); Sodium 280mg; Total Carbohydrate 31g (Dietary Fiber 3g); Protein 18g. EXCHANGES: 1-1/2 Starch, 1/2 Other Carbohydrate, 1/2 Vegetable, 1-1/2 Very Lean Meat, 1-1/2 Fat. CARBOHYDRATE CHOICES: 2.

Grilled Chicken Soft Tacos

PREP TIME: 30 MINUTES (READY IN 40 MINUTES)
SERVINGS: 6

3 tablespoons olive oil

2 tablespoons lime juice

4 teaspoons Montreal chicken grill seasoning

1 ½ lb uncooked chicken breast tenders (not breaded)

1 container (8 oz) refrigerated salsa

1 large mango, seed removed, peeled and chopped

¼ cup chopped fresh cilantro

2 teaspoons chipotle red pepper sauce

6 Old El Paso® flour tortillas for soft tacos & fajitas (6 inch; from 8.2-oz package), heated as directed on package

Crumbled queso fresco or cotija (white Mexican) cheese, if desired

Shredded romaine lettuce, if desired

1) Heat gas or charcoal grill. In resealable food-storage plastic bag, mix oil, lime juice and grill seasoning. Add chicken; seal bag and turn to coat. Refrigerate 10 minutes, turning once.

2) Meanwhile, in small bowl, mix salsa, mango, cilantro and pepper sauce. Cover; refrigerate until serving time.

3) Remove chicken from marinade, discarding marinade. Place chicken on grill over medium heat. Cover grill; cook 12 minutes, turning once, until no longer pink in center. Serve chicken in tortillas with mango salsa. Sprinkle with cheese and lettuce.

1 SERVING: Calories 337; Total Fat 13g (Saturated Fat 3g); Sodium 639mg; Total Carbohydrate 26g (Dietary Fiber 2g); Protein 28g. EXCHANGES: 1 Starch, 1/2 Fruit, 1/2 Vegetable, 3-1/2 Very Lean Meat, 2 Fat. CARBOHYDRATE CHOICES: 1-1/2.

Rustic Pot Roast Pot Pies

PREP TIME: 10 MINUTES (READY IN 35 MINUTES)
SERVINGS: 4

 EASY

1 can (18.5 oz) Progresso® Rich & Hearty beef pot roast with country vegetables soup

½ cup stout beer

¾ cup plain mashed potato mix (dry)

1 box Pillsbury® refrigerated pie crusts, softened as directed on box

2 cups mashed potatoes

1 egg, beaten

Fresh rosemary or thyme sprigs, if desired

1) Heat oven to 450°F. In saucepan, heat soup, beer and potato mix (dry) over medium heat until thickened.

2) Remove pie crusts from pouches; unroll on 2 ungreased cookie sheets. Spoon 1 cup mashed potatoes on center of each crust, spreading to within 2 inches of edge. Top with soup mixture, dividing evenly between crusts. Fold crust over edge to form 2-inch border, pleating crust as necessary. Brush crust with beaten egg.

3) Bake 20 to 25 minutes or until crust is golden brown. Cut each pot pie in half. Garnish with rosemary.

1 SERVING: Calories 660; Total Fat 31g (Saturated Fat 14g); Sodium 1130mg; Total Carbohydrate 83g (Dietary Fiber 3g); Protein 11g. EXCHANGES: 3 Starch, 2 Other Carbohydrate, 1 Vegetable, 6 Fat. CARBOHYDRATE CHOICES: 5-1/2.

tip Crescent roll dough can also work as an easy top crust for any pot pie baked in a traditional pie dish. Roll out the dough to fit the top of the pie. Place over filling, trim the edges and cut slits in top before baking.

Green Chile-Chicken Mac 'n Cheese

PREP TIME: 25 MINUTES (READY IN 55 MINUTES)
SERVINGS: 10

3 ½ cups uncooked elbow macaroni (14 oz)

⅓ cup butter or margarine

⅓ cup all-purpose flour

1 teaspoon salt

1 teaspoon freshly ground pepper

1 ½ cups milk

1 cup water

5 cups shredded sharp Cheddar cheese (20 oz)

2 cups shredded deli rotisserie chicken (from 2-lb chicken)

4 cans (4.5 oz each) Old El Paso® chopped green chiles, drained

2 cups French bread crumbs

⅓ cup butter or margarine, melted

1) Heat oven to 425°F. Spray 3-quart casserole with cooking spray. Cook and drain macaroni as directed on package, using minimum cook time; cover to keep warm.

2) Meanwhile, in Dutch oven or 3-quart saucepan, melt ⅓ cup butter over medium-low heat. Stir in flour, salt and pepper. Cook and stir until smooth and bubbly. Gradually add milk and water, stirring constantly, until mixture boils and thickens. Add 4 cups of the cheese; stir until cheese is melted.

3) Add cooked macaroni to cheese sauce; toss to coat completely. Stir in chicken and chiles. Spoon mixture into casserole. Sprinkle with remaining 1 cup cheese.

4) In small bowl, mix bread crumbs and melted butter. Sprinkle over macaroni mixture.

5) Bake uncovered 25 to 30 minutes or until browned and bubbly.

1 SERVING: Calories 649; Total Fat 36g (Saturated Fat 21g); Sodium 1091mg; Total Carbohydrate 47g (Dietary Fiber 3g); Protein 30g. EXCHANGES: 2-1/2 Starch, 1/2 Other Carbohydrate, 3 High-Fat Meat, 2 Fat. CARBOHYDRATE CHOICES: 3.

Southern Camp Stew

PREP TIME: 15 MINUTES (READY IN 15 MINUTES)
SERVINGS: 6

 EASY LOW FAT

1 ½ cups Green Giant® Valley Fresh Steamers® Niblets® frozen corn (from 12-oz bag), thawed

1 cup Progresso® chicken broth (from 32-oz carton)

2 tablespoons white vinegar

1 tablespoon packed light brown sugar

¼ cup tomato paste

1 can (14.5 oz) Muir Glen® organic diced tomatoes

1 can (15.25 oz) lima beans, drained, rinsed

2 teaspoons red pepper sauce, if desired

3 ½ cups shredded deli rotisserie chicken (from 2-lb chicken)

1) In 5- to 6-quart Dutch oven, stir together all ingredients except chicken. Heat to boiling; reduce heat. Cover; simmer 6 minutes, stirring occasionally.

2) Stir in chicken. Cook 3 minutes longer, stirring occasionally, until thoroughly heated.

1 SERVING: Calories 225; Total Fat 3g (Saturated Fat 1g); Sodium 402mg; Total Carbohydrate 24g (Dietary Fiber 5g); Protein 27g. EXCHANGES: 1 Starch, 1 Other Carbohydrate, 3-1/2 Very Lean Meat. CARBOHYDRATE CHOICES: 1-1/2.

Chicken Tetrazzini

PREP TIME: 20 MINUTES (READY IN 55 MINUTES)
SERVINGS: 12

 EASY

1 package (16 oz) vermicelli

½ cup chicken broth

4 cups chopped cooked chicken

1 can (10 ¾ oz) cream of mushroom soup

1 can (10 ¾ oz) cream of chicken soup

1 can (10 ¾ oz) cream of celery soup

1 container (8 oz) sour cream

1 jar (6 oz) sliced mushrooms, drained

½ cup shredded Parmesan cheese (2 oz)

1 teaspoon pepper

½ teaspoon salt

2 cups shredded Cheddar cheese (8 oz)

1) Heat oven to 350°F. Lightly spray 2 (2-quart) casseroles with cooking spray. Cook and drain vermicelli as directed on package; return to saucepan. Add broth; toss to coat.

2) In large bowl, stir remaining ingredients except Cheddar cheese. Add vermicelli; toss well. Divide mixture evenly between casseroles. Sprinkle with Cheddar cheese.

3) Cover; bake 30 minutes. Uncover; bake 5 minutes longer or until cheese is bubbly.

1 SERVING: Calories 409; Total Fat 17g (Saturated Fat 9g); Sodium 887mg; Total Carbohydrate 35g (Dietary Fiber 2g); Protein 29g. EXCHANGES: 2 Starch, 2 Very Lean Meat, 1/2 High-Fat Meat, 1/2 Fat. CARBOHYDRATE CHOICES: 2.

Mushroom-Herb Stuffed Beef Tenderloin

PREP TIME: 30 MINUTES (READY IN 1 HOUR 15 MINUTES)
SERVINGS: 8

1 beef tenderloin (3 lb), trimmed of fat

1 medium onion, chopped (½ cup)

2 tablespoons butter or margarine

4 cloves garlic, finely chopped

2 packages (4 oz each) wild mushrooms, chopped

1 teaspoon chopped fresh thyme leaves

1 teaspoon chopped fresh rosemary leaves

1 teaspoon salt

2 tablespoons balsamic vinegar

2 teaspoons pepper

Fresh herb sprigs, if desired

1) Heat oven to 450°F. Cut beef lengthwise in half, cutting almost but not completely through; open flat. Pound to ¾-inch thickness.

2) In 12-inch skillet, cook onion in butter over medium-high heat 3 minutes or until tender. Add garlic; cook and stir 30 seconds. Add mushrooms, thyme, rosemary and ½ teaspoon of the salt. Cook 5 minutes or until mushrooms are tender. Stir in vinegar; cook 2 minutes or until liquid has evaporated. Cool. Spoon mushroom mixture over beef to within ½ inch of edges. Roll up beef, starting with long side, and tie with kitchen string at 2-inch intervals. Rub with pepper and remaining ½ teaspoon salt. Place seam side down on rack in roasting pan. Insert ovenproof meat thermometer so tip is in thickest part of beef.

3) Bake uncovered 30 minutes or until thermometer reads at least 140°F. Cover loosely with foil; let stand 15 minutes or until thermometer reads 145°F. Garnish platter with fresh herb sprigs.

1 SERVING: Calories 256; Total Fat 12g (Saturated Fat 5g); Sodium 388mg; Total Carbohydrate 4g (Dietary Fiber 1g); Protein 32g. EXCHANGES: 1/2 Vegetable, 4-1/2 Very Lean Meat. CARBOHYDRATE CHOICES: 0.

Italian Pork Tenderloins 'n Peppers

PREP TIME: 40 MINUTES (READY IN 1 HOUR 40 MINUTES)
SERVINGS: 12

 EASY   LOW FAT

3 pork tenderloins (1 lb each)

1 cup Italian dressing

1 teaspoon garlic powder

1 teaspoon coarse ground black pepper

4 medium bell peppers (any color), cut in half

If you like, cut the peppers into strips and cook in a grill basket. These handy baskets are available at discount and kitchen specialty stores and are great for cooking vegetables and other small foods.

1) In large shallow glass dish or resealable food-storage plastic bag, place pork. Pour dressing over pork; turn to coat pork with dressing. Cover dish or seal bag; refrigerate 1 to 2 hours to marinate.

2) Heat gas or charcoal grill. Remove pork from marinade; reserve marinade. Sprinkle pork with garlic powder and pepper. Add bell peppers to reserved marinade; turn to coat.

3) Place pork and peppers on grill over medium heat. Cover grill; cook 20 to 25 minutes, turning occasionally and brushing with marinade up to last 5 minutes of grilling, until pork has slight blush of pink in center and meat thermometer inserted in center reads 160°F (remove peppers from grill as they become crisp-tender). Discard any remaining marinade.

4) Cut pepper halves lengthwise into strips; cut pork into slices. Serve pork with peppers.

1 SERVING: Calories 200; Total Fat 10g (Saturated Fat 2g); Sodium 410mg; Total Carbohydrate 5g (Dietary Fiber 0g); Protein 22g. EXCHANGES: 1/2 Vegetable, 1/2 Very Lean Meat, 2-1/2 Lean Meat, 1/2 Fat. CARBOHYDRATE CHOICES: 1/2.

Cranberry-Chicken Salad Empanadas

PREP TIME: 25 MINUTES (READY IN 45 MINUTES)
SERVINGS: 8 EMPANADAS

 EASY

1 box Pillsbury® refrigerated pie crusts, softened as directed on box

1 cup deli chicken salad

1/3 cup sweetened dried cranberries

1/3 cup pecan pieces, toasted

1 egg, slightly beaten

1) Heat oven to 400°F. Spray cookie sheet with cooking spray. Remove 1 pie crust from pouch; unroll on lightly floured surface. With 4 ½-inch cutter, cut dough into 4 rounds. Repeat with second pie crust.

2) In medium bowl, stir together chicken salad, cranberries and pecans. Spoon about 2 tablespoons chicken salad in center of each round. Brush edges with beaten egg. Fold dough over filling, pressing edges with fork to seal. Place empanadas on cookie sheet. Brush with egg.

3) Bake 16 minutes or until lightly browned. Serve warm or at room temperature.

1 EMPANADA: Calories 335; Total Fat 23g (Saturated Fat 7g); Sodium 435mg; Total Carbohydrate 31g (Dietary Fiber 1g); Protein 6g. EXCHANGES: 1 1/2 Starch, 1/2 Fruit, 4 Fat. CARBOHYDRATE CHOICES: 2.

Skillet Barbecue Shrimp

PREP TIME: 15 MINUTES (READY IN 15 MINUTES)
SERVINGS: 5

 EASY

1 ¼ cups Italian dressing

2 tablespoons butter

1 tablespoon ground black pepper blend

1 teaspoon dried rosemary leaves, crushed

2 lb uncooked unpeeled large shrimp with tail shells left on

Lemon wedges

Fresh rosemary sprigs, if desired

1) In large skillet, mix dressing, butter, pepper blend and rosemary; heat to boiling. Add shrimp; cook 6 minutes, stirring occasionally, until shrimp are pink.

2) Spoon shrimp and juices into serving bowls. Serve with lemon wedges. Garnish with fresh rosemary.

1 SERVING: Calories 337; Total Fat 23g (Saturated Fat 6g); Sodium 796mg; Total Carbohydrate 7g (Dietary Fiber 1g); Protein 28g. EXCHANGES: 1/2 Other Carbohydrate, 4 Very Lean Meat, 4 Fat. CARBOHYDRATE CHOICES: 1/2.

Cheese-Crusted Pizza Pot Pies

PREP TIME: 40 MINUTES (READY IN 1 HOUR)
SERVINGS: 4

1 package (12 oz) pork sausage links, casings removed, or ¾ lb ground beef round

⅔ cup chopped onion

⅔ cup finely chopped carrots

½ cup chopped green bell pepper

3 cloves garlic, finely chopped

1¼ cups marinara sauce

⅔ cup sliced pepperoni (from 8-oz package)

⅓ cup chopped pimiento-stuffed green olives

1 cup shredded Italian cheese blend (4 oz)

1 can (11 oz) Pillsbury® refrigerated thin pizza crust

1 egg, slightly beaten

8 slices (1 oz each) part-skim mozzarella cheese

Fresh oregano sprigs, if desired

1) Heat oven to 450°F. In 12-inch skillet, cook sausage, onion, carrots, bell pepper and garlic over medium heat 10 to 12 minutes, stirring occasionally, until sausage is thoroughly cooked; drain. Stir in marinara sauce, pepperoni and olives. Simmer 3 to 5 minutes or until thickened. Remove from heat; stir in cheese blend.

2) Spray bottoms, sides and rims of 4 (10-oz) individual baking dishes (ramekins) with cooking spray. Spoon meat mixture into dishes. Place on 15x10x1-inch pan.

3) Unroll dough on large cutting board. Cut in half lengthwise, then cut in half crosswise. Place 1 dough piece over meat mixture in each dish, overlapping rim. Brush with egg. Top each pot pie with 2 slices cheese, overlapping slightly. Bake 16 to 20 minutes or until crust is brown. Garnish with oregano.

1 SERVING: Calories 812; Total Fat 44g (Saturated Fat 19g); Sodium 2603mg; Total Carbohydrate 55g (Dietary Fiber 5g); Protein 47g. EXCHANGES: 2-1/2 Starch, 1 Other Carbohydrate, 1 Vegetable, 5-1/2 High-Fat Meat. CARBOHYDRATE CHOICES: 3-1/2.

Chicken Alfredo Lasagna

PREP TIME: 25 MINUTES (READY IN 1 HOUR 30 MINUTES)
SERVINGS: 12

1   container (16 oz) small-curd cottage cheese

¾   cup shredded Parmesan, Romano and Asiago cheese blend (3 oz)

½   teaspoon garlic salt with parsley

2   tablespoons butter or margarine

1   cup chopped or thinly sliced onion

1   package (8 oz) sliced fresh baby portabella mushrooms

3   cups shredded deli rotisserie chicken (from 2-lb chicken)

2   cups roasted red bell peppers (from two 12-oz jars), drained, cut into ½-inch strips

2   jars (15 oz each) four-cheese Alfredo pasta sauce

9   sheets rectangular instant lasagna noodles (7 ⅛ x 3 ½ inches)

2   cups shredded mozzarella cheese (8 oz)

1) Heat oven to 350°F. Spray 13x9-inch (3-quart) glass baking dish with cooking spray. In medium bowl, mix cottage cheese, cheese blend and garlic salt; set aside.

2) In 12-inch skillet, melt butter over medium-high heat. Add onion; cook until tender. Add mushrooms; cook until tender. Stir in chicken, roasted peppers and Alfredo sauce. Spoon about 2 ⅓ cups chicken mixture in baking dish. Layer with 3 noodles, half of cottage cheese mixture and ½ cup of the mozzarella cheese. Repeat layers. Top with remaining 3 noodles, 2 ⅓ cups chicken mixture and 1 cup mozzarella cheese.

3) Bake uncovered 50 minutes or until golden brown around edges. Let stand 15 minutes before serving.

1 SERVING: Calories 368; Total Fat 19g (Saturated Fat 11g); Sodium 1069mg; Total Carbohydrate 21g (Dietary Fiber 1g); Protein 28g. EXCHANGES: 1 Starch, 1 Vegetable, 2 Very Lean Meat, 1 High-Fat Meat, 1-1/2 Fat. CARBOHYDRATE CHOICES: 1-1/2.

Pork with Cranberry-Port Sauce

PREP TIME: 10 MINUTES (READY IN 35 MINUTES)
SERVINGS: 6

 EASY   LOW FAT

2 pork tenderloins (about 1 lb each)

2 teaspoons chopped fresh rosemary leaves

¾ teaspoon salt

¾ teaspoon freshly ground pepper

1 cup port wine

1 clove garlic, cut in half

½ cup whole berry cranberry sauce

¼ cup crumbled Gorgonzola or blue cheese (1 oz)

1) Heat oven to 400°F. Rub pork on all sides with rosemary, and ½ teaspoon each of the salt and pepper.

2) Heat 12-inch ovenproof cast-iron or nonstick skillet over medium-high heat. Add pork; cook 4 minutes, browning quickly on all sides. Place skillet in oven. Bake 15 minutes or until meat thermometer inserted in center reads 145°F. Cover loosely; let stand 3 minutes.

3) Meanwhile, in 1-quart saucepan, heat wine and garlic to boiling. Cook uncovered 8 minutes or until liquid is reduced by half. Remove and discard garlic. Add cranberry sauce, and remaining ¼ teaspoon each salt and pepper to wine in saucepan, stirring with whisk. Heat to boiling; cook 1 minute, stirring occasionally.

4) Slice pork. Serve pork with sauce; sprinkle with cheese.

1 SERVING: Calories 241; Total Fat 4.5g (Saturated Fat 2g); Sodium 439mg; Total Carbohydrate 10g (Dietary Fiber 1g); Protein 33g. EXCHANGES: 1/2 Other Carbohydrate, 4 Very Lean Meat. CARBOHYDRATE CHOICES: 1/2.

Coffee-Marinated Beef Tenderloin Steaks

PREP TIME: 15 MINUTES (READY IN 8 HOURS 15 MINUTES)
SERVINGS: 4

 EASY   LOW FAT

1 cup strong brewed coffee, room temperature

4 ½ teaspoons packed dark brown sugar

½ teaspoon salt

½ teaspoon black pepper

¼ teaspoon ground red pepper (cayenne)

2 cloves garlic, finely chopped

4 beef tenderloin steaks, ½ inch thick (6 oz each)

1) In large resealable food-storage plastic bag, mix coffee, brown sugar, salt, black pepper, red pepper and garlic. Add steaks; seal bag and turn to coat. Refrigerate to marinate 8 hours, turning occasionally.

2) Heat gas or charcoal grill. Remove steaks from marinade, discarding marinade. Carefully brush oil on grill rack. Place steaks on grill over medium heat. Cover grill; cook 6 minutes, turning once, until of desired doneness.

1 SERVING: Calories 238; Total Fat 10g (Saturated Fat 4g); Sodium 188mg; Total Carbohydrate 3g (Dietary Fiber 0g); Protein 33g. EXCHANGES: 5 Lean Meat. CARBOHYDRATE CHOICES: 0.

Caramelized Pear, Spinach and Chicken Pizza

MARIANNE PIEPER | BEAVER DAM, KY

BAKE-OFF® CONTEST 45, 2012

Pillsbury
Bake-Off®

PREP TIME: 40 MINUTES (READY IN 55 MINUTES)
SERVINGS: 8

2 tablespoons LAND O LAKES® Butter, melted

1 can Pillsbury® refrigerated classic pizza crust

1 medium onion, coarsely chopped

2 medium firm ripe pears, thinly sliced

2 teaspoons packed brown sugar

1 package (6 oz) refrigerated grilled chicken breast strips, coarsely chopped

1 cup Alfredo sauce (from 15-oz jar)

1 package (10 oz) frozen creamed spinach, thawed

3 tablespoons refrigerated basil pesto

½ teaspoon McCormick® Rosemary Leaves

½ teaspoon McCormick® Oregano Leaves

1 ½ cups shredded Italian cheese blend (6 oz)

1) Heat oven to 425°F. Brush 17x11x1-inch pan with 1 teaspoon of the melted butter. Unroll pizza crust dough in pan; press dough to cover bottom and ½ inch up sides.

2) Place pan on lowest oven rack. Bake 6 to 10 minutes or until crust is lightly browned.

3) Meanwhile, in 10-inch skillet, cook remaining butter and onion over medium heat 3 to 5 minutes, stirring frequently, until onion is crisp-tender. Add pears and brown sugar; cook 10 to 15 minutes or until pears and onion are tender and browned, stirring occasionally. Remove from skillet.

4) To same skillet, add chicken, Alfredo sauce, creamed spinach, pesto, rosemary and oregano. Heat over medium heat just until warm. Spread onto baked crust; top with pear mixture. Sprinkle with cheese.

5) Bake on center rack of oven 7 to 12 minutes or until edges of crust are brown and cheese is melted.

1 SERVING: Calories 450; Total Fat 25g (Saturated Fat 13g); Sodium 960mg; Total Carbohydrate 38g (Dietary Fiber 3g); Protein 19g. EXCHANGES: 1-1/2 Starch, 1 Other Carbohydrate, 1-1/2 Very Lean Meat, 1/2 High-Fat Meat, 4 Fat. CARBOHYDRATE CHOICES: 2-1/2.

Slow-Cooked Pot Roast and Vegetables

PREP TIME: 25 MINUTES (READY IN 8 HOURS 25 MINUTES)
SERVINGS: 4

If LOW FAT

4 medium potatoes, peeled, each cut into 6 pieces

4 large carrots, cut into 1-inch pieces

1 large onion, thinly sliced

1 dried bay leaf

1 tablespoon all-purpose flour

½ teaspoon salt

⅛ teaspoon pepper

1 beef top round steak, ½ inch thick (1 ½ lb), cut into 4 serving pieces

1 ¾ cups Progresso® beef-flavored broth (from 32-oz carton)

1 teaspoon Worcestershire sauce

2 tablespoons cornstarch

1) Spray 3 ½- to 4-quart slow cooker with cooking spray. In slow cooker, place potatoes, carrots, onion and bay leaf.

2) In shallow bowl, mix flour, salt and pepper. Add beef pieces; turn to coat both sides. Spray 12-inch skillet with cooking spray; heat over medium-high heat. Add beef and brown on all sides; place in slow cooker. In small bowl, mix 1 ½ cups of the broth and the Worcestershire sauce. Pour over beef.

3) Cover; cook on Low heat setting 8 to 10 hours.

4) With slotted spoon, remove beef and vegetables to serving platter; cover to keep warm. Pour liquid from slow cooker into 2-quart saucepan; discard bay leaf. In small bowl, mix remaining ¼ cup broth and the cornstarch until smooth; add to liquid in saucepan. Heat to boiling over medium-high heat, stirring constantly. Boil 1 minute. Serve sauce with beef and vegetables.

1 SERVING: Calories 370; Total Fat 6g (Saturated Fat 2g); Sodium 860mg; Total Carbohydrate 40g (Dietary Fiber 4g); Protein 39g. EXCHANGES: 2 Starch, 1-1/2 Vegetable, 4-1/2 Very Lean Meat. CARBOHYDRATE CHOICES: 2-1/2.

Harvest Beef and Sweet Potato Stew

PREP TIME: 40 MINUTES (READY IN 4 HOURS 40 MINUTES)
SERVINGS: 6

3 tablespoons vegetable oil

4 cloves garlic, finely chopped

1 large onion, cut into small wedges

1 beef chuck roast (3 lb), trimmed of fat, cut into 1 ½-inch pieces

½ cup all-purpose flour

2 cups Progresso® beef-flavored broth (from 32-oz carton)

½ cup water

2 teaspoons chopped fresh rosemary leaves

2 teaspoons salt

½ teaspoon pepper

2 dried bay leaves

1 lb parsnips, peeled, cut into 2x1-inch pieces

2 lb sweet potatoes, peeled, cut into 1-inch chunks

Additional chopped rosemary, if desired

1) Heat oven to 300°F. In 12-inch skillet, heat 1 tablespoon of the oil over medium-high heat. Cook garlic in oil 1 minute or until golden. In 4-quart Dutch oven, place garlic and onion.

2) In resealable food-storage plastic bag, place beef and flour; seal bag and toss to coat. In same skillet, heat 1 tablespoon oil over medium-high heat. Add half of beef; brown on all sides. Transfer beef to Dutch oven. Repeat with remaining 1 tablespoon oil and beef.

3) Add broth to skillet; heat to boiling, scraping to loosen brown particles. Pour over beef mixture. Stir in water, 2 teaspoons rosemary, the salt, pepper, bay leaves and parsnips.

4) Cover; bake 3 hours. Stir sweet potatoes into stew. Cover; bake 1 hour longer or until beef and vegetables are tender. Remove bay leaves before serving. Garnish with additional rosemary.

1 SERVING: Calories 572; Total Fat 18g (Saturated Fat 5g); Sodium 1230mg; Total Carbohydrate 55g (Dietary Fiber 9g); Protein 47g. EXCHANGES: 3-1/2 Starch, 5 Lean Meat. CARBOHYDRATE CHOICES: 3-1/2.

Bourbon-Fig Glazed Ham

PREP TIME: 10 MINUTES (READY IN 2 HOURS 25 MINUTES)
SERVINGS: 12

 EASY LOW FAT

1 cooked bone-in ham (6 to 8 lb)

1 jar (11.5 oz) fig preserves (1 cup)

½ cup bourbon

¼ cup honey

2 tablespoons Dijon mustard

1) Heat oven to 350°F. Line roasting pan with foil. Trim any excess fat on ham to ¼ inch thick. Place ham, fat side up, in pan. In small bowl, mix fig preserves, bourbon, honey and mustard. Brush half of fig mixture over ham.

2) Bake uncovered 1 hour 30 minutes, basting with remaining fig mixture every 30 minutes. Cover loosely with foil; bake 30 minutes longer or until thoroughly heated. Let stand 15 minutes before slicing.

1 SERVING: Calories 305; Total Fat 7g (Saturated Fat 2g); Sodium 2197mg; Total Carbohydrate 27g (Dietary Fiber 0g); Protein 34g. EXCHANGES: 2 Other Carbohydrate, 5 Very Lean Meat. CARBOHYDRATE CHOICES: 2.

Classic Fried Catfish

PREP TIME: 20 MINUTES (READY IN 8 HOURS 20 MINUTES)
SERVINGS: 6

 EASY

1 ½ lb catfish fillets, cut into 6 serving pieces

1 ½ cups buttermilk

¼ teaspoon red pepper sauce

⅓ cup yellow cornmeal

⅓ cup masa harina flour

⅓ cup all-purpose flour

2 teaspoons salt

1 teaspoon black pepper

1 teaspoon ground red pepper (cayenne)

¼ teaspoon garlic powder

Peanut oil for deep frying

Lemon wedges

1) Place catfish in single layer in 13x9-inch dish. In small bowl, mix buttermilk and pepper sauce with whisk; pour over fish. Cover; refrigerate 8 hours, turning once.

2) Remove fish from refrigerator; let stand at room temperature 10 minutes. Meanwhile, in shallow dish, mix cornmeal, both flours, salt, black pepper, red pepper and garlic powder. Remove fish from buttermilk mixture, allowing excess to drip off. Coat fish with cornmeal mixture, shaking off excess.

3) In deep fryer or heavy saucepan, heat 2 inches oil to 360°F. Line 15x10x1-inch pan with paper towel; place cooling rack in pan. Fry fish in batches 2 minutes on each side or until golden brown. Place on rack in pan. Keep warm in 225°F oven until serving time. Serve with lemon wedges.

1 SERVING: Calories 402; Total Fat 24g (Saturated Fat 5g); Sodium 979mg; Total Carbohydrate 20g (Dietary Fiber 1g); Protein 26g. EXCHANGES: 1-1/2 Starch, 3 Lean Meat, 3 Fat. CARBOHYDRATE CHOICES: 1-1/2.

Parmesan-Pecan Fried Chicken

PREP TIME: 35 MINUTES (READY IN 1 HOUR 35 MINUTES)
SERVINGS: 6

2 lb uncooked chicken breast tenders (not breaded), cut into 1-inch-wide strips

1 cup buttermilk

1 cup ground pecans

⅓ cup yellow cornmeal

⅓ cup grated Parmesan cheese

1 tablespoon Cajun seasoning

1 tablespoon paprika

2 eggs, beaten

Vegetable oil for deep frying

Honey mustard, if desired

1) In large resealable food-storage plastic bag, place chicken and buttermilk. Seal bag; refrigerate 1 hour. Remove chicken from buttermilk, discarding buttermilk.

2) In shallow bowl, mix pecans, cornmeal, cheese, Cajun seasoning and paprika. Dip chicken in eggs; roll in pecan mixture to coat, shaking off excess. In deep fryer or heavy Dutch oven, heat 1 ½ inches oil to 350°F. Fry chicken in batches 2 to 3 minutes or until golden brown. Drain on paper towels. Serve with honey mustard.

1 SERVING: Calories 581; Total Fat 37g (Saturated Fat 6g); Sodium 719mg; Total Carbohydrate 19g (Dietary Fiber 3g); Protein 44g. EXCHANGES: 1 Starch, 6 Very Lean Meat, 6 Fat. CARBOHYDRATE CHOICES: 1.

Loaded Calzones

PREP TIME: 15 MINUTES (READY IN 35 MINUTES)
SERVINGS: 4

 EASY

½ lb bulk Italian pork sausage

1 cup marinara sauce

½ cup bite-size thinly sliced pepperoni

¼ cup shredded fresh basil leaves

1 can (13.8 oz) Pillsbury® refrigerated classic pizza crust

1 ½ cups shredded mozzarella cheese (6 oz)

1) Heat oven to 425°F. Spray cookie sheet with cooking spray. In 10-inch skillet, cook sausage over medium heat, stirring frequently, until no longer pink; drain. Stir in ½ cup of the marinara sauce, the pepperoni and basil. Set aside.

2) Unroll dough. Cut dough in half crosswise; cut each section in half lengthwise. On cookie sheet, press or roll each dough portion into 7x5-inch rectangle. Spoon sausage mixture and cheese on one side of each rectangle. Fold dough over filling; press edges firmly with fork to seal.

3) Bake 15 to 17 minutes or until golden brown. Heat remaining ½ cup marinara sauce; serve with warm calzones.

1 SERVING: Calories 630; Total Fat 32g (Saturated Fat 13g); Sodium 999mg; Total Carbohydrate 55g (Dietary Fiber 3g); Protein 33g. EXCHANGES: 3 Starch, 1-1/2 Medium-Fat Meat, 1-1/2 High-Fat Meat, 1-1/2 Fat. CARBOHYDRATE CHOICES: 4.

tip

Have some family fun time in the kitchen! Let kids make their own calzones using their favorite pizza ingredients.

Greek Meatballs with Spaghetti

PREP TIME: 25 MINUTES (READY IN 45 MINUTES)
SERVINGS: 4

1 lb lean (at least 80%) ground beef

⅓ cup Progresso® plain bread crumbs

2 tablespoons chopped fresh parsley

½ teaspoon chopped fresh oregano leaves

¼ teaspoon ground cinnamon

¼ teaspoon freshly ground pepper

1 clove garlic, finely chopped

2 egg whites

1½ teaspoons olive oil

2 cups marinara sauce

4 oz uncooked spaghetti

¾ cup crumbled feta cheese (3 oz)

Fresh oregano sprigs, if desired

1) In medium bowl, mix beef, bread crumbs, 4 ½ teaspoons of the parsley, the oregano, cinnamon, pepper and garlic until well blended. Add egg whites; mix just until combined. Shape mixture into 12 (1 ½-inch) meatballs; place on plate. Cover; refrigerate 5 minutes.

2) Heat oven to 375°F. In large ovenproof skillet, heat oil over medium-high heat. Cook meatballs in oil 8 minutes, turning frequently, until browned. Drain well; wipe skillet with paper towels. Return meatballs to skillet. Spoon marinara sauce over meatballs. Bake 12 to 13 minutes or until meatballs are thoroughly cooked and no longer pink in center.

3) Meanwhile, cook and drain spaghetti as directed on package. Sprinkle meatballs with remaining 1 ½ teaspoons parsley. Serve meatballs and sauce over spaghetti; sprinkle with cheese. Garnish with oregano sprigs.

1 SERVING: Calories 486; Total Fat 14g (Saturated Fat 6g); Sodium 774mg; Total Carbohydrate 51g (Dietary Fiber 4g); Protein 37g. EXCHANGES: 2 Starch, 1 Other Carbohydrate, 1 Vegetable, 4 Lean Meat. CARBOHYDRATE CHOICES: 3.

Fast & Easy Entrees

Setting a hot and hearty meal on the table is a snap with these recipes that prep in 30 minutes or less!

ORANGE TERIYAKI PORK SKILLET
PG. 175

TURKEY TORTILLA
ROLL-UPS WITH DIP
PG. 170

SHOESTRING POTATO
CHICKEN SALAD
PG. 179

BARBECUE CHICKEN
SANDWICHES
PG. 176

Steak Kabobs with Guacamole Dip

PREP TIME: 20 MINUTES (READY IN 45 MINUTES)
SERVINGS: 4

 EASY   LOW FAT

1 lb beef top sirloin steak, cut into 16 (1-inch) cubes

½ cup mesquite with lime juice marinade

1 red bell pepper, cut into 12 pieces

1 medium sweet onion, cut into 8 wedges

½ cup refrigerated guacamole dip

1) In resealable food-storage plastic bag, place beef and 6 tablespoons of the marinade. Seal bag; turn to coat beef with marinade. Refrigerate 20 minutes.

2) Heat gas or charcoal grill. Remove beef from marinade; reserve marinade. On each of 4 (11-inch) metal skewers, thread bell pepper, beef and onion.

3) Place kabobs on grill over medium-high heat; brush with reserved marinade. Cover grill; cook about 6 minutes, turning once, until beef is slightly pink when cut in center. Remove kabobs from grill to plate; let stand 5 minutes. Discard any reserved marinade.

4) Remove beef and vegetables from skewers; brush with remaining 2 tablespoons marinade. Serve with guacamole dip.

1 SERVING: Calories 240; Total Fat 7g (Saturated Fat 2g); Sodium 920mg; Total Carbohydrate 13g (Dietary Fiber 2g); Protein 33g. EXCHANGES: 1/2 Starch, 1 Vegetable, 2 Very Lean Meat, 2 Lean Meat. CARBOHYDRATE CHOICES: 1.

tip

A side of frozen roasted corn makes a great accompaniment to these skewers. It is available at specialty stores and some supermarkets.

Nacho Beef Skillet

PREP TIME: 15 MINUTES (READY IN 15 MINUTES)
SERVINGS: 6

 EASY

1 lb lean (at least 80%) ground beef

1 can (11 oz) Green Giant® Mexicorn® whole kernel corn with red and green peppers, drained

1 can (14.5 oz) Muir Glen® organic fire roasted diced tomatoes, drained

8 oz Mexican prepared cheese product (from 16-oz loaf), cut into cubes

6 oz nacho-flavored tortilla chips (about 64 chips)

1) In 10-inch skillet, cook beef over medium-high heat 5 to 7 minutes, stirring frequently, until thoroughly cooked; drain. Return beef to skillet.

2) Reduce heat to medium. Add corn and tomatoes; cook until thoroughly heated and desired consistency, stirring occasionally.

3) In small microwavable bowl, microwave cheese cubes and 2 teaspoons water uncovered on High 15 seconds; stir and repeat until cheese is melted and smooth.

4) Divide tortilla chips evenly among 6 plates. Top with beef mixture; drizzle with melted cheese. Garnish with chopped fresh cilantro, if desired.

1 SERVING: Calories 460; Total Fat 25g (Saturated Fat 9g); Sodium 1130mg; Total Carbohydrate 36g (Dietary Fiber 2g); Protein 23g. EXCHANGES: 1-1/2 Starch, 1 Other Carbohydrate, 1/2 Lean Meat, 2 Medium-Fat Meat, 2-1/2 Fat. CARBOHYDRATE CHOICES: 2-1/2.

Apricot-Dijon Chicken Sandwiches

| PREP TIME: | 10 MINUTES (READY IN 10 MINUTES) | EASY | LOW FAT |
| SERVINGS: | 4 | | |

1 loaf ciabatta bread (12 oz)

¼ cup Dijon mustard

¼ cup apricot preserves

4 leaves Bibb or Boston lettuce

¾ lb thinly sliced deli rotisserie chicken

1) Cut loaf in half horizontally. In small bowl, mix mustard and preserves; spread over cut sides of bread.

2) On bread bottom, layer lettuce and chicken. Cover with bread top.

3) Cut lengthwise down center, then cut crosswise in half into 4 sandwiches.

1 SERVING: Calories 400; Total Fat 9g (Saturated Fat 2g); Sodium 1200mg; Total Carbohydrate 50g (Dietary Fiber 2g); Protein 30g. EXCHANGES: 3 Starch, 1/2 Other Carbohydrate, 1 Very Lean Meat, 2 Lean Meat. CARBOHYDRATE CHOICES: 3.

tip

Enjoy these change-of-pace sandwiches with sweet potato chips and pieces of fresh fruit.

Sesame-Crusted Chicken

PREP TIME: 20 MINUTES (READY IN 20 MINUTES)
SERVINGS: 6

 EASY **If** **LOW FAT**

6 **boneless skinless chicken breasts** (1 ¼ lb)

1 ½ **teaspoons grated orange peel**

½ **cup teriyaki baste and glaze**

6 **tablespoons sesame seed, toasted**

2 **medium green onions, chopped** (2 tablespoons)

1) Heat gas or charcoal grill. Between pieces of plastic wrap or waxed paper, place each chicken breast smooth side down; gently pound with flat side of meat mallet or rolling pin until ½ inch thick.

2) In small bowl, stir orange peel into teriyaki glaze. Reserve 2 tablespoons glaze mixture for serving. Brush both sides of chicken with remaining glaze mixture. Sprinkle sesame seed over both sides of chicken; cover chicken with piece of waxed paper and lightly press seed into chicken.

3) Place chicken on grill over medium heat. Cover grill; cook 6 to 8 minutes, turning once, until chicken is no longer pink in center. Remove chicken from grill to serving plate. Spoon reserved 2 tablespoons glaze over chicken. Sprinkle with onions.

1 SERVING: Calories 210; Total Fat 9g (Saturated Fat 1.5g); Sodium 600mg; Total Carbohydrate 9g (Dietary Fiber 1g); Protein 24g. EXCHANGES: 1/2 Other Carbohydrate, 3-1/2 Very Lean Meat, 1-1/2 Fat. CARBOHYDRATE CHOICES: 1/2.

 tip

To toast sesame seed, sprinkle in ungreased heavy skillet. Cook over medium-low heat 5 to 7 minutes, stirring frequently until browning begins, then stirring constantly until golden brown. Remove immediately from hot skillet so seed doesn't continue to toast and become too dark or scorched.

Chicken Satay Salad

PREP TIME: 10 MINUTES (READY IN 10 MINUTES)
SERVINGS: 4

 EASY

2 packages (6 oz each) refrigerated cooked chicken breast strips

¾ cup Thai peanut sauce

1 bag (5 oz) mixed salad greens

1 cup julienne carrots (from 10-oz bag)

¼ cup chopped fresh cilantro

1) In medium microwavable bowl, mix chicken and peanut sauce. Cover; microwave on High 2 to 3 minutes or until hot.

2) Divide salad greens and carrots evenly among 4 plates. Top with chicken mixture and cilantro.

1 SERVING: Calories 280; Total Fat 15g (Saturated Fat 3.5g); Sodium 630mg; Total Carbohydrate 10g (Dietary Fiber 3g); Protein 27g. EXCHANGES: 1/2 Starch, 1/2 Vegetable, 3-1/2 Very Lean Meat, 2-1/2 Fat. CARBOHYDRATE CHOICES: 1/2.

Asian Beef Salad

PREP TIME: 10 MINUTES (READY IN 10 MINUTES)
SERVINGS: 4

 EASY   LOW FAT

1 bag (10 oz) romaine lettuce (6 cups)

12 oz sliced deli roast beef, cut into ½-inch strips

1 medium red bell pepper, chopped

½ cup Asian toasted sesame dressing and marinade

4 medium green onions, sliced (¼ cup)

Dry-roasted peanuts, if desired

1) On 4 plates, evenly divide lettuce, beef and bell pepper.

2) Drizzle each with 2 tablespoons dressing. Sprinkle each with 1 tablespoon onions and dry-roasted peanuts.

1 SERVING: Calories 180; Total Fat 2.5g (Saturated Fat 1g); Sodium 2040mg; Total Carbohydrate 21g (Dietary Fiber 2g); Protein 18g. EXCHANGES: 1/2 Starch, 1/2 Other Carbohydrate, 1 Vegetable, 1-1/2 Very Lean Meat, 1/2 Lean Meat. CARBOHYDRATE CHOICES: 1-1/2.

Shrimp Rolls

PREP TIME: 10 MINUTES (READY IN 10 MINUTES)
SERVINGS: 4

 EASY   LOW FAT

1 small lemon

¼ cup light mayonnaise

2 medium green onions, chopped
(2 tablespoons)

¾ lb cooked deveined peeled
shrimp, chopped

½ cup finely chopped celery

4 leaves Boston lettuce

4 hot dog buns, split

1) Grate ½ teaspoon peel from lemon. Squeeze lemon to measure
4 ½ teaspoons juice. In medium bowl, mix lemon peel, lemon juice,
mayonnaise and onions. Add shrimp and celery; toss gently.

2) Place 1 lettuce leaf in each bun; top evenly with shrimp mixture.
Serve immediately.

1 SERVING: Calories 280; Total Fat 8g; Dietary Fiber 4g. EXCHANGES: 1-1/2 Starch, 1/2 Other
Carbohydrate, 2 Lean Meat. CARBOHYDRATE CHOICES: 2.

Turkey Tortilla Roll-Ups with Dip

PREP TIME: 5 MINUTES (READY IN 5 MINUTES)
SERVINGS: 2

 EASY   **lf** LOW FAT

2 **flour tortillas (7- or 8-inch)**

3 **tablespoons sharp process cheese spread with pimiento (from 5-oz jar)**

1 **package (2.5-oz) smoked turkey breast slices**

4 **leaves leaf lettuce**

¼ **cup fat-free or regular honey Dijon dressing**

1) On each tortilla, spread process cheese spread to edges. Top evenly with turkey and lettuce; roll up. Secure with toothpicks, if desired. Serve with dressing for dipping. Remove toothpicks before serving.

1 SERVING: Calories 290; Total Fat 9g (Saturated Fat 3.5g); Sodium 1220mg; Total Carbohydrate 39g (Dietary Fiber 3g); Protein 12g. EXCHANGES: 2 Starch, 1/2 Other Carbohydrate, 1/2 Vegetable, 1 Very Lean Meat, 1-1/2 Fat. CARBOHYDRATE CHOICES: 2-1/2.

tip
This sandwich makes a great to-go lunch. Just wrap the roll-up in plastic wrap and pour the dressing into a small plastic container with a tight-fitting lid. If you like, try roast beef instead of turkey.

Honey-Lime Mopped Drumsticks

| PREP TIME: | 25 MINUTES (READY IN 25 MINUTES) |
| SERVINGS: | 4 |

 EASY   LOW FAT

8 chicken drumsticks

2 teaspoons garlic-pepper blend

3 tablespoons honey

3 tablespoons fresh lime juice

2 tablespoons chopped fresh cilantro

1) Heat gas or charcoal grill. Sprinkle chicken with garlic-pepper blend. In small bowl, stir honey and lime juice with whisk until blended; set aside.

2) Place chicken on grill over medium heat. Cover grill; cook 15 to 20 minutes, turning frequently and brushing with honey mixture during last 10 minutes of cooking, until juice of chicken is clear when thickest part is cut to bone (at least 165°F).

3) Remove chicken from grill to serving plate; sprinkle with cilantro. Discard any remaining honey mixture.

1 SERVING: Calories 190; Total Fat 4g; Sodium 280mg; Dietary Fiber 0g. EXCHANGES: 3-1/2 Very Lean Meat, 1/2 Fat. CARBOHYDRATE CHOICES: 1.

Tuna Chef's Salad

PREP TIME: 10 MINUTES (READY IN 10 MINUTES)
SERVINGS: 4

 EASY

1 bag (9 oz) leafy salad greens (about 6 cups)

2 cans (5 oz each) albacore tuna in water, drained

4 hard-cooked eggs, sliced

1 cup shredded carrots (from 10-oz bag)

¾ cup Caesar dressing

1) On 4 plates evenly divide salad greens, tuna, eggs and carrots.

2) Drizzle each with 3 tablespoons dressing.

1 SERVING: Calories 400; Total Fat 31g (Saturated Fat 6g); Sodium 770mg; Total Carbohydrate 6g (Dietary Fiber 2g); Protein 23g. EXCHANGES: 1 Vegetable, 2 Very Lean Meat, 1 Medium-Fat Meat, 5 Fat. CARBOHYDRATE CHOICES: 1/2.

Cheese Steak Melts

PREP TIME: 15 MINUTES (READY IN 15 MINUTES)
SERVINGS: 4

 EASY

½ loaf (1 lb) French bread

8 oz Muenster cheese, shredded (2 cups)

¾ lb thinly sliced deli roast beef

1 teaspoon Montreal steak grill seasoning

1 bag (1 lb) frozen bell pepper and onion stir-fry, cooked, drained

1) Set oven control to broil. Cut loaf of bread in half horizontally. Place cut sides up on cookie sheet. Top each bread half with ¼ cup of the cheese. Broil with tops 4 to 6 inches from heat 1 to 2 minutes or until cheese is melted.

2) Layer roast beef on each bread half; sprinkle with grill seasoning. Top with vegetables and remaining cheese; press down.

3) Broil with tops about 4 inches from heat 2 to 3 minutes or until cheese is bubbly. Cut each steak melt into 4 pieces.

1 SERVING: Calories 470; Total Fat 20g (Saturated Fat 12g); Sodium 1790mg; Total Carbohydrate 35g (Dietary Fiber 1g); Protein 37g. EXCHANGES: 2 Starch, 1/2 Other Carbohydrate, 4-1/2 Lean Meat, 1 Fat. CARBOHYDRATE CHOICES: 2.

 tip

Use the shredding disk from your food processor to quickly shred Muenster cheese. Muenster is a soft, meltable cheese, and it is purchased in a block instead of shredded.

Grilled Tomato-Feta Chicken Thighs

PREP TIME: 20 MINUTES (READY IN 25 MINUTES)
SERVINGS: 4

 EASY   lf LOW FAT

8 small bone-in chicken thighs
(1 ½ lb)

1 tablespoon vegetable oil

½ teaspoon garlic-pepper blend

2 plum (Roma) tomatoes, each cut
into 8 slices

½ cup crumbled tomato-basil feta
cheese (2 oz)

1) Heat gas or charcoal grill. Brush chicken with oil; sprinkle with garlic-pepper blend.

2) Place chicken on grill over medium heat. Cover grill; cook 7 minutes. Turn chicken; top each with 2 slices tomato. Cover grill; cook about 7 minutes longer or until juice of chicken is clear when center of thickest part is cut to bone (at least 165°F).

3) Remove chicken from grill to serving plate. Sprinkle cheese over chicken. Cover; let stand 5 minutes to soften cheese.

1 SERVING: Calories 300; Total Fat 21g (Saturated Fat 7g); Sodium 270mg; Total Carbohyrate 2g (Dietary Fiber 0g); Protein 25g. EXCHANGES: 3-1/2 Lean Meat, 2 Fat. CARBOHYDRATE CHOICES: 0.

Cheese and Tomato Omelet

PREP TIME: 15 MINUTES (READY IN 15 MINUTES)
SERVINGS: 2

 EASY　　 **LOW FAT**

2 **whole eggs**

2 **egg whites**

2 **tablespoons water**

1 **tablespoon finely chopped fresh
cilantro**

¼ **teaspoon salt**

⅛ **teaspoon coarse ground black
pepper**

¼ **cup shredded reduced-fat Cheddar
cheese (1 oz)**

1 **small tomato, seeded, diced (½ cup)**

1) In medium bowl, beat whole eggs, egg whites, water, cilantro, salt and pepper with whisk.

2) Heat 8-inch nonstick skillet over medium-high heat. Pour egg mixture into skillet; cook until edges begin to set, lifting edges occasionally to allow uncooked egg mixture to flow to bottom of skillet. Cook 2 minutes or until egg mixture is almost set; sprinkle with cheese. Cover; cook 1 minute longer or until cheese is melted and eggs are set. Spoon tomato over half of omelet; fold in half.

3) Cut omelet in half crosswise, and slide one half onto each of 2 plates. Garnish with additional chopped fresh cilantro and tomato, if desired, and serve immediately.

1 SERVING: Calories 145; Total Fat 8g; Sodium 544mg; Dietary Fiber 0.6g. EXCHANGES: 1-1/2 Medium-Fat Meat, 1/2 Lean Meat. CARBOHYDRATE CHOICES: 0.

Orange Teriyaki Pork Skillet

PREP TIME: 20 MINUTES (READY IN 20 MINUTES)
SERVINGS: 4

 EASY   **f** LOW FAT

1 lb pork tenderloin, cut in half lengthwise, cut crosswise into thin slices

1 bag (19 oz) Green Giant® frozen teriyaki-flavor stir-fry vegetables

¼ cup orange marmalade

1 can (11 oz) mandarin orange segments, drained

2 packages (8.8 oz each) original flavor ready-to-heat rice, heated as directed on package

Sliced green onions, if desired

1) In 12-inch nonstick skillet, cook and stir pork over medium-high heat 4 to 6 minutes or until no longer pink in center.

2) Stir in frozen vegetables, contents of teriyaki sauce pouch and marmalade. Cover; cook 5 to 7 minutes, stirring occasionally, until bubbly and vegetables are crisp-tender. Fold in oranges.

3) Spoon 1 cup rice onto each of 4 serving plates. Top each with about 1 cup pork mixture. Garnish with sliced green onions.

1 SERVING: Calories 470; Total Fat 7g (Saturated Fat 1.5g); Sodium 680mg; Total Carbohydrate 72g (Dietary Fiber 3g); Protein 29g. EXCHANGES: 2-1/2 Starch, 1/2 Fruit, 2 Other Carbohydrate, 1-1/2 Very Lean Meat, 1-1/2 Lean Meat. CARBOHYDRATE CHOICES: 5.

tip

For a bit of spice, stir a little chili paste or crushed red pepper flakes into the pork mixture.

Barbecue Chicken Sandwiches

PREP TIME: 20 MINUTES (READY IN 20 MINUTES)
SERVINGS: 4 SANDWICHES

 EASY

- **4 boneless skinless chicken breasts**
- **¼ cup hickory smoke-flavored barbecue sauce**
- **4 slices (1 oz each) provolone cheese**
- **4 hamburger buns, split**
- **½ cup creamy coleslaw (from deli)**

1) Heat gas or charcoal grill. Between pieces of plastic wrap or waxed paper, place each chicken breast smooth side down; gently pound with flat side of meat mallet or rolling pin until ½ inch thick.

2) Place chicken on grill over medium heat. Cover grill; cook 3 minutes. Turn chicken; brush with barbecue sauce. Cover grill; cook 5 to 7 minutes longer or until chicken is no longer pink in center. Remove chicken from grill; top each with 1 cheese slice. Place buns, cut sides down, on grill. Cover grill; cook 1 minute or until buns are lightly toasted.

3) Spoon 2 tablespoons coleslaw on each bun bottom; top with chicken. Cover with bun tops.

1 SANDWICH: Calories 380; Total Fat 17g (Saturated Fat 7g); Sodium 700mg; Total Carbohydrate 30g (Dietary Fiber 1g); Protein 26g. EXCHANGES: 1-1/2 Starch, 3 Very Lean Meat, 3 Fat. CARBOHYDRATE CHOICES: 2.

tip

For the freshest chicken, check the pack date and "best when used by" date on the package. Refrigerate immediately when home from the grocery store.

Bacon and Sun-Dried Tomato Penne

PREP TIME: 15 MINUTES (READY IN 15 MINUTES)
SERVINGS: 4

 EASY

2 ¼ cups uncooked penne pasta (8 oz)

1 container (10 oz) refrigerated Alfredo pasta sauce

½ cup dry-pack sun-dried tomatoes, cut into julienne strips

6 slices bacon, crisply cooked, crumbled

¼ cup chopped fresh basil leaves

OPTIONAL

Freshly ground pepper

1) Cook and drain pasta as directed on package.

2) Meanwhile, in 1-quart saucepan, heat Alfredo sauce and sun-dried tomatoes over low heat 6 to 8 minutes, stirring occasionally, until thoroughly heated and tomatoes are plump.

3) In large serving bowl, toss cooked pasta with Alfredo sauce mixture. Top with bacon and basil. Sprinkle with freshly ground pepper, if desired.

1 SERVING: Calories 416; Total Fat 17g; Sodium 813mg; Dietary Fiber 3g;. EXCHANGES: 3 Starch, 1 Vegetable, 1/2 Medium-Fat Meat, 3 Fat. CARBOHYDRATE CHOICES: 3.

Chicken-Pear Salad

PREP TIME: 10 MINUTES (READY IN 10 MINUTES)
SERVINGS: 2

 EASY

4 lettuce leaves

2 ripe medium pears, peeled, cut into ¼-inch-thick slices

½ pint (1 cup) creamy chicken salad (from deli)

¼ cup crumbled blue cheese (1 oz)

2 tablespoons chopped smoked almonds

1) Line 2 plates with lettuce. On each plate, stack pear slices alongside lettuce.

2) Spoon ½ cup chicken salad onto lettuce leaves. Sprinkle with cheese and almonds.

1 SERVING: Calories 370; Total Fat 17g (Saturated Fat 5g); Sodium 530mg; Total Carbohydrate 35g (Dietary Fiber 7g); Protein 19g. EXCHANGES: 1/2 Starch, 1/2 Fruit, 1-1/2 Other Carbohydrate, 1 Lean Meat, 1 Medium-Fat Meat, 1/2 High-Fat Meat, 1 Fat. CARBOHYDRATE CHOICES: 2.

Grilled Heirloom Tomato Pizza

PREP TIME: 15 MINUTES (READY IN 15 MINUTES)
SERVINGS: 6

 EASY   **LOW FAT**

1 can (13.8 oz) Pillsbury® refrigerated classic pizza crust

1 clove garlic, cut in half

1 large heirloom tomato, seeded, chopped (about 1 cup)

½ cup shredded reduced-fat mozzarella cheese (2 oz)

3 oz chèvre (goat) cheese with herbs, crumbled (¾ cup)

1) Heat gas or charcoal grill. Spray large cookie sheet with cooking spray. Unroll dough; place on cookie sheet. Starting at center, press out dough with hands to form 12x9-inch rectangle. Lightly spray dough with cooking spray.

2) Carefully brush oil on grill rock. Place dough on grill over medium heat; cook 3 minutes or until bottom of dough is golden brown. Turn dough; grill 1 to 2 minutes longer or until bottom is set. Carefully remove crust from grill. Rub garlic over crust (discard clove); sprinkle with tomato and cheeses. Return crust to grill. Cover grill; cook 3 to 5 minutes longer or until cheese is melted. Serve immediately.

1 SERVING: Calories 242; Total Fat 8g; Sodium 590; Dietary Fiber 0.4g. EXCHANGES: 2 Starch, 1 Medium-Fat Meat. CARBOHYDRATE CHOICES: 2.

Shoestring Potato Chicken Salad

PREP TIME: 10 MINUTES (READY IN 10 MINUTES)
SERVINGS: 4

 EASY

1 bag (12 oz) salad blend with lettuce, carrots and red cabbage

2 packages (6 oz each) refrigerated cooked chicken breast strips, coarsely chopped

1 red bell pepper, cut into ½-inch pieces

1 can (1 ¾ oz) shoestring potatoes

¾ cup ranch dressing

1) In large bowl, mix all ingredients except dressing.

2) Divide salad evenly among 4 plates; drizzle each with 3 tablespoons dressing. Serve immediately.

1 SERVING: Calories 370; Total Fat 26g (Saturated Fat 4.5g); Sodium 910mg; Total Carbohydrate 11g (Dietary Fiber 3g); Protein 23g. EXCHANGES: 1/2 Starch, 1 Vegetable, 2-1/2 Very Lean Meat, 5 Fat. CARBOHYDRATE CHOICES: 1.

tip Cut leftover grilled chicken into strips or cubes. Freeze it in resealable freezer plastic bags to have on hand when you want to make a quick salad such as this. The frozen chicken can be thawed quickly in the microwave.

Grilled Steak with Pineapple Salsa

PREP TIME: 15 MINUTES (READY IN 15 MINUTES)
SERVINGS: 4

 EASY

8 oz sliced fresh pineapple

2 tablespoons packed brown sugar

½ teaspoon salt

1 boneless beef chuck flat-iron steak (1 lb)

3 large green onions

½ cup fresh (refrigerated) salsa

1) Heat gas or charcoal grill. Sprinkle pineapple slices with brown sugar and ¼ teaspoon salt. Sprinkle steak with additional ¼ teaspoon salt.

2) Place steak, pineapple and onions on grill over medium-high heat. Cover grill; cook 6 to 8 minutes, turning once, until steak is of desired doneness and pineapple and onions are tender.

3) Remove steak from grill to cutting board; let stand 5 minutes. Meanwhile, finely chop pineapple and onions; place in small bowl. Stir in salsa. Cut steak diagonally across grain into thin slices. Top steak with pineapple salsa.

1 SERVING: Calories 256; Total Fat 11g; Sodium 404mg; Dietary Fiber 1g. EXCHANGES: 1/2 Other Carbohydrate, 1/2 Fruit, 1/2 Vegetable, 1 Fat. CARBOHYDRATE CHOICES: 1.

Tuna Primavera

PREP TIME:	20 MINUTES (READY IN 20 MINUTES)
SERVINGS:	4 (1-1/4 CUPS EACH)

 EASY

1 package (9 oz) refrigerated fettuccine

1 box (9 oz) Green Giant® Simply Steam® frozen asparagus cuts

1 ½ cups julienne carrots (from 10-oz bag)

1 can (12 oz) solid white tuna in water, drained, flaked

1 jar (15 oz) Alfredo pasta sauce

Chopped fresh parsley, if desired

1) Cook and drain fettuccine as directed on package. Rinse with hot water; cover to keep warm.

2) Meanwhile, in 10-inch nonstick skillet, mix frozen asparagus, carrots and 2 tablespoons water. Cover; cook over medium-high heat 5 to 7 minutes, stirring frequently, until vegetables start to soften. Stir in tuna and Alfredo sauce. Cover; cook until thoroughly heated.

3) In large serving bowl, toss warm fettuccine with tuna mixture. Garnish with fresh parsley.

1 SERVING: Calories 640; Total Fat 36g (Saturated Fat 21g); Sodium 770mg; Total Carbohydrate 47g (Dietary Fiber 4g); Protein 33g. EXCHANGES: 3 Starch, 1/2 Vegetable, 3 Very Lean Meat, 6-1/2 Fat. CARBOHYDRATE CHOICES: 3.

Slow Cooker Standouts

Put a hot dinner on the fast track—let your slow cooker do most of the work for you!

BURGUNDY STEW WITH
HERB DUMPLINGS
PG. 187

TURKEY-SPINACH LASAGNA
PG.186

BARBECUED PULLED-PORK FAJITAS
PG. 200

PORK CHOPS WITH
CORNBREAD STUFFING
PG. 188

Pesto-Ravioli Casserole

PREP TIME: 15 MINUTES (READY IN 3 HOURS 45 MINUTES)
SERVINGS: 6

 EASY

1   cup ricotta cheese

½   cup basil pesto

1   cup shredded mozzarella cheese
    (4 oz)

½   cup freshly grated Parmesan cheese

1   jar (24 oz) chunky pasta sauce

1   package (25 oz) frozen beef-filled
    ravioli (do not thaw)

8   oz fontina cheese, shredded
    (2 cups)

    Fresh basil leaves, if desired

1) In small bowl, mix ricotta cheese and pesto. Stir in mozzarella and Parmesan cheeses.

2) Spray 4-quart slow cooker with cooking spray. Spread 1 cup of the pasta sauce in slow cooker. Layer with half of the ravioli, half of the ricotta mixture and 1 cup of the fontina cheese. Top with 1 cup pasta sauce and remaining ravioli and ricotta mixture. Pour remaining pasta sauce over top.

3) Cover; cook on Low heat setting 3 hours.

4) Sprinkle remaining 1 cup fontina cheese over ravioli. Cover; cook 30 minutes longer or until ravioli is tender. Garnish individual servings with basil.

1 SERVING: Calories 700; Total Fat 38.5g (Saturated Fat 17g); Sodium 1467mg; Total Carbohydrate 47g (Dietary Fiber 3.5g); Protein 40g. EXCHANGES: 2-1/2 Starch, 1-1/2 Vegetable, 1-1/2 Medium-Fat Meat, 3-1/2 High-Fat Meat, 1/2 Fat. CARBOHYDRATE CHOICES: 3.

Teriyaki Chicken Thighs

| PREP TIME: | 10 MINUTES (READY IN 5 HOURS 10 MINUTES) |
| SERVINGS: | 4 |

 EASY

1 medium onion, cut into thin wedges

2 cups fresh pineapple chunks

8 chicken thighs (2 ½ lb), skinned

½ teaspoon salt

½ cup sesame-garlic sauce and glaze

4 medium green onions, sliced (¼ cup)

1 tablespoon sesame seed, toasted

1) Spray 3 ½-quart slow cooker with cooking spray. Place onion and pineapple in slow cooker.

2) Spray a 12-inch skillet with cooking spray; heat over medium-high heat. Cook chicken 4 minutes, turning once, until browned. Place chicken over onion and pineapple in slow cooker. Sprinkle with salt. Pour sauce over chicken.

3) Cover; cook on Low heat setting 5 hours or until chicken is tender. Sprinkle with onions and sesame seed.

1 SERVING: Calories 467; Total Fat 12.5g (Saturated Fat 3g); Sodium 1054mg; Total Carbohydrate 28g (Dietary Fiber 2g); Protein 57g. EXCHANGES: 1/2 Fruit, 1-1/2 Other Carbohydrate, 4 Lean Meat. CARBOHYDRATE CHOICES: 2.

Turkey-Spinach Lasagna

PREP TIME: 15 MINUTES (READY IN 2 HOURS 15 MINUTES)
SERVINGS: 12

 EASY

1 package (8 oz) sliced fresh baby portabella mushrooms

2 boxes (9 oz each) Green Giant® frozen chopped spinach, thawed, squeezed to drain

1 container (15 oz) ricotta cheese

1 ¼ cups shredded Parmesan cheese (5 oz)

½ teaspoon salt

2 jars (15 oz each) Alfredo pasta sauce

6 no-boil lasagna noodles

3 cups chopped cooked turkey

2 cups shredded mozzarella cheese (8 oz)

Chopped fresh parsley

1) Spray 10-inch skillet with cooking spray; heat over medium-high heat. Add mushrooms; cook 3 minutes, stirring often, until tender. Remove from heat; stir in spinach. In medium bowl, mix ricotta cheese, ½ cup of the Parmesan cheese and the salt.

2) Spray 5-quart slow cooker with cooking spray. Spread 1 cup of the Alfredo sauce in slow cooker. Layer with 2 of the noodles, breaking as needed to fit; 1 cup of the turkey; one-third of the spinach mixture; one-third of the ricotta mixture and one-third of the mozzarella cheese. Repeat layers twice. Sprinkle remaining ¾ cup Parmesan cheese and parsley over top.

3) Cover; cook on Low heat setting 2 to 3 hours or until bubbly and noodles are tender.

1 SERVING: Calories 473; Total Fat 33g (Saturated Fat 14.5g); Sodium 1285mg; Total Carbohydrate 14.5g (Dietary Fiber 1g); Protein 31g. EXCHANGES: 1/2 Starch, 1-1/2 Vegetable, 2 Lean Meat, 3 High-Fat Meat, 1/2 Fat. CARBOHYDRATE CHOICES: 1.

Burgundy Stew with Herb Dumplings

PREP TIME: 25 MINUTES (READY IN 8 HOURS 50 MINUTES)
SERVINGS: 8

 LOW FAT

STEW

- 2 lb boneless beef bottom round roast
- 4 carrots, cut into ¼-inch slices (2 cups)
- 2 medium stalks celery, sliced (1 cup)
- 2 medium onions, sliced
- 1 can (14.5 oz) diced tomatoes, undrained
- 2 jars (4.5 oz each) Green Giant® sliced mushrooms, drained
- ¾ cup dry red wine or beef broth
- 1½ teaspoons salt
- 1 teaspoon dried thyme leaves
- 1 teaspoon ground mustard
- ¼ teaspoon pepper
- ¼ cup water
- 3 tablespoons all-purpose flour

DUMPLINGS

- 1½ cups Original Bisquick® mix
- ½ teaspoon dried thyme leaves
- ¼ teaspoon dried sage leaves, crushed
- ½ cup milk

1) Spray 4- to 5-quart slow cooker with cooking spray. Cut beef into 1-inch pieces; place in slow cooker. Stir in remaining stew ingredients except water and flour.

2) Cover; cook on Low heat setting 8 to 10 hours.

3) In small bowl, mix ¼ cup water and the flour; gradually stir into stew. In another bowl, stir Bisquick mix, ½ teaspoon thyme and the sage. Stir in milk just until moistened. Drop dough by spoonfuls onto hot stew.

4) Increase heat setting to High. Cover; cook 25 to 35 minutes or until toothpick inserted in center of dumplings comes out clean. Serve immediately.

1 SERVING: Calories 300; Total Fat 7g (Saturated Fat 2.5g); Sodium 990mg; Total Carbohydrate 28g (Dietary Fiber 3g); Protein 30g. EXCHANGES: 1-1/2 Starch, 1-1/2 Vegetable, 3 Very Lean Meat, 1 Fat. CARBOHYDRATE CHOICES: 2.

tip To make fluffy dumplings, drop the dumpling dough onto the stew pieces rather than directly into the liquid. The dumplings will steam rather than settle into the liquid and become soggy. Also, be sure the stew is piping hot, so the dumplings will start to cook from the steam right away.

Pork Chops with Cornbread Stuffing

PREP TIME: 10 MINUTES (READY IN 4 HOURS 10 MINUTES)
SERVINGS: 6

 EASY

6 boneless pork loin chops, 1 inch thick (about 2 ¼ lb)

2 teaspoons seasoned salt

½ bag (16-oz size) cornbread stuffing (3 cups)

½ cup sweetened dried cranberries

½ medium apple, chopped (½ cup)

½ medium onion, chopped (¼ cup)

¼ cup chopped pecans

1 cup plus 2 tablespoons water

¼ cup butter or margarine, melted

½ cup cranberry relish or sauce

1) Place pork chops in large resealable food-storage plastic bag. Add seasoned salt; seal bag and shake to coat pork.

2) Spray 5- to 6-quart slow cooker with cooking spray. In slow cooker, mix remaining ingredients except cranberry relish. Arrange pork chops on stuffing mixture.

3) Cover; cook on Low heat setting 4 to 5 hours. Serve pork and stuffing with cranberry relish.

1 SERVING: Calories 560; Total Fat 25g (Saturated Fat 10g); Sodium 1220mg; Total Carbohydrate 44g (Dietary Fiber 3g); Protein 39g. EXCHANGES: 2 Starch, 1 Other Carbohydrate, 4-1/2 Lean Meat, 2 Fat. CARBOHYDRATE CHOICES: 3.

tip

If you prefer your stuffing on the dry side, reduce the amount of water by ¼ cup.

Zesty Black Bean Soup

PREP TIME: 25 MINUTES (READY IN 11 HOURS 35 MINUTES)
SERVINGS: 9 (1-1/3 CUPS EACH)

lf LOW FAT

- 1 bag (16 oz) dried black beans (2 cups), sorted, rinsed
- 2 cartons (32 oz each) vegetable broth (8 cups)
- 2 cans (14.5 oz each) diced tomatoes with green chilies, undrained
- 2 medium carrots, coarsely chopped (1 cup)
- 2 medium onions, coarsely chopped (1 cup)
- ¼ cup chopped fresh cilantro
- 4 cloves garlic, finely chopped
- 1 teaspoon salt
- ¼ teaspoon black pepper
- ⅛ teaspoon ground red pepper (cayenne)

  Sour cream, if desired

  Fresh cilantro sprigs, if desired

1) In 4-quart Dutch oven; heat beans and 10 cups water to boiling. Reduce heat; simmer uncovered 10 minutes. Remove from heat. Cover; let stand 1 hour. Drain.

2) Spray 6-quart slow cooker with cooking spray. In slow cooker, mix beans and remaining ingredients except sour cream and cilantro sprigs.

3) Cover; cook on Low heat setting 10 to 12 hours. Garnish individual servings with sour cream and cilantro sprigs.

1 SERVING: Calories 210; Total Fat 0.5g (Saturated Fat 0g); Sodium 1330mg; Total Carbohydrate 39g (Dietary Fiber 12g); Protein 12g. EXCHANGES: 2 Starch, 1-1/2 Vegetable, 1/2 Very Lean Meat. CARBOHYDRATE CHOICES: 2-1/2.

Weeknight Pot Roast

PREP TIME: 10 MINUTES (READY IN 8 HOURS 10 MINUTES)
SERVINGS: 6

 EASY LOW FAT

Cooking spray

1 package (8 oz) sliced fresh mushrooms (about 3 cups)

1 container (8 oz) refrigerated prechopped green bell pepper

1 boneless beef shoulder pot roast (2 lb)

6 tablespoons ketchup

¼ cup water

1 tablespoon Worcestershire sauce

½ teaspoon pepper

¼ teaspoon salt

Hot cooked polenta, if desired

Chopped fresh parsley, if desired

1) Spray 3 ½- to 4-quart slow cooker with cooking spray. Place mushrooms and bell pepper in slow cooker.

2) Spray 12-inch skillet with cooking spray; heat over medium-high heat. Spray roast with cooking spray; add to skillet. Cook 3 minutes on each side or until browned. Place roast over vegetables in slow cooker.

3) In small bowl, stir ketchup, water, Worcestershire sauce, pepper and salt until blended. Pour over roast.

4) Cover; cook on Low heat setting 8 to 9 hours or until beef is very tender. Serve beef with vegetables and sauce and, if desired, hot cooked polenta. Garnish with parsley.

1 SERVING: Calories 228; Total Fat 8g (Saturated Fat 2g); Sodium 397mg; Total Carbohydrate 7.5g (Dietary Fiber 1g); Protein 31.5g. EXCHANGES: 1/2 Other Carbohydrate, 4-1/2 Lean Meat. CARBOHYDRATE CHOICES: 1/2.

Pork and Bean Stew

PREP TIME: 10 MINUTES (READY IN 8 HOURS 10 MINUTES)
SERVINGS: 12 (1 CUP EACH)

 EASY LOW FAT

1 can (55 oz) baked beans with bacon and brown sugar sauce, undrained

2 cups shredded smoked pork

1 can (14.5 oz) fire-roasted diced tomatoes with roasted garlic, undrained

1 bag (12 oz) frozen onions, celery, bell pepper and parsley seasoning blend, thawed

1 box (9 oz) Green Giant® Simply Steam® frozen baby lima beans, thawed

1 cup water

½ cup barbecue sauce

Red pepper sauce, if desired

1) Spray 5- to 6-quart slow cooker with cooking spray. In slow cooker, mix all ingredients except pepper sauce.

2) Cover; cook on Low heat setting 8 hours. Serve with pepper sauce.

1 SERVING: Calories 300; Total Fat 6g (Saturated Fat 2.5g); Sodium 899mg; Total Carbohydrate 43g (Dietary Fiber 9g); Protein 16g. EXCHANGES: 1 Starch, 1-1/2 Other Carbohydrate, 1 Vegetable, 1 Lean Meat. CARBOHYDRATE CHOICES: 3.

Wild Rice and Mushroom Soup

PREP TIME: 15 MINUTES (READY IN 6 HOURS 25 MINUTES)
SERVINGS: 6 (1-1/3 CUPS EACH)

 EASY   LOW FAT

1 lb fresh small whole mushrooms, cut in half

½ cup uncooked whole-grain wild rice (not cracked or broken)

1 medium stalk celery, cut into ½-inch pieces

2 medium carrots, cut into ½-inch pieces

1 package (0.9 oz) onion mushroom soup mix (from 1.8-oz. box)

1 tablespoon sugar

1 cup water

1 carton (32 oz) Progresso® beef-flavored broth (4 cups)

1 cup Green Giant® Valley Fresh Steamers® frozen sweet peas (from 12-oz bag), thawed

1) Spray 3 to 4-quart slow cooker with cooking spray. In slow cooker, layer mushrooms, rice, celery, carrots, soup mix and sugar. Pour water and broth over top.

2) Cover; cook on Low heat setting for 6 to 8 hours.

3) Gently stir thawed peas into soup. Cover; cook 10 minutes longer or until peas are thoroughly heated.

1 SERVING: Calories 140; Total Fat 1g (Saturated Fat 0g); Sodium 1130mg; Total Carbohydrate 25g (Dietary Fiber 4g); Protein 8g. EXCHANGES: 1-1/2 Starch, 1 Vegetable. CARBOHYDRATE CHOICES: 1-1/2.

 tip

Homemade soup makes a great lunch to take to school or work. Transfer leftover cooled soup to single-serving plastic freezer containers and freeze for up to 6 months. Reheat the soup in the microwave.

Chicken in Red Wine

PREP TIME: 20 MINUTES (READY IN 8 HOURS 50 MINUTES)
SERVINGS: 8

 EASY   LOW FAT

6 slices bacon

8 boneless skinless chicken thighs (about 1 ½ lb)

1 bag (16 oz) ready-to-eat baby-cut carrots

8 oz tiny pearl onions

1 teaspoon salt

¼ teaspoon pepper

1 teaspoon dried thyme leaves

2 cloves garlic, finely chopped

2 dried bay leaves

1 ¼ cups dry red wine

¾ cup Progresso® chicken broth (from 32-oz carton)

1 lb fresh small whole mushrooms

2 tablespoons all-purpose flour

2 tablespoons cold water

¼ cup chopped fresh parsley

Hot cooked noodles, if desired

1) Line microwavable plate with microwavable paper towel. Place bacon on plate; cover with paper towel. Microwave on High 3 to 5 minutes or until crisp. Crumble bacon.

2) Spray 5- to 6-quart slow cooker with cooking spray. In slow cooker, place chicken, carrots, onions, bacon, salt, pepper, thyme, garlic, bay leaves, wine and broth.

3) Cover; cook on Low heat setting 8 to 10 hours.

4) Skim any fat from surface of chicken mixture. Stir in mushrooms. In small bowl, mix flour and water until smooth; gradually stir into chicken mixture. Stir in parsley.

5) Increase heat setting to High. Cover; cook about 30 minutes longer or until thickened. Remove bay leaves. Serve chicken mixture over noodles.

1 SERVING: Calories 230; Total Fat 10g (Saturated Fat 3g); Sodium 620mg; Total Carbohydrate 12g (Dietary Fiber 3g); Protein 23g. EXCHANGES: 1/2 Other Carbohydrate, 1 Vegetable, 3 Lean Meat. CARBOHYDRATE CHOICES: 1.

tip

If you prefer not to use red wine, you still can make a delicious chicken dish your family will love. Just increase the chicken broth to 2 cups and leave out the wine.

Veggie-Stuffed Peppers

PREP TIME: 15 MINUTES (READY IN 4 HOURS 15 MINUTES)
SERVINGS: 6

 EASY   LOW FAT

3 large red bell peppers

3 large yellow bell peppers

1 package (8.8 oz) microwavable brown rice

1 can (15 oz) Progresso® cannellini beans, drained, rinsed

1 package (8 oz) sliced fresh mushrooms (about 3 cups)

1 container (8 oz) refrigerated prechopped onion, celery and bell pepper mix

1 tablespoon chopped fresh thyme leaves

½ teaspoon salt

½ teaspoon pepper

1 cup shredded Italian cheese blend (4 oz)

1 cup tomato and basil pasta sauce

1) Cut off stem end of each bell pepper (about ½ inch); remove and discard seeds and membranes. In large bowl, mix rice, beans, mushrooms, prechopped vegetables, thyme, salt, pepper and ½ cup of the cheese. Spoon mixture evenly into bell peppers.

2) Spray 6-quart slow cooker with cooking spray. Spread pasta sauce in slow cooker. Arrange peppers over sauce. Sprinkle with remaining ½ cup cheese.

3) Cover; cook on Low heat setting 4 hours or until peppers are tender.

1 SERVING: Calories 352; Total Fat 6.5g (Saturated Fat 2.5g); Sodium 559mg; Total Carbohydrate 60g (Dietary Fiber 9g); Protein 16g. EXCHANGES: 3 Starch, 1/2 Other Carbohydrate, 1-1/2 Vegetable, 1 High-Fat Meat. CARBOHYDRATE CHOICES: 4.

Chicken Alfredo Stew

PREP TIME: 10 MINUTES (READY IN 6 HOURS 10 MINUTES)
SERVINGS: 6

 EASY

1 jar (16 oz) Alfredo pasta sauce

¾ cup water

½ teaspoon dried basil leaves

½ teaspoon salt

1 bag (20 oz) refrigerated cooked diced potatoes with onions

1 ¼ lb boneless skinless chicken thighs, cut into 1-inch pieces

1 bag (12 oz) Green Giant® Valley Fresh Steamers® frozen mixed vegetables, thawed

1) Spray 3- to 4-quart slow cooker with cooking spray. In medium bowl, mix pasta sauce, water, basil and salt. In slow cooker, layer half each of the potatoes, chicken, vegetables and pasta sauce mixture. Repeat layers, ending with pasta sauce mixture.

2) Cover; cook on Low heat setting 6 to 8 hours.

1 SERVING: Calories 530; Total Fat 31g (Saturated Fat 17g); Sodium 730mg; Total Carbohydrate 33g (Dietary Fiber 5g); Protein 30g. EXCHANGES: 2 Starch, 1 Vegetable, 3 Very Lean Meat, 5-1/2 Fat. CARBOHYDRATE CHOICES: 2.

Beef Burgundy with Sour Cream Spuds

PREP TIME: 10 MINUTES (READY IN 10 HOURS 10 MINUTES)
SERVINGS: 6

 EASY

1 beef chuck roast (3 lb), cut into 1 ½-inch pieces

2 packages (4 oz each) fresh gourmet mushroom blend

3 cloves garlic, finely chopped

1 cup Progresso® beef-flavored broth (from 32-oz carton)

1 cup dry red wine

¼ cup all-purpose flour

1 tablespoon chopped fresh rosemary leaves

½ teaspoon salt

½ teaspoon freshly ground pepper

1 bag (24 oz) refrigerated mashed potatoes with skins

⅓ cup sour cream

Fresh rosemary sprigs, if desired

1) Spray 5-quart slow cooker with cooking spray. In slow cooker, mix beef, mushrooms and garlic. In medium bowl, mix broth, wine, flour, chopped rosemary, salt and pepper with wire whisk until blended. Pour over beef mixture.

2) Cover; cook on Low heat setting 10 hours or until beef is tender and sauce is thickened.

3) Heat mashed potatoes as directed on package; stir in sour cream. Serve beef with mashed potatoes. Garnish with rosemary sprigs.

1 SERVING: Calories 464; Total Fat 18.5g (Saturated Fat 9g); Sodium 743mg; Total Carbohydrate 19.5g (Dietary Fiber 2.5g); Protein 51.5g. EXCHANGES: 1 Starch, 1 Vegetable, 6-1/2 Lean Meat. CARBOHYDRATE CHOICES: 1-1/2.

Turkey and Brown Rice Chili

PREP TIME: 20 MINUTES (READY IN 8 HOURS 35 MINUTES)
SERVINGS: 6

 EASY LOW FAT

1 tablespoon vegetable oil

¾ lb ground turkey breast

1 large onion, chopped (1 cup)

2 cans (14.5 oz each) Muir Glen® organic diced tomatoes, undrained

1 can (15 to 16 oz) chili beans in sauce, undrained

1 can (4.5 oz) Old El Paso® chopped green chiles, drained

½ cup water

1 tablespoon sugar

2 teaspoons chili powder

1 teaspoon ground cumin

½ teaspoon salt

2 cups cooked brown rice

1) Spray 3- to 4-quart slow cooker with cooking spray. In 12-inch skillet, heat oil over medium heat. Cook turkey and onion in oil 8 to 10 minutes, stirring frequently, until turkey is no longer pink; drain. In slow cooker, mix turkey mixture and remaining ingredients except rice.

2) Cover; cook on Low heat setting 8 to 10 hours.

3) Stir rice into chili. Increase heat setting to High. Cover; cook about 15 minutes longer or until rice is hot.

1 SERVING: Calories 240; Total Fat 4g (Saturated Fat 1g); Sodium 1270mg; Total Carbohydrate 38g (Dietary Fiber 7g); Protein 20g. EXCHANGES: 2 Starch, 1 Vegetable, 2 Very Lean Meat. CARBOHYDRATE CHOICES: 2-1/2.

tip

This is a low-fat chili because it is made with ground turkey breast. Check that you are buying ground turkey breast and not regular ground turkey, which includes both light and dark meat and will be higher in fat.

Red Wine-Braised Short Ribs

PREP TIME: 25 MINUTES (READY IN 8 HOURS 25 MINUTES)
SERVINGS: 8

1 ½ cups dry red wine or beef broth

½ cup ketchup

¼ cup packed brown sugar

3   tablespoons soy sauce

5 sprigs fresh thyme

4 lb beef short ribs

¼ teaspoon salt

¼ teaspoon pepper

1 tablespoon canola oil

4 large carrots, cut diagonally into
1 ½-inch slices

2 medium red onions, each cut into
6 wedges

Additional fresh thyme sprigs, if
desired

1) Spray 5- to 6-quart slow cooker with cooking spray. In slow cooker, mix
wine, ketchup, brown sugar and soy sauce. Add 5 thyme sprigs.

2) Sprinkle ribs with salt and pepper. In 12-inch skillet, heat oil over medium-
high heat. Add half of the ribs; cook about 8 minutes until brown on all
sides. Remove from skillet and add to slow cooker. Repeat with remaining
ribs. Place carrots and onions over ribs in slow cooker.

3) Cover; cook on Low heat setting 8 hours or until meat and vegetables are
tender. Garnish with additional thyme.

1 SERVING: Calories 486; Total Fat 25g (Saturated Fat 11g); Sodium 933mg; Total Carbohydrate 18g
(Dietary Fiber 1.5g); Protein 44.5g. Exchanges: 1 Other Carbohydrate, 1/2 Vegetable, 6 High-Fat Meat
CARBOHYDRATE CHOICES: 1.

Beef and Barley Stew

PREP TIME: 20 MINUTES (READY IN 8 HOURS 20 MINUTES)
SERVINGS: 14 (1 CUP EACH)

 EASY

1 boneless beef sirloin tip roast (about 3 lb)

½ cup all-purpose flour

1 teaspoon salt

1 teaspoon pepper

2 tablespoons vegetable oil

2 containers (8 oz each) refrigerated prechopped onion, celery and bell pepper mix

3 medium carrots, chopped (1 ⅓ cups)

2 cans (14.5 oz each) diced tomatoes with garlic, undrained

3 cups reduced-sodium beef broth (from 32-oz carton)

1 cup water

1 cup uncooked pearl barley

1 teaspoon Italian seasoning

1) Spray 5- to 6-quart slow cooker with cooking spray. In large resealable food-storage plastic bag, place beef, flour and ½ teaspoon each of the salt and pepper. Seal bag; shake to coat beef.

2) In 5-quart Dutch oven, heat oil over medium-high heat. Cook beef in oil until brown on all sides. Place in slow cooker. Scatter prechopped vegetables and carrots around beef. Add tomatoes, broth, water, barley, Italian seasoning and remaining ½ teaspoon each salt and pepper.

3) Cover; cook on Low heat setting 8 hours or until beef is tender. Remove beef from slow cooker to plate; shred beef, using 2 forks. Return beef to slow cooker.

1 SERVING: Calories 286; Total Fat 11.5g (Saturated Fat 3.5g); Sodium 456mg; Total Carbohydrate 22g (Dietary Fiber 4g); Protein 23.5g. EXCHANGES: 1 Starch, 1 Vegetable, 2-1/2 Lean Meat, 1 Fat. CARBOHYDRATE CHOICES: 1-1/2.

 tip

Barley absorbs a lot of soup broth. If you like barley in your soup but the leftovers are too thick, add extra chicken, beef or vegetable broth to leftovers while reheating to achieve the desired consistency.

Asian Turkey and Vegetables

PREP TIME: 20 MINUTES (READY IN 7 HOURS 40 MINUTES)
SERVINGS: 6 (1 CUP TURKEY MIXTURE AND 1 CUP RICE EACH)

 EASY   LOW FAT

2 to 2 ½ lb turkey thighs, skinned

1 package (1 ¼ oz) honey teriyaki seasoning mix

1 cup water

2 boxes (9 oz each) Green Giant® frozen Szechuan vegetables, thawed

2 cups uncooked regular long-grain white rice

4 cups water

1) In 3- to 4-quart slow cooker, place turkey. In small bowl, mix dry seasoning mix and 1 cup water; pour over turkey.

2) Cover; cook on Low heat setting 7 to 8 hours.

3) Remove turkey from cooker; place on cutting board. Remove meat from bones; discard bones. Cut turkey into bite-size pieces; return to cooker. Stir in both boxes of vegetables. Increase heat setting to High. Cover; cook 20 to 30 minutes or until vegetables are thoroughly heated.

4) Meanwhile, cook rice in 4 cups water as directed on package. Stir vegetable and turkey mixture. Serve over rice.

1 SERVING: Calories 440; Total Fat 4.5g (Saturated Fat 1.5g); Sodium 1460mg; Total Carbohydrate 68g (Dietary Fiber 4g); Protein 31g. EXCHANGES: 3-1/2 Starch, 1/2 Other Carbohydrate, 1 Vegetable, 2-1/2 Very Lean Meat, 1/2 Fat. CARBOHYDRATE CHOICES: 4-1/2.

Barbecued Pulled-Pork Fajitas

PREP TIME: 15 MINUTES (READY IN 8 HOURS 45 MINUTES)
SERVINGS: 18 FAJITAS

 e EASY   **lf** LOW FAT

FAJITAS

- 1 boneless pork loin roast (2 ½ lb), trimmed of fat
- 1 medium onion, thinly sliced
- 2 cups barbecue sauce
- ¾ cup Old El Paso® Thick 'n Chunky salsa
- 1 tablespoon chili powder
- 1 teaspoon ground cumin
- 1 bag (1 lb) frozen bell pepper and onion stir-fry, thawed
- ½ teaspoon salt
- 18 flour tortillas (8 to 10 inch), heated as directed on package
- Toppings, if desired
- Shredded cheese
- Guacamole
- Sour cream

1) Spray 3- to 4-quart slow cooker with cooking spray. Place pork in slow cooker; top with onion. In small bowl, mix barbecue sauce, salsa, chili powder and cumin; pour over pork and onion.

2) Cover; cook on Low heat setting 8 to 10 hours.

3) Remove pork from slow cooker to plate. Shred pork, using 2 forks. Return pork to slow cooker; mix well. Stir in vegetables and salt. Increase heat setting to High. Cover; cook 30 minutes longer or until mixture is hot and vegetables are tender.

4) Use slotted spoon to spoon ½ cup pork mixture onto each tortilla. Fold one end of tortilla up about 1 inch over filling; fold right and left sides over folded end, overlapping. Fold remaining end down. Serve with cheese, guacamole and sour cream.

1 FAJITA: Calories 290; Total Fat 8g (Saturated Fat 8g); Sodium 620mg; Total Carbohydrate 37g (Dietary Fiber 2g); Protein 18g. EXCHANGES: 2 Starch, 1 Vegetable. CARBOHYDRATE CHOICES: 2-1/2.

Mediterranean Minestrone Casserole

PREP TIME: 20 MINUTES (READY IN 6 HOURS 40 MINUTES)
SERVINGS: 6 (ABOUT 1-1/4 CUPS EACH)

 EASY   LOW FAT

- 3 medium carrots, sliced (1 ½ cups)
- 1 medium onion, chopped (½ cup)
- 1 cup water
- 2 teaspoons sugar
- 1 ½ teaspoons Italian seasoning
- ¼ teaspoon pepper
- 1 can (28 oz) Muir Glen® organic diced tomatoes, undrained
- 1 can (15 oz) Progresso® chick peas (garbanzo beans), drained, rinsed
- 1 can (6 oz) no-salt-added tomato paste
- 2 cloves garlic, finely chopped
- 1 ½ cups Green Giant® Valley Fresh Steamers® frozen cut green beans (from 12-oz bag), thawed
- 1 cup uncooked elbow macaroni (about 4 oz)
- ½ cup shredded Parmesan cheese (2 oz)

1) Spray 3- to 4-quart slow cooker with cooking spray. In slow cooker, mix all ingredients except green beans, macaroni and cheese.

2) Cover; cook on Low heat setting 6 to 8 hours.

3) Stir green beans and macaroni into slow cooker. Increase heat setting to High. Cover; cook about 20 minutes longer or until beans and macaroni are tender. Sprinkle with cheese.

1 SERVING: Calories 340; Total Fat 5g (Saturated Fat 2g); Sodium 510mg; Total Carbohydrate 57g (Dietary Fiber 9g); Protein 16g. EXCHANGES: 2-1/2 Starch, 1 Other Carbohydrate, 1 Vegetable, 1 Very Lean Meat, 1/2 Fat. CARBOHYDRATE CHOICES: 4-1/2.

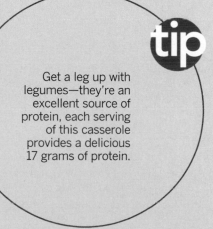

tip

Get a leg up with legumes—they're an excellent source of protein, each serving of this casserole provides a delicious 17 grams of protein.

Fiesta Pot Roast

PREP TIME: 15 MINUTES (READY IN 10 HOURS 15 MINUTES)
SERVINGS: 8

 EASY   LOW FAT

1 beef eye of round roast (3 lb), trimmed of fat

1 teaspoon pepper

½ teaspoon salt

2 tablespoons oil

1 ¾ cups Old El Paso® Thick 'n Chunky salsa

3 teaspoons ground cumin

2 teaspoons chili powder

1) Spray 4-quart slow cooker with cooking spray. Sprinkle beef with ½ teaspoon of the pepper and the salt. In 4-quart Dutch oven, heat oil over medium-high heat. Cook beef in oil until brown on all sides. Place beef in slow cooker.

2) In small bowl, mix salsa, cumin, chili powder and remaining ½ teaspoon pepper. Pour over beef.

3) Cover; cook on Low heat setting 10 hours or until beef is very tender.

1 SERVING: Calories 254; Total Fat 9.5g (Saturated Fat 2.5g); Sodium 609mg; Total Carbohydrate 4.5g (Dietary Fiber 1.5g); Protein 36g. EXCHANGES: 5 Lean Meat. CARBOHYDRATE CHOICES: 0.

tip

Shred the beef and serve on tostada shells with guacamole, chopped tomatoes, shredded lettuce and cheese.

Creole Jambalaya

PREP TIME: 10 MINUTES (READY IN 7 HOURS 40 MINUTES)
SERVINGS: 4 (1 CUP JAMBALAYA AND 3/4 CUP RICE EACH)

 EASY LOW FAT

2 medium stalks celery, chopped (1 cup)

4 cloves garlic, finely chopped

2 cans (14.5 oz each) reduced-sodium diced tomatoes with bell pepper and onion, undrained

½ cup chopped fully cooked turkey smoked sausage

½ teaspoon dried thyme leaves

¼ teaspoon pepper

¼ teaspoon red pepper sauce

¾ lb uncooked medium shrimp (26 to 30 count), thawed if frozen, peeled (tail shells removed), deveined

1 cup uncooked long-grain white or brown rice

2 cups water

1) Spray 3- to 3 ½-quart slow cooker with cooking spray. In slow cooker, mix all ingredients except shrimp, rice and water.

2) Cover; cook on Low heat setting 7 to 8 hours or until vegetables are tender.

3) Stir shrimp into jambalaya. Cover; cook about 30 minutes longer or until shrimp are pink.

4) Meanwhile, cook rice in water as directed on package, omitting butter and salt. Serve jambalaya with rice.

1 SERVING: Calories 300; Total Fat 4g (Saturated Fat 1g); Sodium 370mg; Total Carbohydrate 46g (Dietary Fiber 8g); Protein 21g. EXCHANGES: 2-1/2 Starch, 1 Vegetable, 1 Very Lean Meat, 1/2 Lean Meat. CARBOHYDRATE CHOICES: 3.

Creamy Chicken Risotto

PREP TIME: 15 MINUTES (READY IN 6 HOURS 30 MINUTES)
SERVINGS: 4 (1-1/2 CUPS EACH)

 EASY

1 ½ lb boneless skinless chicken breasts, cut into ¾-inch cubes

1 medium onion, finely chopped (½ cup)

½ cup shredded carrot

1 clove garlic, finely chopped

2 cups water

2 cups uncooked instant white rice

2 tablespoons butter or margarine

1 can (10 ¾ oz) condensed cream of chicken soup

½ cup grated Parmesan cheese

1) Spray 3- to 4-quart slow cooker with cooking spray. In slow cooker, mix chicken, onion, carrot, garlic and water.

2) Cover; cook on Low heat setting 6 to 7 hours.

3) Stir rice and butter into chicken mixture. Increase heat setting to High. Cover; cook 5 minutes or until rice is tender. Stir in soup and cheese. Cover; cook 10 to 15 minutes longer or until thoroughly heated. Serve immediately.

1 SERVING: Calories 580; Total Fat 20g (Saturated Fat 8g); Sodium 900mg; Total Carbohydrate 57g (Dietary Fiber 2g); Protein 43g. EXCHANGES: 3-1/2 Starch, 4-1/2 Very Lean Meat, 3 Fat. CARBOHYDRATE CHOICES: 4.

tip

Serve this rice casserole immediately. Rice continues to absorb moisture as it stands, so the casserole will lose some of its creaminess if it stands too long.

Easy Italian Meatball Stew

PREP TIME: 10 MINUTES (READY IN 6 HOURS 25 MINUTES)
SERVINGS: 4 (1-1/2 CUPS EACH)

 EASY

1 bag (16-oz.) frozen cooked Italian meatballs (32 meatballs), thawed

1 cup frozen pearl onions, thawed

½ teaspoon salt

2 cans (14.5-oz each) Muir Glen® organic diced tomatoes with Italian herbs, undrained

2 tablespoons all-purpose flour

2 tablespoons water

2 ½ cups frozen bell pepper and onion stir-fry (from 1-lb bag), thawed, drained

¼ cup freshly grated Parmesan cheese (1 oz)

1) Spray 3 ½ to 4-quart slow cooker with cooking spray. In slow cooker, mix meatballs, pearl onions, salt and tomatoes.

2) Cover; cook on Low heat setting 6 to 8 hours.

3) In small bowl, mix flour and water until smooth; gradually stir into stew until blended. Stir in bell pepper and onion stir-fry. Increase heat setting to High. Cover; cook 15 to 20 minutes longer or until stew has thickened and bell peppers are thoroughly heated. Sprinkle individual servings with 1 tablespoon cheese.

1 SERVING: Calories 495; Total Fat 25g (Saturated Fat 10g); Sodium 1480mg; Total Carbohydrate 36g (Dietary Fiber 4g); Protein 32g. EXCHANGES: 2 Starch, 2 Other Carbohydrate, 2 Vegetable, 3 Medium-Fat Meat, 2 Fat. CARBOHYDRATE CHOICES: 2-1/2.

Smoky Ham and Navy Bean Stew

PREP TIME: 10 MINUTES (READY IN 10 HOURS 10 MINUTES)
SERVINGS: 4

 EASY

1 lb cooked ham, cut into ½-inch cubes (3 cups)

1 cup dried navy beans, sorted, rinsed

2 medium stalks celery, sliced (1 cup)

2 medium carrots, sliced (1 cup)

1 small onion, chopped (¼ cup)

2 cups water

¼ teaspoon dried thyme leaves

¼ teaspoon liquid smoke

¼ cup chopped fresh parsley

1) Spray 3 ½- to 4-quart slow cooker with cooking spray. In slow cooker, mix all ingredients except parsley.

2) Cover; cook on Low heat setting 10 to 12 hours or until beans are tender. Sprinkle individual servings with parsley.

1 SERVING: Calories 390; Total Fat 11g (Saturated Fat 3.5g); Sodium 1740mg; Total Carbohydrate 37g (Dietary Fiber 9g); Protein 37g. EXCHANGES: 2-1/2 Starch, 4 Very Lean Meat, 1-1/2 Fat. CARBOHYDRATE CHOICES: 2-1/2.

Curried Lamb-Sweet Potato Stew

PREP TIME: 25 MINUTES (READY IN 8 HOURS 25 MINUTES)
SERVINGS: 6 (1 CUP EACH)

¼ cup all-purpose flour

1 ½ teaspoons salt

¼ teaspoon black pepper

2 lb boneless leg of lamb, trimmed, cut into 1-inch cubes

1 tablespoon vegetable oil

1 container (8 oz) refrigerated prechopped onion

3 cloves garlic, finely chopped

3 teaspoons curry powder

½ teaspoon ground red pepper (cayenne)

1 ¾ cups Progresso® beef-flavored broth (from 32-oz carton)

3 medium sweet potatoes, peeled, cut into 2-inch pieces

½ cup whipping cream

Hot cooked couscous

Peanuts, if desired

Chopped fresh parsley, if desired

1) Spray 5-quart slow cooker with cooking spray. In large resealable food-storage plastic bag, place flour, ½ teaspoon of the salt and the black pepper. Add lamb; seal bag and shake to coat with flour mixture. In 12-inch skillet, heat oil over medium-high heat. Cook lamb in oil 5 minutes, stirring occasionally, until browned. Place onion and garlic in slow cooker; sprinkle with curry powder and red pepper. Place lamb over vegetables. Pour broth over lamb.

2) Cover; cook on Low heat setting 6 hours. Stir sweet potatoes into stew. Cover; cook 2 hours longer or until lamb and potatoes are tender. Gently stir in whipping cream and remaining 1 teaspoon salt. Serve stew over couscous. Garnish with peanuts and parsley.

1 SERVING: Calories 454; Total Fat 20g (Saturated Fat 8g); Sodium 965mg; Total Carbohydrate 23g (Dietary Fiber 3g); Protein 43.5g. EXCHANGES: 1-1/2 Starch, 5-1/2 Lean Meat, 1 Fat. CARBOHYDRATE CHOICES: 1-1/2.

Smoked Barbecue Mac 'n Cheese

PREP TIME: 10 MINUTES (READY IN 4 HOURS 10 MINUTES)
SERVINGS: 8

 EASY

1 box (8 oz) elbow macaroni

1 can (12 oz) evaporated milk

1 ½ cups milk

12 oz prepared cheese product (from 16-oz loaf), shredded

1 teaspoon salt

¾ teaspoon ground mustard

½ teaspoon freshly ground black pepper

¼ teaspoon ground red pepper (cayenne)

½ lb shredded smoked pork

¼ cup barbecue sauce

1 cup shredded sharp Cheddar cheese (4 oz)

Additional barbecue sauce, if desired

Sliced green onions, if desired

1) Spray 3-quart slow cooker with cooking spray. Cook and drain macaroni as directed on package—except cook only 6 minutes. In large bowl, mix evaporated milk, milk, cheese product, salt, mustard, black pepper and red pepper. Stir in macaroni. Pour mixture into slow cooker.

2) Cover; cook on Low heat setting 3 hours.

3) In small bowl, mix pork and ¼ cup barbecue sauce. Stir macaroni and cheese in slow cooker. Top with pork. Sprinkle with Cheddar cheese.

4) Cover; cook 1 hour longer or until set in center. Serve with additional barbecue sauce. Garnish with onions.

1 SERVING: Calories 456; Total Fat 24.5g (Saturated Fat 14g); Sodium 1308mg; Total Carbohydrate 34g (Dietary Fiber 1g); Protein 25g. EXCHANGES: 1-1/2 Starch, 1/2 Other Carbohydrate, 1/2 Low-Fat Milk, 2 Medium-Fat Meat, 2-1/2 Fat. CARBOHYDRATE CHOICES: 2-1/2.

Fall & Winter Favorites

When brisk fall and winter days arrive, celebrate with Halloween, Thanksgiving and Christmas treats.

LITTLE MERINGUE GHOSTS
PG. 212

CARAMEL APPLE-PEAR PRALINE PIE
PG. 223

BEEF TENDERLOIN
WITH MARSALA SAUCE
PG. 227

CHOCOLATE CHIP
TREE COOKIES
PG. 228

Elegant Pumpkin-Walnut Layered Pie

PREP TIME: 20 MINUTES (READY IN 1 HOUR 45 MINUTES)
SERVINGS: 12

 EASY

1 box Pillsbury® refrigerated pie crusts, softened as directed on box

3 eggs

1 ¼ cups packed light brown sugar

1 cup walnuts, toasted, chopped

3 tablespoons butter, softened

¼ teaspoon vanilla

1 can (15 oz) pumpkin (not pumpkin pie mix)

1 package (8 oz) cream cheese, softened

2 tablespoons all-purpose flour

1 teaspoon ground cinnamon

½ teaspoon ground ginger

½ teaspoon ground allspice

½ teaspoon ground nutmeg

Whipped cream, if desired

Additional chopped walnuts, if desired

1) Heat oven to 425°F. Unroll 1 pie crust on work surface or cutting board; cut into ½-inch squares with knife. Lightly beat 1 of the eggs; brush over squares. Set aside. Place second pie crust in 9-inch glass pie plate as directed on box for One-Crust Filled Pie. Arrange squares around edge of crust, slightly overlapping. Brush edge with lightly beaten egg.

2) In medium bowl, mix ½ cup of the brown sugar, nuts, the butter and vanilla; spread in crust. In another bowl, beat pumpkin, cream cheese and remaining 2 eggs and ¾ cup brown sugar with electric mixer on medium speed. Beat in flour, cinnamon, ginger, allspice and nutmeg. Spoon over nut mixture. Bake 15 minutes. Reduce oven temperature to 350°F; bake 30 minutes longer or until set. Cool. Garnish with whipped cream and additional nuts.

1 SERVING: Calories 407; Total Fat 25g (Saturated Fat 10g); Sodium 277mg; Total Carbohydrate 43g (Dietary Fiber 2g); Protein 6g. EXCHANGES: 1 Starch, 2 Other Carbohydrate, 1/2 High-Fat Meat, 4 Fat. CARBOHYDRATE CHOICES: 3.

Halloween Sloppy Joes

PREP TIME: 20 MINUTES (READY IN 20 MINUTES)
SERVINGS: 6 SANDWICHES

 EASY

1 lb lean (at least 80%) ground beef round

1 medium onion, chopped (½ cup)

½ cup refrigerated chopped mixed bell peppers (from 8-oz container)

1 can (14.5 oz) fire-roasted diced tomatoes with garlic, undrained

½ cup ketchup

1 teaspoon chili powder

1 teaspoon Worcestershire sauce

¼ teaspoon salt

⅛ teaspoon pepper

6 hamburger buns, split

12 pimiento-stuffed green olives

1) In 10-inch nonstick skillet, cook beef over medium-high heat 5 to 7 minutes, stirring occasionally, until thoroughly cooked. Drain; set aside.

2) Add onion and bell pepper to skillet; cook 5 minutes or until tender. Stir in cooked beef, tomatoes, ketchup, chili powder, Worcestershire sauce, salt and pepper. Cook 2 minutes or until thoroughly heated.

3) Spoon beef mixture onto buns. On top of each bun, place 2 olives to look like eyes; poke toothpick in center of each to hold in place.

1 SANDWICH: Calories 316; Total Fat 11g (Saturated Fat 4g); Sodium 100mg; Total Carbohydrate 33g (Dietary Fiber 2g); Protein 21g. EXCHANGES: 1-1/2 Starch, 1-1/2 Vegetable, 2 Very Lean Meat, 1 Fat. CARBOHYDRATE CHOICES: 2.

Little Meringue Ghosts

PREP TIME: 30 MINUTES (READY IN 9 HOURS 30 MINUTES)
SERVINGS: 48

 LOW FAT

9 egg whites	1 cup plus 2 tablespoons sugar
¾ teaspoon cream of tartar	96 miniature semisweet chocolate chips
¾ teaspoon almond extract	

1) Heat oven to 200°F. Line cookie sheets with cooking parchment paper.

2) In large bowl, beat egg whites, cream of tartar and almond extract with electric mixer on medium speed until soft peaks form. Gradually add sugar, 2 tablespoons at a time, beating on high speed until stiff glossy peaks form and sugar is almost dissolved.

3) Spoon half of meringue mixture into large resealable food-storage plastic bag; seal bag. Cut off corner of bag. Squeeze bag to pipe ghost shapes onto cookie sheets. Repeat with remaining meringue. Insert miniature chocolate chips for eyes.

4) Bake 1 hour. Turn off oven; leave meringues in oven with door closed 8 hours.

1 SERVING: Calories 26; Total Fat 0.5g (Saturated Fat 0g); Sodium 10mg; Total Carbohydrate 5g (Dietary Fiber 0g); Protein 1g. EXCHANGES: 1/2 Other Carbohydrate. CARBOHYDRATE CHOICES: 1/2.

Black Spider Cupcakes

PREP TIME: 20 MINUTES (READY IN 1 HOUR 20 MINUTES)
SERVINGS: 24 CUPCAKES

 EASY

1 box devil's food cake mix with pudding in the mix	48 black candy-coated milk chocolate candies
Water, vegetable oil and eggs called for on cake mix box	16 feet black string licorice, cut into 192 (1-inch) pieces
2 containers (12 oz each) fluffy white whipped ready-to-spread frosting	

1) Heat oven to 350°F. Place paper baking cup in each of 24 regular-size muffin cups or spray with cooking spray.

2) Bake cake as directed on box for cupcakes, using water, oil and eggs. Cool 10 minutes; remove from pans to cooling racks. Cool completely, about 30 minutes.

3) Spread frosting over cupcakes, mounding frosting in center.

4) Top each cupcake with 2 chocolate candies. Attach 4 licorice pieces to both sides of candy to form spider legs.

1 CUPCAKE: Calories 378; Total Fat 15g (Saturated Fat 5g); Sodium 405mg; Total Carbohydrate 56g (Dietary Fiber 1g); Protein 3g. EXCHANGES: 1/2 Starch, 3-1/2 Other Carbohydrate, 2-1/2 Fat. CARBOHYDRATE CHOICES: 4.

Candy Corn Smoothies

PREP TIME: 20 MINUTES (READY IN 20 MINUTES)
SERVINGS: 8

 EASY

1 pint (2 cups) coconut sorbet, slightly softened

6 tablespoons milk

1 pint (2 cups) orange sherbet, slightly softened

1 pint (2 cups) lemon sorbet, slightly softened

4 drops yellow food color

Candy corn, if desired

1) In blender, place coconut sorbet and 2 tablespoons of the milk. Cover; blend on high speed 30 to 60 seconds or until smooth. Divide evenly among 8 glasses. Place glasses in freezer.

2) Rinse blender. In blender, place orange sherbet and 2 tablespoons milk. Cover; blend on high speed 30 to 60 seconds or until smooth. Pour over coconut mixture in glasses, dividing evenly. Return glasses to freezer.

3) Rinse blender. In blender, place lemon sorbet, yellow food color and remaining 2 tablespoons milk. Cover; blend on high speed 30 to 60 seconds or until smooth. Pour over orange mixture in glasses, dividing evenly. Garnish with candy corn. Serve or freeze until serving time.

1 SERVING: Calories 189; Total Fat 4.5g (Saturated Fat 3.5g); Sodium 51mg; Total Carbohydrate 36g (Dietary Fiber 0.5g); Protein 1g. EXCHANGES: 2 Other Carbohydrate, 1/2 Fat. CARBOHYDRATE CHOICES: 2.

Jack-o'-Lantern Beef and Bean Pots

PREP TIME: 20 MINUTES (READY IN 40 MINUTES)
SERVINGS: 4

 EASY

1 lb lean (at least 80%) ground beef

2 teaspoons dried minced onion

1 can (16 oz) pork and beans

1 can (8 oz) Muir Glen® organic tomato sauce

3 tablespoons packed brown sugar

1 cup Original Bisquick® mix

3 tablespoons boiling water

1 tablespoon ketchup

1) Heat oven to 375°F. Grease bottoms and sides of 4 (10- to 12-oz) casseroles or custard cups with shortening. In 10-inch skillet, cook beef over medium-high heat 5 to 7 minutes, stirring occasionally, until thoroughly cooked; drain. Stir in dried minced onion, beans, tomato sauce and brown sugar. Pour into casseroles; set aside.

2) In medium bowl, stir Bisquick mix, water and ketchup until soft dough forms; beat vigorously 20 strokes. Place dough on surface dusted with additional Bisquick mix; gently roll to coat. Shape into ball; knead about 10 times or until smooth. Pat ball into 4 (10-inch) rounds (or size of top of casseroles). Cut jack-o'-lantern shape in crust. Place on beef mixture in casseroles. Bake uncovered 15 to 20 minutes or until crust is light brown.

1 SERVING: Calories 515; Total Fat 22g (Saturated Fat 8g); Sodium 1400mg; Total Carbohydrate 56g (Dietary Fiber 7g); Protein 30g. EXCHANGES: 2 Starch, 2 Other Carbohydrate, 4 Medium-Fat Meat, 1 Fat. CARBOHYDRATE CHOICES: 4.

Slow Cooker Witch's Cider

PREP TIME: 5 MINUTES (READY IN 4 HOURS 5 MINUTES)
SERVINGS: 24 (1/2 CUP EACH)

 EASY LOW FAT

⅓ cup packed brown sugar

2 teaspoons whole allspice

4 cinnamon sticks (3 inch)

1 bottle (48 oz) apple cider (6 cups)

1 bottle (48 oz) cranberry juice cocktail (6 cups)

Cinnamon sticks, if desired

1) In 3 ½- to 6-quart slow cooker, mix all ingredients except additional cinnamon sticks.

2) Cover; cook on Low heat setting 4 to 6 hours. Remove allspice and cinnamon before serving. Garnish with additional cinnamon sticks.

1 SERVING: Calories 80; Total Fat 0g (Saturated Fat 0g); Sodium 0mg; Total Carbohydrate 20g (Dietary Fiber 0g); Protein 0g. EXCHANGES: 1/2 Other Carbohydrate, 1/2 Fruit. CARBOHYDRATE CHOICES: 1.

Chocolate Spiderweb Treats

PREP TIME: 20 MINUTES (READY IN 50 MINUTES)
SERVINGS: 18

 EASY

4 cups packed miniature marshmallows

⅓ cup creamy peanut butter

2 tablespoons butter or margarine

6 cups cocoa-flavored rice cereal

1 bag (11.5 oz) milk chocolate chips (2 cups)

½ cup white vanilla baking chips

1) Lightly spray 15x10x1-inch pan with cooking spray. In large microwavable bowl, microwave marshmallows, peanut butter and butter uncovered on High 2 minutes. Stir vigorously with wooden spoon until smooth. Add cereal; stir until well coated. Quickly spoon mixture into pan and press evenly. Cool until firm. Cut into rounds with 3-inch round cookie cutter.

2) In medium microwavable bowl, microwave chocolate chips uncovered on Medium (50%) 2 minutes, stirring once, until softened and chips can be stirred smooth; set aside. In small resealable freezer plastic bag, place white chips; seal bag. Microwave on Medium (50%) 1 minute or until softened. Gently squeeze bag until chips are smooth. Cut off tiny corner of bag.

3) Spread top of 1 round with melted milk chocolate. Immediately drizzle melted white chips in 3 rings on top of milk chocolate. Starting at center, pull toothpick through rings to look like web. Repeat with remaining rounds. Refrigerate 30 minutes or until chocolate is firm.

1 SERVING: Calories 250; Total Fat 11g (Saturated Fat 6g); Sodium 132mg; Total Carbohydrate 38g (Dietary Fiber 0.5g); Protein 3.5g. EXCHANGES: 1/2 Starch, 1 Other Carbohydrate, 1-1/2 Fat. CARBOHYDRATE CHOICES: 2-1/2.

Goblin's Hot Chocolate

PREP TIME: 10 MINUTES (READY IN 10 MINUTES)
SERVINGS: 4 (ABOUT 1 CUP EACH)

 EASY   LOW FAT

¾ cup instant cocoa mix

¾ teaspoon cherry-flavored soft
  drink mix

4 cups hot water

4 cherry-flavored licorice sticks,
  cut in half

1) In heatproof container, stir cocoa mix and soft drink mix. Add hot water; stir until mixes are dissolved.

2) Pour hot chocolate into mugs. Serve with licorice sticks.

1 SERVING: Calories 135; Total Fat 1g (Saturated Fat 0g); Sodium 130mg; Total Carbohydrate 31g (Dietary Fiber 1g); Protein 1g. EXCHANGES: 2 Starch. CARBOHYDRATE CHOICES: 2.

Bone Crisps with Artichoke Spread

PREP TIME: 30 MINUTES (READY IN 50 MINUTES)
SERVINGS: 30

1 box Pillsbury® refrigerated pie crusts, softened as directed on box

1 egg, slightly beaten

2 ½ cups shredded Parmesan cheese (10 oz)

8 oz chèvre (goat) cheese

4 oz (half of 8-oz package) cream cheese, softened

3 tablespoons whipping cream

½ teaspoon grated lemon peel

1 teaspoon fresh lemon juice

½ teaspoon kosher (coarse) salt

¼ teaspoon ground red pepper (cayenne)

1 can (14 oz) Progresso® artichoke hearts, drained, patted dry

Chopped fresh parsley, if desired

1) Heat oven to 450°F. Remove pie crusts from pouches; unroll on work surface. With 3 ½-inch bone-shaped cookie cutter, cut out 15 bones from each crust; discard scraps. Place dough bones on ungreased large cookie sheet. Brush with egg. Sprinkle 1 cup of the Parmesan cheese in heaping teaspoonfuls over bones.

2) Bake 10 minutes or until cheese is melted and crisps are golden brown. Remove from cookie sheet to cooling rack; cool.

3) Set oven control to broil. In 1-quart microwavable casserole, mix goat cheese, cream cheese, whipping cream, remaining 1 ½ cups Parmesan cheese, the lemon peel, lemon juice, salt and red pepper until blended. Stir in artichokes. Microwave uncovered on High 3 minutes, stirring halfway through. Broil with top about 6 inches from heat 3 minutes or until golden brown. Garnish with parsley. Serve warm with bone crisps.

1 SERVING: Calories 216; Total Fat 15g (Saturated Fat 7g); Sodium 650mg; Total Carbohydrate 8g (Dietary Fiber 0g); Protein 13g. EXCHANGES: 1/2 Starch, 1-1/2 Lean Meat, 2 Fat. CARBOHYDRATE CHOICES: 1/2.

Mummy Head Candy Apples

| PREP TIME: | 25 MINUTES (READY IN 25 MINUTES) |
| SERVINGS: | 8 |

 EASY

8 small apples

8 craft sticks (flat wooden sticks with round ends)

2 ½ cups white candy melts or coating wafers (14 oz), chopped

Black paste icing color (not liquid food color)

tip

Use orange candy melts to make pumpkin heads. Follow the same procedure, painting pumpkin faces with black icing.

1) Wash and dry apples; remove stem and blossom ends. Insert wooden stick into stem end of each apple.

2) In medium microwavable bowl, microwave candy melts uncovered on High 45 seconds or until melted; stir until smooth.

3) Dip each apple in melted coating, turning and spreading to coat. Let stand on waxed paper until firm. With fork, drizzle remaining melted coating (reheat if necessary) across coated apples in zigzag fashion to look like mummies. With black paste icing, pipe eyes on each apple. Let stand until set.

1 SERVING: Calories 313; Total Fat 14g (Saturated Fat 12g); Sodium 55mg; Total Carbohydrate 52g (Dietary Fiber 2g); Protein 3g. EXCHANGES: 1 Fruit, 2-1/2 Other Carbohydrate, 2-1/2 Fat. CARBOHYDRATE CHOICES: 3-1/2.

Frankenstein Reviver

PREP TIME: 5 MINUTES (READY IN 5 MINUTES)
SERVINGS: 2 (1/3 CUP EACH)

 EASY LOW FAT

½ cup slightly crushed ice

3 tablespoons gin

3 tablespoons melon-flavored liqueur

3 tablespoons orange-flavored liqueur

1 tablespoon fresh lemon juice

1 tablespoon simple syrup

1) Place ice in martini shaker or pitcher. Add remaining ingredients; shake or stir until blended. Pour into 2 (3-oz) chilled stemmed glasses, straining out ice.

1 SERVING: Calories 213; Total Fat 0g (Saturated Fat 0g); Sodium 1mg; Total Carbohydrate 21g (Dietary Fiber 0g); Protein 0g. EXCHANGES: 1 Other Carbohydrate, 2 Fat. CARBOHYDRATE CHOICES: 1-1/2.

Pumpkin Pizzas

PREP TIME: 15 MINUTES (READY IN 25 MINUTES)
SERVINGS: 6 PIZZAS

 EASY

1 can (13.8 oz) Pillsbury® refrigerated classic pizza crust

1 cup pizza sauce

½ cup shredded Cheddar cheese (2 oz)

9 slices pepperoni

12 small fresh basil leaves

1) Heat oven to 400°F. Unroll dough on work surface. Roll dough into 13x10-inch rectangle. With 4- or 5-inch pumpkin-shaped cookie cutter, cut dough into 6 pumpkin shapes, rerolling dough if necessary. Place 1 inch apart on ungreased cookie sheet.

2) Spread pizza sauce over shapes to within ¼ inch of edges. Sprinkle with cheese. Cut 6 slices of the pepperoni into triangles; place on pumpkins to create eyes. Cut remaining 3 pepperoni slices in half to look like jack-o'-lantern mouths; place on pumpkins. Place 2 basil leaves on each for stem. Bake 10 minutes or until cheese is melted.

1 PIZZA: Calories 302; Total Fat 11g (Saturated Fat 4g); Sodium 496mg; Total Carbohydrate 28g (Dietary Fiber 1.5g); Protein 24g. EXCHANGES: 1-1/2 Starch, 1 Very Lean Meat, 1/2 Fat. CARBOHYDRATE CHOICES: 2.

Chicken and Rice Cordon Bleu

PREP TIME: 20 MINUTES (READY IN 1 HOUR 25 MINUTES)
SERVINGS: 8

 EASY

2 boxes (6.2 oz each) fast-cooking long-grain and wild rice mix (with seasoning packet)

4 cups water

4 thin slices baked ham, cut into 1-inch strips

1½ lb chicken breast tenders (not breaded)

1 jar (16 oz) Alfredo pasta sauce

½ teaspoon paprika

1 cup finely shredded Swiss cheese (4 oz)

1 tablespoon chopped fresh parsley

1) Heat oven to 350°F. Spray 13x9-inch (3-quart) glass baking dish with cooking spray. In baking dish, mix rice, contents of seasoning packets and water.

2) Place ham over rice. Place chicken tenders over ham. Spoon Alfredo sauce over chicken; sprinkle with paprika.

3) Cover with foil; bake 40 minutes. Uncover; bake about 20 minutes or until rice is tender and chicken is no longer pink in center. Sprinkle with cheese. Bake 5 minutes longer or until cheese is melted. Sprinkle with parsley.

1 SERVING: Calories 350; Total Fat 17g (Saturated Fat 9g); Sodium 580mg; Total Carbohydrate 16g (Dietary Fiber 0g); Protein 33g. EXCHANGES: 1 Starch, 4 Lean Meat, 1 Fat. CARBOHYDRATE CHOICES: 1.

Apple Harvest Pockets

PREP TIME: 25 MINUTES (READY IN 45 MINUTES)
SERVINGS: 8

 EASY

1 box Pillsbury® refrigerated pie
  crusts, softened as directed on box

2 cups chopped peeled apples
  (2 medium)

⅓ cup sugar

1 tablespoon all-purpose flour

1½ teaspoons ground cinnamon

1) Heat oven to 400°F. Remove pie crusts from pouches; unroll on work
   surface. Cut each crust into quarters, making 8 wedges.

2) In medium bowl, toss apples, sugar, flour and cinnamon. Spoon ⅓ cup
   apple mixture on half of each crust wedge. Fold untopped half of wedge
   over filling; press edges with fork to seal. Place on ungreased cookie
   sheet. Cut several small slits in top of each.

3) Bake 15 to 20 minutes or until light golden brown. Serve warm or cool.

1 SERVING: Calories 260; Total Fat 12g (Saturated Fat 5g); Sodium 280mg; Total Carbohydrate 37g
(Dietary Fiber 0g); Protein 0g. EXCHANGES: 2 Starch, 1/2 Other Carbohydrate, 2 Fat.
CARBOHYDRATE CHOICES: 2-1/2.

Apple-Maple Turkey Breast

PREP TIME: 15 MINUTES (READY IN 1 HOUR 55 MINUTES)   EASY
SERVINGS: 8

1 **bone-in whole turkey breast (4 to 5 lb), thawed if frozen**

2 **tablespoons butter or margarine, softened**

1 **teaspoon salt**

1 **teaspoon freshly ground pepper**

⅓ **cup real maple syrup**

¼ **cup apple jelly, melted**

2 **tablespoons butter or margarine, melted**

1 **tablespoon chopped fresh rosemary leaves**

Fresh rosemary sprigs, if desired

Apple wedges, if desired

1) Heat oven to 425°F. Line broiler pan with foil; spray broiler pan rack with cooking spray. Place turkey, breast side up, on rack in pan. Rub turkey all over with softened butter. Sprinkle with ½ teaspoon each of the salt and pepper. Roast uncovered 30 minutes. Reduce oven temperature to 350°F.

2) In small bowl, mix syrup, jelly, melted butter, chopped rosemary and remaining ½ teaspoon each salt and pepper. Baste turkey with some of the syrup mixture.

3) Roast uncovered 55 minutes longer or until thermometer reads at least 165°F, basting with remaining syrup mixture 3 times during last 15 minutes of roasting. Let stand 15 minutes before carving. Garnish platter with rosemary sprigs and apples.

1 SERVING: Calories 444; Total Fat 19g (Saturated Fat 8g); Sodium 447mg; Total Carbohydrate 16g (Dietary Fiber 0g); Protein 50g. EXCHANGES: 1 Other Carbohydrate, 7 Very Lean Meat. CARBOHYDRATE CHOICES: 1.

Caramel Apple-Pear Praline Pie

PREP TIME: 40 MINUTES (READY IN 5 HOURS 35 MINUTES)
SERVINGS: 8

Beth Campbell
Belleville, WI
2010 State Fair Pie Contest Winner

1 box Pillsbury® refrigerated pie crusts, softened as directed on box

½ cup granulated sugar

¼ cup all-purpose flour

½ teaspoon ground nutmeg

½ teaspoon ground cinnamon

Dash salt

2 cups thinly sliced peeled pears

2 cups thinly sliced peeled apples

1 tablespoon lemon juice

2 tablespoons butter, cut into pieces

¾ cup old-fashioned oats

¼ cup packed brown sugar

1 tablespoon all-purpose flour

¼ cup cold butter

18 caramels, unwrapped

5 tablespoons milk

¼ cup chopped pecans

1) Heat oven to 375°F. Make pie crusts as directed on box for Two-Crust Pie using 9-inch glass pie plate. Mix granulated sugar, ¼ cup flour, the nutmeg, cinnamon and salt. Add pears, apples and lemon juice; toss to coat. Pour into crust-lined plate. Dot with 2 tablespoons butter. In small bowl, mix oats, brown sugar and 1 tablespoon flour. Cut in ¼ cup butter until crumbly. Sprinkle over fruit.

2) In 1-quart saucepan, melt caramels with milk over low heat until smooth; stir in pecans. Drizzle over filling. Top with second crust and flute; cut slits in several places. Brush top with additional milk and sprinkle with additional granulated sugar. Cover crust edge with strips of foil. Place pie on middle oven rack; place sheet of foil on lower oven rack. Bake 45 to 55 minutes or until golden brown. Cool.

1 SERVING: Calories 570; Total Fat 26g (Saturated Fat 11g); Sodium 430mg; Total Carbohydrate 80g (Dietary Fiber 3g); Protein 5g. EXCHANGES: 1-1/2 Starch, 1/2 Fruit, 3-1/2 Other Carbohydrate, 5 Fat. CARBOHYDRATE CHOICES: 5.

tip

Purchase pears that are still firm to touch to decrease the chance of mushy pears in the baked pie.

Fruits of Winter Crostata

PREP TIME: 30 MINUTES (READY IN 5 HOURS 50 MINUTES)
SERVINGS: 8

⅔ cup dried pears, chopped

⅔ cup dried apricots, chopped

½ cup dried plums, chopped

¼ cup golden raisins

2 cups apple juice

1 Pillsbury® refrigerated pie crust, softened as directed on box

4 teaspoons cornstarch

⅔ cup chunky applesauce

2 teaspoons lemon juice

¾ teaspoon almond extract

1 teaspoon sugar

⅛ teaspoon ground cinnamon

1) In medium bowl, mix chopped dried fruits, raisins and 1 ½ cups of the apple juice. Refrigerate 4 hours or overnight until fruit plumps up; drain any excess juice.

2) Heat oven to 350°F. Unroll pie crust into ungreased 15x10-inch pan. In 2-quart saucepan, thoroughly mix cornstarch and remaining ½ cup apple juice. Cook and stir over medium heat until mixture thickens and becomes clear. Add applesauce, lemon juice, almond extract and fruit mixture, stirring until well blended.

3) Spoon mixture onto center of crust to within 2 inches of edge. Carefully fold 2-inch edge of crust up over filling, pleating crust slightly as necessary. Sprinkle sugar and cinnamon over crust edge.

4) Bake 50 minutes or until crust is golden brown and filling is bubbly. Cool 30 minutes before serving. Store covered in refrigerator.

1 SERVING: Calories 290; Total Fat 7g (Saturated Fat 2.5g); Sodium 115mg; Total Carbohydrate 54g (Dietary Fiber 3g); Protein 1g. EXCHANGES: 1/2 Starch, 3 Other Carbohydrate, 1-1/2 Fat. CARBOHYDRATE CHOICES: 3-1/2.

Green Bean Amandine Casserole

PREP TIME: 25 MINUTES (READY IN 1 HOUR)
SERVINGS: 8

¾ cup water

⅛ teaspoon salt

2 bags (12 oz each) Green Giant®
Valley Fresh Steamers® frozen cut
green beans

1 tablespoon butter or margarine

1 package (8 oz) sliced fresh
mushrooms (about 3 cups)

1 shallot, finely chopped

1 can (10 ¾ oz) condensed cream of
mushroom soup

½ cup milk

½ teaspoon salt

1 cup freshly grated Parmesan cheese

½ cup Progresso® panko crispy bread
crumbs

½ cup sliced almonds, toasted

¼ cup butter or margarine, melted

1) Heat oven to 350°F. Spray 2-quart casserole with cooking spray. In
3-quart saucepan, heat water and ⅛ teaspoon salt to boiling over
medium-high heat. Add green beans. Cover; cook 5 to 7 minutes
or until tender. Drain; set aside.

2) In 10-inch skillet, melt 1 tablespoon butter over medium-high heat. Cook
mushrooms and shallot in butter 6 to 7 minutes, stirring occasionally,
until tender.

3) In large bowl, mix green beans, mushroom mixture, soup, milk and
½ teaspoon salt. Spread in casserole. In small bowl, mix cheese, bread
crumbs, almonds and ¼ cup butter. Sprinkle over green bean mixture.

4) Bake uncovered 35 minutes or until bubbly and topping is golden.

1 SERVING: Calories 254; Total Fat 16g (Saturated Fat 7g); Sodium 755mg; Total Carbohydrate 16g
(Dietary Fiber 4g); Protein 11g. EXCHANGES: 1/2 Starch, 1-1/2 Vegetable, 1 High-Fat Meat, 1-1/2 Fat.
CARBOHYDRATE CHOICES: 1.

Peppermint Cookie Ice Cream Pie

PREP TIME: 10 MINUTES (READY IN 4 HOURS 10 MINUTES)
SERVINGS: 8

e EASY

½ gallon peppermint ice cream, softened

1 cup chopped creme-filled chocolate sandwich cookies (8 to 10 cookies)

1 creme-filled chocolate sandwich cookie crumb crust (6 oz)

¾ cup chocolate topping that forms hard shell

¼ cup crushed red and green peppermint candies (about 10 candies)

1) In large bowl, stir ice cream and chopped cookies until blended. Spoon into crust.

2) Drizzle chocolate topping over pie; sprinkle with candies. Cover; freeze 4 hours or until firm. Remove from freezer 10 to 15 minutes before serving.

1 SERVING: Calories 608; Total Fat 34g (Saturated Fat 16g); Sodium 343mg; Total Carbohydrate 72g (Dietary Fiber 1g); Protein 6g. EXCHANGES: 5 Other Carbohydrate, 1/2 High-Fat Meat, 6 Fat. CARBOHYDRATE CHOICES: 5.

tip

If you don't have both red and green peppermint candies on hand, one color will work fine.

Beef Tenderloin with Marsala Sauce

PREP TIME: 20 MINUTES (READY IN 1 HOUR 35 MINUTES)
SERVINGS: 8

 EASY

BEEF

- 1 beef tenderloin (3 lb), trimmed of fat
- ½ teaspoon salt
- ½ teaspoon cracked black pepper

SAUCE

- 6 tablespoons butter
- ½ cup finely chopped shallots
- 1 cup Marsala or dry red wine
- 1 cup Progresso® beef-flavored broth (from 32-oz carton)
- ½ teaspoon pepper

1) Heat oven to 400°F. Turn small end of beef under about 6 inches. Tie turned-under portion with kitchen string at 1 ½-inch intervals. Place in shallow roasting pan. Sprinkle with salt and cracked pepper. Insert ovenproof meat thermometer so tip is in thickest part of beef.

2) Bake uncovered 30 to 40 minutes for medium-rare, 40 to 50 minutes for medium, or until thermometer reads 135°F or 150°F. Cover loosely with foil; let stand 15 to 20 minutes. Temperature will continue to rise about 10°F.

3) Meanwhile, in 8-inch skillet, melt 2 tablespoons of the butter over medium-high heat. Cook shallots in butter about 1 minute, stirring frequently. Add wine; cook about 4 minutes until reduced slightly. Stir in broth. Heat to boiling. Reduce heat to medium-low; cook about 10 minutes longer, stirring occasionally, until reduced to about 1 cup. Beat in remaining 4 tablespoons butter, 1 tablespoon at a time, with wire whisk. Stir in ½ teaspoon pepper.

4) Remove string from beef before carving. Serve with sauce.

1 SERVING: Calories 350; Total Fat 20g (Saturated Fat 10g); Sodium 390mg; Total Carbohydrate 1g (Dietary Fiber 0g); Protein 40g. EXCHANGES: 6 Lean Meat, 1/2 Fat. CARBOHYDRATE CHOICES: 0.

Chocolate Chip Tree Cookies

PREP TIME: 50 MINUTES (READY IN 1 HOUR 15 MINUTES)
SERVINGS: 20 COOKIES

 EASY

1 roll (16.5 oz) Pillsbury® refrigerated chocolate chip cookies

½ cup semisweet chocolate chips

Miniature candy-coated chocolate candies

1) Heat oven to 350°F. In large bowl, break up cookie dough. Divide dough in half; wrap each half in plastic wrap. Freeze 10 minutes.

2) Shape half of dough into 10 (1-inch) balls. With floured fingers, roll each ball into 10-inch rope, about ¼ inch wide. Break off small piece from each rope for tree trunk. Carefully place ropes on ungreased cookie sheet. Starting at top of each rope, twist rope back and forth into tree shape, gradually making larger at bottom (rows of dough should touch). If rope breaks, press dough together. Place small piece at bottom of each tree for trunk. Repeat with remaining half of dough.

3) Bake 9 to 11 minutes or until edges are light golden brown. Cool 1 minute; remove from cookie sheet to cooling rack. Cool completely, about 15 minutes.

4) In small microwavable bowl, microwave chocolate chips uncovered on High 30 to 60 seconds, stirring once, until chips can be stirred smooth. Drizzle melted chocolate over cookies; place candies on chocolate to look like ornaments or lights.

1 COOKIE: Calories 100; Total Fat 4g (Saturated Fat 1g); Sodium 70mg; Total Carbohydrate 14g (Dietary Fiber 0g); Protein 0g. EXCHANGES: 1 Other Carbohydrate, 1 Fat. CARBOHYDRATE CHOICES: 1.

Snow-Capped Peppermint Sticks

PREP TIME: 10 MINUTES (READY IN 15 MINUTES)
SERVINGS: 12

 EASY   LOW FAT

3 oz white candy melts or coating wafers (½ cup)

⅓ cup white nonpareils

12 hard peppermint stick candies (5 inch)

1) Line cookie sheet with waxed paper. Melt candy coating as directed on package. In glass pie plate, place nonpareils.

2) Spoon melted coating over each peppermint stick, covering three-fourths of stick. Shake off excess coating. Sprinkle nonpareils over coated sticks. Place on cookie sheet. Let stand until coating is firm.

1 SERVING: Calories 131; Total Fat 3g (Saturated Fat 2g); Sodium 16mg; Total Carbohydrate 26g (Dietary Fiber 0g); Protein 0g. EXCHANGES: 2 Other Carbohydrate, 1/2 Fat. CARBOHYDRATE CHOICES: 2.

Holiday Shake

PREP TIME: 10 MINUTES (READY IN 10 MINUTES)
SERVINGS: 16 (1/2 CUP EACH)

 EASY

½ gallon vanilla ice cream, softened

½ cup bourbon

½ cup brandy

2 tablespoons vanilla

½ teaspoon ground cinnamon

½ teaspoon freshly grated nutmeg

Cinnamon sticks, if desired

Additional freshly grated nutmeg, if desired

1) In blender, place half each of the ice cream, bourbon, brandy, vanilla, cinnamon and nutmeg. Cover; blend on high speed about 30 seconds or until smooth. Pour into punch bowl. Repeat with remaining half of ingredients. Garnish with cinnamon sticks and sprinkle with additional nutmeg.

1 SERVING: Calories 191; Total Fat 9g (Saturated Fat 5g); Sodium 35mg; Total Carbohydrate 15g (Dietary Fiber 0g); Protein 3g. EXCHANGES: 1 Other Carbohydrate, 2 Fat. CARBOHYDRATE CHOICES: 1.

Shepherd's Pie

PREP TIME: 35 MINUTES (READY IN 50 MINUTES)
SERVINGS: 8

1 ½ lb lean (at least 80%) ground beef

1 medium onion, chopped (¾ cup)

2 large cloves garlic, finely chopped

1 package (8 oz) sliced fresh mushrooms (about 3 cups)

1 tablespoon oil

1 cup Cascadian Farm® frozen organic shelled edamame (from 10-oz bag), cooked, drained

½ cup grated carrot

1 tablespoon all-purpose flour

3 teaspoons beef bouillon granules

1 can (14.5 oz) stewed tomatoes, undrained

2 tablespoons balsamic vinegar

1 container (24 oz) refrigerated mashed potatoes

¼ cup chopped fresh parsley

2 tablespoons butter or margarine, softened

1) Heat oven to 400°F. Spray 3-quart casserole with cooking spray. In skillet, cook beef, onion and garlic over medium-high heat 5 minutes or until beef is cooked. Remove to bowl. Cook mushrooms in beef drippings until browned; add to beef mixture. Add oil, edamame and carrot to skillet. Stir in flour and bouillon. Cook and stir over medium heat 1 minute. Stir in tomatoes. Cook 3 minutes or until thickened. Stir in beef mixture and vinegar; heat through. Spoon into casserole.

2) Microwave potatoes as directed on package; stir in parsley and butter. Fill resealable bag with potatoes. Cut off one corner of bag; pipe potatoes over beef mixture. Bake uncovered 15 minutes or until lightly browned.

1 SERVING: Calories 320; Total Fat 17g (Saturated Fat 8g); Sodium 1223mg; Total Carbohydrate 20g (Dietary Fiber 3g); Protein 3g. EXCHANGES: 1 Starch, 1 Vegetable, 2-1/2 Lean Meat, 2 Fat. CARBOHYDRATE CHOICES: 1.

Gingerbread Ice Cream Sandwiches

PREP TIME: 1 HOUR (READY IN 4 HOURS)
SERVINGS: 9

e EASY

1 roll (16.5 oz) Pillsbury® refrigerated gingerbread cookies

½ cup miniature red and green candy-coated chocolate candies or candy sprinkles

2 ¼ cups ice cream (any flavor), slightly softened

1) Heat oven to 350°F. Cut cookie dough into 18 slices. On ungreased cookie sheet, place slices 3 inches apart.

2) Bake 10 to 15 minutes or until golden brown. Cool 1 minute; remove from cookie sheet to cooling rack. Cool completely, about 15 minutes. Cut 9 (12x9-inch) sheets of plastic wrap or waxed paper. In small shallow bowl, place candies.

3) For each sandwich cookie, spoon about ¼ cup ice cream onto bottom of 1 cookie. Top with second cookie, bottom side down; gently press together. Roll outer edge of ice cream in candies. Quickly wrap each sandwich in plastic wrap. Freeze about 3 hours or until firm. Remove from freezer 10 minutes before serving.

1 SERVING: Calories 340; Total Fat 16g (Saturated Fat 7g); Sodium 190mg; Total Carbohydrate 46g (Dietary Fiber 0g); Protein 3g. EXCHANGES: 1/2 Starch, 2-1/2 Other Carbohydrate, 3 Fat. CARBOHYDRATE CHOICES: 3.

Pomegranate Party Punch

PREP TIME: 5 MINUTES (READY IN 5 MINUTES)
SERVINGS: 32 (1/2 CUP EACH)

 EASY   LOW FAT

6 cups cranberry-pomegranate juice blend, chilled

1 bottle (16 oz) pomegranate juice, chilled

½ cup pomegranate-flavored liqueur, chilled

1 bottle (750 ml) vodka, chilled

1 bottle (750 ml) sparkling white wine or champagne, chilled

Fresh cranberries, if desired

Pomegranate seeds, if desired

1) In punch bowl, mix juices, liqueur and vodka. Just before serving, pour in sparkling wine. Garnish with cranberries and pomegranate seeds.

1 SERVING: Calories 111; Total Fat 0g (Saturated Fat 0g); Sodium 8mg; Total Carbohydrate 7g (Dietary Fiber 0g); Protein 0g. EXCHANGES: 1/2 Other Carbohydrate. CARBOHYDRATE CHOICES: 1/2.

Holiday Goat Cheese Log

PREP TIME: 15 MINUTES (READY IN 1 HOUR 15 MINUTES)
SERVINGS: 14 (2 TABLESPOONS EACH)

 EASY

1 log (10.5 oz) chèvre (goat) cheese

1 package (3 oz) cream cheese, softened

½ teaspoon cracked black pepper

⅓ cup chopped dried cranberries

¼ cup chopped fresh Italian (flat-leaf) parsley

1 tablespoon chopped fresh rosemary leaves

Assorted crackers

1) In medium bowl, mix cheeses and pepper. Using hands, roll mixture into 10-inch log.

2) In shallow dish, mix dried cranberries, parsley and chopped rosemary. Roll log in mixture, coating all sides and gently pressing to adhere. Cover; refrigerate at least 1 hour. Garnish with rosemary sprigs and fresh cranberries. Serve with crackers.

1 SERVING: Calories 84; Total Fat 6g (Saturated Fat 4g); Sodium 104mg; Total Carbohydrate 3g (Dietary Fiber 0g); Protein 4g. EXCHANGES: 1/2 High-Fat Meat, 1/2 Fat. CARBOHYDRATE CHOICES: 0.

Easy Gingerbread Friends

PREP TIME: 30 MINUTES (READY IN 50 MINUTES)
SERVINGS: 20 COOKIES

 EASY

1 roll (16.5 oz) Pillsbury® refrigerated gingerbread cookies

¼ cup all-purpose flour

½ cup white or creamy vanilla ready-to-spread frosting

100 red cinnamon candies or other small red candies

1) Heat oven to 350°F. Remove half of cookie dough from wrapper; refrigerate remaining dough until needed.

2) Sprinkle about ¼ cup flour onto work surface; coat sides of half of dough with flour. With rolling pin, roll out dough to ¼-inch thickness, adding additional flour as needed to prevent sticking. With floured 2 ½- to 3-inch gingerbread boy or girl cutter, cut out dough boys or girls. Gently brush excess flour from shapes; place 2 inches apart on ungreased cookie sheet. Repeat with remaining half of dough.

3) Bake 7 to 9 minutes or until light golden brown. Cool 1 minute; remove from cookie sheet to cooling racks. Cool completely. Place icing in piping bag, decorate with icing and candies for eyes and buttons, as desired.

1 COOKIE: Calories 140; Total Fat 6g (Saturated Fat 2.5g); Sodium 80mg; Total Carbohydrate 21g (Dietary Fiber 0g); Protein 0g. EXCHANGES: 1-1/2 Other Carbohydrate, 1 Fat. CARBOHYDRATE CHOICES: 1-1/2.

Ornament Cupcakes

PREP TIME: 20 MINUTES (READY IN 1 HOUR 20 MINUTES)
SERVINGS: 24 CUPCAKES

e EASY

1 box white cake mix with pudding in the mix

Water, vegetable oil and egg whites called for on cake box

6 cups powdered sugar

⅔ cup butter or margarine, softened

1 tablespoon vanilla

3 to 4 tablespoons milk

24 small candy canes

Red and green jelly beans

Red cinnamon candies

Red string licorice

Red and green candy-coated chocolate-covered sunflower seeds

1) Heat oven to 350°F. Place paper baking cup in each of 24 regular-size muffin cups or spray with cooking spray.

2) Make and bake cake as directed on box for cupcakes, using water, oil and egg whites. Cool 10 minutes; remove from pans to cooling racks. Cool completely, about 30 minutes.

3) In large bowl, mix powdered sugar and butter with spoon or electric mixer on low speed. Stir in vanilla and 3 tablespoons milk. Gradually beat in just enough remaining milk to make frosting smooth and spreadable. Frost cupcakes generously.

4) Create ornament designs using assorted candies. Use top of candy cane to create a "hook" on each cupcake.

1 CUPCAKE: Calories 325; Total Fat 11g (Saturated Fat 4g); Sodium 199mg; Total Carbohydrate 58g (Dietary Fiber 0.5g); Protein 1.5g. EXCHANGES: 1 Starch, 3 Other Carbohydrate, 2 Fat. CARBOHYDRATE CHOICES: 4.

Holiday Star Cookies

PREP TIME: 30 MINUTES (READY IN 45 MINUTES)
SERVINGS: 24 COOKIES

 EASY

1 roll (16.5 oz) Pillsbury® refrigerated sugar cookies

¼ to ½ cup all-purpose flour

Ready-to-spread frosting (any white variety)

Colored sugar or coarse white sparkling sugar

1) Heat oven to 350°F. In large bowl, break up cookie dough. Stir or knead in ¼ cup of the flour until well blended. Sprinkle about 1 tablespoon flour onto work surface; coat all sides of dough with flour. With rolling pin, roll out dough to ¼-inch thickness, adding additional flour as needed to prevent sticking.

2) With floured 2-inch star-shaped cookie cutter, cut out stars. Gently brush off excess flour. On ungreased cookie sheet, place stars 2 inches apart.

3) Bake 7 to 9 minutes or until light golden brown. Cool 1 minute; remove from cookie sheet to cooling rack. Cool completely, about 15 minutes. Frost cookies with frosting. Sprinkle with sugar.

1 COOKIE (UNFROSTED): Calories 90; Total Fat 4.5g (Saturated Fat 1.5g); Sodium 50mg; Total Carbohydrate 12g (Dietary Fiber 0g); Protein 1g. EXCHANGES: 1 Other Carbohydrate, 1 Fat. CARBOHYDRATE CHOICES: 1.

Eggnog Pudding

PREP TIME: 15 MINUTES (READY IN 3 HOURS 15 MINUTES)
SERVINGS: 4

EASY

⅓ cup granulated sugar

2 tablespoons cornstarch

¼ teaspoon salt

2 ¼ cups eggnog

3 egg yolks

2 tablespoons bourbon, if desired

¼ cup whipping cream

1 teaspoon powdered sugar

Ground nutmeg

1) In 2-quart heavy saucepan, mix granulated sugar, cornstarch and salt. Gradually stir in eggnog and egg yolks with whisk. Cook over medium heat, stirring constantly, until pudding thickens and coats back of spoon, about 5 minutes. Remove from heat; stir in bourbon. Spoon into small bowl. Place plastic wrap directly on surface of pudding. Refrigerate until set, about 3 hours.

2) Just before serving, in chilled small bowl, beat whipping cream and powdered sugar with electric mixer on high speed until stiff peaks form. Divide pudding evenly among 4 serving bowls. Top each with whipped cream; sprinkle with nutmeg.

1 SERVING: Calories 320; Total Fat 15g (Saturated Fat 8.5g); Sodium 237mg; Total Carbohydrate 34g (Dietary Fiber 0g); Protein 9g. EXCHANGES: 1 Other Carbohydrate, 1 Milk, 1-1/2 Fat. CARBOHYDRATE CHOICES: 1-1/2.

Spring & Summer Specialties

Breeze into seasonal menus with refreshing recipes, from Easter treats to Fourth of July favorites.

SAVORY VEGETABLE TART
PG. 260

BLUEBERRY-LEMONADE COOLERS
PG. 258

BALSAMIC-BROWN SUGAR
BAKED HAM
PG. 238

STRAWBERRY DAIQUIRI
COCKTAIL PIE
PG. 254

Balsamic-Brown Sugar Baked Ham

PREP TIME: 15 MINUTES (READY IN 2 HOURS 25 MINUTES)
SERVINGS: 16

 EASY

1 **fully cooked smoked bone-in ham (8 lb)**

1 **cup packed brown sugar**

2 **tablespoons balsamic or cider vinegar**

½ **teaspoon ground mustard**

   Orange slices, if desired

1) Heat oven to 325°F. On rack in shallow roasting pan, place ham, fat side up. Insert ovenproof meat thermometer so tip is in thickest part of ham and does not touch bone or rest in fat. Cover loosely; bake 1 hour 30 minutes.

2) Remove ham from oven. Pour drippings from pan. Remove any skin from ham. In small bowl, mix brown sugar, vinegar and mustard. Pat or brush mixture on ham.

3) Bake uncovered 20 to 30 minutes more or until thermometer reads 140°F. Cover loosely; let stand 10 minutes before carving. Garnish with orange slices.

1 SERVING: Calories 260; Total Fat 11g (Saturated Fat 3.5g); Sodium 1770mg; Total Carbohydrate 14g (Dietary Fiber 0g); Protein 27g. EXCHANGES: 1 Other Carbohydrate, 4 Lean Meat. CARBOHYDRATE CHOICES: 1.

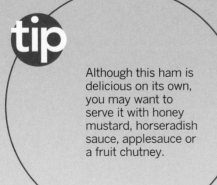

tip

Although this ham is delicious on its own, you may want to serve it with honey mustard, horseradish sauce, applesauce or a fruit chutney.

Coconut Cream Pie

PREP TIME:	20 MINUTES (READY IN 1 HOUR 35 MINUTES)
SERVINGS:	12

 EASY

1 Pillsbury® refrigerated pie crust, softened as directed on box

½ cup sugar

¼ cup cornstarch

2 cups half-and-half

4 egg yolks

3 tablespoons butter

1 cup flaked coconut

2 ½ teaspoons vanilla

2 cups whipping cream

⅓ cup sugar

Toasted coconut, if desired

1) Heat oven to 450°F. Make pie crust as directed on box for One-Crust Baked Shell using 9-inch glass pie plate. Cool completely.

2) Meanwhile, in large heavy saucepan, mix ½ cup sugar and the cornstarch. In small bowl, beat half-and-half and egg yolks with whisk. Gradually add egg mixture to sugar mixture; heat to boiling over medium heat, stirring constantly. Boil 1 minute; remove from heat. Stir in butter, 1 cup coconut and 1 teaspoon of the vanilla. Cover with plastic wrap, placing plastic wrap directly on custard; let stand 30 minutes. Spoon custard into cooled baked shell. Cover; refrigerate 30 minutes or until set.

3) In medium bowl, beat whipping cream with electric mixer on high speed until foamy; gradually add ⅓ cup sugar and remaining 1 ½ teaspoons vanilla, beating until soft peaks form. Spread whipped cream over pie. Sprinkle with toasted coconut. Store in refrigerator.

1 SERVING: Calories 384; Total Fat 28g (Saturated Fat 17g); Sodium 171mg; Total Carbohydrate 31g (Dietary Fiber 1g); Protein 4g. EXCHANGES: 1/2 Starch, 1-1/2 Other Carbohydrate, 1/2 High-Fat Meat, 4-1/2 Fat. CARBOHYDRATE CHOICES: 2.

Salmon with Lemon-Dill Butter

PREP TIME: 20 MINUTES (READY IN 20 MINUTES)
SERVINGS: 2

 EASY

3 tablespoons butter, softened

½ teaspoon finely chopped fresh dill weed

½ teaspoon grated lemon peel

½ teaspoon fresh lemon juice

2 salmon fillets (4 oz each)

1) Heat gas or charcoal grill. In small bowl, mix butter, dill weed, lemon peel and lemon juice; set aside until serving time.

2) Carefully brush oil on grill rack. Place salmon, skin side up, on grill over medium heat. Cover grill; cook 3 minutes. Turn skin side down. Cover grill; cook 8 to 10 minutes longer or until fish flakes easily with fork.

3) Serve salmon with lemon-dill butter.

1 SERVING: Calories 310; Total Fat 24g (Saturated Fat 13g); Sodium 190mg; Total Carbohydrate 0g (Dietary Fiber 0g); Protein 24g. EXCHANGES: 3-1/2 Lean Meat, 2-1/2 Fat. CARBOHYDRATE CHOICES: 0.

tip To broil salmon, place skin side down on broiler pan; broil with tops 4 to 6 inches from heat using times above as a guide, turning once.

Coconut-Macadamia Key Lime Pie

PREP TIME: 15 MINUTES (READY IN 3 HOURS 15 MINUTES)   ⓔ EASY
SERVINGS: 12

CRUST

- 1 cup macadamia nuts, finely chopped
- 2 cups graham cracker crumbs
- 1 cup flaked coconut, toasted
- ½ cup butter or margarine, melted

FILLING

- 2 cans (14 oz each) sweetened condensed milk (not evaporated)
- 1 tablespoon grated Key lime peel
- ½ cup Key lime juice
- 3 egg yolks
- 1 to 2 drops green food color, if desired
- 1 container (8 oz) frozen whipped topping, thawed

Garnish, if desired

Additional macadamia nuts, toasted

Additional toasted coconut

Key lime slices

1) Heat oven to 350°F. In small bowl, mix crust ingredients. Press in bottom and up side of 9-inch glass pie plate. Bake 12 minutes or until golden brown; cool.

2) In large bowl, beat condensed milk, grated lime peel, lime juice, egg yolks and food color with electric mixer on medium speed about 1 minute or until well blended. Pour into partially baked crust.

3) Bake 15 to 20 minutes or until center is set. Cool on cooling rack 15 minutes. Cover; refrigerate until chilled, at least 2 hours but no longer than 3 days. Spread whipped topping over pie. Garnish with toasted macadamia nuts, coconut and lime slices.

1 SERVING: Calories 529; Total Fat 29g (Saturated Fat 15g); Sodium 225mg; Total Carbohydrate 60g (Dietary Fiber 2g); Protein 8g. EXCHANGES: 1/2 Starch, 3-1/2 Other Carbohydrate, 1 High-Fat Meat, 4 Fat. CARBOHYDRATE CHOICES: 4.

Herb and Garlic Roast Leg of Lamb

PREP TIME: 15 MINUTES (READY IN 2 HOURS 50 MINUTES)
SERVINGS: 10

 EASY

1 boneless leg of lamb (5 to 6 lb)

¼ cup finely chopped fresh parsley

1 tablespoon chopped fresh or
1 teaspoon dried rosemary leaves,
crushed

1 tablespoon chopped fresh or
1 teaspoon dried thyme leaves,
crushed

3 tablespoons olive or vegetable oil

2 teaspoons kosher (coarse) salt

½ teaspoon pepper

2 cloves garlic, finely chopped

1) Heat oven to 325°F. Place lamb in shallow roasting pan (keep netting or string on lamb).

2) In small bowl, mix remaining ingredients. Spread mixture over entire surface of lamb. Insert meat thermometer so tip is in thickest part of lamb and does not rest in fat.

3) Roast uncovered 2 hours 5 minutes to 2 hours 15 minutes or until thermometer reads 140°F for medium-rare (155°F for medium). Cover loosely with foil. Let stand 15 to 20 minutes or until thermometer reads 145°F (160°F for medium). Remove netting or string before slicing. Serve with pan juices, if desired.

1 SERVING: Calories 370; Total Fat 20g (Saturated Fat 6g); Sodium 590mg; Total Carbohydrate 0g (Dietary Fiber 0g); Protein 48g. EXCHANGES: 7 Lean Meat. CARBOHYDRATE CHOICES: 0.

Chive-Egg Salad Mini Sandwiches

PREP TIME: 20 MINUTES (READY IN 2 HOURS 20 MINUTES)
SERVINGS: 12 MINI SANDWICHES

 EASY

6 thin slices (½ inch) English muffin toasting bread

1 cup refrigerated egg salad (½ pint)

⅓ cup reduced-fat chives-and-onion cream cheese (from 8-oz container)

¼ cup chopped fresh chives

1) Trim crusts from bread, creating squares; discard crusts. Spread ⅓ cup egg salad on each of 3 bread slices; top with remaining bread. Cut each sandwich in half diagonally; cut each half diagonally, making 4 triangles from each sandwich.

2) On 15-inch rectangular serving tray, arrange mini sandwiches, cut sides down, in 1 long row. Pick up each sandwich, 1 at a time, and spread cream cheese on 1 side of sandwich edges; sprinkle evenly with chives. Press chives lightly into cream cheese. Cover with plastic wrap; refrigerate 2 hours for easier serving.

1 MINI SANDWICH: Calories 90; Total Fat 6g (Saturated Fat 1.5g); Sodium 170mg; Total Carbohydrate 7g (Dietary Fiber 0g); Protein 3g. EXCHANGES: 1/2 Starch, 1 Fat. CARBOHYDRATE CHOICES: 1/2.

tip

English muffin toasting bread has a firmness that works beautifully for this recipe.

Extreme Cheese Tart with Apricot Cream

ROLAND PORTILLO | CAMBRIA, CA

Pillsbury Bake-Off®

PREP TIME: 25 MINUTES (READY IN 1 HOUR 20 MINUTES)
SERVINGS: 12

- 1 box Pillsbury® refrigerated pie crusts, softened as directed on box
- 1 ½ cups shredded mozzarella cheese (6 oz)
- 1 package (8 oz) cream cheese, softened
- ½ cup finely crumbled feta cheese (2 oz)
- ½ cup grated Parmigiano-Reggiano cheese (2 oz)
- 3 LAND O LAKES® Eggs
- ¼ cup chopped fresh parsley
- 2 tablespoons chopped fresh dill weed
- ½ teaspoon McCormick® Italian Seasoning
- ⅛ teaspoon McCormick® Ground Black Pepper
- 2 teaspoons Dijon mustard
- 1 tablespoon LAND O LAKES® Butter, melted
- 1 tablespoon Crisco® Pure Olive Oil
- 2 tablespoons McCormick® Sesame Seed
- ¼ cup Smucker's® Apricot Preserves
- ½ cup sour cream

1) Heat oven to 375°F. Place cookie sheet in oven. Unroll 1 pie crust; place in ungreased 10-inch tart pan with removable bottom. Press crust in bottom and up side of pan; trim and discard excess crust.

2) In large bowl, stir together mozzarella, cream cheese, feta and Parmigiano-Reggiano until well mixed. Add eggs, parsley, dill, Italian seasoning, pepper and mustard; blend well. Spread in crust-lined pan. Top with second crust; trim and discard excess crust. In small bowl, stir together melted butter and olive oil. Brush top crust with butter mixture. Sprinkle with sesame seed.

3) Place tart on cookie sheet in oven. Bake 35 to 45 minutes or until golden brown. Cool 15 minutes.

4) Meanwhile, in small bowl, combine preserves and sour cream; blend well. Cut warm tart into wedges; top with apricot cream.

1 SERVING: Calories 370; Total Fat 26g (Saturated Fat 13g); Sodium 510mg; Total Carbohydrate 23g (Dietary Fiber 0g); Protein 10g. EXCHANGES: 1 Starch, 1/2 Other Carbohydrate, 1 Medium-Fat Meat, 4 Fat. CARBOHYDRATE CHOICES: 1-1/2.

Orange Ham Rolls

PREP TIME:	15 MINUTES (READY IN 35 MINUTES)
SERVINGS:	8 ROLLS

 EASY

1 can (13.9 oz) Pillsbury® refrigerated orange flavor sweet rolls with icing

2 teaspoons Dijon mustard

½ lb sliced smoked ham (from deli)

8 slices (1 oz each) Swiss cheese

¼ cup orange marmalade

1) Heat oven to 350°F. Line cookie sheet with foil; spray foil with cooking spray.

2) Unroll log of dough onto waxed paper, but do not separate into rolls. Set icing aside for another use. Spread mustard evenly over dough. Top with ham and cheese, overlapping slices. Carefully reroll dough jelly-roll fashion, starting with long side. Cut along perforations into 8 rolls. Place 1 ½ inches apart on cookie sheet.

3) Bake 20 minutes or until golden brown. Spread marmalade over rolls. Serve warm.

1 ROLL: Calories 339; Total Fat 17g (Saturated Fat 7g); Sodium 637mg; Total Carbohydrate 33g (Dietary Fiber 1g); Protein 15g. EXCHANGES: 1 Starch, 1 Other Carbohydrate, 1-1/2 High-Fat Meat, 1 Fat. CARBOHYDRATE CHOICES: 0.

Herb-Crusted Pork Tenderloin

PREP TIME: 15 MINUTES (READY IN 50 MINUTES)
SERVINGS: 6

 EASY   **LOW FAT**

---

2   pork tenderloins (about ¾ lb each)

1   cup soft bread crumbs (about 1 ½ slices bread)

¼   cup chopped fresh parsley

2   tablespoons chopped fresh or 1 teaspoon dried thyme leaves, crushed

1   tablespoon olive or vegetable oil

½   teaspoon salt

½   teaspoon fennel seed

¼   teaspoon coarse ground black pepper

2   cloves garlic, finely chopped

1) Heat oven to 450°F. Spray shallow roasting pan and rack with cooking spray. Place pork tenderloins on rack in pan.

2) In small bowl, mix remaining ingredients. Spoon herb mixture evenly over pork.

3) Bake 20 minutes; remove foil. Bake uncovered 10 minutes longer or until meat thermometer inserted in center reads 145°F. Cover pork loosely with foil and let stand 3 minutes before slicing.

1 SERVING: Calories 230; Total Fat 8g (Saturated Fat 2g); Sodium 400mg; Total Carbohydrate 13g (Dietary Fiber 0g); Protein 28g. EXCHANGES: 1 Starch, 3-1/2 Very Lean Meat, 1 Fat. CARBOHYDRATE CHOICES: 1.

Lemon Crumb Tart

JACKIE TERMONT | RUTHER GLEN, VA

BAKE-OFF® CONTEST 45, 2012

PREP TIME: 15 MINUTES (READY IN 2 HOURS 20 MINUTES)
SERVINGS: 12

EASY

- 1 roll Pillsbury® refrigerated sugar cookie dough
- 1 cup Pillsbury BEST® All Purpose Flour
- ¾ cup Hershey's® premier white baking chips
- 1 jar (10 oz) lemon curd

1) Heat oven to 350°F. Let cookie dough stand at room temperature 10 minutes to soften. In large bowl, knead cookie dough and flour with hands until well blended. Stir in white chips. Reserve 1 cup of the mixture for topping. Press remaining mixture in 10- or 11-inch tart pan with removable bottom.

2) Bake 13 to 18 minutes or until edges just begin to brown. Cool 5 minutes. In small microwavable bowl, microwave lemon curd on High 20 to 30 seconds or until softened; stir until smooth and of spreading consistency. Spread to within 1 inch of crust edge. Sprinkle reserved crumb mixture evenly over top of tart.

3) Bake an additional 20 to 30 minutes or until light golden brown. Cool completely, about 1 hour. To serve, cut into 12 wedges. Store covered.

1 SERVING: Calories 340; Total Fat 12g (Saturated Fat 6g); Sodium 170mg; Total Carbohydrate 54g (Dietary Fiber 0g); Protein 3g. EXCHANGES: 1 Starch, 2-1/2 Other Carbohydrate, 2-1/2 Fat. CARBOHYDRATE CHOICES: 3-1/2.

Lime Cooler Mini Ice Cream Pies

PREP TIME: 20 MINUTES (READY IN 4 HOURS 30 MINUTES)
SERVINGS: 12

 EASY

1 box Pillsbury® refrigerated pie crusts, softened as directed on box

1 cup lime sherbet

1 cup vanilla ice cream

½ cup frozen (thawed) whipped topping

1) Heat oven to 450°F. Remove pie crusts from pouches; unroll on work surface. Cut 6 (4-inch) rounds from each crust. Firmly press each round in bottom and up side of each of 12 ungreased regular-size muffin cups. Prick with fork. Bake 8 to 10 minutes or until lightly browned. Cool completely, about 1 hour.

2) In small bowl, gently mix sherbet and ice cream. Divide mixture evenly among pie crust cups. Freeze uncovered until firm, about 3 hours.

3) Remove from freezer 5 minutes before serving. Garnish with whipped topping.

1 SERVING: Calories 190; Total Fat 10g (Saturated Fat 5g); Sodium 190mg; Total Carbohydrate 23g (Dietary Fiber 0g); Protein 1g. EXCHANGES: 1/2 Starch, 1 Other Carbohydrate, 2 Fat. CARBOHYDRATE CHOICES: 1-1/2.

Peach-Glazed Ham

PREP TIME: 5 MINUTES (READY IN 8 HOURS 20 MINUTES)
SERVINGS: 14

 EASY   LOW FAT

1 fully cooked smoked bone-in ham (7 lb)

¾ cup peach preserves

¾ cup packed brown sugar

½ cup Dijon mustard

¼ cup white cranberry and peach juice

Fresh peach slices, if desired

1) Spray 7-quart oval slow cooker with cooking spray. Remove excess fat from ham. Make cuts about ½ inch apart and ¼ inch deep in diamond pattern around top and sides of ham. Place ham in slow cooker. In small bowl, mix preserves, brown sugar, mustard and cranberry juice until smooth. Spread or brush mixture over ham in slow cooker.

2) Cover; cook on Low heat setting 8 hours or until meat thermometer reads 140°F. Remove ham from slow cooker; cover with foil and let stand 10 to 15 minutes before carving.

3) Meanwhile, pour juices from slow cooker into 2-quart saucepan. Heat to simmering; cook until slightly thickened. Serve ham with sauce. Garnish serving platter with peach slices.

1 SERVING: Calories 274; Total Fat 7g (Saturated Fat 2g); Sodium 1380mg; Total Carbohydrate 27g (Dietary Fiber 0g); Protein 25g. EXCHANGES: 2 Other Carbohydrate, 3-1/2 Lean Meat. CARBOHYDRATE CHOICES: 2.

Pineapple-Coconut Bread Pudding

PREP TIME: 15 MINUTES (READY IN 3 HOURS 45 MINUTES)
SERVINGS: 10

 EASY

1 tablespoon butter, softened

8 eggs

2 cans (13.5 oz each) coconut milk (not cream of coconut)

1 ½ cups flaked coconut

1 cup chopped dried pineapple

¾ cup sugar

2 tablespoons vanilla

¼ teaspoon salt

1 loaf (1 lb) French bread, cut into 1-inch cubes

1 can (8 oz) unsweetened crushed pineapple in juice, drained, juice reserved

1 tablespoon cornstarch

1 tablespoon honey

2 tablespoons dark rum or 2 teaspoons rum extract

¼ cup butter, cubed

Toasted coconut, if desired

1) Grease bottom and side of 6-quart slow cooker with 1 tablespoon butter. In very large bowl, mix eggs, coconut milk, 1 ½ cups coconut, dried pineapple, sugar, vanilla and salt. Add bread cubes; toss to coat. Pour mixture into slow cooker. Let stand 30 minutes or cover and refrigerate up to 18 hours.

2) Cover; cook on High heat setting 1 hour. Reduce heat setting to Low. Cover; cook 2 hours longer or until puffed and set.

3) In 2-cup microwavable measuring cup, place reserved pineapple juice and enough water to equal ¾ cup. Stir in cornstarch and honey with wire whisk until smooth. Microwave uncovered on High 2 minutes 30 seconds or until thickened. Stir in rum. Microwave on High 30 seconds. Add crushed pineapple and ¼ cup butter; stir until butter is melted. Serve warm bread pudding with pineapple sauce. Garnish with toasted coconut.

1 SERVING: Calories 583; Total Fat 30.5g (Saturated Fat 23g); Sodium 452mg; Total Carbohydrate 66.5g (Dietary Fiber 3g); Protein 12.5g. EXCHANGES: 1-1/2 Starch, 1 Fruit, 2 Other Carbohydrate, 1 Medium-Fat Meat, 5 Fat. CARBOHYDRATE CHOICES: 4-1/2.

Peach-Plum Cobbler

PREP TIME: 20 MINUTES (READY IN 4 HOURS 35 MINUTES)
SERVINGS: 8

 EASY

1 ½ lb peaches, peeled, sliced

1 ½ lb plums, sliced

 ¾ cup granulated sugar

4 ½ teaspoons cornstarch

1 ½ teaspoons fresh lemon juice

 ½ teaspoon almond extract

2 ¼ cups baking mix

 ½ cup milk

 ¼ cup butter or margarine, melted

2 tablespoons cinnamon-sugar

 ⅓ cup sliced almonds, toasted

1) Spray 3 ½- to 4-quart slow cooker with cooking spray. In large bowl, mix peaches, plums, ½ cup of the granulated sugar, the cornstarch, lemon juice and almond extract. Transfer mixture to slow cooker.

2) In medium bowl, stir baking mix, remaining ¼ cup granulated sugar, the milk and butter just until blended. Drop heaping tablespoons of dough into 8 mounds on fruit in slow cooker.

3) Cover; cook on High heat setting 3 hours 30 minutes or until topping is dry in center and fruit is bubbly.

4) Sprinkle cinnamon-sugar over topping. Cover; cook 30 minutes longer. Let stand 15 minutes before serving. Sprinkle with almonds.

1 SERVING: Calories 397; Total Fat 13.5g (Saturated Fat 5.5g); Sodium 477mg; Total Carbohydrate 70g (Dietary Fiber 5g); Protein 5g. EXCHANGES: 1-1/2 Starch, 1-1/2 Fruit, 1-1/2 Other Carbohydrate, 2-1/2 Fat. CARBOHYDRATE CHOICES: 4-1/2.

Ultimate Fresh Fruit Tart

PREP TIME: 30 MINUTES (READY IN 5 HOURS)
SERVINGS: 10

1 Pillsbury® refrigerated pie crust, softened as directed on box

2 oz unsweetened baking chocolate

1 ¼ cups whipping cream

6 tablespoons butter

⅓ cup sugar

1 tablespoon cornstarch

4 egg yolks, beaten

3 teaspoons vanilla

1 ½ cups fresh fruit (such as raspberries, blackberries, sliced nectarines and kiwifruit)

½ cup apricot jam

1 tablespoon water

1) Heat oven to 450°F. Place pie crust in 10-inch tart pan with removable bottom; prick bottom and side with fork. Bake 10 minutes. Reduce oven temperature to 350°F; bake 10 minutes longer or until golden. In small saucepan, melt chocolate and ¼ cup of the whipping cream over low heat. Stir until smooth; spread in crust. Refrigerate. In heavy 2-quart saucepan, cook butter, sugar and cornstarch over medium-high heat, stirring constantly, until mixture thickens and boils; boil 1 minute. Stir small amount of sugar mixture into egg yolks. Slowly stir egg mixture into remaining sugar mixture in saucepan. Cook 1 minute over low heat. Remove from heat; stir in vanilla. Cover; refrigerate 3 hours.

2) In small bowl, beat remaining 1 cup whipping cream with electric mixer on high speed until stiff peaks form. Fold cold egg mixture into whipped cream with whisk. Spoon filling into crust. Top with fruit. In small microwavable bowl, microwave jam and water uncovered on High 1 minute. Brush jam mixture over fruit. Refrigerate 1 hour 30 minutes.

1 SERVING: Calories 384; Total Fat 28g (Saturated Fat 16g); Sodium 186mg; Total Carbohydrate 32g (Dietary Fiber 2g); Protein 3g. EXCHANGES: 1/2 Starch, 1-1/2 Other Carbohydrate, 5-1/2 Fat. CARBOHYDRATE CHOICES: 2.

Plum Crostata

| PREP TIME: | 20 MINUTES (READY IN 1 HOUR 55 MINUTES) | EASY |
| SERVINGS: | 8 | |

1 ½ lb fresh plums, sliced

½ cup sugar

⅓ cup plum preserves

1 teaspoon vanilla

¼ teaspoon ground allspice

1 Pillsbury® refrigerated pie crust, softened as directed on box

1 tablespoon all-purpose flour

1 egg

1 tablespoon water

1 tablespoon sugar

1) In large bowl, stir together plums, ½ cup sugar, the plum preserves, vanilla and allspice. Let stand 30 minutes, stirring occasionally.

2) Heat oven to 425°F. Line cookie sheet with cooking parchment paper; spray paper with cooking spray. Unroll pie crust on cookie sheet; roll into 12-inch round.

3) Drain plum mixture, reserving liquid. In same bowl, toss plums with flour. Arrange plums in center of crust, leaving 3-inch border. Fold crust up and over plums, pleating as you go. In small bowl, beat egg and water. Brush crust with egg mixture; sprinkle with 1 tablespoon sugar.

4) Bake 25 minutes or until filling is bubbly and crust is golden. Cool on cooling rack 15 minutes before serving. Meanwhile, in 1-quart saucepan, heat reserved plum liquid to boiling over medium heat. Boil 1 to 2 minutes or until slightly thickened. Cool slightly. Brush 1 to 2 tablespoons plum syrup over exposed fruit in center of tart. Serve immediately with remaining plum syrup.

1 SERVING: Calories 246; Total Fat 8g (Saturated Fat 3g); Sodium 147mg; Total Carbohydrate 45g (Dietary Fiber 1g); Protein 2g. EXCHANGES: 1 Starch, 1/2 Fruit, 1-1/2 Other Carbohydrate, 1-1/2 Fat. CARBOHYDRATE CHOICES: 3.

Carrot Cake Tart

LAURA MAJCHRZAK | HUNT VALLEY, MD

Pillsbury Bake-Off®

BAKE-OFF® CONTEST 45, 2012

PREP TIME: 30 MINUTES (READY IN 3 HOURS 10 MINUTES)
SERVINGS: 12

e EASY

TART

- 1 Pillsbury® refrigerated pie crust, softened as directed on box
- ¼ cup LAND O LAKES® Unsalted Butter, melted, cooled slightly
- 1 cup packed light brown sugar
- ⅓ cup light corn syrup
- 2 LAND O LAKES® Eggs
- ⅔ cup Pillsbury BEST® All Purpose Flour
- 1 teaspoon McCormick® Ground Cinnamon
- ½ teaspoon baking soda
- ½ teaspoon salt
- 1 ½ cups shredded carrots
- ½ cup raisins
- ½ cup Fisher® Chef's Naturals® Chopped Pecans

FROSTING

- 2 packages (3 oz each) cream cheese, softened
- 2 tablespoons LAND O LAKES® Unsalted Butter, softened
- 1 ½ cups powdered sugar
- ½ teaspoon McCormick® Pure Vanilla Extract

GARNISH

- 12 whole Fisher® Praline Pecans
- ½ cup Hershey's® caramel syrup
- 12 carrot curls, if desired

1) Heat oven to 350°F. Place large cookie sheet on middle oven rack. Unroll pie crust; place in ungreased 10-inch tart pan with removable bottom. Press crust firmly against bottom and side of pan; trim edges.

2) In large bowl, beat ¼ cup melted butter, brown sugar and corn syrup with electric mixer on medium speed until blended; beat in eggs until blended. Add flour, cinnamon, baking soda and salt; beat on low speed until blended. Stir in carrots, raisins and chopped pecans. Spread mixture evenly over bottom of crust-lined pan. Place tart on cookie sheet in oven.

3) Bake 30 to 40 minutes or until filling is set and deep golden brown. Cool completely on cooling rack, about 1 hour. Remove side of pan; place tart on serving plate.

4) In medium bowl, beat cream cheese and 2 tablespoons butter with electric mixer on high speed until smooth. Add powdered sugar and vanilla; beat on low speed until creamy. Frost cooled tart. Place praline pecans evenly around edge of tart. Refrigerate 1 hour.

5) To serve, cut into 12 wedges. Drizzle each serving with 2 teaspoons caramel syrup; garnish each with carrot curl. Store covered in refrigerator.

1 SERVING: Calories 500; Total Fat 22g (Saturated Fat 9g); Sodium 380mg; Total Carbohydrate 71g (Dietary Fiber 2g); Protein 4g. EXCHANGES: 1 Starch, 3-1/2 Other Carbohydrate, 4-1/2 Fat. CARBOHYDRATE CHOICES: 5.

tip

To make carrot curls, cut thin strips of peeled, medium-size carrots with a vegetable peeler. Roll each strip and fasten with a toothpick. Chill in ice water 2 to 3 hours. Remove toothpicks before garnishing.

Strawberry Daiquiri Cocktail Pie

PREP TIME: 20 MINUTES (READY IN 3 HOURS 20 MINUTES)
SERVINGS: 8

 EASY

1 Pillsbury® refrigerated pie crust, softened as directed on box

2 cups strawberry sorbet, softened

2 containers (6 oz each) Yoplait® 99% Fat Free strawberry yogurt

1 cup frozen strawberries, thawed, chopped

¼ cup rum

½ cup fresh strawberries

¼ cup sugar

1) Heat oven to 450°F. Place pie crust in ungreased 9-inch pie plate. Press crust firmly against side and bottom; flute. Bake 9 to 11 minutes or until light brown. Cool completely, about 1 hour.

2) Mix sorbet, yogurt, chopped strawberries and rum until blended. Spoon into crust. Freeze uncovered until firm, about 3 hours.

3) Let stand at room temperature 10 minutes before cutting. Roll moistened fresh strawberries in sugar; garnish each slice of pie with sugared strawberries.

1 SERVING: Calories 380; Total Fat 12g (Saturated Fat 5g); Sodium 290mg; Total Carbohydrate 59g (Dietary Fiber 1g); Protein 3g. EXCHANGES: 1 Starch, 3 Other Carbohydrate, 2-1/2 Fat. CARBOHYDRATE CHOICES: 4.

Rice Pudding with Cherries

PREP TIME: 10 MINUTES (READY IN 2 HOURS 55 MINUTES)
SERVINGS: 16 (1/2 CUP EACH)

 EASY

2 ½ cups milk

1 cup sugar

2 ½ cups whipping cream

1 ½ cups uncooked short-grain Arborio rice

1 ½ cups dried cherries

2 teaspoons vanilla

½ teaspoon almond extract

Grated orange peel, if desired

Sliced almonds, if desired

1) Spray 4- to 5-quart slow cooker with cooking spray. In 2-quart saucepan, heat milk to simmering over medium heat. Stir in sugar until dissolved. Remove from heat. In slow cooker, mix milk mixture and whipping cream with whisk. Stir in rice.

2) Cover; cook on Low heat setting 2 hours 30 minutes, stirring twice, until pudding is just set in center.

3) Stir cherries, vanilla and almond extract into pudding. Cover; cook 15 minutes longer. Serve warm, or cool completely, then cover and refrigerate at least 3 hours until chilled. Garnish with orange peel and almonds. Store covered in refrigerator.

1 SERVING: Calories 315; Total Fat 15g (Saturated Fat 9.5g); Sodium 33mg; Total Carbohydrate 41g (Dietary Fiber 3.5g); Protein 4.5g. EXCHANGES: 1 Starch, 1/2 Fruit, 1 Other Carbohydrate, 3 Fat. CARBOHYDRATE CHOICES: 2-1/2.

Orange-Glazed Ham

PREP TIME: 10 MINUTES (READY IN 1 HOUR 50 MINUTES)
SERVINGS: 10

 EASY   LOW FAT

1 fully cooked smoked boneless ham (4 lb)

1 cup orange marmalade

1 cup orange juice

¼ cup packed brown sugar

2 tablespoons creamy Dijon mustard-mayonnaise spread

1 teaspoon ground ginger

1) Heat oven to 350°F. Line 13x9-inch pan with foil. Place ham in pan.

2) In small bowl, stir together remaining ingredients; spoon mixture over ham.

3) Bake uncovered on lowest oven rack 1 hour 30 minutes, basting with pan juices every 30 minutes. Let stand 10 minutes before slicing.

1 SERVING: Calories 275; Total Fat 5g (Saturated Fat 2g); Sodium 2168mg; Total Carbohydrate 35g (Dietary Fiber 0g); Protein 26g. EXCHANGES: 2-1/2 Other Carbohydrate, 4 Very Lean Meat. CARBOHYDRATE CHOICES: 2-1/2.

Blueberry-White Chocolate Cream Ginger Tart

ALICE WILSON | FAIRPORT, NY

BAKE-OFF® CONTEST 45, 2012

PREP TIME: 20 MINUTES (READY IN 2 HOURS 20 MINUTES)
SERVINGS: 8

🅔 EASY

- 1 roll Pillsbury® refrigerated sugar cookie dough
- ¼ cup Pillsbury BEST® All Purpose Flour
- 1 tablespoon McCormick® Ground Ginger
- 1 tablespoon McCormick® Crystallized Ginger
- 1 teaspoon McCormick® Ground Cinnamon
- 1 teaspoon McCormick® Ground Nutmeg
- 1 bag (12 oz) Hershey's® premier white baking chips
- 1 package (8 oz) cream cheese, softened
- ¼ cup heavy whipping cream
- 2 teaspoons grated lemon peel
- 2 cups fresh blueberries

1) Heat oven to 350°F. Let cookie dough stand at room temperature 10 minutes to soften. Spray 12-inch pizza pan with Crisco® Original No-Stick Cooking Spray.

2) In medium bowl, break up cookie dough. Add flour, ground ginger, crystallized ginger, cinnamon and nutmeg. Mix with wooden spoon or knead with hands, until well blended. Press dough evenly in bottom of pan.

3) Bake 15 to 20 minutes or until golden brown. Cool completely, about 30 minutes.

4) In medium microwavable bowl, microwave white chips on High 1 minute to 1 minute 45 seconds, stirring every 30 seconds, until smooth. Add cream cheese, cream and lemon peel; beat with electric mixer on medium speed until smooth. Spread mixture over cooled crust. Arrange blueberries over cream cheese mixture; press into filling.

5) Refrigerate 1 hour. Cut into wedges. Store in refrigerator.

1 SERVING: Calories 640; Total Fat 34g (Saturated Fat 20g); Sodium 370mg; Total Carbohydrate 76g (Dietary Fiber 1g); Protein 7g. EXCHANGES: 2 Starch, 3 Other Carbohydrate, 6-1/2 Fat. CARBOHYDRATE CHOICES: 5.

Strawberries & Cream Sugar Cookie Sandwiches

CHRISTENA ROOKS | CINCINNATI, OH

BAKE-OFF® CONTEST 45, 2012

PREP TIME: 1 HOUR 15 MINUTES (READY IN 1 HOUR 15 MINUTES)
SERVINGS: 12

1 package Pillsbury® Ready to Bake!™ refrigerated sugar cookies

1 package (2 oz) Fisher® Chef's Naturals® Pecan Chips (½ cup)

1 container (8 oz) mascarpone cheese

2 tablespoons powdered sugar

½ teaspoon McCormick® Pure Vanilla Extract

¼ cup Smucker's® Strawberry Preserves

2 tablespoons Hershey's® milk chocolate baking chips

2 tablespoons Hershey's® premier white baking chips

6 small strawberries, cut in half

1) Heat oven to 350°F. Shape cookies into balls; roll 12 of the cookies in pecans, pressing into dough. Place all of the cookies 2 inches apart on large ungreased cookie sheets.

2) Bake 11 to 15 minutes or until golden brown. Cool on cookie sheets 2 minutes; remove from cookie sheets to cooling racks. Cool completely, about 20 minutes.

3) Meanwhile, in small bowl, stir together mascarpone, powdered sugar and vanilla until blended. Spread 1 heaping tablespoonful mascarpone mixture on bottom of each plain cookie; top each with 1 teaspoon preserves. Top with pecan-coated cookies, bottom side down; press slightly.

4) In small resealable freezer plastic bag, place milk chocolate chips; seal bag. Microwave on High 20 to 30 seconds or until softened. Gently squeeze bag until chocolate is smooth; cut off tiny corner of bag. Repeat with another bag and white chips.

5) Squeeze bag to drizzle milk chocolate and white chocolate over top of cookie sandwiches. Top each sandwich with strawberry half. Store in refrigerator.

1 SERVING: Calories 260; Total Fat 13g (Saturated Fat 4g); Sodium 105mg; Total Carbohydrate 32g (Dietary Fiber 0g); Protein 1g. EXCHANGES: 1/2 Starch, 1-1/2 Other Carbohydrate, 2-1/2 Fat. CARBOHYDRATE CHOICES: 2.

Blueberry-Lemonade Coolers

PREP TIME: 10 MINUTES (READY IN 30 MINUTES)
SERVINGS: 8

 EASY   LOW FAT

1 pint fresh blueberries

½ cup sugar

1 can (12 oz) frozen lemonade concentrate, thawed

3 ½ cups water

2 cups vodka

8 lemon slices

1) In large bowl, crush blueberries with sugar, using potato masher. Set aside 20 minutes for syrup to form. Place strainer over small bowl; pour berry mixture into strainer. Press mixture with back of spoon to get as much syrup as possible; discard pulp.

2) In large pitcher, stir together blueberry syrup, lemonade concentrate, 3 ½ cups water and the vodka.

3) To serve, fill highball glasses with ice. Pour blueberry-lemonade mixture into glasses. Garnish with lemon slices. Serve immediately.

1 SERVING: Calories 280; Total Fat 0g (Saturated Fat 0g); Sodium 5mg; Total Carbohydrate 38g (Dietary Fiber 1g); Protein 0g. EXCHANGES: 2-1/2 Other Carbohydrate. CARBOHYDRATE CHOICES: 2-1/2.

Star-Spangled Blueberry Squares

PREP TIME: 25 MINUTES (READY IN 3 HOURS)
SERVINGS: 18

 EASY

2 cans (8 oz each) Pillsbury®
refrigerated crescent dinner rolls or
2 cans (8 oz each) Pillsbury®
Crescent Recipe Creations®
refrigerated seamless dough sheet

½ cup sugar

2 packages (8 oz each) cream cheese

2 eggs

1 can (21 oz) blueberry pie filling with
more fruit

tip

The dough scraps can
be sprinkled with
cinnamon-sugar,
baked and used to
top pudding or ice
cream.

1) Heat oven to 375°F. Unroll 1 can of dough (if using crescent rolls, press perforations to seal). Using 1-inch and 2 ¼-inch star-shaped cookie cutters, cut 18 stars of each size out of dough. Place stars on ungreased cookie sheet; sprinkle with 1 tablespoon of the sugar. Set aside. Unroll remaining can of dough. Press in ungreased 13x9-inch pan. Bake about 5 minutes or until crust is puffed.

2) In large bowl, beat remaining sugar, the cream cheese and eggs with electric mixer on high speed until well blended. Gently spread over partially baked crust. Bake dessert and star cutouts about 7 minutes or until stars are puffed and edges are light golden brown. Remove stars to cooling rack. Bake dessert 9 to 13 minutes longer or until cream cheese mixture is set. Cool 40 minutes. Carefully spread blueberry filling over cream cheese layer. Cover; refrigerate at least 2 hours until completely chilled. Cut into 6 rows by 3 rows. Top each square with stars as desired. Store any leftover stars in an airtight container. Cover and refrigerate any remaining dessert.

1 SERVING: Calories 270; Total Fat 15g (Saturated Fat 7g); Sodium 280mg; Total Carbohydrate 30g (Dietary Fiber 0g); Protein 4g. EXCHANGES: 1/2 Starch, 1-1/2 Other Carbohydrate, 1/2 High-Fat Meat, 2 Fat. CARBOHYDRATE CHOICES: 2.

Savory Vegetable Tart

HOLLY DEAK | BROOKLINE, MA

BAKE-OFF® CONTEST 45, 2012

PREP TIME: 35 MINUTES (READY IN 1 HOUR 50 MINUTES)
SERVINGS: 6

1 Pillsbury® refrigerated pie crust, softened as directed on box

3 tablespoons Crisco® 100% Extra Virgin Olive Oil

1 ½ cups chopped onions

2 cloves garlic, sliced

2 small unpeeled red potatoes, cut into thin slices

3 small plum (Roma) tomatoes, cut into ¼-inch slices

1 small unpeeled Japanese (or other small) eggplant (about 5 oz), cut into ¼-inch slices

1 small zucchini, cut into ¼-inch slices

½ teaspoon salt

¼ teaspoon McCormick® Ground Black Pepper

¼ teaspoon McCormick® Thyme Leaves

3 oz Gruyère cheese, shredded (¾ cup)

¼ cup Progresso® panko bread crumbs

1) Heat oven to 375°F. Make pie crust as directed on box for One-Crust Filled Pie using 9-inch glass pie plate; flute edge.

2) In 10-inch skillet, heat 2 tablespoons of the oil over medium-low heat until hot. Add onions; cook 10 minutes, stirring occasionally, or until onions are slightly golden in color. Add garlic; cook an additional minute. Spread onions and garlic evenly in bottom of pie crust. Arrange vegetables in tight spiral pattern over onion mixture, alternating vegetables. Sprinkle with salt, pepper and thyme. Drizzle with remaining 1 tablespoon of oil. Cover with foil.

3) Bake 30 minutes. Remove foil; bake 15 minutes. Sprinkle vegetables with cheese and bread crumbs. Bake an additional 10 to 20 minutes or until cheese begins to brown.

4) Cool 15 minutes. To serve, cut into wedges.

1 SERVING: Calories 370; Total Fat 20g (Saturated Fat 7g); Sodium 430mg; Total Carbohydrate 39g (Dietary Fiber 4g); Protein 8g. EXCHANGES: 2 Starch, 1-1/2 Vegetable, 4 Fat. CARBOHYDRATE CHOICES: 2-1/2.

tip

One and one half cups sliced and quartered eggplant can be substituted for the Japanese eggplant.

Turkey Brats with Sweet Slaw

PREP TIME: 15 MINUTES (READY IN 15 MINUTES)
SERVINGS: 5

 EASY

5 fresh turkey bratwurst

5 bratwurst or hoagie buns, split

5 teaspoons honey mustard

1 ¼ cups sweet cabbage salad (from deli)

1) Heat gas or charcoal grill. Place bratwurst on grill over medium heat. Cover grill; cook 6 to 8 minutes, turning occasionally, until bratwurst are no longer pink in center. During last 1 to 2 minutes of cooking time, place buns, cut sides down, on grill; cook until lightly toasted.

2) Spread 1 teaspoon mustard on each bun bottom. Top each with bratwurst and ¼ cup cabbage salad; cover with bun tops.

1 SERVING: Calories 440; Total Fat 25g (Saturated Fat 9g); Sodium 1110mg; Total Carbohydrate 29g (Dietary Fiber 1g); Protein 23g. EXCHANGES: 1-1/2 Starch, 1/2 Other Carbohydrate, 1/2 Vegetable, 2-1/2 Lean Meat, 3-1/2 Fat. CARBOHYDRATE CHOICES: 2.

Tomato Basil Bruschetta

PREP TIME: 10 MINUTES (READY IN 10 MINUTES)
SERVINGS: 16 APPETIZERS

 EASY   LOW FAT

1 can (14.5 oz) Muir Glen® organic diced tomatoes, drained

2 tablespoons chopped fresh basil leaves

1 tablespoon extra-virgin olive oil

1 clove garlic, finely chopped

16 slices (½ inch thick) baguette (about 6 oz), toasted

1) In medium bowl, mix tomatoes, basil, olive oil and garlic.

2) Spoon mixture onto toasted bread slices. Serve immediately.

1 APPETIZER: Calories 40; Total Fat 1g (Saturated Fat 0g); Sodium 85mg; Total Carbohydrate 6g (Dietary Fiber 0g); Protein 1g. EXCHANGES: 1/2 Starch. CARBOHYDRATE CHOICES: 1/2.

Cookies, Bars & More

What's not to love? Indulge in decadent brownies, fudge, toffee, pinwheels and more!

GINGERBREAD PINWHEELS
PG. 281

PEANUT BUTTER CREME
COOKIE CUPS
PG. 278

CHEWY PEANUT
BUTTER-CARAMEL BARS
PG. 286

MAPLE BROWN SUGAR
GRANOLA COOKIES
PG. 282

Sweet-and-Salty Truffle Bars

PREP TIME: 10 MINUTES (READY IN 1 HOUR 10 MINUTES)
SERVINGS: 24 BARS

 EASY

1 roll (16.5 oz) Pillsbury® refrigerated sugar cookies

1 package (11.5 or 12 oz) semisweet chocolate chunks (2 cups)

2 cups small pretzel twists, coarsely chopped

1 cup caramel bits (from 11-oz bag)

1 tablespoon whipping cream

¾ teaspoon coarse sea salt

1) Heat oven to 350°F. In ungreased 13x9-inch pan, break up cookie dough. With floured fingers, press dough evenly in bottom of pan.

2) Bake 20 to 25 minutes or until light golden brown. Immediately sprinkle chocolate chunks over crust. Let stand 5 minutes or until chocolate is melted. Spread chocolate with knife and sprinkle with chopped pretzels.

3) In small microwavable bowl, microwave caramel bits and whipping cream on High 1 to 2 minutes, stirring every 30 seconds, until mixture can be stirred smooth. Drizzle caramel mixture over bars. Sprinkle with salt. Cool completely. Cut into 6 rows by 4 rows.

1 BAR: Calories 214; Total Fat 9g (Saturated Fat 4g); Sodium 232mg; Total Carbohydrate 33g (Dietary Fiber 1g); Protein 2g. EXCHANGES: 2 Other Carbohydrate, 2 Fat. CARBOHYDRATE CHOICES: 2.

tip

If you don't have bite-sized caramel bits on hand, you can chop regular-sized caramels into small pieces. Use a sharp paring knife to make clean, even cuts.

Chocolate-Hazelnut Cookies

PREP TIME: 50 MINUTES (READY IN 1 HOUR 25 MINUTES)
SERVINGS: 2-1/2 DOZEN COOKIES

 EASY

1 roll (16.5 oz) Pillsbury® refrigerated sugar cookies

⅓ cup unsweetened baking cocoa

⅔ cup hazelnut spread with cocoa

½ cup coarsely chopped hazelnuts

1) In large bowl, break up cookie dough. Let stand at room temperature 15 minutes to soften.

2) Heat oven to 350°F. Stir or knead cocoa into cookie dough until well blended. Shape dough into 30 (1 ¼-inch) balls. On ungreased cookie sheets, place balls 2 inches apart.

3) Bake 7 to 9 minutes or until edges of cookies are barely set. Cool 2 minutes; remove from cookie sheets to cooling racks. Cool completely, about 20 minutes.

4) Frost each cookie with about 1 teaspoon hazelnut spread. Sprinkle with hazelnuts.

1 COOKIE: Calories 120; Total Fat 6g (Saturated Fat 1g); Sodium 55mg; Total Carbohydrate 15g (Dietary Fiber 1g); Protein 1g. EXCHANGES: 1/2 Starch, 1/2 Other Carbohydrate, 1 Fat. CARBOHYDRATE CHOICES: 1.

Freeze the cookies in a single layer on a cookie sheet, and then stack them between layers of waxed paper in a sealed container for longer freezer storage.

Oatmeal-Toffee Cookies

PREP TIME: 1 HOUR (READY IN 1 HOUR)
SERVINGS: 48 COOKIES

1 ½ cups old-fashioned oats

1 ½ cups all-purpose flour

½ teaspoon baking soda

¼ teaspoon salt

¾ cup butter, softened

1 cup packed brown sugar

2 eggs

1 teaspoon vanilla

½ cup chopped pecans

1 bag (8 oz) toffee bits

1) Heat oven to 350°F. Line cookie sheets with cooking parchment paper. In medium bowl, mix oats, flour, baking soda and salt; set aside.

2) In large bowl, beat butter and brown sugar with electric mixer on medium speed 2 to 3 minutes or until light and fluffy. Add eggs and vanilla; beat until blended. On low speed, beat in oat mixture just until blended. Stir in pecans and toffee bits.

3) Onto cookie sheets, drop dough by heaping tablespoonfuls about 2 inches apart.

4) Bake 10 to 12 minutes or until light golden brown. Remove from cookie sheets to cooling racks.

1 COOKIE: Calories 101; Total Fat 6g (Saturated Fat 3g); Sodium 74mg; Total Carbohydrate 12g (Dietary Fiber 0g); Protein 1g. EXCHANGES: 1/2 Starch, 1/2 Other Carbohydrate, 1 Fat. CARBOHYDRATE CHOICES: 1.

Espresso Cheesecake Bars

PREP TIME: 15 MINUTES (READY IN 4 HOURS 5 MINUTES)
SERVINGS: 25 BARS

 EASY

1 ½ cups chocolate wafer cookie crumbs

1 teaspoon instant espresso coffee powder or granules

¼ cup butter or margarine, melted

1 package (8 oz) cream cheese, softened

¼ cup sugar

½ teaspoon vanilla

1 egg

1) Heat oven to 350°F. In small bowl, mix cookie crumbs, ½ teaspoon of the coffee powder and the melted butter. Reserve ¼ cup mixture for topping. Press remaining mixture in bottom of ungreased 8-inch square pan.

2) In medium bowl, beat cream cheese with electric mixer on medium speed until smooth and creamy. Beat in sugar, remaining ½ teaspoon coffee powder, the vanilla and egg until well blended, scraping bowl occasionally. Pour filling over crust. Sprinkle with reserved ¼ cup crumb mixture.

3) Bake 15 to 20 minutes or just until center is set. Cool completely on cooling rack, about 30 minutes. Cover loosely; refrigerate until firm, 3 to 4 hours. With hot, wet knife, cut into 5 rows by 5 rows. Store in refrigerator.

1 BAR: Calories 90; Total Fat 6g (Saturated Fat 3.5g); Sodium 80mg; Total Carbohydrate 7g (Dietary Fiber 0g); Protein 1g. EXCHANGES: 1/2 Other Carbohydrate, 1 Fat. CARBOHYDRATE CHOICES: 1/2.

Peanut Butter Crunch Layer Bars

BECKY PIFER | BLANCHARD, MI

BAKE-OFF® CONTEST 45, 2012

PREP TIME: 15 MINUTES (READY IN 2 HOURS 10 MINUTES)
SERVINGS: 36

 EASY

2 rolls Pillsbury® refrigerated peanut butter cookie dough

¾ cup Heath® Bits 'O Brickle® toffee bits

1 cup Reese's® peanut butter baking chips

1 ¾ cups Fisher® Nut Topping

1 teaspoon McCormick® Pure Vanilla Extract

1 bag (12 oz) Hershey's® semi-sweet chocolate baking chips

1 bag (11 oz) Hershey's® butterscotch baking chips

¼ cup Jif® Creamy Peanut Butter

1) Heat oven to 350°F. Spray 13x9-inch pan (dark pan not recommended) with Crisco® Original No-Stick Cooking Spray. In large bowl, break up 1 ½ rolls of cookie dough. (Refrigerate ½ roll cookie dough for another use.) Add toffee bits, peanut butter chips, ½ cup of the nut topping and vanilla. Mix with wooden spoon or knead with hands until well blended. Press evenly in bottom of pan.

2) Bake for 18 to 24 minutes or until golden brown. Remove from oven to cooling rack. Cool completely, about 1 hour.

3) In large microwavable bowl, microwave chocolate chips and butterscotch chips on High 2 to 2 minutes 30 seconds, stirring every 30 seconds, until smooth. Stir in peanut butter until smooth. Spread over cooled bars. Sprinkle with remaining 1 ¼ cups nut topping; press in lightly. Refrigerate 30 minutes or until firm.

4) For bars, cut into 6 rows by 6 rows. Store covered.

1 SERVING: Calories 320; Total Fat 18g (Saturated Fat 7g); Sodium 190mg; Total Carbohydrate 34g (Dietary Fiber 1g); Protein 4g. EXCHANGES: 1 Starch, 1-1/2 Other Carbohydrate, 3-1/2 Fat. CARBOHYDRATE CHOICES: 2.

tip

Before putting peanut butter in a measuring cup, lightly coat the inside with water or oil. The peanut butter will slide right out without you having to scrape the cup.

Salted Chocolate Almond Fudge

PREP TIME: 15 MINUTES (READY IN 2 HOURS 30 MINUTES)
SERVINGS: 36

 EASY

1 tablespoon butter

¼ cup packed brown sugar

1 can (6 oz) smoked almonds, coarsely chopped

1 bag (12 oz) semisweet chocolate chips (2 cups)

1 cup milk chocolate chips (6 oz)

1 can (14 oz) sweetened condensed milk (not evaporated)

1 cup chopped dried cherries

½ teaspoon fleur de sel or coarse sea salt

1) Line cookie sheet with foil. In 8-inch nonstick skillet, melt butter over medium-high heat. Stir in brown sugar; cook until bubbly. Cook and stir 1 minute longer. Add almonds; stir to coat. Spread almonds on cookie sheet. Cool completely, about 15 minutes. Break into small pieces.

2) Line 8-inch square pan with foil. In large microwavable bowl, microwave semisweet and milk chocolate chips with condensed milk uncovered on High 1 to 2 minutes, stirring once, until melted and smooth. Add almonds and cherries; stir until blended. Spread evenly in pan. Sprinkle with salt. Refrigerate about 2 hours until firm. Cut into 6 rows by 6 rows. Store covered at room temperature.

1 SERVING: Calories 160; Total Fat 8g (Saturated Fat 3.5g); Sodium 35mg; Total Carbohydrate 21g (Dietary Fiber 1g); Protein 2g. EXCHANGES: 1/2 Starch, 1 Other Carbohydrate, 1-1/2 Fat. CARBOHYDRATE CHOICES: 1-1/2.

tip Smoked almonds, dried cherries and sea salt combine with chocolate and sweetened condensed milk to give this traditional fudge a high-end, flavor-forward makeover. A great gift for your nearest and dearest.

Mint Chocolate Chip Meringues

PREP TIME: 35 MINUTES (READY IN 26 HOURS 35 MINUTES)
SERVINGS: 24 COOKIES

2 egg whites

¼ teaspoon cream of tartar

⅓ cup sugar

¼ teaspoon spearmint extract

4 drops green food color

1 ½ cups miniature semisweet chocolate chips

2 teaspoons shortening

1) Heat oven to 200°F. Line 2 large cookie sheets with cooking parchment paper.

2) In medium bowl, beat egg whites and cream of tartar with electric mixer on low speed until foamy. Gradually add sugar, beating on high speed just until stiff peaks form. Beat in spearmint extract and food color. Fold in ½ cup of the chocolate chips. Onto cookie sheets, drop meringue by tablespoonfuls about 1 inch apart. Bake 2 hours. Turn oven off; let meringues stay in oven with door closed overnight.

3) In small microwavable bowl, microwave shortening and remaining 1 cup chocolate chips uncovered on High 1 to 2 minutes, stirring every 30 seconds, until melted and chips can be stirred smooth. Dip bottom of each cookie into melted chocolate. Return to cookie sheets; let stand 2 hours until chocolate is set. Store loosely covered at room temperature.

1 COOKIE: Calories 67; Total Fat 3.5g (Saturated Fat 2g); Sodium 6mg; Total Carbohydrate 10g (Dietary Fiber 0.5g); Protein 1g. EXCHANGES: 1/2 Other Carbohydrate, 1/2 Fat. CARBOHYDRATE CHOICES: 1/2.

Bittersweet-Ginger Brownies

PREP TIME: 15 MINUTES (READY IN 2 HOURS 50 MINUTES)
SERVINGS: 24 BROWNIES

 EASY

6 tablespoons butter or margarine

2 packages (11.5 oz each) bittersweet chocolate chips (4 cups)

3 eggs

1 tablespoon freshly grated gingerroot

⅓ cup all-purpose flour

½ cup granulated sugar

½ cup packed dark brown sugar

½ teaspoon baking powder

1) Heat oven to 375°F. Spray 13x9-inch pan with cooking spray.

2) In large microwavable bowl, microwave butter and 2 cups of the chocolate chips uncovered on High 1 minute; stir. Microwave 30 seconds to 1 minute longer until melted and mixture can be stirred smooth. Cool slightly. Stir in eggs and gingerroot.

3) In medium bowl, mix flour, granulated sugar, brown sugar and baking powder with wire whisk. Add flour mixture to chocolate mixture, stirring just until blended. Stir in remaining 2 cups chocolate chips. Spread batter in pan.

4) Bake 30 to 33 minutes or until edges are set and toothpick inserted in center comes out almost clean. Cool completely in pan on cooling rack, about 2 hours. Cut into 6 rows by 4 rows.

1 BROWNIE: Calories 201; Total Fat 14.5g (Saturated Fat 9.5g); Sodium 47mg; Total Carbohydrate 23g (Dietary Fiber 2g); Protein 3g. EXCHANGES: 1/2 Starch, 1 Other Carbohydrate, 3 Fat. CARBOHYDRATE CHOICES: 1-1/2.

Raspberry-Almond Bars

PREP TIME: 25 MINUTES (READY IN 1 HOUR 40 MINUTES)
SERVINGS: 16 BARS

 EASY   LOW FAT

½ roll (16.5-oz) Pillsbury® refrigerated sugar cookies

½ cup seedless raspberry preserves

1 teaspoon cornstarch

¼ cup sliced almonds

1) Heat oven to 350°F. Break up cookie dough into ungreased 8-inch square pan. With floured fingers, press dough evenly in bottom of pan to form crust. Bake 12 to 17 minutes or until edges are golden brown.

2) Meanwhile, in 1-quart saucepan, mix preserves and cornstarch. Cook and stir over medium heat just until mixture comes to a boil. Pour preserves mixture evenly over crust; spread to within ¼ inch of edges. Sprinkle with almonds.

3) Bake 10 minutes longer. Cool completely on cooling rack, about 1 hour. Cut into 4 rows by 4 rows.

1 BAR: Calories 100; Total Fat 3g (Saturated Fat 1g); Sodium 50mg; Total Carbohydrate 16g (Dietary Fiber 0g); Protein 1g. EXCHANGES: 1/2 Starch, 1/2 Other Carbohydrate, 1/2 Fat. CARBOHYDRATE CHOICES: 1.

Chocolate Chip-Candy Bar Treats

PREP TIME: 20 MINUTES (READY IN 2 HOURS 10 MINUTES)
SERVINGS: 24 BARS

 EASY

2 rolls (16.5 oz each) Pillsbury® refrigerated chocolate chip cookies

25 bars (fun-size) milk chocolate-covered peanut, caramel and nougat candy (from 11.5-oz bag), unwrapped, cut in half diagonally

2 cups miniature marshmallows

½ cup caramel topping (from 12 oz jar)

1) Heat oven to 350°F. Cut cookie dough from 1 roll into ½-inch slices. Arrange slices in bottom of ungreased 13x9-inch pan. Press dough evenly to form crust. Bake 11 to 13 minutes or until puffed and light golden brown.

2) Break remaining roll of cookie dough into chunks; sprinkle evenly over partially baked crust. Bake 23 to 28 minutes or until dough is golden brown.

3) Sprinkle with candy bars and marshmallows. Bake 5 minutes longer or until marshmallows are puffed and chocolate begins to melt. Cool on cooling rack about 1 hour. Drizzle with caramel topping. Cut into 6 rows by 4 rows.

1 BAR: Calories 270; Total Fat 11g (Saturated Fat 4.5g); Sodium 180mg; Total Carbohydrate 39g (Dietary Fiber 0g); Protein 2g. EXCHANGES: 1 Starch, 1-1/2 Other Carbohydrate, 2 Fat. CARBOHYDRATE CHOICES: 2-1/2.

 tip

Substitute your favorite fun-size candy bars for those called for in this recipe.

Crunchy Chocolate Bonbons

PREP TIME: 20 MINUTES (READY IN 1 HOUR 20 MINUTES)
SERVINGS: 24 BONBONS

 EASY

⅓ cup butter or margarine

1 bag (10.5 oz) miniature marshmallows (5 ½ cups)

5 cups corn flakes cereal

1 ½ cups semisweet chocolate chips

1 tablespoon shortening

1) Line cookie sheet with waxed paper. In 4-quart saucepan, melt butter and marshmallows over low heat, stirring constantly, until smooth. Remove from heat; add cereal. Stir until completely coated. Using buttered hands, shape mixture into 24 (1 ½-inch) balls. Place on cookie sheet. Refrigerate 30 minutes.

2) In 1-quart saucepan, melt chocolate chips and shortening over low heat, stirring constantly. Dip half of each ball into melted chocolate, allowing excess to drip off. Return to cookie sheet. Refrigerate about 30 minutes or until firm. Store loosely covered in refrigerator.

1 BONBON: Calories 163; Total Fat 7g (Saturated Fat 4.5g); Sodium 80mg; Total Carbohydrate 24.5g (Dietary Fiber 1g); Protein 1.5g. EXCHANGES: 1/2 Starch, 1 Other Carbohydrate, 1-1/2 Fat. CARBOHYDRATE CHOICES: 1-1/2.

tip

Store miniature marshmallows in the freezer to keep them from turning hard. When thawed, they're like fresh.

Red Velvet Pinwheel Cookies

PREP TIME: 35 MINUTES (READY IN 2 HOURS 35 MINUTES)
SERVINGS: 28 COOKIES

 EASY

- 1 pouch (1 lb 1.5 oz) sugar cookie mix
- ¼ cup butter or margarine, softened
- 1 package (3 oz) cream cheese, softened
- 1 egg
- 2 tablespoons unsweetened baking cocoa
- ½ teaspoon red gel food color

1) In large bowl, stir cookie mix, butter, cream cheese and egg with spoon until dough forms. Divide dough in half. Add cocoa and food color to 1 half; mix until well blended and uniform in color. Place red dough between 2 (17x12-inch) sheets of waxed paper; roll out to 12x7-inch rectangle. Repeat with plain dough; remove top sheet of waxed paper from both doughs. Invert plain dough onto red dough. Gently press out layered dough and trim edges. Remove top sheet of waxed paper from plain dough. Starting with short side, roll up dough in bottom sheet of waxed paper. Wrap tightly; freeze 2 hours or until very firm.

2) Heat oven to 350°F. Unwrap dough; cut into ¼-inch slices. On ungreased cookie sheet, place slices 2 inches apart. Bake 12 to 15 minutes or until set. Cool 2 minutes; remove from cookie sheet to cooling rack.

1 COOKIE: Calories 105; Total Fat 4.5g (Saturated Fat 2g); Sodium 68mg; Total Carbohydrate 14.5g (Dietary Fiber 0g); Protein 1g. EXCHANGES: 1 Other Carbohydrate, 1 Fat. CARBOHYDRATE CHOICES: 1.

White Peanut Butter Fudge Bars

PREP TIME: 10 MINUTES (READY IN 1 HOUR 10 MINUTES)
SERVINGS: 36 BARS

 EASY

- 1 cup crunchy peanut butter
- 1 cup butter, melted
- ⅔ cup graham cracker crumbs (10 squares)
- 1 box (1 lb) powdered sugar (4 cups)
- 8 oz white chocolate baking bars or squares, chopped
- ⅓ cup chopped peanuts

1) Line bottom and sides of 9-inch pan with foil, leaving foil overhanging at 2 opposite sides of pan. In large bowl, mix peanut butter, butter, graham cracker crumbs and powdered sugar until well blended. Press in bottom of pan.

2) In medium microwavable bowl, microwave white chocolate uncovered on High 1 to 2 minutes, stirring every 30 seconds, until melted and chocolate can be stirred smooth. Pour melted white chocolate over peanut butter mixture and spread to edges. Sprinkle with peanuts. Refrigerate 1 hour or until chocolate is set. Use foil to lift out of pan. Cut into 6 rows by 6 rows.

1 BAR: Calories 186; Total Fat 11.5g (Saturated Fat 5.5g); Sodium 94mg; Total Carbohydrate 19g (Dietary Fiber 0.5g); Protein 3g. EXCHANGES: 1 Other Carbohydrate, 2 Fat. CARBOHYDRATE CHOICES: 1.

Linzer Jam Sandwiches

PREP TIME: 1 HOUR 15 MINUTES (READY IN 1 HOUR 30 MINUTES)
SERVINGS: 14 SANDWICH COOKIES

⅓ cup sliced almonds, toasted

1 pouch (1 lb 1.5 oz) sugar cookie mix

½ teaspoon ground cinnamon

⅛ teaspoon ground nutmeg

⅓ cup butter, softened

1 egg

½ cup apricot, plum or seedless raspberry jam

1) Heat oven to 350°F. In food processor, place almonds. Cover; process until almonds are finely ground. In medium bowl, mix almonds, cookie mix, cinnamon and nutmeg. Add butter and egg; stir until stiff dough forms. Divide dough in half (refrigerate half until ready to use). On floured surface, roll out other half of dough to ¼-inch thickness. Cut with 2 ½-inch round fluted cookie cutter. On ungreased cookie sheet, place cutouts 2 inches apart.

2) Bake 10 to 12 minutes. Cool 5 minutes; remove from cookie sheet. Cool on cooling rack. On floured surface, roll out remaining dough to ¼-inch thickness. Cut with the same fluted cookie cutter. With 1-inch round fluted cookie cutter, cut out center of each cookie. On cookie sheet, place cutouts 2 inches apart. Bake 12 to 15 minutes. Cool 5 minutes; remove from cookie sheet. Cool on cooling rack. Spread about 1 ½ teaspoons jam on bottom of each whole cookie; top each with cutout cookie.

1 SANDWICH COOKIE: Calories 237; Total Fat 9g (Saturated Fat 3.5g); Sodium 126mg; Total Carbohydrate 36g (Dietary Fiber 0.5g); Protein 2g. EXCHANGES: 1/2 Starch, 2 Other Carbohydrate, 2 Fat. CARBOHYDRATE CHOICES: 2-1/2.

Triple Chocolate-Covered Nut Clusters

PREP TIME: 15 MINUTES (READY IN 2 HOURS 30 MINUTES)
SERVINGS: 60 CANDIES

 EASY

1 jar (16 oz) salted dry-roasted peanuts

1 jar (16 oz) unsalted dry-roasted peanuts

36 oz chocolate-flavored candy coating, chopped

1 bag (12 oz) semisweet chocolate chips (2 cups)

1 bar (4 oz) sweet baking chocolate, chopped

1 can (9.75 oz) salted whole cashews

1 teaspoon vanilla

1) Spray 3 ½- to 4-quart slow cooker with cooking spray. In slow cooker, mix all ingredients except cashews and vanilla.

2) Cover; cook on Low heat setting 2 hours.

3) Line cookie sheets with waxed paper. Stir mixture in slow cooker until smooth. Add cashews and vanilla; stir until cashews are coated. Drop mixture by heaping tablespoonfuls onto cookie sheets. Let stand until firm. Store tightly covered at room temperature.

1 CANDY: Calories 244; Total Fat 17g (Saturated Fat 6.5g); Sodium 56mg; Total Carbohydrate 20.5g (Dietary Fiber 1.5g); Protein 5g. EXCHANGES: 1-1/2 Other Carbohydrate, 1/2 High-Fat Meat, 2-1/2 Fat. CARBOHYDRATE CHOICES: 1-1/2.

Double Chocolate Brownies

PREP TIME: 15 MINUTES (READY IN 3 HOURS)
SERVINGS: 32 BROWNIES

 EASY

2 oz unsweetened baking chocolate, chopped

2 oz semisweet baking chocolate, chopped

1 cup butter, softened

2 cups sugar

4 eggs

1 cup all-purpose flour

½ teaspoon salt

1 teaspoon vanilla

¾ cup chopped pecans, toasted

¾ cup semisweet chocolate chips

1) Heat oven to 350°F. Grease 13x9-inch pan with shortening; lightly flour. In small microwavable bowl, microwave baking chocolate on Medium (50%) 1 minute to 1 minute 30 seconds, stirring every 30 seconds, until softened and chocolate can be stirred smooth.

2) In medium bowl, beat butter and sugar with electric mixer on medium speed until light and fluffy. Add eggs, one at a time, beating after each addition just until blended. Add melted chocolate; beat just until blended. On low speed, beat in flour and salt just until blended. Stir in vanilla and ½ cup each of the pecans and chocolate chips. Spread batter in pan. Sprinkle with remaining ¼ cup each pecans and chocolate chips.

3) Bake 40 minutes or until set. Cool completely on cooling rack. Cut into 8 rows by 4 rows.

1 BROWNIE: Calories 183; Total Fat 11g (Saturated Fat 6g); Sodium 97mg; Total Carbohydrate 21g (Dietary Fiber 1g); Protein 2g. EXCHANGES: 1/2 Starch, 1 Other Carbohydrate, 2 Fat. CARBOHYDRATE CHOICES: 1-1/2.

Cashew-Fudge Bars

PREP TIME: 20 MINUTES (READY IN 1 HOUR 45 MINUTES)
SERVINGS: 36 BARS

 EASY

1 ¾ cups cashew halves

1 roll (16.5 oz) Pillsbury® refrigerated chocolate chip cookies

½ cup old-fashioned oats

1 can (14 oz) sweetened condensed milk (not evaporated)

1 bag (12 oz) semisweet chocolate chips

1 teaspoon vanilla

1) Heat oven to 350°F (325°F for dark or nonstick pan). Chop 1 cup of the cashews. In large bowl, break up cookie dough. Stir in chopped cashews and oats. In ungreased 13x9-inch pan, press dough evenly to form crust. Bake 12 minutes.

2) Meanwhile, in 1 ½-quart saucepan, cook condensed milk and chocolate chips over low heat about 6 minutes, stirring constantly, until chips are melted and smooth. Stir in vanilla.

3) Spread chocolate mixture evenly over partially baked crust. Sprinkle with remaining ¾ cup cashews; press gently into chocolate.

4) Bake 18 to 23 minutes longer or until edges and center begin to crack. Cool completely on cooling rack, about 1 hour. Cut into 9 rows by 4 bars.

1 BAR: Calories 200; Total Fat 10g (Saturated Fat 4g); Sodium 90mg; Total Carbohydrate 24g (Dietary Fiber 1g); Protein 4g. EXCHANGES: 1-1/2 Starch, 2 Fat. CARBOHYDRATE CHOICES: 1-1/2.

For gift-giving, pack tiny squares of these not-quite-candy bars in holiday candy/cookie boxes (available where cake and candy-making supplies are sold). Wrap each box with a pretty ribbon before presenting as a gift.

Black-and-White Chunk Cookies

| PREP TIME: | 50 MINUTES (READY IN 50 MINUTES) |
| SERVINGS: | 36 COOKIES |

¾ cup packed brown sugar

½ cup granulated sugar

½ cup butter or margarine, softened

½ cup shortening

1 ½ teaspoons vanilla

1 egg

1 ¾ cups all-purpose flour

1 teaspoon baking soda

¼ teaspoon salt

4 oz semisweet baking chocolate, chopped

4 oz white chocolate baking bars or squares, chopped

1 cup chopped pecans

1) Heat oven to 375°F. In large bowl, beat brown sugar, granulated sugar, butter and shortening with electric mixer on medium speed until light and fluffy. Beat in vanilla and egg until well blended. On low speed, beat in flour, baking soda and salt until well blended. Stir in semisweet chocolate, white chocolate and pecans.

2) Onto ungreased cookie sheets, drop dough by tablespoonfuls 2 inches apart.

3) Bake 9 to 12 minutes or until light golden brown. Cool 1 minute; remove from cookie sheets to cooling racks.

1 COOKIE: Calories 160; Total Fat 10g (Saturated Fat 3.5g); Sodium 75mg; Total Carbohydrate 16g (Dietary Fiber 0g) EXCHANGES: 1/2 Starch, 1/2 Other Carbohydrate, 2 Fat. CARBOHYDRATE CHOICES: 1.

Peanut Butter Creme Cookie Cups

MARY FIELDS | GILBERT, AZ

PREP TIME: 10 MINUTES (READY IN 1 HOUR)
SERVINGS: 12

 EASY

½ cup Fisher® Chef's Naturals® Pecan Chips

1 package Pillsbury® Big Deluxe refrigerated chocolate chip cookies

½ cup Hershey's® premier white baking chips

¼ cup Jif® Natural Creamy Peanut Butter Spread

1) Heat oven to 350°F. Place paper or foil baking cup in each of 12 regular-size muffin cups.

2) In small bowl, place pecan chips. Lightly coat each cookie with pecans; press into dough. Place each cookie, flat side down, in muffin cup.

3) Bake 18 to 22 minutes or until edges are golden brown. Cool in muffin cups on cooling rack 30 minutes. (Centers of cookies will sink slightly.)

4) In small microwavable bowl, microwave white chips on Medium 1 minute to 1 minute 30 seconds, stirring every 30 seconds, until smooth. Stir peanut butter into melted chips until blended.

5) Spoon about 2 teaspoons peanut butter mixture into each cookie cup. Store in covered container.

1 SERVING: Calories 290; Total Fat 17g (Saturated Fat 6g); Sodium 170mg; Total Carbohydrate 31g (Dietary Fiber 0g); Protein 4g. EXCHANGES: 1 Starch, 1 Other Carbohydrate, 3-1/2 Fat. CARBOHYDRATE CHOICES: 2.

Pecan-Cream Cheese Bars

PREP TIME: 10 MINUTES (READY IN 2 HOURS 20 MINUTES)
SERVINGS: 15 BARS

 EASY

1 box yellow cake mix with pudding in the mix

1 cup chopped pecans

½ cup butter, melted

3 eggs

1 package (8 oz) cream cheese, softened

1 bag (1 lb) powdered sugar

1) Heat oven to 325°F. Lightly grease 13x9-inch pan with shortening or cooking spray.

2) In large bowl, stir cake mix, pecans, butter and 1 of the eggs with spoon until well blended. Press mixture in bottom of pan.

3) In medium bowl, beat remaining 2 eggs, the cream cheese and powdered sugar with electric mixer on medium speed until smooth. Pour over cake mix base.

4) Bake 40 minutes or until set. Cool completely on cooling rack. Cut into 5 rows by 3 rows.

1 BAR: Calories 436; Total Fat 22g (Saturated Fat 8g); Sodium 343mg; Total Carbohydrate 59g (Dietary Fiber 1g); Protein 4g. EXCHANGES: 1 Starch, 3 Other Carbohydrate, 4 Fat. CARBOHYDRATE CHOICES: 4.

Vanilla-Malt-Toffee Triangles with Sea Salt

VALERIE SCHUCHT | GLASTONBURY, CT

BAKE-OFF® CONTEST 45, 2012

PREP TIME: 20 MINUTES (READY IN 2 HOURS 30 MINUTES)
SERVINGS: 24

Ⓔ EASY

1 roll Pillsbury® refrigerated sugar cookie dough

½ cup original-flavor malted milk powder

1 can (14 oz) Eagle Brand® Sweetened Condensed Milk

1 LAND O LAKES® Egg

1 ½ teaspoons McCormick® Imitation Vanilla Extract-Premium Extract

1 bag (8 oz) Heath® Bits 'O Brickle® toffee bits

½ teaspoon McCormick® Sea Salt

1) Heat oven to 350°F. Let cookie dough stand at room temperature 10 minutes to soften. Line bottom and sides of 13x9-inch pan (dark pan not recommended) with foil, extending foil 2 inches over short sides of pan. Spray foil with Crisco® Original No-Stick Cooking Spray.

2) In large bowl, break up cookie dough. Add ¼ cup of the malted milk powder. Mix with wooden spoon or knead with hands, until well blended. Press dough evenly in bottom of pan.

3) Bake 13 to 15 minutes or until crust is light golden brown and puffed.

4) Meanwhile, in same bowl, beat condensed milk, remaining ¼ cup malted milk powder, egg and vanilla with wire whisk until blended. Stir in ⅓ cup of the toffee bits. Carefully pour mixture over partially baked crust.

5) Bake 18 to 23 minutes or until edges are golden brown and filling is set. Remove from oven; sprinkle evenly with remaining toffee bits. Bake an additional 3 to 5 minutes or until toffee bits just begin to melt. Sprinkle bars with sea salt. Cool completely, about 1 hour 30 minutes.

6) Remove bars from pan using edges of foil as handles. Cut into 4 rows by 3 rows. Cut each bar in half diagonally to form triangles. Store loosely covered.

1 SERVING: Calories 150; Total Fat 5g (Saturated Fat 2g); Sodium 140mg; Total Carbohydrate 23g (Dietary Fiber 0g); Protein 2g. EXCHANGES: 1/2 Starch, 1 Other Carbohydrate, 1 Fat. CARBOHYDRATE CHOICES: 1-1/2.

Luscious Caramel-Brownie Bites

MARJEAN BIGELOW | PORTLAND, OR

BAKE-OFF® CONTEST 45, 2012

PREP TIME: 1 HOUR 5 MINUTES (READY IN 2 HOURS 35 MINUTES)
SERVINGS: 36

- 1 bag (14 oz) caramels, unwrapped
- ½ cup whipping cream
- 1 box Pillsbury® refrigerated pie crusts, softened as directed on box
- ½ cup Fisher® Chef's Naturals® Chopped Pecans, finely chopped
- 1 box (15.9 oz) Pillsbury® Chocolate Extreme Premium Brownie Mix
- ⅓ cup Crisco® Pure Canola Oil
- 3 tablespoons water
- 1 LAND O LAKES® Egg
- ⅔ cup Hershey's® semi-sweet chocolate baking chips
- 1 tablespoon light corn syrup

1) In medium microwavable bowl, microwave caramels and ¼ cup of the cream on High 2 to 3 minutes, stirring every 30 seconds, until melted and smooth. Cool 30 minutes.

2) Meanwhile, spray 36 mini muffin cups with Crisco® Original No-Stick Cooking Spray. Unroll pie crusts; roll each into 13-inch round. Using 2 ½-inch round cookie cutter, cut 18 rounds from each crust, rerolling dough if necessary. Gently press each round on bottom and up side of muffin cup. Spoon scant ½ teaspoon pecans in bottom of each cup. Spoon about 1 teaspoon caramel mixture over pecans in each cup (cup will be ½ full); reserve remaining caramel mixture.

3) Heat oven to 350°F. In medium bowl, stir brownie mix (with syrup packet), oil, water and egg 50 strokes with spoon. Spoon 1 level tablespoon brownie batter into each cup.

4) Bake 18 to 24 minutes or until toothpick inserted into edge of brownie comes out clean. Cool in pans on cooling racks 10 minutes. Run knife around edges of cups to loosen; carefully remove from cups. Place on cooking racks. Cool completely, about 30 minutes.

5) Meanwhile, to make ganache glaze, in small microwavable bowl, microwave remaining ¼ cup cream and chocolate chips on High 1 to 2 minutes, stirring every 30 seconds, until melted and smooth. Stir in corn syrup until blended. Spoon ganache over each brownie. Refrigerate about 30 minutes or until ganache is set.

6) Microwave reserved caramel mixture on High 20 to 30 seconds if necessary for drizzling consistency. Drizzle each brownie with about ½ teaspoon caramel mixture. Store loosely covered in refrigerator.

1 SERVING: Calories 180; Total Fat 9g (Saturated Fat 3g); Sodium 90mg; Total Carbohydrate 24g (Dietary Fiber 0g); Protein 1g. EXCHANGES: 1-1/2 Other Carbohydrate, 2 Fat. CARBOHYDRATE CHOICES: 1-1/2.

Russian Tea Cakes

PREP TIME: 35 MINUTES (READY IN 55 MINUTES)
SERVINGS: 4 1/2 DOZEN COOKIES

 EASY   LOW FAT

1 roll (16.5 oz) Pillsbury®
refrigerated sugar cookies

½ cup all-purpose flour

¾ cup finely chopped pecans

½ teaspoon vanilla

½ cup plus 1 tablespoon
powdered sugar

1) Heat oven to 350°F. In large bowl, break up cookie dough. Stir or knead in flour, pecans and vanilla until well blended.

2) Shape dough into 54 (1-inch) balls. On ungreased cookie sheets, place balls 1 inch apart.

3) Bake 10 to 14 minutes or until set but not brown. Remove from cookie sheets to cooling racks; cool slightly.

4) Roll warm cookies in powdered sugar; cool on cooling rack. Roll in powdered sugar again.

1 COOKIE: Calories 60; Total Fat 3g (Saturated Fat 0.5g); Sodium 25mg; Total Carbohydrate 8g (Dietary Fiber 0g); Protein 0g. EXCHANGES: 1/2 Other Carbohydrate, 1/2 Fat. CARBOHYDRATE CHOICES: 1/2.

Gingerbread Pinwheels

PREP TIME: 1 HOUR (READY IN 2 HOURS)
SERVINGS: 4-1/2 DOZEN COOKIES

 EASY   LOW FAT

1 roll (16.5 oz) Pillsbury®
refrigerated gingerbread
cookies

1 roll (16.5 oz) Pillsbury®
refrigerated sugar cookies

1 tablespoon sugar

1) Place 17x12-inch sheet of waxed paper on cookie sheet. Cut gingerbread cookie dough in half lengthwise. Arrange halves, side by side, on cookie sheet. Top with second sheet of waxed paper. Roll dough to form 15x9-inch rectangle.

2) Repeat on work surface with sheets of waxed paper and sugar cookie dough. Remove top sheet of waxed paper. Lifting dough with waxed paper, invert sugar cookie rectangle onto gingerbread rectangle. Gently pat doughs together. Refrigerate 15 minutes.

3) Remove and discard waxed paper from top of dough. Using remaining waxed paper and starting with 1 long side, roll up stacked dough jelly-roll fashion, without rolling paper into roll. Wrap roll of dough securely with waxed paper. Freeze 45 minutes or until very firm.

4) Heat oven to 350°F. Unwrap dough; cut into 4 equal rolls. Keep rolls in freezer until ready to slice. Cut each roll into ¼-inch slices. On ungreased cookie sheets, place slices 2 inches apart, reshaping into rounds as necessary. Sprinkle with sugar.

5) Bake 10 to 12 minutes or until edges are golden brown. Cool 2 minutes; remove from cookie sheets to cooling racks.

1 COOKIE: Calories 75; Total Fat 3g (Saturated Fat 1g); Sodium 55mg; Total Carbohydrate 11g (Dietary Fiber 0g); Protein 1g. EXCHANGES: 1 Other Carbohydrate, 1/2 Fat. CARBOHYDRATE CHOICES: 1.

Maple Brown Sugar Granola Cookies

PREP TIME: 1 HOUR 15 MINUTES (READY IN 1 HOUR 15 MINUTES)
SERVINGS: 48 COOKIES

1 cup butter, softened

¾ cup granulated sugar

¾ cup packed brown sugar

2 teaspoons vanilla

2 eggs

2 ¼ cups all-purpose flour

1 teaspoon baking soda

¼ teaspoon salt

4 cups Cascadian Farm® organic
   maple brown sugar granola

¾ cup raisins

¾ cup chopped pecans

1) Heat oven to 350°F. In large bowl, beat butter, granulated sugar, brown sugar, vanilla and eggs with electric mixer on low speed until light and fluffy. Beat in flour, baking soda and salt until well blended.

2) Stir in granola, raisins and pecans. Onto ungreased cookie sheets, drop dough by rounded tablespoonfuls 2 inches apart.

3) Bake 11 to 13 minutes or until light golden brown. Cool 1 minute; remove from cookie sheets to cooling racks.

1 COOKIE: Calories 140; Total Fat 6g (Saturated Fat 2.5g); Sodium 90mg; Total Carbohydrate 18g (Dietary Fiber 0g); Protein 2g. EXCHANGES: 1 Starch, 1-1/2 Fat. CARBOHYDRATE CHOICES: 1.

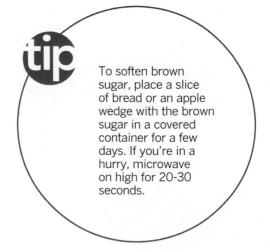

tip

To soften brown sugar, place a slice of bread or an apple wedge with the brown sugar in a covered container for a few days. If you're in a hurry, microwave on high for 20-30 seconds.

Salted Caramel Macaroons

SARAH MEUSER | NEW MILFORD, CT

BAKE-OFF® CONTEST 45, 2012

PREP TIME: 30 MINUTES (READY IN 1 HOUR 50 MINUTES)
SERVINGS: 60

- 1 can (14 oz) Eagle Brand® Sweetened Condensed Milk
- 1 jar (12.25 oz) Smucker's® Caramel Ice Cream Topping
- 1 cup Pillsbury BEST® All Purpose Unbleached Flour
- 1 ¼ teaspoons McCormick® Sea Salt
- 2 bags (14 oz each) shredded coconut
- 1 ½ cups Fisher® Chef's Naturals® Chopped Pecans
- 1 cup Hershey's® semi-sweet chocolate baking chips

1) Heat oven to 325°F. Line 2 large cookie sheets with cooking parchment paper; spray with Crisco® Original No-Stick Cooking Spray. In large bowl, combine condensed milk, caramel topping, flour and ¾ teaspoon of the sea salt; mix well. Stir in coconut, pecans and chocolate chips until well mixed.

2) Drop dough by rounded tablespoonfuls 1 inch apart onto cookie sheets. Lightly sprinkle tops with remaining ½ teaspoon sea salt.

3) Bake 15 to 25 minutes or until golden brown. Immediately remove from cookie sheets to cooling racks. Cool completely, about 30 minutes. Store in airtight container.

1 SERVING: Calories 150; Total Fat 8g (Saturated Fat 5g); Sodium 110mg; Total Carbohydrate 17g (Dietary Fiber 1g); Protein 1g. EXCHANGES: 1/2 Starch, 1/2 Other Carbohydrate, 1-1/2 Fat. CARBOHYDRATE CHOICES: 1.

Nutty Chocolate-Irish Cream Cookies

ANITA VAN GUNDY | DES MOINES, IA

BAKE-OFF® CONTEST 45, 2012

PREP TIME: 30 MINUTES (READY IN 1 HOUR 10 MINUTES)
SERVINGS: 20

1 package Pillsbury® Ready to Bake!™ refrigerated sugar cookies

⅓ cup Hershey's® baking cocoa

4 tablespoons Irish cream-flavored coffee syrup or Irish cream-flavored creamer

1 ¼ cups Fisher® Deluxe Mixed Nuts, chopped

2 cups powdered sugar

3 tablespoons LAND O LAKES® Unsalted or Salted Butter

½ teaspoon McCormick® Pure Vanilla Extract

1 to 2 tablespoons milk

1) Heat oven to 350°F. Spray cookie sheets with Crisco® Original No-Stick Cooking Spray. In large bowl, mix cookie dough, cocoa and 2 tablespoons of the flavored syrup with wooden spoon or knead with hands until well blended. Stir in ¾ cup of the nuts. Drop dough by rounded tablespoonfuls onto cookie sheets.

2) Bake 10 to 15 minutes or until edges are set. Cool 5 minutes. Remove from cookie sheets to cooling racks. Cool completely, about 20 minutes.

3) Meanwhile, in medium bowl, beat powdered sugar, butter, remaining 2 tablespoons flavored syrup, vanilla and enough milk for desired frosting consistency with electric mixer on medium speed 2 minutes or until smooth.

4) Frost cooled cookies; sprinkle with remaining ½ cup nuts. Store loosely covered.

1 SERVING: Calories 240; Total Fat 12g (Saturated Fat 3.5g); Sodium 85mg; Total Carbohydrate 30g (Dietary Fiber 0g); Protein 2g. EXCHANGES: 1 Starch, 1 Other Carbohydrate, 2-1/2 Fat. CARBOHYDRATE CHOICES: 2.

tip

Baking cocoa is the powdery residue that remains after the cocoa butter is removed from the chocolate liquor. This form of chocolate contains the least amount of fat.

Chocolate-Hazelnut-Coconut Bars

TERESA BERKEY | HANOVER, NH

BAKE-OFF® CONTEST 45, 2012

PREP TIME: 25 MINUTES (READY IN 3 HOURS 30 MINUTES)
SERVINGS: 24

1 roll Pillsbury® refrigerated chocolate flavored chip cookie dough

1 ¼ cups hazelnut spread with cocoa (from 13-oz jar)

1 package (8 oz) cream cheese, softened

1 LAND O LAKES® Egg White

1 can (14 oz) Eagle Brand® Sweetened Condensed Milk

3 cups shredded coconut

1 teaspoon McCormick® Pure Vanilla Extract

3 tablespoons LAND O LAKES® Butter

½ cup toasted shredded coconut, if desired

1) Heat oven to 350°F. Spray 13x9-inch pan (dark pan not recommended) with Crisco® Original No-Stick Cooking Spray. Let cookie dough stand at room temperature 10 minutes to soften. In large bowl, break up cookie dough. Stir in ¾ cup of the hazelnut spread until blended. Press dough evenly in bottom of pan.

2) Bake 10 to 15 minutes or until light golden brown. Cool 30 minutes.

3) In large bowl, beat cream cheese and egg white with electric mixer on medium speed until smooth. Add condensed milk, 3 cups coconut and vanilla; beat until well blended. Pour over crust.

4) Bake 35 to 40 minutes or until light golden brown and set. Cool completely, about 1 hour.

5) In 1-quart saucepan, heat remaining ½ cup hazelnut spread and butter over low heat, stirring constantly, until melted. Spread over cooled bars; sprinkle with toasted coconut. Refrigerate 30 minutes or until topping is set. For bars, cut into 6 rows by 4 rows. Store covered in refrigerator.

1 SERVING. Calories 350, Total Fat 20g (Saturated Fat 10g); Sodium 170mg; Total Carbohydrate 37g (Dietary Fiber 1g); Protein 4g. EXCHANGES: 1 Starch, 1-1/2 Other Carbohydrate, 4 Fat. CARBOHYDRATE CHOICES: 2-1/2.

Chewy Peanut Butter-Caramel Bars

SANDRA HILBERT | FORT LITTLETON, PA

 Bake-Off   BAKE-OFF® CONTEST 45, 2012

PREP TIME: 20 MINUTES (READY IN 2 HOURS
SERVINGS: 36

e EASY

1 package Pillsbury® Ready to Bake!™ refrigerated sugar cookies

½ cup LAND O LAKES® Butter

1 can (14 oz) Eagle Brand® Sweetened Condensed Milk

1 cup packed light brown sugar

1 cup granulated sugar

1 ¾ cups graham cracker crumbs

1 bag (11.5 oz) Hershey's® milk chocolate baking chips

½ cup Jif® Creamy Peanut Butter

½ cup finely chopped Fisher® Dry Roasted Peanuts

1) Heat oven to 350°F. Spray 13x9-inch pan (dark pan not recommended) with Crisco® Original No-Stick Cooking Spray or line with nonstick foil. Evenly arrange cookie rounds in pan.

2) Bake 24 to 26 minutes or until light golden brown. Cool 15 minutes on cooling rack.

3) Meanwhile, in 2-quart heavy saucepan, melt butter over medium heat. Stir in condensed milk, brown sugar and granulated sugar until blended. Add graham cracker crumbs; mix well (mixture will be thick). Bring to a boil, stirring constantly. Reduce heat to low; cook 5 minutes, stirring constantly, or until slightly thickened. Pour caramel mixture over warm cookie crust, spreading evenly.

4) In medium microwavable bowl, microwave chocolate chips on High 1 minute to 1 minute 20 seconds, stirring every 30 seconds, until smooth. Stir in peanut butter until blended. Spread evenly over caramel layer. Sprinkle with chopped peanuts. Refrigerate 1 hour or until chocolate is set. For bars, cut into 6 rows by 6 rows. Store covered in refrigerator.

1 SERVING: Calories 260; Total Fat 12g (Saturated Fat 5g); Sodium 130mg; Total Carbohydrate 35g (Dietary Fiber 1g); Protein 3g. EXCHANGES: 1 Starch, 1-1/2 Other Carbohydrate, 2 Fat. CARBOHYDRATE CHOICES: 2.

Chocolate-Marshmallow Cookie Treats

PREP TIME: 20 MINUTES (READY IN 1 HOUR)
SERVINGS: 36

 EASY

1 pouch (1 lb 1.5 oz) double chocolate chunk cookie mix

Water, vegetable oil and egg called for on cookie mix package

18 large marshmallows

1 cup hot fudge topping

Candy sprinkles, if desired

1) Heat oven to 350°F. Make cookies as directed on package, using water, oil and egg. Onto ungreased cookie sheet, drop dough by tablespoonfuls 2 inches apart.

2) Bake 10 to 12 minutes. With serrated knife, cut marshmallows crosswise in half. Immediately top each hot cookie with marshmallow half, cut side down, pressing down firmly. Remove cookies from cookie sheet to cooling rack; cool completely.

3) In small microwavable bowl, microwave fudge topping uncovered on High 30 seconds or until warm. Spoon topping over each marshmallow-topped cookie. Decorate with candy sprinkles.

1 SERVING: Calories 240; Total Fat 8g (Saturated Fat 3.5g); Sodium 190mg; Total Carbohydrate 40g (Dietary Fiber 0g); Protein 2g. EXCHANGES: 1/2 Starch, 2 Other Carbohydrate, 1-1/2 Fat. CARBOHYDRATE CHOICES: 2-1/2.

tip

These whimsical cookies would be delightful served atop an ice cream sundae.

Pies & Tarts

From fruit-filled classics to silky cream creations, these pies and tarts bake to flaky perfection.

ALMOND-APRICOT GALETTE
PG. 298

ORANGE CREAM-CHOCOLATE TARTS
PG. 296

HAZELNUT-FRENCH SILK TURTLE PIE
PG. 301

DOUBLE-BOTTOM
BLUEBERRY-PECAN PIE
PG. 300

White Chocolate-Raspberry Pie

PREP TIME: 35 MINUTES (READY IN 3 HOURS 5 MINUTES)
SERVINGS: 8

1 Pillsbury® refrigerated pie crust, softened as directed on box

5 oz white chocolate baking squares

3 tablespoons milk

5 oz cream cheese, softened

½ cup powdered sugar

½ to 1 teaspoon grated orange peel

1 cup whipping cream, whipped

3 cup fresh raspberries

1) Heat oven to 450°F. Make pie crust as directed on box for One-Crust Baked Shell, using 9-inch pie plate. Cool completely.

2) In small microwavable bowl, microwave 4 squares of the white chocolate and the milk uncovered on Medium (50%) about 2 minutes or until softened and chocolate can be stirred smooth. Cool to room temperature.

3) In small bowl, beat cream cheese, powdered sugar and orange peel with electric mixer on low speed until smooth. Beat in white chocolate mixture. Fold in whipped cream. Spread filling in cooled baked shell. Arrange raspberries on filling.

4) Melt remaining 1 square white chocolate; drizzle over pie. Refrigerate about 2 hours or until set. Cover and refrigerate any remaining pie.

1 SERVING: Calories 410; Total Fat 27g (Saturated Fat 15g); Sodium 220mg; Total Carbohydrate 37g (Dietary Fiber 3g); Protein 4g. EXCHANGES: 1 Starch, 1/2 Fruit, 1 Other Carbohydrate, 5-1/2 Fat. CARBOHYDRATE CHOICES: 2-1/2.

White chocolate is made of a mixture of sugar, cocoa butter, milk solids, lecithin and vanilla. Check to see if the label states it contains cocoa butter; if not, it's not white chocolate.

Chocolate-Macadamia Tart

PREP TIME:	10 MINUTES (READY IN 2 HOURS 45 MINUTES)
SERVINGS:	8

 EASY

1 Pillsbury® refrigerated pie crust, softened as directed on box

1 egg

½ cup packed brown sugar

2 tablespoons unsalted butter or margarine, melted

¼ cup light corn syrup

1 tablespoon dark rum or rum extract

1 cup macadamia nuts, coarsely chopped

½ cup miniature semisweet chocolate chips

2 oz bittersweet baking chocolate, chopped, melted

1) Heat oven to 450°F. Place pie crust in 9-inch tart pan with removable bottom as directed on box for One-Crust Filled Pie. Press in bottom and up sides of pan. Trim edges if necessary. Do not prick crust.

2) Bake 10 to 12 minutes or until golden brown. If crust puffs in center, flatten gently with back of wooden spoon. Cool. Reduce oven temperature to 375°F.

3) In medium bowl, beat egg and brown sugar with electric mixer on medium speed until well blended. Beat in butter, corn syrup and rum. Stir in macadamia nuts and chocolate chips. Pour filling into partially baked crust.

4) Bake 25 minutes or until deep golden brown and center is almost set. Cool completely on cooling rack. Remove side of pan; cut tart into 8 wedges. Drizzle with melted chocolate.

1 SERVING: Calories 442; Total Fat 29g (Saturated Fat 11g); Sodium 162mg; Total Carbohydrate 46g (Dietary Fiber 2g); Protein 4g. EXCHANGES: 1/2 Starch, 2-1/2 Other Carbohydrate, 6 Fat. CARBOHYDRATE CHOICES: 3.

Jam Pie

PREP TIME:	35 MINUTES (READY IN 2 HOURS 20 MINUTES)
SERVINGS:	8

1 Pillsbury® refrigerated pie crust, softened as directed on box

3 egg yolks

1 whole egg

½ cup granulated sugar

¼ cup crumbled almond paste

½ cup butter or margarine, melted, cooled

⅓ cup seedless raspberry or blackberry jam

Powdered sugar, if desired

Frozen (thawed) whipped topping, if desired

Fresh raspberries or blackberries, if desired

1) Heat oven to 325°F. Place pie crust in 9-inch glass pie plate as directed on box for One-Crust Filled Pie.

2) In medium bowl, beat egg yolks and egg with electric mixer on medium speed until thickened. Add granulated sugar and almond paste; beat well. (Filling will be slightly lumpy.) Add melted butter, beating just until blended. Stir jam well; spread in crust-lined plate. Stir egg mixture and pour over jam.

3) Bake 30 to 45 minutes or until set and a golden crust has formed on top. Cool completely on cooling rack. Sprinkle with powdered sugar. Garnish with whipped topping and berries. Serve at room temperature. Store in refrigerator.

1 SERVING: Calories 354; Total Fat 23g (Saturated Fat 11g); Sodium 252mg; Total Carbohydrate 37g (Dietary Fiber 0g); Protein 3.5g. EXCHANGES: 1 Starch, 1-1/2 Other Carbohydrate, 4-1/2 Fat. CARBOHYDRATE CHOICES: 2-1/2.

Mincemeat Pie

PREP TIME: 25 MINUTES (READY IN 14 HOURS 10 MINUTES)
SERVINGS: 8

1 jar (20.5 oz) ready-to-use mincemeat (2 cups)

1 ½ cups chopped pecans

1 Gala apple, peeled, chopped (1 ½ cups)

½ cup chopped dried Calimyrna figs

⅓ cup packed brown sugar

⅓ cup brandy

2 teaspoons grated lemon peel

1 box Pillsbury® refrigerated pie crusts, softened as directed on box

1) In medium bowl, stir together mincemeat, pecans, apple, figs, brown sugar, brandy and lemon peel. Cover; refrigerate at least 8 hours.

2) Let pie filling stand at room temperature 30 minutes. Meanwhile, heat oven to 425°F. Make pie crusts as directed on box for Two-Crust Pie using 9-inch pie plate. Stir filling well; pour into crust-lined plate. Top with second crust and flute; cut slits in several places.

3) Bake on lowest oven rack 40 to 45 minutes or until pastry is golden brown. Cool completely on cooling rack, about 5 hours.

1 SERVING: Calories 556; Total Fat 31g (Saturated Fat 7g); Sodium 433mg; Total Carbohydrate 70g (Dietary Fiber 3g); Protein 4g. EXCHANGES: 1-1/2 Fruit, 3 Other Carbohydrate, 1/2 High-Fat Meat, 7-1/2 Fat. CARBOHYDRATE CHOICES: 4-1/2.

Harvest Medley Pie

PREP TIME: 20 MINUTES (READY IN 3 HOURS 5 MINUTES)
SERVINGS: 8

 EASY

Mary Campbell Crutchfield
Collierville, TN
1st Place, Mid-South Fair Tennessee

1 box Pillsbury® refrigerated pie crusts, softened as directed on box

3 ½ cups chopped peeled Granny Smith apples

1 cup mixed dried apricots, cranberries and blackberries

¼ cup chopped walnuts

⅔ cup packed brown sugar

¼ cup all-purpose flour

1 ½ teaspoons pumpkin pie spice

1 to 2 tablespoons granulated sugar

1) Heat oven to 425°F. Unroll 1 pie crust in ungreased 9-inch glass pie plate. Press firmly against side and bottom. In large bowl, mix apples, dried fruit and walnuts. In small bowl, mix brown sugar, flour and pumpkin pie spice. Add sugar mixture to fruit and gently toss; spoon into crust-lined plate.

2) Cut second crust into ½-inch-wide strips with pastry cutter. Place half of the strips across filling in pie plate. Place remaining strips crosswise across first strips. Trim ends of strips even with edge of bottom crust. Fold trimmed edge of bottom crust over ends of strips, forming a high stand-up rim. Seal and flute. Bake 30 minutes; sprinkle top with granulated sugar. Cover edge of crust with strips of foil to prevent excessive browning. Bake 10 to 15 minutes longer or until apples are tender and crust is golden brown. Cool 2 hours before serving. Refrigerate remaining pie.

1 SERVING: Calories 400; Total Fat 16g (Saturated Fat 5g); Sodium 210mg; Total Carbohydrate 63g (Dietary Fiber 2g); Protein 1g. EXCHANGES: 1/2 Starch, 1/2 Fruit, 3 Other Carbohydrate, 3 Fat. CARBOHYDRATE CHOICES: 4.

Cookie Chess Pie

| PREP TIME: | 10 MINUTES (READY IN 5 HOURS 10 MINUTES) |
| SERVINGS: | 10 |

 EASY

1 Pillsbury® refrigerated pie crust, softened as directed on box

2 cups sugar

½ cup butter or margarine, melted

¼ cup half-and-half

2 tablespoons yellow cornmeal

1 tablespoon all-purpose flour

¼ teaspoon salt

1 tablespoon white vinegar

1 teaspoon vanilla

4 eggs, slightly beaten

1 package (7.5 oz) double chocolate-filled sandwich cookies, chopped

1) Heat oven to 325°F. Place pie crust in 9-inch pie plate as directed on box for One-Crust Filled Pie.

2) In large bowl, mix sugar, butter, half-and-half, cornmeal, flour, salt, vinegar, vanilla and eggs with whisk or spoon. Stir in cookie pieces. Pour into crust-lined plate.

3) Bake 55 to 60 minutes or until center is slightly puffed and almost set. Cover pie with foil during last 25 minutes of baking to prevent excessive browning. Cool completely on cooling rack, about 4 hours. Store in refrigerator.

1 SERVING: Calories 482; Total Fat 24g (Saturated Fat 12g); Sodium 337mg; Total Carbohydrate 66g (Dietary Fiber 1g); Protein 5g. EXCHANGES: 1 Starch, 3-1/2 Other Carbohydrate, 4-1/2 Fat. CARBOHYDRATE CHOICES: 4-1/2.

tip

Omit the sandwich cookies, if desired, for a purist's version of chess pie. Bake time will be slightly less.

Spiced Gingered Pear Pie

PREP TIME: 25 MINUTES (READY IN 1 HOUR 40 MINUTES)
SERVINGS: 8

CRUST

1 box Pillsbury® refrigerated pie crusts, softened as directed on box

FILLING

½ cup packed light brown sugar

¼ cup granulated sugar

2 tablespoons cornstarch

3 tablespoons finely chopped crystallized ginger

1 teaspoon finely grated lemon peel

6 cups thinly sliced peeled pears (6 medium)

1 tablespoon butter, cut into small pieces

TOPPING

1 tablespoon water

4 teaspoons granulated sugar

1) Heat oven to 425°F. Make pie crusts as directed on box for Two-Crust Pie using 9-inch glass pie plate.

2) In large bowl, mix brown sugar, ¼ cup granulated sugar and the cornstarch. Stir in ginger and lemon peel. Add pears; toss gently. Spoon into crust-lined plate. Dot with butter. Top with second crust; seal edge and flute. Cut slits or shapes in several places in top crust. Brush crust with water; sprinkle with 4 teaspoons sugar.

3) Bake 40 to 45 minutes or until pears are tender and crust is golden brown. After 15 to 20 minutes of baking, cover crust edge with strips of foil to prevent excessive browning. Cool 30 minutes before cutting. Store covered in refrigerator.

1 SERVING: Calories 420; Total Fat 14g (Saturated Fat 6g); Sodium 280mg; Total Carbohydrate 74g (Dietary Fiber 3g); Protein 2g. EXCHANGES: 1 Starch, 1-1/2 Fruit, 2-1/2 Other Carbohydrate, 2-1/2 Fat. CARBOHYDRATE CHOICES: 5.

Orange Cream-Chocolate Tarts

LENORE KLASS | KOLOA, HI

BAKE-OFF® CONTEST 45, 2012

PREP TIME: 55 MINUTES (READY IN 2 HOURS 15 MINUTES)
SERVINGS: 6 TARTS

1 teaspoon unflavored gelatin

2 tablespoons cold water

4 LAND O LAKES® Egg Yolks, beaten

½ cup sugar

2 tablespoons grated orange peel

¼ cup freshly squeezed orange juice

1 ½ teaspoons lemon juice

¼ teaspoon salt

3 tablespoons LAND O LAKES® Butter

1 ½ teaspoons McCormick® Pure Vanilla Extract

1 ¼ cups whipping cream

1 box Pillsbury® refrigerated pie crusts, softened as directed on box

¼ cup Hershey's® semi-sweet chocolate baking chips

1) In small bowl, soften gelatin in cold water. In 2-quart heavy saucepan, stir together egg yolks, sugar, 1 tablespoon of the orange peel, orange juice, lemon juice and ⅛ teaspoon of the salt. Cook over low heat, 8 to 10 minutes, stirring constantly, or until slightly thickened; remove from heat. Add 2 tablespoons of the butter, gelatin and 1 teaspoon of the vanilla; stir until butter is melted. Fill large bowl with ice water; place saucepan in water. Cool egg mixture, stirring occasionally, about 10 minutes or until thickened.

2) In medium bowl, beat whipping cream with electric mixer on high speed until stiff peaks form. Reserve ½ cup of the whipped cream; refrigerate. Carefully fold orange mixture into remaining whipped cream. Refrigerate while preparing tart shells.

3) Heat oven to 425°F. Cover outsides of 6 (6-oz) custard cups or ramekins with foil; spray with Crisco® Original No-Stick Cooking Spray. Place cups upside down on 15x10-inch pan with sides. Unroll pie crusts; roll each into 12-inch round. Using 4 ½-inch scalloped or round cookie cutter, cut 3 rounds from each crust. Place dough round over back of each custard cup, pressing dough to fit around cup. Prick dough several times with fork.

4) Bake shells 10 to 13 minutes or until golden brown. Cool 15 minutes. Carefully remove shells from ramekins; place open side up, on cooling rack.

5) In small microwavable bowl, microwave baking chips and remaining 1 tablespoon butter on High 10 to 20 seconds, stirring every 10 seconds, until smooth. Stir in remaining ⅛ teaspoon salt and ½ teaspoon vanilla. Brush thick coating of chocolate mixture over bottom and up side of inside of each shell. Let stand 5 minutes or until set.

6) Evenly divide orange filling among 6 tart shells. Top tarts with reserved whipped cream and remaining 1 tablespoon orange peel. Refrigerate 1 hour (filling will be soft). Store covered in refrigerator.

1 SERVING: Calories 470; Total Fat 33g (Saturated Fat 18g); Sodium 300mg; Total Carbohydrate 38g (Dietary Fiber 0g); Protein 4g. EXCHANGES: 1 Starch, 1-1/2 Other Carbohydrate, 6-1/2 Fat. CARBOHYDRATE CHOICES: 2-1/2.

Pineapple Meringue Pie

PREP TIME: 30 MINUTES (READY IN 7 HOURS)
SERVINGS: 10

2 cups pecan shortbread cookie crumbs (about 18 cookies)

1 ⅓ cups flaked coconut

¼ cup butter, melted

2 cups milk

¼ cup cornstarch

3 eggs, separated

1 ¼ cups sugar

1 can (20 oz) crushed pineapple, drained

1 tablespoon butter

1 teaspoon vanilla

1) Heat oven to 350°F. Spray 9-inch glass pie plate with cooking spray. In small bowl, mix cookie crumbs, 1 cup of the coconut and the melted butter; firmly press in bottom, up side and onto rim of pie plate. Bake 10 to 12 minutes or until lightly browned. Cool completely. Reduce oven temperature to 325°F.

2) In heavy saucepan, stir milk and cornstarch with whisk until cornstarch is dissolved. Stir in 3 egg yolks and ¾ cup of the sugar. Cook over medium-low heat 8 to 10 minutes, stirring constantly, until mixture begins to bubble and is thick enough to hold soft peaks. Remove from heat; stir in pineapple, 1 tablespoon butter and the vanilla. Spoon into crust.

3) In medium bowl, beat egg whites with electric mixer on high speed until foamy. Add remaining ½ cup sugar, 1 tablespoon at a time, beating until stiff peaks form. Spread meringue over hot filling, sealing edges. Sprinkle remaining ⅓ cup coconut over meringue. Bake 20 to 25 minutes or until golden brown. Cool completely. Refrigerate 4 hours before serving.

1 SERVING: Calories 413; Total Fat 20g (Saturated Fat 10g); Sodium 218mg; Total Carbohydrate 55g (Dietary Fiber 2g); Protein 6g. EXCHANGES: 1/2 Starch, 1/2 Fruit, 2-1/2 Other Carbohydrate, 1/2 High-Fat Meat, 3 Fat. CARBOHYDRATE CHOICES: 3-1/2.

Almond-Apricot Galette

ANGELIKA HARDER | EAGLE RIVER, AK

BAKE-OFF® CONTEST 44, 2010

PREP TIME: 20 MINUTES (READY IN 1 HOUR 20 MINUTES)
SERVINGS: 8

1   Pillsbury® refrigerated pie crust, softened as directed on box

1 ½ cups natural sliced almonds

½   cup sugar

1   egg

1   tablespoon whipping cream

½   cup apricot preserves

1   tablespoon lemon juice

½ to 1 teaspoon ground ginger

1   tablespoon cornstarch

2   tablespoons unsalted or salted butter, melted

2   teaspoons sugar

1) Heat oven to 400°F. Unroll pie crust in ungreased 9- or 10-inch glass pie plate, pressing on bottom and up side (crust will extend over edge of plate).

2) In food processor, place almonds and ½ cup sugar. Cover; process with on-and-off pulses until almonds are very finely chopped. Add egg and whipping cream. Cover; process until thick paste forms. Spread in bottom of crust-lined plate. Wipe out processor with paper towel. Add preserves, lemon juice, ginger and cornstarch to food processor. Cover; process with on-and-off pulses until smooth. Spread evenly over almond mixture.

3) Fold edge of crust over filling, pleating crust as necessary. Brush crust with melted butter; sprinkle with 2 teaspoons sugar.

4) Bake 20 to 30 minutes or until golden brown. Cool 30 minutes. Remove from pie plate to serving plate. Serve warm or cool.

1 SERVING: Calories 360; Total Fat 19g (Saturated Fat 5g); Sodium 160mg; Total Carbohydrate 44g (Dietary Fiber 2g); Protein 4g. EXCHANGES: 1 Starch, 2 Other Carbohydrate, 3-1/2 Fat. CARBOHYDRATE CHOICES: 3.

Almond Bing Cherry Pie

PREP TIME: 35 MINUTES (READY IN 3 HOURS 35 MINUTES)
SERVINGS: 10

Lola Nebel
Cambridge, Minnesota
2009 Minnesota State Fair Contest Winner

1 box Pillsbury® refrigerated pie crusts, softened as directed on box

4 cups fresh or frozen (partially thawed) halved pitted dark sweet cherries (2 lb)

1 tablespoon lemon juice

½ teaspoon almond extract

¾ cup sugar

3 tablespoons cornstarch

1 tablespoon cold butter, cut into small pieces

2 tablespoons milk

2 tablespoons sugar

¼ cup sliced almonds

1) Heat oven to 350°F. Make pie crusts as directed on box for Two-Crust Pie using 9-inch glass pie plate.

2) In large bowl, mix cherries, lemon juice and almond extract. In small bowl, mix ¾ cup sugar and the cornstarch; stir into cherry mixture. Spoon into crust-lined plate; dot with butter.

3) Cut second crust into ½-inch-wide strips. Arrange strips in lattice design over filling. Trim and fold edge under to form standing rim; flute edges. In small saucepan, heat milk, 2 tablespoons sugar and the almonds to boiling over medium heat; cook 2 minutes, stirring constantly. Brush over lattice strips.

4) Bake 20 minutes. Cover crust edge with strips of foil to prevent excessive browning; bake 30 to 40 minutes longer or until golden brown. Cool at least 2 hours before serving.

1 SERVING: Calories 354; Total Fat 13g (Saturated Fat 6g); Sodium 233mg; Total Carbohydrate 60g (Dietary Fiber 1g); Protein 4g. EXCHANGES: 1 Starch, 1 Fruit, 2 Other Carbohydrate, 1/2 High-Fat Meat, 1-1/2 Fat. CARBOHYDRATE CHOICES: 4.

tip

For easy lattice top, place second half of strips crosswise across first strips instead of weaving. Trim end of strips.

Double-Bottom Blueberry-Pecan Pie

PREP TIME: 40 MINUTES (READY IN 2 HOURS)
SERVINGS: 10

Marina Heppner
Orchard Park, NY
2007 State Fair Pie Contest Winner

1 box Pillsbury® refrigerated pie crusts, softened as directed on box

⅓ cup sugar

2 ½ teaspoons ground cinnamon

¼ cup butter, melted

¾ cup coarsely chopped pecans

3 cups fresh or frozen blueberries

½ teaspoon finely grated lemon peel

¼ cup fresh lemon juice

1 teaspoon quick-cooking tapioca

2 tablespoons sugar

¾ cup canned lemon pie filling

Lemon peel twists, if desired

1) Heat oven to 425°F. Unroll 1 pie crust in ungreased 9-inch glass pie plate. Press firmly against side and bottom. In small bowl, mix ⅓ cup sugar and the cinnamon. Brush side and top edge of crust with melted butter. Sprinkle buttered areas with cinnamon-sugar. Stir remaining cinnamon-sugar and the pecans into remaining melted butter. Sprinkle mixture into crust-lined plate. Top with second crust; seal and flute. Prick crust several times with fork. Bake 20 minutes or until golden brown. Cool completely.

2) In 1-quart saucepan, mash 1 cup of the blueberries, the grated lemon peel, lemon juice, tapioca and 2 tablespoons sugar. Cook over medium-low heat about 15 minutes, stirring frequently, until thickened. Stir in remaining 2 cups blueberries. Spread lemon pie filling over cooled pie. Top with blueberry mixture. Garnish with lemon peel twists. Store in refrigerator.

1 SERVING: Calories 322; Total Fat 17g (Saturated Fat 5g); Sodium 269mg; Total Carbohydrate 43g (Dietary Fiber 2g); Protein 3g. EXCHANGES: 1 Starch, 1/2 Fruit, 1-1/2 Other Carbohydrate, 3 Fat. CARBOHYDRATE CHOICES: 3.

Hazelnut-French Silk Turtle Pie

CRAIG PARTIN | FUQUAY-VARINA, NC

 Bake-Off®

BAKE-OFF® CONTEST 45, 2012

PREP TIME: 20 MINUTES (READY IN 1 HOUR 50 MINUTES)
SERVINGS: 8

e EASY

1 Pillsbury® refrigerated pie crust, softened as directed on box

1 package (8 oz) cream cheese, softened

1 cup hazelnut spread with cocoa (from 13-oz jar)

1 tablespoon packed brown sugar

1 container (8 oz) frozen whipped topping, thawed

¼ cup graham cracker crumbs

⅓ cup Hershey's® Caramel Syrup

2 oz Hershey's® semi-sweet baking chocolate, chopped

2 tablespoons Fisher® Chef's Naturals® Chopped Hazelnuts (filberts)

1) Heat oven to 450°F. Make pie crust as directed on box for One-Crust Baked Shell using 9-inch glass pie plate. Cool completely.

2) Meanwhile, in large bowl, beat cream cheese, hazelnut spread and brown sugar with electric mixer on medium speed until smooth. Carefully fold in whipped topping and graham cracker crumbs until blended. Reserve 1 tablespoon of the caramel syrup; set aside. Pour remaining caramel syrup into cooled pie crust; spread evenly. Spoon and spread cream cheese mixture over caramel layer.

3) Freeze 1 hour or until firm. Remove from freezer 15 minutes before serving.

4) Meanwhile, in small microwavable bowl, microwave chocolate on High 30 to 60 seconds, stirring every 10 seconds, until smooth. Drizzle melted chocolate and reserved caramel syrup over top of pie; sprinkle with hazelnuts. Store covered in refrigerator.

1 SERVING: Calories 600; Total Fat 38g (Saturated Fat 17g); Sodium 310mg; Total Carbohydrate 58g (Dietary Fiber 4g); Protein 7g. EXCHANGES: 2 Starch, 2 Other Carbohydrate, 7-1/2 Fat. CARBOHYDRATE CHOICES: 4.

Cherry-Plum-Berry Tart

PREP TIME: 30 MINUTES (READY IN 2 HOURS 20 MINUTES)
SERVINGS: 8

Denise Pounds
Hutchinson, KS
2008 State Fair Contest Winner

CRUST AND TOPPING

- 1 box Pillsbury® refrigerated pie crusts
- ¼ cup chopped almonds
- 3 tablespoons turbinado sugar (raw sugar)

FILLING

- ½ cup dried cranberries
- ½ cup dried cherries
- ¾ cup amaretto
- 1 ¼ cups fresh blueberries
- 2 plums, cut into pieces
- 4 ½ teaspoons cornstarch

WHITE AMARETTO TRUFFLE SAUCE

- ⅓ cup white vanilla baking chips
- ½ cup whipping cream
- 2 tablespoons amaretto

1) Heat oven to 425°F. Let 1 pie crust stand at room temperature 15 minutes; unroll crust into 9-inch tart pan. Lightly press into edge of pan; trim edges. Prick side and bottom of crust with fork. Bake 10 minutes. Meanwhile, in 2-quart saucepan, heat cranberries, cherries and ¾ cup amaretto over medium heat 5 minutes. Add blueberries and plums. Cook 15 minutes. Stir in cornstarch. Pour into partially baked crust.

2) Chop second crust while cold into small pieces, adding almonds and sugar while chopping. Sprinkle over filling. Bake 30 to 35 minutes. Cool. Place baking chips in small bowl. In 1-quart saucepan, heat whipping cream over low heat. As soon as bubbles form around edge of pan, remove from heat; pour warm cream over chips. Stir until smooth. Stir in 2 tablespoons amaretto. Refrigerate 1 hour, stirring every 15 minutes. Stir sauce well before serving.

1 SERVING: Calories 500; Total Fat 22g (Saturated Fat 9g); Sodium 240mg; Total Carbohydrate 64g (Dietary Fiber 2g); Protein 2g. EXCHANGES: 1 Starch, 1 Fruit, 2-1/2 Other Carbohydrate, 4-1/2 Fat. CARBOHYDRATE CHOICES: 4.

Ginger-Praline Pumpkin Tart

PREP TIME: 15 MINUTES (READY IN 2 HOURS 15 MINUTES)
SERVINGS: 10

 EASY

CRUST

- 1 Pillsbury® refrigerated pie crust, softened as directed on box
- ⅓ cup chopped glazed pecans (from 5-oz bag)
- 1 tablespoon chopped crystallized ginger

FILLING

- 2 eggs
- ½ cup sugar
- 1 teaspoon ground cinnamon
- ¾ cup whipping cream
- 1 can (15 oz) pumpkin (not pumpkin pie mix)

GARNISH

- ½ cup whipping cream, whipped
- ⅓ cup chopped glazed pecans (from 5-oz bag)
- 2 tablespoons chopped crystallized ginger

1) Place cookie sheet in oven on middle oven rack; heat oven to 425°F. Place pie crust in 10-inch tart pan with removable bottom as directed on box for One-Crust Filled Pie. Sprinkle ⅓ cup pecans and 1 tablespoon ginger in bottom of crust; press in lightly. Place tart pan on preheated cookie sheet. Bake 8 to 10 minutes or until set but not brown. Meanwhile, in large bowl, mix filling ingredients until well blended. Pour into partially baked crust.

2) Reduce oven temperature to 350°F; bake 45 to 50 minutes or until knife inserted in center comes out clean. Cool on cooling rack 1 hour. Top each serving with whipped cream; sprinkle evenly with ⅓ cup pecans and 2 tablespoons ginger.

1 SERVING: Calories 340; Total Fat 17g (Saturated Fat 8g); Sodium 140mg; Total Carbohydrate 42g (Dietary Fiber 1g); Protein 3g. EXCHANGES: 1 Starch, 2 Other Carbohydrate, 3-1/2 Fat. CARBOHYDRATE CHOICES: 3.

Individual Mixed-Berry Pies

PREP TIME: 10 MINUTES (READY IN 1 HOUR 5 MINUTES)
SERVINGS: 4

 EASY

- 1 cup fresh or frozen (thawed and drained) strawberries
- ¾ cup fresh or frozen (thawed and drained) blueberries
- ¾ cup fresh or frozen (thawed and drained) raspberries
- ⅓ cup sugar
- 2 tablespoons cornstarch
- 1 Pillsbury® refrigerated pie crust, softened as directed on box
- 1 teaspoon sugar

1) Heat oven to 425°F. In large bowl, mix berries, ⅓ cup sugar and the cornstarch. Divide mixture among 4 (6 oz) custard cups or ramekins.

2) Remove pie crust from pouch; unroll on work surface. Cut 4 (5-inch) rounds from crust. Place 1 round over filling in each cup, draping over edge of cup. Cut slits or shapes on top of each. Sprinkle with 1 teaspoon sugar. Place custard cups on 15x10x1-inch pan.

3) Bake 17 to 23 minutes or until edges are deep golden brown. Cool on cooling rack about 30 minutes. Serve warm.

1 SERVING: Calories 330; Total Fat 11g (Saturated Fat 4g); Sodium 170mg; Total Carbohydrate 57g (Dietary Fiber 5g); Protein 0g. EXCHANGES: 1/2 Fruit, 3-1/2 Other Carbohydrate, 2 Fat. CARBOHYDRATE CHOICES: 4.

English Toffee-Cappuccino Pie

PREP TIME: 15 MINUTES (READY IN 2 HOURS 50 MINUTES)
SERVINGS: 10

 EASY

CRUST

1 roll (16.5 oz) Pillsbury® refrigerated chocolate chip cookies

FILLING

1 package (8 oz) cream cheese, softened

¼ cup powdered sugar

3 tablespoons English toffee cappuccino instant hot drink mix

¼ cup chocolate-flavor syrup

1 container (8 oz) frozen whipped topping, thawed

½ cup toffee bits

1) Heat oven to 350°F. Lightly grease bottom only of 9-inch glass pie plate with shortening. Press three-fourths of the dough in bottom and up side of pie plate to form crust. Bake 15 to 17 minutes or until golden brown. Cool completely, about 1 hour.

2) Meanwhile, shape remaining dough into ½-inch balls. Place on ungreased cookie sheet 2 inches apart. Bake 6 to 8 minutes or until golden brown. Cool 5 minutes. Remove from cookie sheet. Cool completely.

3) In large bowl using electric mixer, beat cream cheese, powdered sugar, instant drink mix and 2 tablespoons of the chocolate syrup on medium speed until smooth. Fold in whipped topping and 6 tablespoons of the toffee bits. Spoon filling into cooled crust. Top with baked cookies and remaining 2 tablespoons toffee bits. Drizzle with remaining 2 tablespoons chocolate syrup. Refrigerate at least 1 hour before serving. Cover and refrigerate any remaining pie.

1 SERVING: Calories 590; Total Fat 35g (Saturated Fat 18g); Sodium 310mg; Total Carbohydrate 66g (Dietary Fiber 0g); Protein 4g. EXCHANGES: 1 Starch, 3-1/2 Other Carbohydrate, 7 Fat. CARBOHYDRATE CHOICES: 4-1/2.

Pumpkin-Caramel-Toffee Pie

PREP TIME: 10 MINUTES (READY IN 3 HOURS)
SERVINGS: 8

 EASY

- 1 Pillsbury® refrigerated pie crust, softened as directed on box
- ¾ cup canned dulce de leche (caramelized sweetened condensed milk)
- 2 eggs
- 1 can (15 oz) pumpkin (not pumpkin pie mix)
- 1 cup packed brown sugar
- 2 tablespoons all-purpose flour
- 1 tablespoon vanilla or vanilla bean paste
- ½ teaspoon salt
- 1 teaspoon ground cinnamon
- ¾ teaspoon ground ginger
- ¼ teaspoon ground nutmeg
- 1 can (12 oz) evaporated milk
- Sweetened whipped cream, if desired
- Toffee bits, if desired

1) Heat oven to 375°F. Place pie crust in 9 ½-inch glass deep-dish pie plate as directed on box for One-Crust Filled Pie. Spoon dollops of dulce de leche into crust, spreading to edges. Place in refrigerator. In medium bowl, beat eggs, pumpkin, brown sugar, flour, vanilla, salt, cinnamon, ginger and nutmeg with whisk until smooth. Beat in milk. Pour filling over dulce de leche in crust.

2) Bake on lower oven rack 48 to 50 minutes or until pie is just set (center will still jiggle slightly). Cool completely on cooling rack, about 2 hours. Garnish with whipped cream and toffee bits.

1 SERVING: Calories 382; Total Fat 13g (Saturated Fat 6g); Sodium 381mg; Total Carbohydrate 61g (Dietary Fiber 2g); Protein 8g. EXCHANGES: 1 Starch, 3 Other Carbohydrate, 1/2 High-Fat Meat, 1-1/2 Fat. CARBOHYDRATE CHOICES: 4.

Caramel-Pecan Tart

PREP TIME: 15 MINUTES (READY IN 2 HOURS)
SERVINGS: 12

 EASY

3 ½ cups coarsely chopped pecans

2 cups all-purpose flour

⅔ cup powdered sugar

¾ cup butter, cut into pieces

½ cup packed brown sugar

½ cup honey

⅔ cup butter

3 tablespoons whipping cream

1) Heat oven to 350°F. Spread pecans in ungreased shallow pan. Bake uncovered 6 to 10 minutes, stirring occasionally, until light brown. Cool completely.

2) Lightly grease 11-inch tart pan with removable bottom with shortening or cooking spray. In food processor, place flour, powdered sugar and ¾ cup butter. Cover; process with on-and-off pulses until consistency of coarse meal. Pat mixture evenly on bottom and up side of pan. Bake 20 minutes or until edges are lightly browned. Cool 15 minutes.

3) Meanwhile, in 3-quart saucepan, heat brown sugar, honey, ⅔ cup butter and the whipping cream to boiling over medium-high heat. Stir in toasted pecans; spoon hot filling into partially baked crust. Bake 25 to 30 minutes or until golden and bubbly. Cool completely on cooling rack, about 30 minutes.

1 SERVING: Calories 598; Total Fat 46g (Saturated Fat 16.5g); Sodium 196mg; Total Carbohydrate 48g (Dietary Fiber 3g); Protein 5g. EXCHANGES: 1 Starch, 2 Other Carbohydrate, 9 Fat. CARBOHYDRATE CHOICES: 3.

Fresh Blackberry Pie

PREP TIME: 20 MINUTES (READY IN 10 HOURS 40 MINUTES)
SERVINGS: 8

 EASY

1 ½ cups fresh blackberries

1 ¼ cups sugar

1 Pillsbury® refrigerated pie crust, softened as directed on box

3 tablespoons cornstarch

1 ¼ cups water

½ teaspoon vanilla

1 box (4-serving size) raspberry-flavored gelatin

4 drops blue food color

1) In large bowl, gently toss berries and ¼ cup of the sugar. Cover; refrigerate 8 hours.

2) Heat oven to 450°F. Make pie crust as directed on box for One-Crust Baked Shell using 9-inch glass pie plate. Prick bottom and sides of crust with fork. Bake 7 to 9 minutes or until lightly browned. Cool completely on cooling rack, about 15 minutes.

3) Meanwhile, in small saucepan, stir together cornstarch and remaining 1 cup sugar; slowly stir in water and vanilla with whisk. Cook over medium heat 7 to 8 minutes, stirring constantly, until mixture thickens. In small bowl, mix gelatin and food color; stir into warm cornstarch mixture.

4) Drain blackberries; spoon into cooled baked shell. Pour glaze evenly over berries, pressing down gently with spoon to be sure all berries are covered. Refrigerate 2 hours before serving.

1 SERVING: Calories 293; Total Fat 7g (Saturated Fat 3g); Sodium 177mg; Total Carbohydrate 58g (Dietary Fiber 1g); Protein 2g. EXCHANGES: 1 Starch, 3 Other Carbohydrate, 1-1/2 Fat. CARBOHYDRATE CHOICES: 4.

Apple Upside-Down Pie

PREP TIME: 25 MINUTES (READY IN 2 HOURS 40 MINUTES)
SERVINGS: 12

Marina Heppner
Orchard Park, NY
2007 State Fair Pie Contest Winner

1 cup chopped pecans

½ cup packed brown sugar

⅓ cup butter, melted

1 box Pillsbury® refrigerated pie crusts, softened as directed on box

4 medium Granny Smith apples (about 1 ¾ lb), peeled, cut into 1-inch chunks

2 large Jonagold apples (about 1 ¼ lb), peeled, cut into 1-inch chunks

¼ cup granulated sugar

2 tablespoons all-purpose flour

1 teaspoon ground cinnamon

½ teaspoon ground nutmeg

1) Heat oven to 375°F. In medium bowl, mix pecans, brown sugar and butter. Spread in bottom of 9-inch glass pie plate. Place 1 pie crust over pecan mixture, allowing excess crust to hang over sides. In large bowl, toss apples, granulated sugar, flour, cinnamon and nutmeg. Spoon apple mixture onto crust, packing tightly and mounding in center. Unroll second pie crust over filling; press edges together, fold under and crimp. Cut slits in several places.

2) Place pie on cookie sheet on lower oven rack. Bake 50 minutes. If necessary, cover crust edge with strips of foil to prevent excessive browning; bake 10 to 15 minutes longer or until juices are bubbly and crust is golden brown. Cool on cooling rack 10 minutes. Invert pie plate onto heatproof serving plate. Remove pie plate; replace any pecans in pie plate onto top of pie. Cool completely.

1 SERVING: Calories 352; Total Fat 21g (Saturated Fat 8g); Sodium 231mg; Total Carbohydrate 43g (Dietary Fiber 2g); Protein 3g. EXCHANGES: 1 Starch, 1 Fruit, 1 Other Carbohydrate, 4 Fat. CARBOHYDRATE CHOICES: 3.

Chocolate, Ginger-Cream and Pear Tart

MARIA SCOTTO DI SANTOLO | BERLIN, NJ

PREP TIME: 35 MINUTES (READY IN 3 HOURS 35 MINUTES)
SERVINGS: 12

TART

- 1 Pillsbury® refrigerated pie crust, softened as directed on box
- 2 cans (15 oz each) pear halves in juice, drained
- 1 tablespoon turbinado sugar (raw sugar)
- 2 ½ teaspoons McCormick® Ground Ginger
- 2 tablespoons Progresso® bread crumbs
- 4 oz (half of 8-oz package) cream cheese, softened
- ½ cup mascarpone cheese (from 8-oz container), softened
- ¾ cup Eagle Brand® Sweetened Condensed Milk (from 14-oz can)
- ¼ cup LAND O LAKES® Unsalted or Salted Butter, softened
- 1 LAND O LAKES® Egg
- 1 LAND O LAKES® Egg Yolk
- ⅓ cup heavy whipping cream
- ⅓ cup Hershey's® Special Dark® chocolate baking chips
- 1 teaspoon corn syrup

GARNISH

- ¾ cup heavy whipping cream, whipped
- ¼ cup Fisher® Chef's Naturals® Chopped Walnuts

1) Heat oven to 450°F. In ungreased 10- or 9-inch tart pan with removable bottom, press pie crust evenly in bottom and up side of pan. Generously prick crust with fork.

2) Bake 6 to 9 minutes or until golden brown. Reduce oven temperature to 325°F. Cool crust 15 minutes.

3) Meanwhile, reserve 2 pear halves for garnish; refrigerate. Slice remaining pear halves; place in small bowl. Add raw sugar, ½ teaspoon of the ginger and bread crumbs; toss gently to coat. In medium bowl, beat cream cheese and mascarpone with electric mixer on high speed until smooth. Add condensed milk, butter, remaining 2 teaspoons ginger, 1 whole egg and 1 egg yolk; beat on medium speed until well blended. Spread 1 cup filling over cooled crust; arrange pear slices on top. Spread remaining filling over pears.

4) Bake at 325°F 40 to 50 minutes or until set and golden brown around edge. Cool 30 minutes.

5) In small microwavable bowl, microwave ⅓ cup whipping cream and chocolate chips on High 1 to 2 minutes, stirring every 30 seconds, or until smooth. Stir in corn syrup until well blended. Spread over cooled tart. Refrigerate 1 hour 30 minutes or until set.

6) Cut reserved pear halves into 12 slices. Remove side of pan. To serve, cut into 12 wedges. Top each wedge with 2 tablespoons whipped cream, 1 pear slice and 1 teaspoon walnuts. Store covered in refrigerator.

1 SERVING: Calories 330; Total Fat 22g (Saturated Fat 12g); Sodium 160mg; Total Carbohydrate 29g (Dietary Fiber 1g); Protein 4g. EXCHANGES: 1 Starch, 1 Other Carbohydrate, 4 Fat. CARBOHYDRATE CHOICES: 2.

Mango-Pineapple Pie

Regina Ferris
Mesquite, TX
2008 State Fair Contest Winner

PREP TIME: 45 MINUTES (READY IN 3 HOURS 35 MINUTES)
SERVINGS: 10

1 box Pillsbury® refrigerated pie crusts, softened as directed on box

¾ cup coarsely chopped macadamia nuts

2 cups fresh or frozen (thawed) mango chunks

2 cups chopped fresh pineapple

¾ cup sugar

¼ cup canned cream of coconut (not coconut milk)

3 tablespoons cornstarch

½ teaspoon salt

1 tablespoon butter or margarine

3 tablespoons milk

1 tablespoon sugar

1) Heat oven to 350°F. Make pie crusts as directed on box for Two-Crust Pie using 9-inch glass pie plate. Place second crust on lightly floured sheet of waxed paper. Using pastry cutter, gently mark lines on crust 1 inch apart. Sprinkle macadamia nuts between lines on crust; use rolling pin to gently press nuts into crust. Cut into strips along lines; set aside.

2) In 2-quart saucepan, mix mango, pineapple, ¾ cup sugar and the cream of coconut. In small bowl, mix cornstarch and salt; stir into fruit mixture. Cook over medium-low heat until thickened. Stir in butter; pour into crust-lined plate.

3) Place 5 to 7 pie crust strips across filling. Place cross-strips over first strips. Seal and flute edges. Brush with milk; sprinkle with 1 tablespoon sugar. Bake 45 to 50 minutes or until golden brown. Cool on cooling rack at least 2 hours.

1 SERVING: Calories 394; Total Fat 21g (Saturated Fat 8g); Sodium 355mg; Total Carbohydrate 52g (Dietary Fiber 2g); Protein 3g. EXCHANGES: 1 Starch, 1 Fruit, 1-1/2 Other Carbohydrate, 4 Fat. CARBOHYDRATE CHOICES: 3-1/2.

Delectable Desserts

There's always room for dessert, and these sweet sensations make it easy to whip up a winner!

ALMOND-CREAM PUFF PASTRIES
PG. 313

MOCHA MOUSSE
PG. 334

PINEAPPLE UPSIDE-DOWN CAKE
PG. 334

CARAMEL IN-BETWEEN
FUDGE CAKE
PG. 340

Cream-Filled Strawberry-Brownie Cake

DORIS WALLACE | DES ARC, AR

BAKE-OFF® CONTEST 45, 2012

PREP TIME: 40 MINUTES (READY IN 3 HOURS 20 MINUTES)
SERVINGS: 16

BROWNIE LAYER

- 1 box (19.5 oz) Pillsbury® Chocolate Fudge Brownie Mix
- ½ cup Crisco® Pure Vegetable Oil
- ¼ cup water
- 3 LAND O LAKES® Eggs

CAKE LAYER

- 1 box (18.25 oz) Pillsbury® Strawberry Cake Mix
- ¾ cup water
- ¼ cup Crisco® Pure Vegetable Oil
- 3 LAND O LAKES® Eggs
- ½ cup diced fresh strawberries

FILLING

- 1 package (8 oz) cream cheese, softened
- ½ cup LAND O LAKES® Butter, softened
- 3 cups powdered sugar
- 1 container (8 oz) frozen whipped topping, thawed

FROSTING AND GARNISH

- 1 container (16 oz) frozen whipped topping, thawed
- ⅔ cup powdered sugar
- 3 cups sliced fresh strawberries

1) Heat oven to 350°F. Spray 3 (9-inch) round cake pans with Crisco® Original No-Stick Cooking Spray. Line bottoms of pans with cooking parchment paper; spray paper with cooking spray. In medium bowl, stir all brownie layer ingredients 50 strokes with spoon. Spread about 1 cup batter in each of 3 pans.

2) In large bowl, beat all cake layer ingredients except diced strawberries with electric mixer on low speed 30 seconds. Beat on high speed 2 minutes or until blended. Fold in diced strawberries. Pour and spread about 1 ⅓ cups mixture evenly over brownie batter in each pan.

3) Bake 20 to 30 minutes or until toothpick inserted in center comes out clean. Cool in pans 10 minutes. Carefully invert cake layers from pans onto cooling racks; remove parchment paper. Cool completely, about 1 hour.

4) Meanwhile, to make filling, in medium bowl, beat cream cheese and butter with electric mixer on high speed until smooth and creamy. Beat in 3 cups powdered sugar until creamy. Carefully fold in 8 oz whipped topping.

5) To make frosting, in another medium bowl, beat 16 oz whipped topping and ⅔ cup powdered sugar with electric mixer on low speed until blended.

6) To assemble cake, place 1 cake layer, brownie side down, on serving plate. Spread half of filling to within ¼ inch of edge; top with ¾ cup of the strawberry slices. Repeat with second layer, remaining filling and ¾ cup strawberry slices. Top with remaining cake layer, top side up. Frost sides and top of cake with frosting. Garnish with remaining 1 ½ cups strawberry slices. Refrigerate 1 hour before serving. Store in refrigerator.

1 SERVING: Calories 570; Total Fat 32g (Saturated Fat 15g); Sodium 330mg; Total Carbohydrate 65g (Dietary Fiber 1g); Protein 5g. EXCHANGES: 2 Starch, 2-1/2 Other Carbohydrate, 6 Fat. CARBOHYDRATE CHOICES: 4.

Almond-Cream Puff Pastries

PREP TIME:	30 MINUTES (READY IN 1 HOUR)
SERVINGS:	12

2 packages (10 oz each) frozen puff pastry shells

1 cup milk

2 egg yolks

⅓ cup sugar

2 tablespoons cornstarch

½ teaspoon vanilla

¼ teaspoon almond extract

1 cup whipping cream

3 tablespoons sliced almonds, toasted

12 raspberries

1) Heat oven to 400°F. Bake puff pastry shells as directed on package. Cool on cooling rack, removing and reserving tops.

2) In 1-quart saucepan, heat milk to simmering; remove from heat. In medium bowl, beat egg yolks and ¼ cup of the sugar with whisk. Sift cornstarch over mixture; beat with whisk until well blended. Stir in ½ cup warm milk. Slowly pour egg mixture into pan, stirring constantly. Heat to boiling over medium-high heat; cook and stir 4 to 5 minutes until thickened. Remove from heat; stir in vanilla and almond extract. Pour pudding into clean medium bowl; place plastic wrap directly on surface of pudding. Refrigerate 30 minutes.

3) In large bowl, beat whipping cream and remaining 4 teaspoons sugar with electric mixer on high speed until stiff peaks form. Gently fold two-thirds of the whipped cream into pudding. Divide evenly among pastry shells. Replace pastry tops; dollop with remaining whipped cream. Top with almonds and raspberries.

1 SERVING: Calories 316; Total Fat 22g (Saturated Fat 9g); Sodium 250mg; Total Carbohydrate 25g (Dietary Fiber 1g); Protein 6g. EXCHANGES: 1 Starch, 1/2 Other Carbohydrate, 1/2 High-Fat Meat, 3-1/2 Fat CARBOHYDRATE CHOICES: 1-1/2.

Banana-Caramel Sundaes

PREP TIME: 10 MINUTES (READY IN 10 MINUTES)
SERVINGS: 4

EASY

2 large bananas

1 ⅓ cups vanilla ice cream

¼ cup caramel topping

⅓ cup coarsely chopped cinnamon-coated almonds

1) Cut each banana in half crosswise and then in half lengthwise to make 8 quarters. Place 2 banana quarters in each of 4 stemmed glasses or individual serving bowls.

2) Top each serving with ⅓ cup ice cream and 1 tablespoon caramel topping; sprinkle each sundae with about 1 tablespoon almonds.

1 SERVING: Calories 263; Total Fat 11g (Saturated Fat 4g); Sodium 96mg; Total Carbohydrate 41g (Dietary Fiber 3g); Protein 5g. EXCHANGES: 1 Fruit, 1-1/2 Other Carbohydrate, 1/2 High-Fat Meat, 1-1/2 Fat. CARBOHYDRATE CHOICES: 2-1/2.

tip Cinnamon-coated almonds are great to use for embellishing recipes that need only a few ingredients. Try them on desserts like ice cream sundaes or in sweet-and-savory recipes such as salads. Look for the almonds either with the other nuts in your supermarket or near the produce section.

Coconut Cake

PREP TIME: 30 MINUTES (READY IN 10 HOURS)
SERVINGS: 16

1 box butter recipe yellow cake mix with pudding in the mix

½ cup butter, softened

¾ cup canned coconut milk (not cream of coconut)

½ cup water

3 eggs

1 bag (14 oz) flaked coconut

2 cups sugar

1 container (16 oz) sour cream

1 container (8 oz) frozen whipped topping, thawed

¼ teaspoon coconut extract

1) Heat oven to 350°F. Generously grease bottoms and sides of 2 (8-inch) round cake pans with shortening. Line pans with waxed paper; grease paper and lightly flour.

2) In large bowl, beat cake mix, butter, coconut milk, water and eggs with electric mixer on low speed 30 seconds. Beat on medium speed 2 minutes. Pour batter into pans. Bake 33 to 38 minutes or until toothpick comes out clean. Cool 10 minutes; remove from pans to cooling racks. Remove waxed paper. Cool completely, about 40 minutes.

3) In medium bowl, mix 2 cups of the coconut, the sugar and sour cream. Spoon 2 cups of the mixture into large bowl; stir in whipped topping, coconut extract and 1 cup coconut. Cut each cake horizontally to make 2 layers. Spread one-third (about ⅔ cup) of the coconut-sour cream mixture on cut side of 1 layer. Repeat layers twice. Top with remaining layer, cut side down. Frost top and side of cake with coconut topping mixture. Press remaining coconut into top and side of cake. Cover; refrigerate 8 hours before serving.

1 SERVING: Calories 529; Total Fat 27g (Saturated Fat 20g); Sodium 359mg; Total Carbohydrate 66g (Dietary Fiber 2g); Protein 5g. EXCHANGES: 1 Starch, 3-1/2 Other Carbohydrate, 5 Fat. CARBOHYDRATE CHOICES: 4-1/2.

Tiramisu Toffee Trifle Pie

PREP TIME: 15 MINUTES (READY IN 8 HOURS 15 MINUTES)
SERVINGS: 10

 EASY

4 ½ teaspoons instant coffee granules or crystals

¾ cup warm water

1 package (10.75 oz) frozen pound cake loaf, thawed

1 package (8 oz) cream cheese or 1 container (8 oz) mascarpone cheese, softened

½ cup powdered sugar

½ cup chocolate-flavor syrup

1 container (12 oz) frozen whipped topping, thawed

2 bars (1.4 oz each) chocolate-covered English toffee candy, coarsely chopped

1) In small bowl, stir coffee granules in warm water until dissolved. Cool.

2) Cut pound cake into 14 slices. Cut each slice in half diagonally. Place cake pieces on bottom and up side of 9 ½-inch glass deep-dish pie plate. Drizzle coffee over cake pieces.

3) In medium bowl, beat cream cheese, powdered sugar and chocolate syrup with electric mixer on medium speed until smooth. Add 2 ½ cups of the whipped topping; beat until light and fluffy.

4) Spread filling evenly into cake-lined pie plate. Spoon remaining whipped topping over pie. Sprinkle with chopped candy. Refrigerate 8 hours before serving.

1 SERVING: Calories 396; Total Fat 21g (Saturated Fat 14g); Sodium 253mg; Total Carbohydrate 47g (Dietary Fiber 0g); Protein 4g. EXCHANGES: 1/2 Starch, 2-1/2 Other Carbohydrate, 1/2 High-Fat Meat, 3-1/2 Fat. CARBOHYDRATE CHOICES: 3.

Baked Fruit Turnovers

PREP TIME: 10 MINUTES (READY IN 25 MINUTES)
SERVINGS: 6 TURNOVERS

 EASY

1 box Pillsbury® refrigerated pie crusts, softened as directed on box

1 cup cherry, apple or peach pie filling (from 21-oz can)

¼ cup chopped pecans, toasted

1 tablespoon sugar

½ teaspoon ground cinnamon

1) Heat oven to 425°F. Spray cookie sheet with cooking spray. Remove pie crusts from pouches; unroll on work surface or cutting board. Cut each crust into 6 wedges.

2) In medium bowl, stir together pie filling and pecans; spoon mixture evenly in center of 6 wedges. Top each with another wedge. Moisten edges of pastry with water; press edges with fork to seal. Place turnovers on cookie sheet.

3) Bake 12 to 14 minutes or until golden brown. In small bowl, mix sugar and cinnamon; sprinkle evenly over turnovers. Serve warm.

1 TURNOVER: Calories 372; Total Fat 22g (Saturated Fat 8g); Sodium 374mg; Total Carbohydrate 45g (Dietary Fiber 1g); Protein 3g. EXCHANGES: 2 Starch, 1 Other Carbohydrate, 4 Fat. CARBOHYDRATE CHOICES: 3.

Candy Cane Angel Cake

PREP TIME: 10 MINUTES (READY IN 2 HOURS 50 MINUTES)
SERVINGS: 12

 EASY   LOW FAT

1 box (16 oz) angel food cake mix

1 ¼ cups cold water

½ teaspoon red paste food color

1 teaspoon peppermint extract

¾ cup powdered sugar

1 to 2 tablespoons milk

½ cup finely crushed soft peppermint candies

1) Move oven rack to lowest position (remove other racks). Heat oven to 350°F. In extra-large glass or metal bowl, beat cake mix and cold water with electric mixer on low speed 30 seconds. Beat on medium speed 1 minute.

2) Pour about 3 cups batter into ungreased 10-inch angel food (tube) cake pan. Into small bowl, pour about ¾ cup batter; stir in food color and peppermint extract until blended. Carefully spoon red batter over white batter in pan. Carefully spoon remaining white batter over red batter and swirl with knife.

3) Bake 40 minutes or until top springs back when lightly touched. Immediately turn pan upside down onto heatproof funnel or bottle. Cool completely, about 2 hours. Loosen cake by running long metal spatula along edge of pan. Place serving plate upside down on pan. Turn plate and pan over; remove pan.

4) In small bowl, mix powdered sugar and 1 tablespoon milk; stir in enough remaining milk, 1 teaspoon at a time, until thin enough to drizzle. Drizzle over cake; top with crushed candies.

1 SERVING: Calories 181; Total Fat 0g (Saturated Fat 0g); Sodium 186mg; Total Carbohydrate 42g (Dietary Fiber 0g); Protein 3g. EXCHANGES: 1 Starch, 2 Other Carbohydrate. CARBOHYDRATE CHOICES: 3.

Easy Lane Cake

PREP TIME: 25 MINUTES (READY IN 2 HOURS 25 MINUTES)
SERVINGS: 12

1 box white cake mix with pudding in the mix

1 cup water

⅓ cup vegetable oil

3 whole eggs

½ cup butter (do not use margarine)

1 cup sugar

8 egg yolks

1 cup chopped pecans, toasted

1 cup raisins

1 cup flaked coconut

¼ cup bourbon

Maraschino cherries or candied cherries, if desired

Whipping cream, whipped, if desired

1) Heat oven to 350°F. Grease bottom only of 13x9-inch pan with shortening or cooking spray.

2) In large bowl, beat cake mix, water, oil and whole eggs with electric mixer on low speed 30 seconds. Beat on medium speed 2 minutes, scraping bowl occasionally. Pour batter into pan.

3) Bake 28 to 32 minutes or until toothpick inserted in center comes out clean. Cool completely on cooling rack, about 1 hour.

4) Meanwhile, in 2-quart saucepan, melt butter. Stir in sugar and egg yolks with whisk. Cook over medium heat, stirring constantly, 5 to 8 minutes or until thickened and a thermometer reads 160°F. Remove from heat. Stir in pecans, raisins, coconut and bourbon. Cool completely, about 30 minutes.

5) Spread custard evenly over top of cake. Garnish with cherries and whipped cream. Store covered in refrigerator.

1 SERVING: Calories 573; Total Fat 31g (Saturated Fat 10g); Sodium 401mg; Total Carbohydrate 68g (Dietary Fiber 2.5g); Protein 6.5g. EXCHANGES: 1 Starch, 3 Other Carbohydrate, 6 Fat. CARBOHYDRATE CHOICES: 4-1/2.

Apple Butter-Pecan Cupcakes

PREP TIME:	20 MINUTES (READY IN 1 HOUR 20 MINUTES)
SERVINGS:	24 CUPCAKES

 EASY

CUPCAKES

- 1 box golden vanilla cake mix with pudding in the mix
- 1 cup water
- ⅓ cup butter, softened
- 3 eggs
- ½ cup chopped pecans, toasted
- ⅓ cup apple butter
- 1 teaspoon pumpkin pie spice

FROSTING

- ½ cup butter, softened
- 1 tablespoon apple butter
- 1 package (8 oz) cream cheese, softened
- 3 cups powdered sugar
- ½ cup chopped pecans, toasted

1) Heat oven to 350°F. Place paper baking cup in each of 24 regular-size muffin cups.

2) In large bowl, beat cake mix, water, ⅓ cup butter and the eggs with electric mixer on low speed 30 seconds. Beat on medium speed 2 minutes, scraping bowl occasionally. Stir in ½ cup pecans, ⅓ cup apple butter and the pumpkin pie spice. Divide batter evenly among muffin cups.

3) Bake 25 to 30 minutes or until toothpick inserted in center comes out clean. Cool 10 minutes; remove from pans to cooling racks. Cool completely, about 30 minutes.

4) In medium bowl, beat ½ cup butter, 1 tablespoon apple butter and the cream cheese with electric mixer on medium speed until creamy. Gradually beat in powdered sugar until smooth. Frost cupcakes. Sprinkle each with 1 teaspoon pecans.

1 CUPCAKE: Calories 297; Total Fat 15g (Saturated Fat 7g); Sodium 241mg; Total Carbohydrate 39g (Dietary Fiber 0.5g); Protein 3g. EXCHANGES: 1/2 Starch, 2 Other Carbohydrate, 3 Fat. CARBOHYDRATE CHOICES: 2-1/2.

Frozen Orange Swirl Pie

PREP TIME: 10 MINUTES (READY IN 2 HOURS 10 MINUTES)
SERVINGS: 8

 EASY

1 pint (2 cups) vanilla ice cream, slightly softened

1 pint (2 cups) orange sherbet, slightly softened

1 chocolate flavor crumb crust (6 oz)

½ cup hot fudge topping (from 16 oz jar), if desired

1) Place heaping spoonfuls of ice cream and sherbet in crumb crust. Using back of spoon, lightly press and smooth top. Freeze about 2 hours or until firm.

2) Cut into wedges. Drizzle fudge topping over each wedge.

1 SERVING: Calories 220; Total Fat 9g (Saturated Fat 3.5g); Sodium 150mg; Total Carbohydrate 33g (Dietary Fiber 1g); Protein 3g. EXCHANGES: 1-1/2 Starch, 1/2 Other Carbohydrate, 1-1/2 Fat. CARBOHYDRATE CHOICES: 2.

Peach Dumplings with Raspberry Sauce

PREP TIME: 15 MINUTES (READY IN 50 MINUTES)
SERVINGS: 4

 EASY

1 Pillsbury® refrigerated pie crust, softened as directed on box

1 can (16 oz) peach halves in light syrup, drained, syrup reserved

1 egg white, slightly beaten

1 tablespoon sugar

½ cup red raspberry preserves

¼ teaspoon almond extract

1) Heat oven to 425°F. Remove pie crust from pouch; unroll on floured work surface. Cut crust into quarters.

2) Divide peaches evenly onto crust quarters. Brush crust edges lightly with reserved peach syrup. Bring sides of crust up over peaches; press edges to seal, making 3 seams. Place seam side up in ungreased 8-inch square or 12x8-inch (2-quart) glass baking dish. Brush crust with egg white; sprinkle with sugar.

3) Bake 22 to 32 minutes or until golden brown. Immediately remove from baking dish; place in individual dessert dishes.

4) In 1-quart saucepan, mix preserves and almond extract. Heat over low heat, stirring occasionally, until warm. Serve sauce with warm dumplings.

1 SERVING: Calories 400; Total Fat 14g (Saturated Fat 5g); Sodium 250mg; Total Carbohydrate 67g (Dietary Fiber 1g); Protein 1g. EXCHANGES: 1/2 Starch, 4 Other Carbohydrate, 2-1/2 Fat. CARBOHYDRATE CHOICES: 4-1/2.

Orange Cream-Macadamia Torte

BRETT YOUMANS | READING, PA

BAKE-OFF® CONTEST 45, 2012

PREP TIME: 40 MINUTES (READY IN 2 HOURS 50 MINUTES)
SERVINGS: 16

TORTE

- 1 roll Pillsbury® refrigerated sugar cookie dough
- 1 package (8 oz) cream cheese, softened
- 1 teaspoon McCormick® Pure Vanilla Extract
- 1 ¼ cups flaked coconut, toasted*
- 1 ¼ cups Fisher® Chef's Naturals® Chopped Macadamia Nuts, toasted**
- 3 tablespoons grated orange peel
- 2 tablespoons grated lemon peel
- 1 can (14 oz) Eagle Brand® Sweetened Condensed Milk
- ¼ cup freshly squeezed orange juice
- 2 tablespoons LAND O LAKES® Butter

ICING

- 1 cup Hershey's® premier white baking chips
- 1 tablespoon Crisco® All-Vegetable Shortening

  Garnish, if desired

- 1 large orange, cut into 16 thin slices

1) Heat oven to 350°F. Let cookie dough stand at room temperature 10 minutes to soften. In large bowl, break up cookie dough. Add ¼ of the cream cheese and vanilla; beat with electric mixer on medium speed until well blended. Add 1 cup of the coconut, ¾ cup of the nuts, 1 tablespoon of the orange peel and 1 tablespoon of the lemon peel; beat until well blended. Spread evenly in bottom and up side of ungreased 10-inch nonstick tart pan with removable bottom.

2) Bake 18 to 23 minutes or until light golden brown. Cool completely, about 1 hour.

3) Meanwhile, in 2-quart heavy saucepan, add condensed milk, orange juice, butter, remaining cream cheese, orange peel and lemon peel. Cook over low heat, 20 to 25 minutes, stirring constantly with wire whisk, until mixture is bubbly and thickened. Remove from heat; spread over cooled crust. Refrigerate until cooled, about 1 hour.

4) In small microwavable bowl, combine icing ingredients, microwave on High 30 to 40 seconds, stirring every 10 seconds, until smooth. Drizzle over cooled torte to cover. Sprinkle with remaining ¼ cup coconut and ½ cup nuts, lightly pressing into icing. To serve, cut into 16 wedges; top each with orange slice. Store loosely covered in refrigerator.

1 SERVING: Calories 450; Total Fat 27g (Saturated Fat 13g); Sodium 250mg; Total Carbohydrate 46g (Dietary Fiber 1g); Protein 5g. EXCHANGES: 1-1/2 Starch, 1-1/2 Other Carbohydrate, 5-1/2 Fat. CARBOHYDRATE CHOICES: 3.

* To toast coconut, spread in shallow pan. Bake at 350°F 8 to 10 minutes, stirring occasionally, or until golden brown. Remove from pan.
** Chop larger macadamia nuts. To toast nuts, spread in shallow pan. Bake at 350°F 6 to 10 minutes, stirring occasionally, or until light brown. Remove from pan.

Biscuit Bread Pudding

PREP TIME: 20 MINUTES (READY IN 1 HOUR 15 MINUTES)
SERVINGS: 12

 EASY

12 Pillsbury® Grands!® frozen buttermilk biscuits (from 16 oz bag)

8 eggs

4 ½ cups milk

⅔ cup sugar

⅔ cup raisins

2 teaspoons ground cinnamon

2 teaspoons vanilla

Caramel topping, warmed, if desired

1) Heat oven to 350°F. Generously spray 12 (10-oz) custard cups with cooking spray.

2) Bake biscuits as directed on bag. Cool completely, about 20 minutes.

3) Meanwhile, in large bowl, beat eggs. Add milk, sugar, raisins, cinnamon and vanilla; mix well. Cut baked biscuits into 1-inch cubes. Add to egg mixture; stir until well coated. Let stand 5 minutes. Divide biscuit mixture evenly among custard cups.

4) Bake 20 to 25 minutes or until set. Run knife or metal spatula around edge of cups to loosen; slide bread pudding onto dessert plates. Drizzle with caramel topping. Serve warm.

1 SERVING: Calories 350; Total Fat 14g (Saturated Fat 5g); Sodium 640mg; Total Carbohydrate 44g (Dietary Fiber 0g); Protein 11g. EXCHANGES: 3 Starch, 1/2 Medium-Fat Meat, 1-1/2 Fat. CARBOHYDRATE CHOICES: 3.

tip You can bake the biscuits up to 2 days before preparing the pudding. After they have cooled, store in a sealed food-storage plastic bag at room temperature. It won't matter if they're no longer as soft as fresh-baked—the milk and sugar mixture will work its magic either way.

Incredible Peach Cobbler

BECKY BEUS | KUNA, ID

BAKE-OFF® CONTEST 39, 2000

Bake-Off®

PREP TIME: 15 MINUTES (READY IN 1 HOUR 25 MINUTES)
SERVINGS: 15

 EASY

½ cup butter or margarine

1 box Pillsbury® cranberry quick bread and muffin mix

2 tablespoons grated orange peel

2 cans (29 oz each) peach slices in light syrup, drained, 1 cup liquid reserved

1 egg

⅓ cup sweetened dried cranberries

⅓ cup sugar

Vanilla ice cream, if desired

1) Heat oven to 375°F. In ungreased 13x9-inch pan, melt butter in oven.

2) Meanwhile, in large bowl, place quick bread mix, 1 tablespoon of the orange peel, 1 cup reserved peach liquid and the egg; stir 50 to 75 strokes with spoon until mix is moistened. Drop mixture by spoonfuls over butter in pan; spread slightly without stirring. Arrange peaches over mixture. Sprinkle with cranberries.

3) In small bowl, mix sugar and remaining 1 tablespoon orange peel; sprinkle over fruit.

4) Bake 45 to 50 minutes or until edges are deep golden brown. Cool 20 minutes. Serve warm with ice cream.

1 SERVING: Calories 260; Total Fat 9g (Saturated Fat 4.5g); Sodium 190mg; Total Carbohydrate 41g (Dietary Fiber 2g); Protein 3g. EXCHANGES: 1 Starch, 1-1/2 Other Carbohydrate, 1-1/2 Fat. CARBOHYDRATE CHOICES: 3.

Mini Chocolate Rum Cakes

PREP TIME: 30 MINUTES (READY IN 1 HOUR 25 MINUTES)
SERVINGS: 12

CAKES

- 1 box devil's food cake mix with pudding in the mix
- ³/₄ cup fat-free buttermilk
- ²/₃ cup vegetable oil
- ½ cup dark rum
- 3 eggs
- 1 ½ cups miniature semisweet chocolate chips

GANACHE GLAZE

- 6 oz bittersweet baking chocolate, chopped
- ½ cup whipping cream
- 1 tablespoon dark rum

DRIZZLE

- 4 oz white baking chocolate bars or squares, chopped

1) Heat oven to 350°F. Grease 2 (6-cup) miniature fluted tube cake pans with shortening; lightly flour. In medium bowl, beat cake ingredients except chocolate chips with electric mixer on low speed 30 seconds. Beat on medium speed 2 minutes, until smooth. Stir in chocolate chips. Divide batter evenly among pans.

2) Bake 18 minutes or until toothpick inserted in center comes out clean. Cool 5 minutes. Carefully invert each pan onto cooling rack; lift pan from cakes. Cool completely, about 30 minutes.

3) Place bittersweet chocolate in medium bowl. In 1-quart saucepan, heat whipping cream to simmering; pour over chocolate. Let stand 3 minutes. Stir in 1 tablespoon rum. Spoon glaze over cakes.

4) In small resealable freezer plastic bag, place white chocolate; seal bag. Microwave on High about 1 minute or until softened. Gently squeeze bag until chocolate is smooth; cut off tiny corner of bag. Squeeze bag to drizzle chocolate over cakes.

1 SERVING: Calories 657; Total Fat 39g (Saturated Fat 16g); Sodium 376mg; Total Carbohydrate 65g (Dietary Fiber 2g); Protein 9g. EXCHANGES: 1 Starch, 3-1/2 Other Carbohydrate, 8 Fat. CARBOHYDRATE CHOICES: 4-1/2.

Chocolate-Butterscotch Lava Cake

PREP TIME: 15 MINUTES (READY IN 5 HOURS)
SERVINGS: 12

 EASY

- 1 box dark chocolate cake mix with pudding in the mix
- 1 box (4-serving size) chocolate instant pudding and pie filling mix
- 1 cup sour cream
- ⅓ cup butter or margarine, melted
- 1 teaspoon vanilla
- 3 ¼ cups milk
- 3 eggs
- 1 bag (8 oz) toffee bits
- 1 box (4-serving size) butterscotch instant pudding and pie filling mix
- 1 container (8 oz) frozen whipped topping, thawed

1) Spray 5-quart oval slow cooker with cooking spray. In large bowl, beat cake mix, chocolate pudding mix, sour cream, butter, vanilla, 1 ¼ cups of the milk and the eggs with electric mixer on medium speed 2 minutes, scraping sides of bowl as needed. Stir in 1 cup of the toffee bits. Pour batter into slow cooker.

2) In 2-quart saucepan, heat remaining 2 cups milk over medium heat 3 to 5 minutes, stirring frequently, until hot and bubbly. Remove from heat. Sprinkle butterscotch pudding mix over batter in slow cooker. Slowly pour hot milk over pudding.

3) Cover; cook on Low heat setting 4 hours 30 minutes or until edge of cake is set at least 2 inches from edge of slow cooker but center still jiggles slightly when moved. Turn off slow cooker. Let stand 15 minutes. Garnish with whipped topping and remaining toffee bits.

1 SERVING: Calories 534; Total Fat 23.5g (Saturated Fat 13.5g); Sodium 736mg; Total Carbohydrate 70.5g (Dietary Fiber 1.5g); Protein 8g. EXCHANGES: 4-1/2 Other Carbohydrate, 1 Medium-Fat Meat, 3-1/2 Fat. CARBOHYDRATE CHOICES: 4-1/2.

Cranberry-Orange Cake

PREP TIME: 10 MINUTES (READY IN 2 HOURS 15 MINUTES)
SERVINGS: 8

 EASY

1 package (16.6 oz) date quick bread mix

⅔ cup water

½ cup sweetened dried cranberries

2 tablespoons vegetable oil

1 ½ teaspoons grated orange peel

2 eggs

4 oz (half of 8-oz container) mascarpone cheese

¼ cup powdered sugar

1 tablespoon milk

Orange peel twists, if desired

1) Heat oven to 350°F. Spray 7-inch tube pan with cooking spray; lightly flour. Place pan on cookie sheet.

2) In large bowl, stir bread mix, water, dried cranberries, oil, grated orange peel and eggs until blended. Pour batter into pan.

3) Bake 40 to 50 minutes or until toothpick inserted in center comes out clean. Cool 15 minutes; remove from pan to cooling rack. Cool completely, about 1 hour.

4) In small bowl, mix mascarpone cheese, powdered sugar and milk until smooth. Pour over cake. Garnish with orange peel twists.

1 SERVING: Calories 376; Total Fat 14g (Saturated Fat 5g); Sodium 226mg; Total Carbohydrate 60g (Dietary Fiber 2g); Protein 6g. EXCHANGES: 2-1/2 Starch, 1 Fruit, 1 Other Carbohydrate, 3 Fat. CARBOHYDRATE CHOICES: 4.

Maple Crème Brûlée

PREP TIME: 10 MINUTES (READY IN 9 HOURS 50 MINUTES)
SERVINGS: 6

 EASY

2 cups whipping cream

2 whole eggs

2 egg yolks

⅔ cup real maple syrup

Dash salt

6 tablespoons maple sugar

1) Heat oven to 325°F. In 2-quart saucepan, heat whipping cream to simmering over medium heat; remove from heat. In medium bowl, beat whole eggs, egg yolks, syrup and salt with whisk. Gradually stir in warm whipping cream. Pour into 6 (4-oz) ramekins or custard cups. Place ramekins in 13x9-inch pan. Place pan in oven. Pour hot water into pan to within ½ inch of tops of cups.

2) Bake 1 hour 10 minutes or until knife comes out clean. Remove cups from water. Place on cooling rack; cool 30 minutes. Cover tightly with plastic wrap; refrigerate until well chilled. Set oven control to broil. In food processor, place maple sugar. Cover; process until sugar is finely chopped. Uncover custard cups; gently blot any condensation on custards with paper towel. Sprinkle custards evenly with sugar. Place in 15x10x1-inch pan. Broil with tops 4 inches from heat about 3 minutes or until sugar is caramelized. Serve immediately.

1 SERVING: Calories 463; Total Fat 33g (Saturated Fat 20g); Sodium 113mg; Total Carbohydrate 40g (Dietary Fiber 0g); Protein 5g. EXCHANGES: 2-1/2 Other Carbohydrate, 1/2 High-Fat Meat, 6 Fat. CARBOHYDRATE CHOICES: 2-1/2.

tip

To cut bars easily, line bottom and sides of 9-inch square pan with foil, leaving foil overhanging at 2 opposite sides of pan. Make bars as directed. Use foil to lift bars from pan, then pull foil from sides of bars before cutting.

Chocolate-Macadamia Shortbread

PREP TIME:	20 MINUTES (READY IN 3 HOURS 20 MINUTES)	**e** EASY
SERVINGS:	36 BARS	

³⁄₄ cup butter, softened

¼ cup packed brown sugar

1 ½ cups all-purpose flour

½ teaspoon salt

½ cup chopped dry-roasted macadamia nuts

1 can (14 oz) sweetened condensed milk (not evaporated)

1 bag (12 oz) white vanilla baking chips (2 cups)

4 oz dried pineapple, finely chopped (³⁄₄ cup)

1 bag (12 oz) semisweet chocolate chips (2 cups)

1 tablespoon butter

¼ cup whipping cream

1) Heat oven to 350°F. In medium bowl, beat ³⁄₄ cup butter and the brown sugar with electric mixer on medium speed until creamy. Add flour and salt; beat until soft dough forms. Stir in nuts. Press in 9-inch square pan. Bake 25 to 30 minutes. Cool 10 minutes.

2) In medium microwavable bowl, microwave condensed milk and vanilla baking chips uncovered on High 1 to 2 minutes, stirring every 30 seconds, until chips are melted and mixture can be stirred smooth. Stir in dried pineapple. Pour over shortbread. Refrigerate 1 hour 30 minutes or until set. In small microwavable bowl, microwave chocolate chips, 1 tablespoon butter and the whipping cream uncovered on High 1 to 2 minutes, stirring every 30 seconds, until chips are melted and mixture can be stirred smooth. Spread over pineapple layer. Refrigerate 1 hour or until set. Cut into 6 rows by 6 rows. Store covered in refrigerator.

1 BAR: Calories 220; Total Fat 12g (Saturated Fat 8g); Sodium 100mg; Total Carbohydrate 26g (Dietary Fiber 1g); Protein 2g. EXCHANGES: 1/2 Starch, 1 Other Carbohydrate, 2-1/2 Fat. CARBOHYDRATE CHOICES: 2.

Butter Pecan Ice Cream Cake

PREP TIME: 15 MINUTES (READY IN 3 HOURS)
SERVINGS: 12

 EASY

1 roll (16.5 oz) Pillsbury® refrigerated chocolate chip cookies

6 cups (1 ½ quarts) butter pecan ice cream, slightly softened

2 cups miniature marshmallows

½ cup hot fudge topping (from 16 oz jar)

½ cup caramel topping (from 12 oz jar)

1) Heat oven to 350°F. Spray 13x9-inch pan with cooking spray. Cut cookie dough into ½-inch slices. Arrange slices in bottom of pan. Press dough evenly to form crust. Bake 11 to 13 minutes or until puffed and edges are starting to turn golden brown. Cool completely on cooling rack, about 30 minutes.

2) Spoon ice cream over cooled crust, spreading evenly. Sprinkle marshmallows over ice cream. In small microwavable measuring cup, heat fudge topping on High 30 seconds; stir and drizzle over marshmallows. In small microwavable measuring cup, heat caramel topping on High 30 seconds; stir and drizzle over marshmallows.

3) Freeze at least 2 hours or overnight. Let stand 10 minutes before serving. Cut into 4 rows by 3 rows.

1 SERVING: Calories 460; Total Fat 21g (Saturated Fat 11g); Sodium 270mg; Total Carbohydrate 63g (Dietary Fiber 0g); Protein 4g. EXCHANGES: 1-1/2 Starch, 2-1/2 Other Carbohydrate, 4 Fat. CARBOHYDRATE CHOICES: 4.

tip

For a birthday celebration, top the cake with colorful candy sprinkles. You can use multi-colored sprinkles or any color that matches the theme of your party.

Caramel-Spice Cupcakes

PREP TIME: 30 MINUTES (READY IN 1 HOUR 30 MINUTES)
SERVINGS: 24 CUPCAKES

CUPCAKES

1 box yellow cake mix with pudding in the mix

Water, vegetable oil and eggs called for on cake mix box

1 teaspoon apple pie spice

CARAMEL FROSTING

1 cup packed brown sugar

½ cup whipping cream

½ cup butter, cut into pieces

3 cups powdered sugar

½ teaspoon apple pie spice

Apple slices, if desired

1) Heat oven to 350°F. Place paper baking cup in each of 24 regular-size muffin cups.

2) In large bowl, beat cupcake ingredients with electric mixer on low speed 30 seconds. Beat on medium speed 2 minutes, scraping bowl occasionally. Divide batter evenly among muffin cups.

3) Bake 18 to 20 minutes or until toothpick inserted in center comes out clean. Cool 10 minutes; remove from pans to cooling racks. Cool completely, about 30 minutes.

4) In 2-quart saucepan, heat brown sugar, whipping cream and butter to boiling over medium heat, stirring constantly. Boil 1 minute. Remove from heat. Add powdered sugar; stir with wooden spoon until spreadable. Frost cupcakes. Sprinkle with ½ teaspoon apple pie spice.

1 CUPCAKE: Calories 285; Total Fat 12g (Saturated Fat 4.5g); Sodium 189mg; Total Carbohydrate 45g (Dietary Fiber 0.5g); Protein 2g. EXCHANGES: 1 Starch, 2 Other Carbohydrate, 2 Fat. CARBOHYDRATE CHOICES: 3.

Pumpkin Ravioli with Salted Caramel Whipped Cream

CHRISTINA VERRELLI | DEVON, PA

BAKE-OFF® CONTEST 45, 2012

PREP TIME: 1 HOUR 10 MINUTES (READY IN 1 HOUR 10 MINUTES)
SERVINGS: 12 (2 RAVIOLI EACH)

4 tablespoons LAND O LAKES® Butter, melted

2 packages (3 oz each) cream cheese, softened

½ cup canned pumpkin

1 LAND O LAKES® Egg Yolk

½ teaspoon McCormick® Pure Vanilla Extract

¼ cup sugar

5 tablespoons Pillsbury BEST® All Purpose Flour

½ teaspoon McCormick® Pumpkin Pie Spice

⅓ cup Fisher® Chef's Naturals® Chopped Pecans, finely chopped

2 cans Pillsbury® Crescent Recipe Creations® refrigerated seamless dough sheet

1 cup heavy whipping cream

⅛ teaspoon salt

5 tablespoons Hershey's® caramel syrup

4 tablespoons McCormick® Cinnamon Sugar

1) Heat oven to 375°F. Brush 2 large cookie sheets with 2 tablespoons of the melted butter. In large bowl, beat cream cheese and pumpkin with electric mixer on medium speed about 1 minute or until smooth. Add egg yolk, vanilla, sugar, 3 tablespoons of the flour and pumpkin pie spice; beat on low speed until blended. Reserve 4 teaspoons of the pecans; set aside. Stir remaining pecans into pumpkin mixture.

2) Lightly sprinkle work surface with 1 tablespoon of the flour. Unroll 1 can of dough on floured surface with 1 short side facing you. Press dough into 14x12-inch rectangle. With paring knife, lightly score the dough in half horizontally. Lightly score bottom half of dough into 12 squares (3x2 ¼-inch each). Spoon heaping tablespoon of the pumpkin filling onto center of each square. Gently lift and position unscored half of dough over filling. Starting at the top folded edge, press handle of wooden spoon firmly between mounds and along edges of pumpkin filling to seal. Using toothpick, poke small hole in top of each ravioli. Using a pizza cutter or sharp knife, cut between each ravioli; place 1 inch apart on cookie sheets. Repeat with remaining 1 tablespoon flour, dough sheet and filling. Brush ravioli with remaining 2 tablespoons melted butter.

3) Bake 9 to 14 minutes or until golden brown.

4) Meanwhile, in medium bowl, beat whipping cream and salt with electric mixer on high speed until soft peaks form. Beat in 2 tablespoons of the caramel syrup until stiff peaks form. Transfer to serving bowl; cover and refrigerate.

5) Remove ravioli from oven. Sprinkle ravioli with 2 tablespoons cinnamon sugar; turn. Sprinkle with remaining cinnamon sugar.

6) To serve, place 2 ravioli on each of 12 dessert plates. Drizzle each serving with scant teaspoon of the caramel syrup; sprinkle with reserved chopped pecans. With spoon, swirl remaining 1 tablespoon caramel syrup into bowl of whipped cream. Serve warm ravioli with whipped cream.

1 SERVING: Calories 380; Total Fat 25g (Saturated Fat 13g); Sodium 440mg; Total Carbohydrate 35g (Dietary Fiber 1g); Protein 4g. EXCHANGES: 1-1/2 Starch, 1 Other Carbohydrate, 4-1/2 Fat. CARBOHYDRATE CHOICES: 2.

Toffee Apple Turnover Pie

PREP TIME: 40 MINUTES (READY IN 1 HOUR 50 MINUTES)
SERVINGS: 4

PASTRY

- 1 cup all-purpose flour
- ¼ teaspoon salt
- ⅓ cup plus 1 tablespoon shortening
- 2 to 3 tablespoons cold water

FILLING

- 1 ½ cups sliced peeled apples (2 small)
- 1 tablespoon all-purpose flour
- ½ cup toffee bits (from 10 oz bag)
- 1 egg, beaten
- 1 tablespoon coarse white sparkling sugar

1) Heat oven to 375°F. Line 15x10x1-inch pan with foil. In medium bowl, mix 1 cup flour and the salt. Cut in shortening, using pastry blender or fork, until particles are size of small peas. Sprinkle with water, 1 tablespoon at a time, tossing with fork until moistened. Gather into a ball. On lightly floured surface, shape into flattened round. Roll into 12-inch round, about ⅛ inch thick. Place in pan.

2) In medium bowl, toss apples and 1 tablespoon flour. Mound apple mixture on half of pastry to within ¾ inch of edge. Sprinkle with toffee bits. Fold pastry in half over apple mixture. Fold ½ inch of sealed edge of pastry over; press tines of fork firmly around edge to seal. Brush top with egg. Cut 3 slits, 1 inch long, in top to vent steam. Sprinkle with sugar. Bake 30 to 40 minutes or until golden brown. Immediately remove from pan to serving plate. Cool 30 minutes before cutting.

1 SERVING: Calories 500; Total Fat 31g (Saturated Fat 11g); Sodium 280mg; Total Carbohydrate 50g (Dietary Fiber 2g); Protein 5g. EXCHANGES: 1 Starch, 2-1/2 Other Carbohydrate, 6 Fat. CARBOHYDRATE CHOICES: 3.

FOOD PROCESSOR DIRECTIONS FOR MAKING PASTRY: Into small bowl, measure 2 tablespoons water. In food processor, place shortening, flour and salt. Cover; process with on-and-off pulses until mixture is crumbly. With food processor running, pour water all at once through feed tube, processing just until dough leaves side of bowl (dough should not form a ball).

Chocolate-Dipped Peanut Butter Empanadas

SUSAN HUBICKEY | WEST CHESTER, PA

BAKE-OFF® CONTEST 45, 2012

PREP TIME: 35 MINUTES (READY IN 1 HOUR 35 MINUTES)
SERVINGS: 24

1 roll Pillsbury® refrigerated peanut butter cookie dough

4 oz (half of 8-oz package) cream cheese, softened

3 Pillsbury® refrigerated pie crusts (from 2 boxes), softened as directed on box

1 LAND O LAKES® Egg, beaten

1 bag (10 oz) Hershey's® peanut butter baking chips

4 tablespoons Crisco® All-Vegetable Shortening

1 bag (12 oz) Hershey's® semi-sweet chocolate baking chips

1 teaspoon powdered sugar

tip

If you like, toss in a few peanut butter baking chips and semi-sweet chocolate baking chips to the cookie dough mixture to make these treats even more indulgent.

1) Heat oven to 375°F. Let ½ roll of cookie dough stand at room temperature 10 minutes to soften. (Refrigerate ½ roll cookie dough for another use.) In large bowl, break up cookie dough. Add cream cheese; beat on medium speed with electric mixer until smooth. Set aside.

2) Unroll 1 pie crust; roll into 12-inch round. Using 4-inch round cookie cutter, cut into 8 rounds, rerolling dough as necessary. Repeat with second and third crusts.

3) Spoon scant 1 tablespoon cookie dough mixture on half of each round; flatten slightly. Bring dough over filling; press edges with fork to seal. Cut small slit on top of each empanada; place on ungreased cookie sheets. Brush tops with beaten egg.

4) Bake 12 to 16 minutes or until golden brown. Cool 2 minutes. Remove from cookie sheets to cooling racks. Cool completely, about 15 minutes.

5) Meanwhile, in small microwavable bowl, microwave peanut butter chips and 2 tablespoons of the shortening on High 1 minute to 1 minute 30 seconds, stirring every 30 seconds, until smooth. Dip 1 corner of each empanada into melted chips on an angle, creating a diagonal line. Place on waxed paper; let stand 10 minutes or until coating is set.

6) Meanwhile, in another small microwavable bowl, microwave chocolate chips and remaining 2 tablespoons shortening on High 1 to 2 minutes, stirring every 30 seconds, until smooth. Holding undipped corner, dip the peanut butter-coated empanadas into melted chocolate on opposite angle so that some peanut butter coating is still visible. Refrigerate 10 minutes or until chocolate is set. Sprinkle with powdered sugar. Store covered in refrigerator.

1 SERVING: Calories 330; Total Fat 20g (Saturated Fat 8g); Sodium 230mg; Total Carbohydrate 33g (Dietary Fiber 1g); Protein 4g. EXCHANGES: 1 Starch, 1 Other Carbohydrate, 4 Fat. CARBOHYDRATE CHOICES: 2.

Tunnel of Fudge Cake

ELLA RITA HELFRICH | HOUSTON, TX

BAKE OFF® CONTEST 17, 1966

PREP TIME: 35 MINUTES (READY IN 4 HOURS 55 MINUTES)
SERVINGS: 16

CAKE

1 ¾ cups butter or margarine, softened

1 ¾ cups granulated sugar

6 eggs

2 cups powdered sugar

2 ¼ cups all-purpose flour

¾ cup unsweetened baking cocoa

2 cups chopped walnuts*

GLAZE

¾ cup powdered sugar

¼ cup unsweetened baking cocoa

4 to 6 teaspoons milk

1) In large bowl, beat butter and granulated sugar with electric mixer on medium speed until light and fluffy. Add eggs, one at a time, beating well after each addition. On low speed, gradually beat in 2 cups powdered sugar until blended. With spoon, stir in flour, cocoa and nuts until well blended. Spread batter evenly in pan.

2) Bake 45 to 50 minutes or until top is set and edge begins to pull away from side of pan.** Cool upright in pan on cooling rack 1 hour 30 minutes. Invert cake onto serving plate; cool at least 2 hours.

3) In small bowl, mix glaze ingredients, adding enough milk for desired drizzling consistency. Spoon glaze over top of cake, allowing some to run down sides. Store tightly covered.

1 SERVING: Calories 570; Total Fat 33g (Saturated Fat 15g); Sodium 170mg; Total Carbohydrate 61g (Dietary Fiber 3g); Protein 8g. EXCHANGES: 2 Starch, 2 Other Carbohydrate, 6 Fat. CARBOHYDRATE CHOICES: 4.

*Nuts are essential for the success of this recipe.
**Since this cake has a soft filling, an ordinary doneness test cannot be used. Accurate oven temperature and baking times are essential.

Mocha Mousse

PREP TIME: 15 MINUTES (READY IN 15 MINUTES)
SERVINGS: 6 (1/2 CUP EACH)

 EASY LOW FAT

2 tablespoons light chocolate soymilk

1 tablespoon instant espresso coffee powder or granules

1 oz semisweet or bittersweet baking chocolate

1 cup light chocolate soymilk

1 box (4-serving size) chocolate instant pudding and pie filling mix

2 cups frozen (thawed) fat-free whipped topping

Chocolate-covered coffee beans, if desired

1) In 1-quart saucepan, mix 2 tablespoons soymilk, the coffee powder and chocolate. Cook over medium heat, stirring constantly, until chocolate is completely melted and mixture is well blended. Cool slightly.

2) In medium bowl, beat 1 cup soymilk and the pudding mix with electric mixer on medium speed or wire whisk 1 to 2 minutes or until mixture is well blended and thickened.

3) Stir melted chocolate mixture into pudding mixture. Fold in whipped topping. Divide evenly among 6 dessert dishes; serve or refrigerate. Cover and refrigerate any remaining mousse. Garnish with chocolate-covered coffee beans.

1 SERVING: Calories 140; Total Fat 2.5g (Saturated Fat 1.5g); Sodium 280mg; Total Carbohydrate 28g (Dietary Fiber 1g); Protein 2g. EXCHANGES: 1 Starch, 1 Other Carbohydrate. CARBOHYDRATE CHOICES: 2.

Pineapple Upside-Down Cake

PREP TIME: 15 MINUTES (READY IN 1 HOUR 10 MINUTES)
SERVINGS: 9

 EASY

¼ cup butter or margarine

⅔ cup packed brown sugar

9 slices pineapple in juice (from 14-oz can), drained

9 maraschino cherries without stems

1 ⅓ cups all-purpose flour

1 cup granulated sugar

⅓ cup shortening

1 ½ teaspoons baking powder

½ teaspoon salt

¾ cup milk

1 egg

1) Heat oven to 350°F. In 9-inch square pan, melt butter in oven. Sprinkle brown sugar evenly over melted butter. Arrange pineapple slices over brown sugar. Place cherry in center of each pineapple slice.

2) In medium bowl, beat remaining ingredients with electric mixer on low speed 30 seconds, scraping bowl constantly. Beat on high speed 3 minutes, scraping bowl occasionally. Pour batter over pineapple and cherries.

3) Bake 50 to 55 minutes or until toothpick inserted in center comes out clean. Immediately place heatproof serving plate upside down over pan; turn plate and pan over. Leave pan over cake a few minutes so brown sugar mixture can drizzle over cake; remove pan. Serve cake warm. Store loosely covered.

1 SERVING: Calories 390; Total Fat 14g (Saturated Fat 6g); Sodium 270mg; Total Carbohydrate 62g (Dietary Fiber 1g); Protein 4g. EXCHANGES: 1-1/2 Starch, 1 Fruit, 1-1/2 Other Carbohydrate, 2-1/2 Fat. CARBOHYDRATE CHOICES: 4.

Peanut Butter Boston Cream Cake

MARY BETH MANDOLA | HOUSTON, TX

PREP TIME: 35 MINUTES (READY IN 2 HOURS 45 MINUTES)
SERVINGS: 12

¾ cup heavy whipping cream

½ cup powdered sugar

1 ½ teaspoons McCormick® Pure Vanilla Extract

¼ cup Simply Jif® Peanut Butter

2 LAND O LAKES® Eggs

1 roll Pillsbury® refrigerated peanut butter cookie dough

¼ cup Pillsbury BEST® All Purpose Flour

1 ½ teaspoons baking powder

½ teaspoon baking soda

1 cup sour cream

¾ cup Hershey's® milk chocolate baking chips

2 tablespoons chopped Fisher® Lightly Salted, Dry Roasted Peanuts

1) To make filling, in medium bowl, beat ½ cup whipping cream and powdered sugar with electric mixer on medium speed until stiff peaks form. Add ½ teaspoon of the vanilla and peanut butter; beat on low speed just until blended, being careful not to overmix. Refrigerate.

2) Heat oven to 350°F. Spray 2 (8- or 9-inch) round cake pans with Crisco® No-Stick Butter Spray. In large bowl, beat eggs with electric mixer on high speed, about 5 minutes or until thick and lemon colored. Break up cookie dough into eggs; beat on low speed until creamy. Add remaining 1 teaspoon vanilla; beat on low speed until blended.

3) In small bowl, stir together flour, baking powder and baking soda. Add flour mixture gradually to egg mixture, beating with electric mixer on medium speed, until blended. Add sour cream; beat on low speed until mixed. Divide batter evenly between pans.

4) Bake 18 to 28 minutes or until toothpick inserted in center comes out clean. Cool in pans 10 minutes. Carefully invert cake layers from pans onto cooling racks. Cool completely, about 30 minutes.

5) Meanwhile, to make ganache, in small microwavable bowl, microwave remaining ¼ cup whipping cream and chocolate chips on High 30 to 60 seconds, stirring every 30 seconds, until smooth. Set aside.

6) To assemble cake, place 1 cake layer, bottom side up, on serving plate. Spread peanut butter filling on top to within ½ inch of edge. Top with remaining cake layer, rounded side up. Spread ganache over cake, covering top and allowing ganache to run down side of cake. Sprinkle peanuts around top edge of cake. Refrigerate 1 hour. Store covered in refrigerator.

1 SERVING: Calories 400; Total Fat 25g (Saturated Fat 11g); Sodium 360mg; Total Carbohydrate 37g (Dietary Fiber 1g); Protein 7g. EXCHANGES: 2 Starch, 1/2 Other Carbohydrate, 5 Fat. CARBOHYDRATE CHOICES: 2-1/2.

Mini Carrot-Spiced Cupcakes with Molasses Buttercream

NATALIE MORALES | OAKLEY, CA

BAKE-OFF® CONTEST 45, 2012

PREP TIME: 35 MINUTES (READY IN 1 HOUR 40 MINUTES)
SERVINGS: 32

CUPCAKES

- 1 roll Pillsbury® refrigerated sugar cookie dough
- 1 tablespoon LAND O LAKES® Unsalted or Salted Butter, melted
- 1 tablespoon full-flavor (dark) molasses
- 2 tablespoons milk
- 2 teaspoons McCormick® Ground Ginger
- 1 ½ teaspoons McCormick® Ground Cinnamon
- ⅛ teaspoon McCormick® Ground Nutmeg
- 2 cups shredded carrots
- ½ cup Fisher® Chef's Naturals® Chopped Pecans

FROSTING

- 7 tablespoons LAND O LAKES® Unsalted or Salted Butter, softened
- 1 tablespoon full-flavor (dark) molasses
- 2 ½ cups powdered sugar
- ½ teaspoon McCormick® Ground Cinnamon
- 2 tablespoons milk

1) Heat oven to 350°F. Let cookie dough stand at room temperature 10 minutes to soften. Spray 32 mini muffin cups with Crisco® No-Stick Cooking Spray with Flour.

2) In large bowl, beat cookie dough, melted butter, 1 tablespoon molasses, 2 tablespoons milk, ginger, 1 ½ teaspoons cinnamon, and nutmeg with electric mixer on medium speed until blended. Add carrots and pecans; beat on low speed just until blended. Spoon 1 heaping tablespoonful batter into each muffin cup.

3) Bake 16 to 21 minutes or until toothpick inserted in center comes out clean. Cool in pan 10 minutes; remove from pans to cooling racks. Cool completely, about 30 minutes.

4) To make frosting, in large bowl, beat 7 tablespoons butter and 1 tablespoon molasses with electric mixer on medium speed until creamy. Add powdered sugar, ½ teaspoon cinnamon and 2 tablespoons milk, beat on medium speed until smooth. Spread or pipe frosting onto cupcakes. Store in covered container.

1 SERVING: Calories 150; Total Fat 7g (Saturated Fat 2.5g); Sodium 55mg; Total Carbohydrate 21g (Dietary Fiber 0g); Protein 0g. EXCHANGES: 1-1/2 Other Carbohydrate, 1-1/2 Fat. CARBOHYDRATE CHOICES: 1-1/2.

Strawberries and Cream Butter Cake

LAURIE BENDA | MADISON, WI

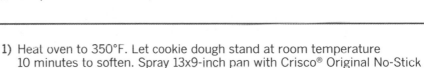

BAKE-OFF® CONTEST 45, 2012

PREP TIME: 30 MINUTES (READY IN 2 HOURS 30 MINUTES)
SERVINGS: 16

1 roll Pillsbury® refrigerated sugar cookie dough

1 ¼ cups LAND O LAKES® Unsalted or Salted Butter, softened

¾ cup granulated sugar

3 LAND O LAKES® Eggs

3 ½ teaspoons McCormick® Pure Vanilla Extract

2 ¼ cups Pillsbury BEST® All Purpose Unbleached Flour

1 can (14 oz) Eagle Brand® Sweetened Condensed Milk

⅓ cup Smucker's® Strawberry Preserves

2 cups heavy whipping cream

2 tablespoons powdered sugar

1 lb fresh strawberries, sliced (2 ½ cups)

1) Heat oven to 350°F. Let cookie dough stand at room temperature 10 minutes to soften. Spray 13x9-inch pan with Crisco® Original No-Stick Cooking Spray. Break up cookie dough in pan; press to cover bottom of pan.

2) In large bowl, beat butter and granulated sugar with electric mixer on medium speed until light and fluffy. Beat in eggs and 2 teaspoons of the vanilla until well blended. On low speed, alternately beat in about ⅓ of the flour and ½ of the condensed milk, ending with flour addition, until blended. Pour batter over dough in pan, spreading gently to cover.

3) Drop teaspoonfuls preserves onto batter; with knife, swirl preserves into batter.

4) Bake 45 to 55 minutes or until edges are golden brown and toothpick inserted in center comes out clean. Cool until slightly warm, about 1 hour.

5) In small bowl, beat whipping cream, powdered sugar and remaining 1 ½ teaspoons vanilla with electric mixer on high speed until soft peaks form.

6) Serve warm cake with whipped cream and strawberries. Store covered.

1 SERVING: Calories 590; Total Fat 34g (Saturated Fat 19g); Sodium 150mg; Total Carbohydrate 63g (Dietary Fiber 1g); Protein 7g. EXCHANGES: 2 Starch, 2 Other Carbohydrate, 6-1/2 Fat. CARBOHYDRATE CHOICES: 4.

Streusel Fruit Custard

PREP TIME: 15 MINUTES (READY IN 1 HOUR 10 MINUTES)
SERVINGS: 6

 EASY

FRUIT MIXTURE

1 can (15.25 oz) sliced pears, drained

1 can (15.25 oz) sliced peaches, drained

2 eggs

¼ cup all-purpose flour

¼ cup granulated sugar

1 container (8 oz) sour cream

1 teaspoon vanilla

TOPPING

¾ cup all-purpose flour

½ cup packed brown sugar

½ teaspoon ground nutmeg

¼ cup butter or margarine, softened

Vanilla ice cream, if desired

1) Heat oven to 325°F. In ungreased 8-inch square or 11x7-inch (2-quart) glass baking dish, arrange pears and peaches. In medium bowl, beat eggs with wire whisk until blended. Beat in ¼ cup flour, the granulated sugar, sour cream and vanilla until smooth. Pour over fruit in baking dish.

2) In small bowl, mix all topping ingredients until crumbly. Sprinkle over fruit mixture.

3) Bake 30 to 40 minutes or until topping is golden brown and center is set. Cool at least 15 minutes. Serve warm with ice cream, if desired. Cover and refrigerate any remaining custard.

1 SERVING: Calories 390; Total Fat 17g (Saturated Fat 10g); Sodium 100mg; Total Carbohydrate 54g (Dietary Fiber 3g); Protein 6g. EXCHANGES: 2 Starch, 1-1/2 Other Carbohydrate, 3 Fat. CARBOHYDRATE CHOICES: 3-1/2.

Strawberry-Cherry Tartlets

PREP TIME: 25 MINUTES (READY IN 1 HOUR)
SERVINGS: 10 (1 TARTLET)

 EASY

1 box Pillsbury® refrigerated pie crusts, softened as directed on box

2 cups sliced fresh strawberries

1 can (21 oz) cherry pie filling

3 snack-size containers (3.5 oz each) vanilla pudding

⅔ cup frozen (thawed) whipped topping

1) Heat oven to 450°F. Spray backs of two 12-cup regular-size muffin pans with cooking spray. Cut 5 (4-inch) rounds from each pie crust. Fit rounds alternately over backs of muffin cups. Pinch 6 equally spaced pleats around side of each cup.

2) Bake 5 to 7 minutes or until lightly browned. Cool 5 minutes. Carefully remove tart shells from muffin cups. Cool completely, about 20 minutes.

3) In medium bowl, gently mix strawberries and pie filling. Spoon 1 rounded tablespoonful pudding into each cooled tartlet. Spoon ⅓ cup fruit filling over pudding in each. Top each with about 1 tablespoon whipped topping.

1 SERVING: Calories 280; Total Fat 8g (Saturated Fat 3.5g); Sodium 170mg; Total Carbohydrate 51g (Dietary Fiber 2g); Protein 2g. EXCHANGES: 1/2 Starch, 1/2 Fruit, 2-1/2 Other Carbohydrate, 1-1/2 Fat. CARBOHYDRATE CHOICES: 3-1/2.

Hot Fudge Brownie Cake

PREP TIME:	15 MINUTES (READY IN 1 HOUR 25 MINUTES)
SERVINGS:	0

 EASY

1 cup all-purpose flour

6 tablespoons unsweetened baking cocoa

2 teaspoons baking powder

¼ teaspoon salt

1 ¼ cups granulated sugar

½ cup milk, room temperature

3 tablespoons vegetable oil

1 teaspoon vanilla

½ cup packed light brown sugar

1 ½ cups boiling water

Frozen (thawed) whipped topping or ice cream, if desired

Fresh raspberries, if desired

1) Heat oven to 350°F. Lightly grease 8-inch square pan with shortening or cooking spray.

2) In medium bowl, mix flour, 2 tablespoons of the cocoa, the baking powder, salt and ¾ cup of the granulated sugar; stir in milk, oil and vanilla. Spread batter in pan.

3) In small bowl, mix brown sugar and remaining ¼ cup cocoa and ½ cup granulated sugar. Sprinkle over batter. Using a spoon, gently drizzle boiling water over batter, being careful not to disturb layers. (Do not stir.)

4) Bake 45 minutes or until cake layer forms on top and springs back when lightly touched. Cool 25 minutes. Serve cake warm with whipped topping and raspberries.

1 SERVING: Calories 292; Total Fat 6g (Saturated Fat 1g); Sodium 223mg; Total Carbohydrate 60g (Dietary Fiber 1g); Protein 3g. EXCHANGES: 1 Starch, 3 Other Carbohydrate, 1 Fat. CARBOHYDRATE CHOICES: 4.

Caramel In-Between Fudge Cake

JUDEE DISCO | NORWICH, CT

BAKE-OFF® CONTEST 21, 1970

PREP TIME: 35 MINUTES (READY IN 2 HOURS 20 MINUTES)
SERVINGS: 18

FILLING

- 28 caramels, unwrapped
- 1 tablespoon butter or margarine
- 1 can (14 oz) sweetened condensed milk (not evaporated)

CAKE

- 1 box Pillsbury® Moist Supreme® dark chocolate cake mix with pudding
- 1 cup water
- 3 eggs

FROSTING AND GARNISH

- ½ cup butter or margarine, softened
- 2 envelopes (1 oz each) premelted unsweetened baking chocolate
- 3 tablespoons half-and-half
- 1 teaspoon vanilla
- 2 cups powdered sugar
- ⅓ cup sliced almonds, toasted

1) Heat oven to 350°F. Grease bottom only of 13x9-inch pan with shortening; lightly flour. In 2-quart saucepan, cook and stir filling ingredients over medium-low heat until caramels are melted. Set aside.

2) In large bowl, beat cake ingredients with electric mixer on low speed 30 seconds. Beat on medium speed 2 minutes. Spread half of batter in pan. Bake 20 minutes. Spread filling over partially baked cake; cover with remaining batter. Bake 20 to 25 minutes or until toothpick inserted in center comes out clean. Cool completely.

3) In small bowl, beat ½ cup butter, the chocolate, half-and-half and vanilla with electric mixer on medium speed until well blended. Beat in powdered sugar until light and fluffy. Frost cooled cake; sprinkle with almonds.

1 SERVING: Calories 390; Total Fat 14g (Saturated Fat 8g); Sodium 360mg; Total Carbohydrate 60g (Dietary Fiber 2g); Protein 6g. EXCHANGES: 1 Starch, 3 Other Carbohydrate, 2-1/2 Fat. CARBOHYDRATE CHOICES: 4.

tip If you're serving someone with a nut allergy, skip the almonds and instead garnish with fresh small strawberries or raspberries or chocolate curls. Or for real chocolate lovers, press mini chocolate chips onto the top of the frosted cake.

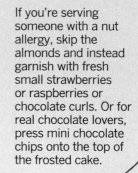

Easy Blackberry Cobbler

PREP TIME: 10 MINUTES (READY IN 1 HOUR 5 MINUTES)
SERVINGS: 6

 EASY

4 cups frozen blackberries

1 tablespoon lemon juice

1 egg

1 cup sugar

1 cup all-purpose flour

6 tablespoons butter, melted

Vanilla ice cream, if desired

1) Heat oven to 375°F. Lightly grease 8-inch square (2-quart) glass baking dish with shortening or cooking spray. Place blackberries in dish; drizzle with lemon juice.

2) In medium bowl, stir egg, sugar and flour until mixture looks like coarse meal. Sprinkle over fruit. Drizzle melted butter over topping.

3) Bake 40 to 45 minutes or until topping is lightly browned and filling is bubbly. Cool 10 minutes. Serve warm with ice cream.

1 SERVING: Calories 368; Total Fat 13g (Saturated Fat 8g); Sodium 114mg; Total Carbohydrate 63g (Dietary Fiber 5g); Protein 4g. EXCHANGES: 1 Starch, 1 Fruit, 2 Other Carbohydrate, 2-1/2 Fat. CARBOHYDRATE CHOICES: 4.

Chocolate Streusel Banana-Carrot Cake

PREP TIME: 20 MINUTES (READY IN 2 HOURS)
SERVINGS: 12

 EASY

STREUSEL

½ cup chopped walnuts

¼ cup packed brown sugar

2 tablespoons all-purpose flour

2 tablespoons butter, melted

½ cup semisweet chocolate chips

CAKE

1 ½ cups sliced very ripe bananas (about 3 medium)

½ cup sour cream

4 eggs

1 box carrot cake mix with pudding in the mix

½ cup semisweet chocolate chips

1) Heat oven to 350°F. Grease 13x9-inch pan with shortening; lightly flour. In medium bowl, mix streusel ingredients except chocolate chips. Stir in ½ cup chocolate chips; set aside.

2) In large bowl, beat bananas, sour cream and eggs with electric mixer on medium speed until well blended. Add cake mix; beat on low speed until combined. Beat on medium speed 2 minutes. Stir in ½ cup chocolate chips. Spread in pan. Sprinkle with streusel.

3) Bake 30 to 40 minutes or until toothpick inserted in center comes out clean. Cool completely on cooling rack, about 1 hour.

1 SERVING: Calories 380; Total Fat 18g (Saturated Fat 7g); Sodium 300mg; Total Carbohydrate 49g (Dietary Fiber 1g); Protein 5g. EXCHANGES: 1-1/2 Starch, 2 Other Carbohydrate, 3-1/2 Fat. CARBOHYDRATE CHOICES: 3.

Cappuccino Pudding

| PREP TIME: | 15 MINUTES (READY IN 2 HOURS 15 MINUTES) | EASY |
| SERVINGS: | 6 (1/2 CUP EACH) | |

½ cup packed light brown sugar

¼ cup cornstarch

2 tablespoons instant espresso coffee powder or granules

¼ teaspoon salt

2 ½ cups whipping cream

1 cup milk

3 egg yolks

2 tablespoons powdered sugar

1 tablespoon unsweetened baking cocoa

1) In 2-quart heavy saucepan, mix brown sugar, cornstarch, coffee powder and salt. Add 2 cups of the whipping cream, the milk and egg yolks; stir with whisk until blended. Heat to boiling over medium heat; boil 1 minute until pudding thickens and coats back of spoon. Remove from heat.

2) Divide pudding evenly among 6 serving bowls or custard cups. Cover tops of pudding with plastic wrap to prevent skin from forming; refrigerate 2 hours or until chilled.

3) Just before serving, in chilled small bowl, beat remaining ½ cup whipping cream and the powdered sugar with electric mixer on high speed until stiff peaks form. Top each serving of pudding with whipped cream; sprinkle with cocoa.

1 SERVING: Calories 500; Total Fat 40g (Saturated Fat 24g); Sodium 166mg; Total Carbohydrate 32g (Dietary Fiber 0.5g); Protein 5g. EXCHANGES: 1 Other Carbohydrate, 1/2 Milk, 7-1/2 Fat. CARBOHYDRATE CHOICES: 1-1/2.

Oatmeal Raisin Cookie Cheesecake

PREP TIME: 15 MINUTES (READY IN 8 HOURS 45 MINUTES)
SERVINGS: 16

 EASY

1 package (16 oz) Pillsbury® Big Deluxe® refrigerated oatmeal raisin cookies

3 packages (8 oz each) cream cheese, softened

1 container (8 oz) sour cream

1 cup granulated sugar

4 eggs

3 tablespoons all-purpose flour

1 teaspoon vanilla

⅛ teaspoon salt

2 large graham cracker crumb crusts (9 oz each)

1 cup whipping cream

3 tablespoons powdered sugar

1) Heat oven to 350°F. Bake cookies as directed on package for 16 minutes. Cool 10 minutes. Crumble cookies into pieces.

2) Reduce oven temperature to 300°F. In large bowl, beat cream cheese, sour cream and granulated sugar with electric mixer on medium speed until smooth. Beat in eggs, one at a time, just until blended. On low speed, beat in flour, vanilla and salt. Fold in crumbled cookies. Pour batter evenly into crusts.

3) Bake 1 hour or until almost set. Cool completely on cooling rack, about 1 hour. Refrigerate at least 6 hours or overnight.

4) In chilled large bowl, beat whipping cream with electric mixer on low speed until soft peaks form. Add powdered sugar; beat on high speed until stiff peaks form. Cut cheesecakes into wedges. Pipe or spoon whipped cream onto each wedge just before serving.

1 SERVING: Calories 576; Total Fat 36g (Saturated Fat 16g); Sodium 364mg; Total Carbohydrate 56g (Dietary Fiber 1g); Protein 8g. EXCHANGES: 2 Starch, 2 Other Carbohydrate. CARBOHYDRATE CHOICES: 4.

Alphabetical Index

General Recipe Index

This handy index lists every recipe by food category and/or major ingredient, so you can easily locate recipes to suit your needs.

Desserts (continued)

Plum Crostata, 252
Pumpkin Ravioli with Salted Caramel
    Whipped Cream, 330
Rice Pudding with Cherries, 255
Snow-Capped Peppermint Sticks, 229
Star-Spangled Blueberry Squares, 259
Streusel Fruit Custard, 338
Vanilla-Malt-Toffee Triangles with Sea
    Salt, 279

Dips & Spreads

Artichoke-Crab Spread, 56
Baked Clam Dip with Crusty French Bread
    Dippers, 42
Caramelized Onion Dip, 49
Cheesy Bean Dip, 73
Five-Layer Mexican Dip, 64
Holiday Goat Cheese Log, 232
Monster Ball, 64
Pepperoni Pizza Dip, 71
Roasted Lemon-White Bean Dip, 51

Eggs

Bacon-Egg Breakfast Bites, 12
Breakfast Crostatas, 16
Cheese and Tomato Omelet, 174
Chive-Egg Salad Mini Sandwiches, 243
Eggnog Pudding, 235
Italian Biscuit Strata, 15
Panko-Topped Curried Eggs Breakfast
    Pizza, 28
Sausage and Cheese Frittata, 11

Fish & Seafood

Artichoke-Crab Spread, 56
Baked Clam Dip with Crusty French Bread
    Dippers, 42
Citrus-Shrimp Wraps, 98
Classic Fried Catfish, 159
Cold Thai Noodles with Shrimp, 144
Crab Cake Crostini with Corn and Bacon
    Salsa, 41
Creole Jambalaya, 203
Mango-Shrimp Salad, 125
Orange-Coconut Fish Po'Boys, 104
Salmon Crescent Sushi Rolls, 34
Salmon with Lemon-Dill Butter, 240
Shrimp and Dill Toasts, 39
Shrimp, Peas and Pesto Pasta, 143
Shrimp Rolls, 169
Skillet Barbecue Shrimp, 152
Sushi-Style Crescent Crab Rolls, 37
Sweet and Spicy Shrimp Cups, 35
Tuna Chef's Salad, 172
Tuna Primavera, 181

Fruit

(also see specific kinds)
Baked Fruit Turnovers, 317
Cherry-Plum-Berry Tart, 302
Citrus in Vanilla Syrup, 16
Citrus Mimosas, 26
Fruits of Winter Crostata, 224
Grapefruit Tart, 23
Mango-Pineapple Pie, 309
Mincemeat Pie, 293

Pomegranate Party Punch, 232
Streusel Fruit Custard, 338
Ultimate Fresh Fruit Tart, 251

Grapefruit

Citrus in Vanilla Syrup, 16
Citrus Mimosas, 26
Grapefruit Tart, 23

Green Beans

Green Bean Amandine Casserole, 225
Mediterranean Minestrone Casserole, 201

Ground Beef

(also see Beef)
Greek Meatballs with Spaghetti, 161
Halloween Sloppy Joes, 211
Home-Style Meat Loaf, 141
Jack-o'-Lantern Beef and Bean Pots, 214
Loaded Nacho Burgers, 132
Meatball Minestrone Bake, 136
Nacho Beef Skillet, 165
Shepherd's Pie, 230
Sloppy Jose Gorditas, 115
Spicy Cheeseburger Soup, 117
Stuffed Onion Packets with Cheese Sauce, 130
Texas No-Bean Chili, 100

Ham & Prosciutto

Balsamic-Brown Sugar Baked Ham, 238
Bourbon-Fig Glazed Ham, 159
Breakfast Crostatas, 16
Chicken and Rice Cordon Bleu, 220
Orange Ham Rolls, 245
Orange-Glazed Ham, 255
Peach-Glazed Ham, 248
Prosciutto-Spinach Spirals, 32
Smoky Ham and Navy Bean Stew, 205

Lamb

Curried Lamb-Sweet Potato Stew, 206
Herb and Garlic Roast Leg of Lamb, 242

Lemon & Lime

Blueberry-Lemonade Coolers, 258
Chicken "Pho" Noodle Soup, 126
Citrus-Shrimp Wraps, 98
Coconut-Macadamia Key Lime Pie, 241
Honey-Lime Mopped Drumsticks, 171
Key Lime Pie Cinnamon Rolls, 24
Lemon Crumb Tart, 247
Lime Cooler Mini Ice Cream Pies, 248
Mango-Lemon Drop Sunshine Puffs, 95
Roasted Lemon-White Bean Dip, 51
Salmon with Lemon-Dill Butter, 240

Mangoes

Grilled Chicken Soft Tacos, 145
Mango-Lemon Drop Sunshine Puffs, 95
Mango-Pineapple Pie, 309
Mango Salsa Appetizer Bites, 33
Mango-Shrimp Salad, 125

Mushrooms

Beef Burgundy with Sour Cream Spuds, 195
Chicken Alfredo Lasagna, 154

Chicken in Red Wine, 192
Chicken Tetrazzini, 148
Green Bean Amandine Casserole, 225
Italian Biscuit Strata, 15
Mushroom-Herb Stuffed Beef Tenderloin, 149
Shepherd's Pie, 230
Weeknight Pot Roast, 190
Wild Rice and Mushroom Soup, 191

Nuts & Peanut Butter

Almond-Apricot Galette, 298
Almond Bing Cherry Pie, 299
Almond-Chicken Crescent Crostini, 53
Almond-Cream Puff Pastries, 313
Almond-Macaroon Coffee Cake, 8
Apple Butter-Pecan Cupcakes, 319
Banana-Walnut Pancakes, 22
Candied Spiced Nut Mix, 69
Caramel Apple-Pear Praline Pie, 223
Caramel-Pecan Tart, 306
Cashew-Fudge Bars, 276
Chocolate-Dipped Peanut Butter
    Empanadas, 332
Chocolate-Hazelnut Cookies, 265
Chocolate-Hazelnut-Coconut Bars, 285
Chocolate-Macadamia Shortbread, 327
Chocolate-Macadamia Tart, 291
Chocolate-Peanut Butter Haystacks, 75
Cilantro-Peanut Slaw, 114
Coconut-Macadamia Key Lime Pie, 241
Crunchy Curried Snack Mix, 72
Double-Bottom Blueberry-Pecan Pie, 300
Elegant Pumpkin-Walnut Layered Pie, 210
Ginger-Praline Pumpkin Tart, 303
Hazelnut-French Silk Turtle Pie, 301
Indonesian Chicken Turnovers with Spicy
    Peanut Sauce, 133
Nutty Chocolate-Irish Cream Cookies, 284
Orange Cream-Macadamia Torte, 321
Parmesan-Pecan Fried Chicken, 160
Peanut Butter Boston Cream Cake, 335
Peanut Butter Creme Cookie Cups, 278
Peanut Butter Crunch Layer Bars, 267
Peanut Butter-Graham Cereal Bars, 62
Pecan-Cream Cheese Bars, 278
Praline-Topped Sweet Potatoes, 94
Raspberry-Almond Bars, 270
Salted Chocolate Almond Fudge, 268
Triple Chocolate-Covered Nut Clusters, 274
White Peanut Butter Fudge Bars, 273

Onions & Leeks

Bacon and Leek Tart, 46
Bacon-Chicken Sliders with Raspberry-Onion
    Spread, 116
Beef and Caramelized Onion Canapés, 48
Beefy French Onion Soup, 99
Caramelized Onion and Peppered Bacon
    Flatbread, 38
Caramelized Onion Dip, 49
Roasted Rosemary-Onion Potatoes, 82
Stuffed Onion Packets with Cheese
    Sauce, 130

Oranges

Citrus in Vanilla Syrup, 16
Citrus Mimosas, 26
Cranberry-Orange Cake, 326